Mission on the Road to Emmaus

Constants, Context and Prophetic Dialogue

Edited by

Cathy Ross and Stephen B. Bevans

scm press

Published in 2015 by SCM Press
Editorial office
3rd Floor
Invicta House
108-114 Golden Lane
London EC1Y OTG

SCM Press is an imprint of Hymns Ancient & Modern Ltd
(a registered charity)
13A Hellesdon Park Road
Norwich NR6 5DR, UK
www.scmpress.co.uk

The publisher acknowledges with thanks permission to use the
following copyright material:

The poem 'Beginners' by Denise Levertov, from *Candles in Babylon*, is
copyright © 1982 by Denise Levertov. Reprinted by permission of New
Directions Publishing Corp.

Eucharistic prayer, *A New Zealand Prayer Book, He Karakia Mihinare o
Aotearoa*, Auckland: William Collins, 1989. Used by permission.

Scripture quotations are from the New Revised Standard Version of the
Bible, Anglicized Edition, copyright © 1989, 1995 by the Division of
Christian Education of the National Council of the Churches of Christ in
the USA. Used by permission. All rights reserved.

British Library Cataloguing in Publication data

A catalogue record for this book is available
from the British Library

978 0 334 04909 8

Typeset by Regent Typesetting, London
Printed and bound by
CPI Group (UK) Ltd, Croydon

Contents

Contributors

Frances S. Adeney is the William A. Benfield Jr Professor Emerita of Evangelism and Global Mission at Louisville Presbyterian Theological Seminary. Adeney's interest in Christian mission focuses on the interstices between culture and religions and a focus on giftive mission – mission as a giving and receiving of gifts. Her books include *Christian Women in Indonesia: A Narrative Study of Gender and Religion* (2003), *Christianity and Human Rights: Ideas and Issues* (2007), *Christianity Encountering World Religions* (2009) and *Graceful Evangelism: Christian Witness in a* Complex World (2010).

Jonny Baker is Mission Education Director for the Church Mission Society, Britain. He connects with pioneers, leaders who have the gift of not fitting in as they are called by God to new forms of mission and ministry often beyond the edges of the Church. The main focus of his work in the last few years has been setting up and leading the innovative Pioneer Mission Leadership Training.

Stephen Bevans is a Roman Catholic priest in the Society of the Divine Word (SVD) and Louis J. Luzbetak, SVD Professor of Mission and Culture at Catholic Theological Union, Chicago. He has worked as a missionary to the Philippines (1972–81) and has taught and lectured in many places throughout the world. He is the author of *Models of Contextual Theology* (1992/2002), *An Introduction to Theology in Global Perspective* (2009) and, with Roger P. Schroeder, *Constants in Context* (2004) and *Prophetic Dialogue* (2011).

Maria Cimperman RSCJ, is Visiting Associate Professor of Ethics at Catholic Theological Union, Chicago. Working at the intersection of social ethics, moral theology and spirituality, Maria is completing a manuscript on *Social Analysis for the 21st Century: Faith in Action for a Socially Conscious Spirituality* (2015). She also presents and writes on topics in consecrated religious life.

S. Mark Heim is the Samuel Abbot Professor of Christian Theology at Andover Newton Theological School in Newton Centre, MA. He is deeply involved in issues of religious pluralism, Christian ecumenism and the relation of theology and science. His books include *Salvations: Truth and Difference in Religion* (1995), *The Depth of the Riches: A Trinitarian Theology of Religious Ends* (2001) and *Saved from Sacrifice: A Theology of the Cross* (2006). He is a member of the American Theological Society and has received both a Pew Evangelical Scholars Research Fellowship and a Henry Luce III Fellowship in Theology. He is an ordained American Baptist minister.

Joe Kapolyo is the Lead Minister at Edmonton Baptist Church in north London. He is a trustee and member of the National Council of the Baptist Union of Great Britain. He has been Principal of All Nations Christian College and worked with the Scripture Union in Zambia (1976–84) before ordination in 1985.

Kirsteen Kim is Professor of Theology and World Christianity at Leeds Trinity University. She is the author of several books, including *Joining in with the Spirit: Connecting World Church and Local Mission* (2012) and *A History of Korean Christianity* (2014). She is currently the editor of *Mission Studies*, the journal of the International Association for Mission Studies.

Tim Naish is Dean of the Oxford Ministry Course and Lecturer in Missiology at Ripon College Cuddesdon, Oxford. Between 1980 and 2000 he was a mission partner of the Church Mission Society in South India, England, Zaire and Uganda. Among his interests are the interface of missiology with systematic theology and contemporary poetry in relation to mission.

Dawn M. Nothwehr OSF, is a member of the Sisters of St Francis, Rochester, MN (Profession of Life Vows, 1984). She is currently Professor of Catholic Theological Ethics at Catholic Theological Union, Chicago, where she holds The Erica and Harry John Family Endowed Chair in Catholic Ethics. Nothwehr's research focuses on global climate change, environmental ethics and ecotheology. She is the author of numerous book chapters and articles, as well as several books, including: *Ecological Footprints: An Essential Franciscan Guide to Sustainable Living* (2012).

Cathy Ross is Tutor in Contextual Theology at Ripon College Cuddesdon and Lecturer in Mission at Regent's Park College, Oxford. She also teaches Pioneer Leaders at the Church Mission Society, Britain. Her recent publications include *Mission in the 21ˢᵗ Century, Exploring the Five Marks of Global Mission* (ed. with Andrew Walls, 2008), *Life-Widening Mission: Global Anglican Perspectives* (2012) and *Mission in Context* (with John Corrie, 2012). Her research interests are in the areas of contextual theologies, World Christianity, feminist theologies and hospitality.

Robert Schreiter holds the Vatican Council II Professorship in Theology at Catholic Theological Union in Chicago. He has written widely on mission, inculturation and reconciliation. His most recent book (with Knud Jorgensen) is *Mission as Ministry of Reconciliation* (2013).

Roger Schroeder is Professor of Intercultural Studies and Ministry and holder of the Bishop Francis X. Ford, MM, Chair of Catholic Missiology at Catholic Theological Union, Chicago. He has authored *What is the Mission of the Church?* (2008) and co-authored with Stephen Bevans, *Constants in Context: A Theology of Mission for Today* (2004) and *Prophetic Dialogue: Reflections on Christian Mission Today* (2011). Schroeder is a past president of the American Society of Missiology and is serving his third three-year term as the International Coordinator of Anthropos Institute. He is a member of Catholic missionary order of the Society of the Divine Word (SVD) and worked for six years in Papua New Guinea.

vanThanh Nguyen SVD is Associate Professor of New Testament Studies and Director of the Master of Divinity Program at Catholic Theological Union, Chicago. He is an associate editor of the *Journal of the International Association of Mission Studies*. He is the author of *Peter and Cornelius: A Story of Conversion and Mission* (2012) and *Stories of Early Christianity: Creative Retellings of Faith and History* (2013).

Emma Wild-Wood migrated to the Democratic Republic of Congo in 1993 to teach at the Anglican Theological College (now the Université Anglicane du Congo) and also taught in Uganda. She returned to her native Britain in 2000 and is now Director of the Cambridge Centre for Christianity World-wide.

Amos Yong is Professor of Theology and Mission and Director of Center for Missiological Research at Fuller Theological Seminary. He has authored or edited two dozen volumes on a wide range of topics.

Introduction

Mission as Prophetic Dialogue

STEPHEN B. BEVANS AND CATHY ROSS

The Road to Emmaus

These last few days had probably been the worst of their lives. Just a few days ago they had been so happy, so full of hope. They had been disciples of Jesus of Nazareth, a truly amazing man. They had never heard anyone talk the way he had talked. They would never forget his beautiful, provocative stories. They would never forget his teachings about God that brought new light to their old traditions. They had never seen anyone so powerful. Not powerful like the Romans who occupied the land, or like their puppet Herod, but powerful in a totally different way. It was a power that was at the same time absolutely gentle – the way he smiled, the way he dealt with people, assuring them that they were loved and forgiven by God. It was an awesome power too, a power to heal, a power to drive out demons, even a power to bring the dead back to life. He used to say, like the prophet Isaiah, that the Spirit of the Lord was upon him, and it had to be true! Like their many friends who followed Jesus as he journeyed around Israel, they thought that this was it. He was the one. He was the long-awaited Messiah.

But in these last few days the bottom had fallen out. He was dead. He was never popular with the authorities. In fact, what he said and did challenged their authority to the core. But this last week, during Passover in Jerusalem, they arrested him, turned him over to the Romans, and they executed him – had him crucified. It was over. They had had enough. Better go back to their old lives. Gradually they would get over their disillusionment. Sure – some of the women said that the tomb in which he was buried was empty and that they had had a vision of angels who said he was alive. For a while there was hope as they rushed to the tomb. Sure enough it was empty. But there was no Jesus. Just a gaping tomb. It was over. They were leaving Jerusalem for good.

They talked about these things as they walked along. It helped to share their grief. At least they had each other to talk to as they followed the road that left the city – the same road that just a week ago was filled with crowds who welcomed Jesus with songs and palms as he entered the city. All of a sudden, as if out of nowhere, another man joined them. 'What are you talking about?' he asked. 'About all those terrible things that have happened in Jerusalem in these past days,' they answered. 'What things?' he asked. And so they told him, and he listened. When they had finished their terrible story, the stranger just shook his head and sighed. 'Don't you see?' he said. 'Look more closely at the Scriptures. You'll see a pattern there – the one who is Messiah is supposed to suffer before he is fully revealed.' Then he went through the entire Scriptures, from the Torah through the prophets, and showed them the pattern. They were fascinated, consoled – they could hardly believe it, though. Who was this learned stranger?

They had left Jerusalem at midday, and they had walked all afternoon. With the stranger guiding them through the Scriptures, though, the time had flown, and they found themselves at dusk approaching the small village of Emmaus. The stranger began to take his leave, but the two begged him to stay with them overnight. So they went in and began to eat supper. And then it happened. The stranger took bread, said the blessing, broke the bread – just like ... Jesus! It was Jesus!

This story – told with beautiful economy in Luke 24.13–35 – is a passage in the Gospels that Christians deeply cherish. The risen Lord is known 'in the breaking of the bread' (Luke 24.35). It follows the same pattern of several of the resurrection appearances: Jesus is seen but not recognized, then does something or says something that triggers instant, powerful recognition. The disciples on the mountain still doubt, but Jesus gives the 'Great Commission'. Magdalene confuses Jesus with the gardener, until he addresses her as 'Mary'. The disciples obey the shadowy stranger and cast the nets to the right side of the boat and know the Lord in the astonishing catch of fish. See Matthew 28.16–20; John 20.11–18; and John 21.1–14.

Prophetic Dialogue

The Emmaus story, however, also seems to us to be a wonderful illustration of the theme of this book: Mission as prophetic dialogue. We discern in this familiar story the way a stranger becomes a friend, a guest becomes a host, one who listens becomes one who proclaims. The story begins with sharing a journey and sharing a story. It ends with a shared meal and a shared recognition. Besides being a great story of resurrection faith, it is also a model of sharing the gospel, and the model is the Lord himself. Jesus asks what the disciples are discussing. He listens to their tale of woe. In that context he teaches, leading the disciples to a moment of insight and revelation. The story calls to mind other stories – of Jesus asking blind Bartimaeus what he could do for him (Mark 10.51), of Jesus listening to the plight – at first unwillingly – of the Canaanite/Syro-Phoenician woman (Mark 7.24–30/ Matt. 15.21–28), of a patient conversation with a Samaritan woman at Jacob's well (John 4.1–42). It is echoed in Philip's dialogue with the Ethiopian Eunuch (Acts 8.26–39), in Peter's answering the summons of Cornelius (Acts 10.1–48), of the anonymous evangelists taking Greek culture seriously in Antioch (Acts 11.19–26; see Acts 15.1–35), of Paul swallowing his anger and meeting the Athenians on their own terms (Acts 17.16–34). It is modelled by Paul as he writes to the Thessalonians. When he came among them, he reminds them, he 'had courage ... to declare to you the gospel of God', but he was nevertheless gentle among them, 'like a nurse tenderly caring for her own children' (1 Thess. 2.2, 7; see 2.1–12).

'Prophetic dialogue', of course, is not a biblical term, but we believe it is deeply rooted in the Bible. The biblical message of God offering a covenant to Israel, castigating them for their unfaithfulness and assuring them of an everlasting love despite their sins, of offering hope in the depth of exile, of the proclamation and witness to the reign of God, of the good news of Jesus' lordship and of the reconciling work of the cross is the essence of prophecy. The patient, loving, persistent, adaptable divine method is 'one long, varied dialogue, which marvellously begins with God and which God prolongs with women and men in so many different ways'.[1] 'Prophetic Dialogue' is a new term to describe mission, but the method and, indeed, spirituality that it describes is not new at all. Not only is it rooted in the Bible, it is rooted as well in history, implicit in the best missiological thinking and practice of the past: in Justin Martyr, in Benedict and Scholastica, in Cyril and Methodius, in Matteo Ricci, in William Carey, in Lottie Moon, in Henry Martyn, in Pandita Ramabai and in the martyrs of the Tibhurine monastery in Algeria.

'Prophetic Dialogue' has its origin in the reflections on mission at the 2000 General Chapter of Stephen B. Bevans' religious congregation of the Society of the Divine Word (SVD).[2] When Steve and Roger Schroeder were writing their book *Constants in Context*, prophetic dialogue was the term they chose to describe what they proposed was a synthesis – or a creative tension, as Roger later has called it – among current Trinitarian, regno-centric and kerygmatic understandings of mission.[3] If mission is a dance, they write in their subsequent book *Prophetic Dialogue* – the dance of the Trinity through the world, a dance to which all creation is called as a partner – the *name* of the dance is prophetic dialogue. 'It is based on the beautiful but complex rhythm of dialogue and prophecy, boldness and humility, learning and teaching, letting go and speaking out.'[4] The key thing as Christians engage in mission is to discern the kind of rhythm and posture that is needed for a particular version of the dance. As Steve insists in the chapter that he wrote for this book, every act of prophetic dialogue is an exercise of contextual theology.

---

1 Paul VI, Encyclical Letter *Ecclesiam Suam* (ES), www.vatican.va/holy_father/paul_vi/encyclicals/documents/hf_p-vi_enc_06081964_ecclesiam_en.html, 70.

2 Society of the Divine Word, Fifteenth General Chapter 2000, 'Listening to the Spirit: Our Missionary Response Today', Rome: Society of the Divine Word, 2000.

3 Stephen B. Bevans and Roger P. Schroeder, *Constants in Context: A Theology of Mission for Today*, Maryknoll, NY: Orbis, 2004, esp. 348–52.

4 Stephen B. Bevans and Roger P. Schroeder, *Prophetic Dialogue: Reflections on Christian Mission Today*, Maryknoll, NY: Orbis, 2011.

Mission as Dialogue

On the one hand, mission is dialogue or conversation. As a Roman document put it powerfully in 1984, 'dialogue is ... the norm and necessary manner of every form of Christian mission, as well as of every aspect of it'.[5] The latest WCC statement, 'Together Towards Life' affirms that dialogue is essential for mission, claiming that 'dialogue provides for an honest encounter'[6] and that dialogue begins 'with the wider context in order to discern how Christ is already present and where God's Spirit is already at work'.[7] To speak of mission as dialogue is by no means arbitrary, therefore. We do mission this way because this is the way *God* is in mission. Mission in dialogue is nothing less than a Trinitarian practice. And so, if the triune God carries out the divine mission *in* dialogue and *for* dialogue, so must those women and men baptized in the Trinity's name.

What does it mean to do mission in dialogue? Primarily, it means that we must have a heart 'so open', as African American novelist Alice Walker describes it, 'that the wind blows through it'.[8] Steve's colleague at Catholic Theological Union Claude Marie Barbour explains such openness and vulnerability as 'mission in reverse'. Rather than arriving somewhere and right away serving or preaching or teaching, Barbour has insisted over 40 years that the minister/missionary needs first to be evangelized by those whom she or he evangelizes. The people that we serve, she insists, must be the teachers before we dare to teach.[9]

The first step in evangelization, then, is that deep listening, docility (the ability to be taught), gentleness, the ability to forge real relationships. Australian missiologist Noel Connolly suggests that 'most people listen more willingly to people who appreciate them and are learning along with them'.[10] 'Give us FRIENDS' was the heartfelt cry of Indian churchman A. S. Azariah in his famous speech about missionaries at the 1910 Edinburgh

5 Secretariat for Non-Christians, 'The Attitude of the Church toward the Followers of Other Religions: Reflections and Orientations on Dialogue and Mission', 29. Quoted in US Bishops, *To the Ends of the Earth*, New York: Society for the Propagation of the Faith, 1986, 29 (para. 40).

6 World Council of Churches, 'Together Towards Life': Mission and Evangelism in Changing Landscapes', 2013, www.oikoumene.org/en/resources/documents/wcc-commissions/mission-and-evangelism/together-towards-life-mission-and-evangelism-in-changing-landscapes?set_language=en, paragraph 94.

7 WCC, 'Together Towards Life', paragraph 97.

8 Alice Walker, 'A Wind through the Heart: A Conversation with Alice Walker and Sharon Salzburg on Loving Kindness in a Painful World', *Shambhala Sun* (January 1997), 1–5.

9 See Claude Marie Barbour, 'Seeking Justice and Shalom in the City', *International Review of Mission* 73 (1984), 303–9.

10 Noel Connolly, 'New Evangelisation in Australia', draft paper to be presented at the SEDOS Conference, April 2013, 8.

World Mission Conference.[11] Connolly writes, 'we are most missionary when we move out to discover what God is doing around us. Then we will be a more authentic and convincing sign of God's hopes for the world.'[12] This same idea was expressed in an editorial in the American *National Catholic Reporter* during the 2012 Synod of (Roman Catholic) Bishops on the New Evangelization. Most lapsed Catholics, the editorial observed, or that rising group of people not affiliated with any church (whom sociologists call 'nones') are not particularly interested if we simply come to them with ready-made answers.[13] The editorial asks, 'Is it possible that "nones" can teach us something about God? Or at least can we learn something from listening to their questions? The Church's challenge is not to supply answers but to accompany people on their spiritual quests.'[14]

In February, 2013, Annie Selak, a young Catholic lay minister, contributed to a blog in the *Washington Post* in which she asked the question 'What do young Catholics want?'[15] She offered four answers, and all of them revolved around the idea that the Church needs to be a community of openness and dialogue. Selak was speaking for 'young Catholics'. Our own sense is that the relevance of what she said articulates the wants of a much wider age group as well and transcends denominational lines.

'We want the Church to ask the questions we are asking', she says. These are questions, she explains, that deal with some of the hard issues in today's world and Church. These are questions about women's equality and participation in the Church, about sexuality, including homosexuality, and about truth outside the pale of Christianity. In this way, she says, the Church would begin to model to the world the inclusivity of Jesus. 'There is an urgency to these issues, as these are not nameless people on the margins, these are our friends, family members, mentors and leaders.' This generation of young adults has grown up with non-Christians, and Selak says that they are among 'the holiest people we know'. Selak's words are reminiscent of the intervention of Archbishop – now Cardinal – Luis Antonio Tagle at the 2012 Roman Synod. Perhaps rather than always speaking, Tagle said, the Church needs to keep silent and listen: 'The Church must discover the power of silence. Confronted with the sorrows, doubts and uncertainties of people she cannot pretend to give easy solutions. In Jesus, silence becomes

---

11 Brian Stanley, *The World Missionary Conference, Edinburgh 1910*, Grand Rapids, MI: Eerdmans, 2009.

12 Connolly, 'New Evangelisation in Australia', 9.

13 *National Catholic Reporter*, Editorial, 27 October 2012, cited in Connolly, 'New Evangelisation in Australia', 10.

14 *National Catholic Reporter*, Editorial, 27 October 2012, cited in Connolly, 'New Evangelisation in Australia', 10.

15 Annie Selak, 'The Church Young Catholics Want', www.washingtonpost.com/blogs/guest-voices/post/the-church-young-catholics-want/2013/02/14/deo8eae2-760a-11e2-95e4-6148e45d7adb_blog.html.

the way of attentive listening, compassion and prayer.'[16] Bishop John Taylor quotes Ivan Illich's plea, 'only the very brave ... dare ... to go back to the helpless silence of being learners and listeners – "the holding of hands of the lovers" – from which deep communication may grow. Perhaps it is the one way of being together with others and with the Word in which we have no more foreign accent.'[17]

Dialogue is the *sine qua non* of mission. It is about presence. It is about relationship. It is about hospitality. It is about openness. It is humble, vulnerable, joyful.

Mission as Prophecy

But, on the other hand, mission is prophecy. Like the God of the Covenant, the God of salvation, mission has something to do and something to say. 'Woe to me', Paul exclaims, 'if I do not preach the gospel!' (1 Cor. 9.16). The rhythm of dialogue is not complete without the counter-rhythm of prophecy.

Prophecy, however, is quite complex. First of all, it is rooted in dialogue. The prophet is a woman or man who listens, who is in relationship, who is committed to a community. Prophets speak boldly and clearly – and some-times angrily – not because they are against people, but because they are so totally for them. Karl Barth wrote powerfully of God's 'No' which is ulti-mately God's 'Yes.'[18] In Barth's spirit, Hendrik Kraemer spoke of how the gospel offered to the world's cultures their 'subversive fulfilment'.[19]

Second, prophecy is done in both word and deed; it is spoken and unspo-ken. The books of Israel's prophets are certainly full of words, but the prophets also act prophetically. Hosea is instructed to marry a prostitute (Hos. 1.2); Jeremiah wears and buries and exhumes a linen loincloth (Jer. 13.1–11), buys and breaks an earthenware jug (Jer. 19.1–13) and walks through Jerusalem wearing a yoke (Jer. 27.1–22). Throughout the Old Testament, Israel is called to be a sign of God's holiness to the surrounding peoples – a royal priesthood, a holy people, a light to the nations (Ex. 19.6; Isa. 49.6) – in whom all nations will find a blessing (Gen. 12.2–3). Jesus not only tells stories and teaches wisdom. He performs 'mighty deeds' of healing

---

16 Thirteenth Synod of Bishops, 7–28 October 2012, on the New Evangelization, www. vatican.va/news_services/Press/sinodo/documents/bollettino_25_xiii-ordinaria-2012/xx_ plurilingue/b07_xx.html, (unofficial translation).

17 J. V. Taylor, *The Go-Between God: The Holy Spirit and the Christian Mission*, London: SCM Press, 1972, 229.

18 See Karl Barth, 'The Word of God and the Task of Ministry', in *The Word of God and the Word of Man*, New York: Harper Torchbooks, 1957, 207–8.

19 Hendrik Kraemer, *The Authority of Faith: The Madras Series*, vol. 1, London: Interna-tional Missionary Council, 1939, 4. These are quoted from Michael Goheen, '*As The Father Has Sent Me, I Am Sending You': J. E. Lesslie Newbigin's Missionary Ecclesiology*, Zoetermeer, Netherlands: Boekencentrum Publishing House, 2001, 357.

and exorcism and is himself a parable, as Edward Schillebeeckx has noted, in that he stands on the side of the poor and the marginalized, welcoming all. The early community preaches whenever it gets a chance (e.g. Acts 5.42) and yet witnesses as well (Acts 3.41–47).

Third, prophecy is both about 'speaking forth' and 'speaking out' – acting, as we have said, both with and without words. Christian communities, by their joyful, life-giving, vibrant community life, are, as Lesslie Newbigin has written famously, the best interpretation of the gospel to those who do not believe.[20] With great contextual sensitivity, preachers and evangelists communicate the gospel message, making sure that it can truly be heard and understood by those to whom it is taught and proclaimed. In both word and deed, Christians offer a message of hope to a world that often finds itself in what seems a hopeless situation – violence, greed, poverty, oppression. And Christian individuals and communities live as counter-witnesses and 'contrast communities' in a world that values success over authenticity, wealth over sharing, exploitation of creation over its protection and care.[21] Christians also dare to speak 'truth to power' by mobilizing for justice and fearlessly speaking out against any injustice or oppression – of women, of the poor, of migrants, against human trafficking.

Prophecy is about living Christian life and Christian community authentically. It is about the communication of the gospel, about offering a word of hope, about commitment to justice, peacemaking and reconciliation.

Prophetic Dialogue as Spiritual Discipline

Bringing dialogue and prophecy together in the practice of mission is no easy task. It requires discipline – spiritual discipline. Steve and Roger Schroeder paraphrase Robert Schreiter's insistence about reconciliation, insisting themselves that prophetic dialogue is more of a *spirituality* than a *strategy*.[22] Mission can only be done, in the final analysis, by women and men who pray regularly, who spend time in contemplation, who share their faith in theological reflection, who study and read the Bible individually and in community, who steep themselves in the wisdom of the Christian tradition, who constantly hone their skills in reading cultures and contexts, who understand cultural trends and current events. Mission is also done with a posture of curiosity, creativity, imagination – being curious about the world and the context, rejoicing in 'strange' ways of being and doing, imagining that another world is possible (to pick up the Occupy slogan) or indeed already here!

---

20 Lesslie Newbigin, *The Gospel in a Pluralist Society*, Grand Rapids, MI: Eerdmans, 1989, 222–33.

21 Gerhard Lohfink, *Jesus and Community*, Philadelphia: Fortress Press, 1984.

22 Robert J. Schreiter, *The Ministry of Reconciliation: Spirituality and Strategies*, Maryknoll, NY: Orbis, 1998.

Only in constant discernment can Christians in mission decide whether a situation calls for a more prophetic stance or a more dialogical one. How are Lebanese Christians to live out and witness to their faith? How can Africans preach the gospel within their rich cultures but often corrupt governments? How are US Americans to decide what the Church's position should be in regard to migration, or health care, or same sex marriage? What should be the stance of Anglicans in Britain over a declining church attendance? How do Chinese Christians live authentically as Christians in a hostile political environment? There are no easy answers, but both prophecy and dialogue are needed in each case, and only those who are attuned to God's movement in the world can really know. As Rowan Williams has said so wonderfully, 'mission is finding out where the Spirit is at work and joining in'.[23] 'Finding out' is the work of spirituality.

This Book: Continuing the Reflection

In the second chapter of *Constants in Context*, Steve and Roger Schroeder propose six 'Constants' that are constitutive of mission as it has been practised throughout history and in today's context. These six constants are: (1) the *centrality of Christ* and implicitly the centrality of *Trinitarian faith*; (2) the importance of the *communal or ecclesial nature* of mission; (3) the connection between missionary reflection and practice and a person's or community's *eschatological vision*; (4) closely connected to this, a person's or a community's conviction about the *nature of salvation*; (5) the perspective on the nature of humanity, or *anthropology*; and (6) the appreciation or suspicion of *culture*. It is to further the reflection on prophetic dialogue that we, Stephen B. Bevans and Cathy Ross, have conceived this present book. Specifically, we and the authors in these pages propose to offer a deeper reflection on the prophetic and dialogical possibilities of the six constants that Stephen and Roger proposed over a decade ago. To thicken this approach yet even more, we have correlated the six sections of this book in a way that each would include the six elements of mission that were reflected on in the final section of *Constants in Context*: witness and proclamation, liturgy, prayer and contemplation; justice, peace and the integrity of creation; interreligious dialogue; inculturation and reconciliation.

The first section on Christology, includes an essay by Amos Yong on the question of the uniqueness of Jesus, as well as an essay by vanThanh Nguyen on Jesus as Prophet and one on the Holy Spirit in mission by Kirsteen Kim.

The second section is on ecclesiology where Emma Wild-Wood presents an intercultural ecclesiology through the lens of migration and Cathy Ross

---

23 Rowan Williams, 'Fresh Expressions' website, www.freshexPressions.org.uk/guide/about/principles/transform. Cited also in Kirsteen Kim, *Joining in with the Spirit: Connecting World Church and Local Mission*, London: SCM Press, 2010, 1.

writes on the Church as a hospitable mother where there is space for all. The third section deals with eschatology and features an essay by Dawn Nothwehr on the Church's mission of ecojustice affirming that we must relate humbly to all of God's creation. There is also an essay by Tim Naish where he muses on Christian approaches to justice in our complex world. The fourth section is soteriology with an essay on reconciliation and one on salvation. Robert Schreiter challenges us to see the salvific and mystagogic insights of reconciliation as a posture for mission and Mark Heim offers salvation as healing of broken relations and structures in a Trinitarian context. The fifth section offers three essays in the area of anthropology and what it means to be human. Frances Adeney considers this question from women's perspectives and what distinctive perspectives women can offer in mission engagement. Maria Cimperman offers a beautiful and encouraging anthropology of hope to root our practice of prophetic dialogue while Joe Kapolyo considers what it means to be human from an African (Zambian) perspective. The final section is on culture. Jonny Baker reflects on what prophetic dialogue has to offer contemporary culture while Roger Schroeder brings interculturality and prophetic dialogue into conversation to shape each other. Stephen B. Bevans rounds off the volume with an expansion of his well-known thesis of theology as contextual theology being expanded and shaped by interaction with prophetic dialogue.

Over the years, we have been struck by Sedmak's metaphor as theologian as the local village cook[24] – concocting a meal with a variety of differing ingredients and cooking methods – with all the associated resonances around eating, hospitality, warmth, convivial conversation – good meals enjoyed with friends. All these writers are our friends and we believe that this volume offers and reflects something of that metaphor – a rich and varied diet of theological reflection on mission as prophetic dialogue.

---

24 C. Sedmak, *Doing Local Theology: A Guide for Artisans of a New Humanity*, Maryknoll, NY: Orbis, 2002.

PART I

Christology: The Mission of Jesus as Prophetic Dialogue

Prophetic Christology in the New Testament

VANTHANH NGUYEN

Introduction

'What sort of man is this?' is the question that the disciples asked themselves about Jesus (Matt. 8.27). Over the past 2,000 years, this same question has frequently been raised by Christians as well as non-believers. Who was Jesus really and what did he actually say and do? For Christians and especially for biblical scholars the quest to know what sort of man Jesus really was is an important and even a necessary endeavour. However, scholars down through the ages have wondered whether we can really know and uncover the real Jesus. It is true that the New Testament in general and the four Gospels in particular give us many portraits of Jesus. But the question is, how much is the Jesus from the New Testament writings a historical depiction of Jesus and how much of it is really the authors' description of the 'Christ of faith'?

Consequently, this chapter seeks to uncover a reliable portrait of Jesus attested broadly in the New Testament. Since any historical investigation of Jesus is intricately related to Christology, the aim is to establish a consistent Christological portrait of Jesus.[1] Jesus as prophet is a reliable portrait of Jesus since this is well attested in all four Gospels and throughout the New Testament. More importantly, Jesus saw himself as a Spirit-filled prophet whose mission was to bring about the reign of God here and now. The programmatic passage of Luke 4.16–21 will provide the key for unlocking the door to understand Jesus' entire prophetic mission and ministry and the framework for establishing a prophetic Christology in the New Testament.

This chapter contains four main sections. The first part shows that the canonical Gospels are essentially Christological narratives, which portray Jesus according to each evangelist's perspective or the community's profession of faith. To reconstruct the historical Jesus, a careful examination of

---

1 R. David Kaylor states: 'If the truth be known, every study of the historical Jesus is a Christology in disguise.' *Jesus the Prophet: His Vision of the Kingdom of God*, Louisville, KY: Westminster John Knox Press, 1994, 231.

these Christological claims is required. The second part will focus on how Jesus is presented in the Gospels and more specifically in the Gospel of Luke. I will examine the mission proclamation in Luke 4.16–21 to see whether Jesus' self-understanding as the 'anointed' and 'spirit-filled' prophet corroborates what other characters perceive about him. The third section will demonstrate that Jesus was truly a mighty prophet whose words and deeds paralleled ancient biblical prophets. Finally, I will conclude by proposing that prophetic Christology can support a suitable model for doing Christian mission today.

Gospels as Christological Narratives

The quest for the historical Jesus must begin with the examination of the sources that are available to us.[2] The best surviving sources to help us reconstruct the life and teachings of Jesus are obviously the four canonical Gospels.[3] Richard Burridge's influential study, *What Are the Gospels?* convincingly demonstrates that the four canonical Gospels remarkably resemble the genre of Graeco-Roman biographies. In his analysis of the Fourth Gospel, Burridge shows that like the Synoptics, John's approach also resembles Graeco-Roman *bioi* or 'lives' in length, description of the life of the hero, grammatical style – in which the hero is also the grammatical subject of a high proportion of verbs – and many other literary features.[4] While it is true that the Gospels bear a resemblance to Graeco-Roman biography, they are not exactly the same. The Gospels are noticeably cohesive narratives of Jesus' life from birth to death. Lives of philosophers however are compilations of anecdotes, which are arranged according to themes rather

---

2 Unfortunately surviving pagan as well as Jewish sources, such as the Dead Sea Scrolls, contribute little to the historical quest. While Josephus' two brief references of Jesus helped validate the existence of Jesus of Nazareth, his references add very little information about the life of Jesus. Some scholars even questioned the validity of the details that are contained therein. See John P. Meier, *A Marginal Jew: Rethinking the Historical Jesus*, vol. 1: *The Roots of the Problem and the Person*, New York: Doubleday, 1991, 61. The references coincide basically with the Gospel accounts of Jesus.

3 The Apostle Paul, to whom tradition has attributed 13 epistles, is far more concerned about faith in Jesus' death and resurrection than in the details of his life. Outside the Gospels, Paul said the most about Jesus, but interestingly, the total information would fit on a three-by-five-inch index card. In Galatians 4.4 Paul tells us that Jesus was born of a woman and that he was a Jew. In 1 Corinthians 9.5 Paul tells us that Jesus had brothers one of whom is called James (see also Gal. 1.19). In 1 Corinthians 11, Paul alluded that Jesus was betrayed, although he did not say that it was by Judas. Furthermore, Paul obviously knows what Jesus said at the Last Supper. Paul tells us that Jesus was crucified but did not say by Pontius Pilate. That is about all that we can know about Jesus from Paul. Paul tells us nothing about Jesus' birth, temptations, baptism, transfiguration, miracles, parables and so on.

4 Richard A. Burridge, *What Are the Gospels? A Comparison with Graeco-Roman Biography*, 2nd edition, Grand Rapids, MI: Eerdmans, 2004, especially 213–32.

than in a chronological and unified narrative. Besides, the most significant element that is missing is 'the good news that is essential to the gospels'.[5]

In a nutshell, the four canonical Gospels are good tidings written in story form about Jesus from Nazareth who lived in first-century Palestine, preached the message of eternal life and compassion, established an alternative egalitarian community of fellowship, was betrayed by one of his own, put to death by means of Roman crucifixion, but was raised to life after three days. Having witnessed the resurrection, his disciples were convinced and therefore even testified with their own lives that Jesus was the Messiah/Christ, who fulfilled the Old Testament prophecy. The proclamation of Jesus as the Christ was first preached orally, but as time evolved, especially when the eyewitnesses were no longer around, traditions and Christological claims about him were gradually collected and written down for preservation, authentication, evangelization and legitimation of the position of Christ. In other words, the written Gospels are essentially *Christological narratives* from four different perspectives emerging from four distinct social locations and historical circumstances. Although we inherit four different Christological portraits of Jesus, there is but one Jesus Christ.[6]

The Gospel of Mark, which was the first to have been written, most likely in Rome around AD 70, portrays Jesus as a suffering Christ who was the Son of God, yet he was misunderstood by the people and even by his own disciples, rejected and persecuted by the religious leaders of the time and left to die alone on the cross. Mark's portrayal of Jesus as the *crucified Christ and Son of God* purposely provided meaning and encouragement for a community that was being persecuted for its beliefs. For this evangelist, discipleship literally means picking up one's cross daily and following him (Mark 8.34). Since Matthew and Luke used Mark and another hypothetical source called 'Q' (from the German word *Quelle* meaning source), both Gospels attribute many similar features and characteristics of Jesus, yet at the same time portray Jesus in a very different light. The Gospel of Matthew, which was composed for a more Jewish audience, possibly located in Upper Galilee or more likely Antioch, Syria, depicts Jesus as the *Jewish Messiah*, who was a prophet and teacher par excellence. Matthew's portrayal of Jesus as the obedient Messiah, who came not to abolish the old Jewish ways but to fulfil the Scriptures, provided meaning for Christians to follow and practise the new way within the existing Jewish heritage and traditions. For this evangelist, discipleship can be compared to a scribe who has been trained for the kingdom of heaven who brings out of his treasury 'what is new and what is old' (Matt. 13.52). As for Luke, Jesus is distinctively characterized as the *universal Saviour* who delivers humanity from the consequences of

---

5 Loveday Alexander, 'What is a Gospel', in Stephen C. Barton (ed.), *The Cambridge Companion to the Gospels*, Cambridge: Cambridge University Press, 2006, 13–30 (26).

6 vanThanh Nguyen SVD, 'Luke's Passion as Story of Good News', *The Bible Today* 48:2 (2010), 61–7 (61–2).

sin and offers salvation to all people. Luke's unique portrait of Jesus makes much sense for a predominantly Gentile audience who were continually challenged by the mystery cults and imperial theology that claimed ancient gods and emperors as 'god and saviour'. For this evangelist, discipleship is bearing witness to Jesus as the one and only Son of God who is light and salvation for all people (Luke 2.29, 32).

Independent of the Synoptic Gospels, the Gospel of John portrays Jesus in a unique way. Many stories in this Gospel are not told elsewhere in the New Testament.[7] Noticeably, the Johannine Jesus does not tell parables, cast out demons or eat with outcasts. Rather, Jesus performs seven 'signs'[8] and delivers long philosophical discourses. He repeatedly describes himself by using the expression 'I am' (egō eimi).[9] Contrasting with Mark's portrayal, Jesus publicly and openly reveals his true identity as the Messiah, King, Lamb of God, Son of Man, Saviour of the world, resurrection and life, the only begotten Son, to name just a few important titles.[10] Moreover, since he embodies divine qualities and essence, Jesus, the *personified divine Wisdom* or the incarnate *Logos* or 'Word', is one with the Father and therefore is eternal and God. Many scholars have noted the 'high Christology' that is presented in this Gospel.

As I have briefly shown, the Gospels are basically Christological narratives representing four distinct traditions of the same basic story of Jesus who is the Christ. Consequently, each Gospel depicts Jesus differently according to the evangelist's or community's profession of faith. But the question is, did Jesus perceive himself to be the Messiah, Son of God or God? A close examination reveals that Mark, being the earliest Gospel, never had Jesus himself claiming to be God nor even Messiah. This seems to be the consensus of biblical scholars today. How then can we get behind the Christological portrayals of Jesus in these accounts to discover what he was really like? In other words, how do we move from the 'Christ of faith' to get to the 'Jesus of history'? This is definitely a difficult task but not necessarily impossible.[11]

---

7 Some of the most noted stories are: calling of Andrew, Philip and Nathanael (1.35–51); changing of water into wine at Cana (2.1–12); conversation with Nicodemus (3.1–21); encountering the Samaritan woman at a well (4.1–42); healing of a crippled man at the Pool of Bethesda (5.1–18); healing of a man born blind (9.1–41); raising of Lazarus (11.1–44); washing of the disciples' feet (13.1–20); resurrection appearance to Thomas (20.24–29).

8 There are seven or eight miracle stories (2.1–12; 4.46–54; 5.1–9; 6.1–13; 9.1–7; 11.1–44; 21.1–6; maybe 6.15–25).

9 Jesus is the bread of life (6.35, 51), the light of the world (8.12; 9.5), the door (10.7, 9), the good shepherd (10.11, 14), the resurrection and the life (11.25), the way, the truth and the life (14.6), the true vine (15.1, 5).

10 Christological titles of Jesus in John's Gospel are numerous. Here are just a few titles and their references: Messiah (1.41; 7.41); King of Israel (1.49; 18.37; 19.19); Lamb of God (1.29, 35); Son of Man (1.51; 6.27; 13.13); Prophet par excellence (4.44; 6.14; 9.17); Saviour of the world (4.42); God's eternal Son (1.18); light of the world (8.12; 9.5; 12.46); good shepherd (10.14); the way, truth and life (14.6).

11 For a concise summary of the best methods and criteria for discerning traditions that

To discover the real Jesus, we need to peel away the various layers of traditions in order to unveil what Jesus really thought and said about himself. The task requires us literally to turn the stones upside down and exegetically sift through the multiple layers of the texts to reconstruct his life.[12]

Jesus the 'Messianic' Prophet

Our quest for a historical–Christological portrait of Jesus begins with an examination of what people in the Gospels perceived him to be. The earliest written source, the Gospel of Mark, records Jesus asking his disciples: '"Who do people say that I am?" And they answered him, "John the Baptist; and others, Elijah; and still others, one of the prophets"' (8.27–28; also Matt. 16.14; Luke 9.19). People obviously saw Jesus as a prophet. When Jesus entered Jerusalem, for example, the crowds rejoiced, singing hymns and chanting, 'This is the prophet Jesus from Nazareth in Galilee' (Matt. 21.10). Matthew recounts that the chief priests and the Pharisees were greatly offended by what Jesus said and therefore wanted to arrest him, but they feared the crowds, 'because they regarded him as a prophet' (Matt. 21.46). The crowd's recognition of Jesus' prophetic character actually prevented him from getting arrested. Even Jesus' opponents saw him as a prophet. Herod Antipas believed that Jesus was the prophet John, whom he had beheaded and had been raised from the dead (Mark 6.16). In the story of the repentant woman who anointed his feet, Simon the Pharisee considered Jesus a prophet when he asked himself, 'If this man were a prophet, he would have known who and what kind of woman this is who is touching him – that she is a sinner' (Luke 7.39). Jesus' own disciples also identified him as a prophet. As the two distraught disciples travelled to Emmaus, a stranger appeared and enquired of them about the things that they were discussing. They replied, 'The things about Jesus of Nazareth, who was a prophet mighty in deed and word before God and all the people' (Luke 24.19). Likewise, the Gospel of John bears witness to the identification of Jesus as a prophet. Already in the Prologue, the Fourth Evangelist introduces Jesus as a prophet (John 1.14–18) and more explicitly as *the* prophet 'about whom Moses in the law and also the prophets wrote' (John 1.45). In the story of the Samaritan woman, after Jesus told her about her past history, she became amazed and said to him, 'Sir, I see that you are a prophet' (John

---

originate with Jesus, see James H. Charlesworth, *The Historical Jesus: An Essential Guide*, Nashville, TN: Abingdon, 2008, 15–32.

12 John D. Crossan and Jonathan L. Reed make an interesting observation about the task of excavating Jesus, which is 'Digging down archaeologically amidst the stones to reconstruct his world and digging down exegetically amidst the texts to reconstruct his life. It is, above all else, about integrating those twin excavations in order to locate his life in its world, to place his vision and his program in its time and place.' *Excavating Jesus: Beneath the Stones, Behind the Texts*, revised and updated; New York: HarperOne, 2001, 1.

4.19). Having been healed by Jesus, the man born blind confidently declared to his interrogators, the Pharisees, that Jesus is a 'prophet' (John 9.17). Jesus also seemed to refer to himself as a prophet when he testified, 'a prophet has no honour in the prophet's own country' (John 4.44).[13]

Among the four Gospels, however, Luke provides the finest presentation of Jesus as a prophet.[14] To get a better sense of how Jesus thought of himself and his mission as a prophet, let us briefly turn to the programmatic passage of Luke 4.16–21. I believe that this text is the key for unlocking the door of Luke's Christology and provides the framework for Jesus' entire prophetic mission and ministry.

Luke 4.16–21 is Jesus' 'homecoming' and 'inaugural address'.[15] As Jesus was making his way home to Nazareth, he performed many deeds, and a report about him had begun to spread 'through all the surrounding country' (Luke 4.14). Obviously, his fame and popularity had not gone unnoticed at Nazareth as well. Jesus' family and neighbours probably expected him to do even greater things in his own hometown. One can imagine the commotion at his arrival. The streets were probably filled with excitement as his family, friends and neighbours joyfully welcomed one of their very own into the synagogue. As a quiet settled over the congregation, an air of anticipation arose as to what Jesus might say or do. When the time came, Jesus stood up, unrolled the sacred scroll that was given to him and read a selected passage from the prophet Isaiah:

'The Spirit of the Lord is upon me,
　because he has anointed me
　　to bring good news to the poor.
He has sent me to proclaim release to the captives
　and recovery of sight to the blind,
　　to let the oppressed go free,
to proclaim the year of the Lord's favour.' (Luke 4.18–19)

The reading that Jesus selected is actually a combination of Isaiah 61.1–2 and 58.6. This composite quotation is the heart of this passage, which Jesus intentionally chose to identify and define his own prophetic mission.[16] First

---

13 See J. D. Atkins, 'The Trial of the People and the Prophet: John 5:30–47 and the True and False Prophet Traditions', *Catholic Biblical Quarterly* 75.2 (2013), 279–96 (281–2).

14 Robert F. O'Toole, *Luke's Presentation of Jesus: A Christology*, Rome: Editrice Pontificio Istituto Biblico, 2004, 29–54.

15 In the Markan account, Jesus' visit to his hometown appears later in his ministry (Mark 6.1–6a), which Matthew follows closely (Matt. 13.53–58). Luke however placed the event at the beginning of Jesus' ministry, which is noticeably different from the Markan chronology.

16 Fitzmyer suggests that the passage was not assigned for there is no clear evidence for a cycle of prophetic readings in first-century Palestine. Thus, Jesus must have deliberately handpicked the passage. See Joseph A. Fitzmyer, *The Gospel according to Luke I–IX*, Garden City, NY: Doubleday, 1981, 531–2.

and foremost, Jesus was imbued with the Spirit of God because he had been 'anointed'. The event obviously happened at baptism (3.22).[17] Since the verb 'anoint' (*chrio*) is a cognate with *Christos* in Greek and *Messiah* in Hebrew, exegetes often misinterpret this as a royal anointing, turning Jesus into a royal Messiah. However, Joseph Fitzmyer is correct in pointing out that this passage does not contain any reference to the Davidic dynasty or kingly function of Jesus. Furthermore, the quotation from Isaiah makes no reference or allusion to a priestly function belonging to Jesus. Thus, I agree with Fitzmyer that Jesus referred to his 'anointing' as a *prophetic* and not a royal or priestly anointing.[18] Through the words of the prophet Isaiah, Jesus explicitly claims that he is the one who embodies and fulfils the Old Testament prophecy. Just as his birth had been characterized by Spirit and power (1.35), Jesus now enters into his ministry by the same 'power of the Spirit of God' (4.1–2, 14–15), which allows him to teach, heal and drive out demons. Indeed, it is the power of the Spirit that directs Jesus' activity and therefore authorizes him as the prophet of God mighty in words and deeds.

The quotation from Isaiah defines the character of Jesus' prophetic ministry. First and foremost, Jesus proclaims good news to the poor. This echoes the theme already highlighted in the *Magnificat* whereby Mary praised the Lord for lifting the lowly, filling the hungry with good things and sending the rich away empty (1.52–53). In the Beatitudes, Jesus declares that the poor are blessed (6.20). Notably, the poor have a very prominent place in Jesus' teaching, especially in the Gospel of Luke.[19] Second, Jesus has been commissioned to release those who are oppressed and in captivity. The term 'release' (*aphesis*) probably means more than just the forgiveness of sins. It could imply a liberation 'from various forms of bondage and oppression: economic (the poor), physical (the lame, the crippled), political (the condemned), and demonic'.[20] Jesus also restores sight to the blind (7.21–22; 18.35). Jesus' restoration of sight to the blind not only fulfils Simeon's prediction as the one who would be a 'light for the nations' (2.32) but also fulfils the prophetic vision of Isaiah (Isa. 35.5; 42.6–7).

The reference to the proclamation of the 'year of the Lord's favour' comes from Isaiah 61, which is connected with the Jubilee year legislation in Leviticus 25.10. David Tiede describes the Jubilee year as follows:

---

17 Later Peter also mentions the anointing of Jesus with the Holy Spirit in his speech at Cornelius' house (Acts 10.38).

18 See Fitzmyer, *Luke I–IX*, 529–30. While Robert C. Tannehill (*The Narrative Unity of Luke–Acts: A Literary Interpretation*, 2 vols, Philadelphia: Fortress Press, 1986, vol. 1, 63) does not exclude the prophetic anointing, he claims that it is a royal anointing, reaffirming Jesus as God's son and Davidic Messiah. Luke Timothy Johnson seems to recognize that it is a prophetic anointing; nevertheless, he identifies Jesus as the 'prophetic Messiah' (*The Gospel of Luke*, Sacra Pagina Series 3, Collegeville, MN: Liturgical Press, 1991, 81).

19 See Luke 14.13, 21; 16.20, 22; 18.22; 21.3.

20 R. Alan Culpepper, 'The Gospel of Luke', in *The New Interpreter's Bible Commentary*, vol. IX, Nashville, TN: Abingdon Press, 1995, 3–490 (106).

The Jubilee Year was to be a time of restitution and restoration for all Israel. Debts were to be forgiven, land returned to families who had leased them or used them as collateral. On the anniversary of the 7x7th year or the 50th year, this program of land reform and forgiveness was to be God's way of renewing the society of Israel. But this program of God's reign remained a hope rather than a practice.[21]

Unfortunately, the Jubilee legislation – namely the economic and social reform that includes slave release, interest-free loans, debt release and the restoration of land to the original owner – was a utopian vision and was never really practised in Israel's history. It is not certain whether Jesus sought to inaugurate the Jubilee year through his reading of Isaiah 61. It is more likely that Jesus saw that his prophetic mission and ministry fulfilled the vision and hope of the Jubilee year.[22] Luke states that after Jesus made the prophetic proclamation, he rolled up the scroll, gave it back to the attendant and sat down. The eyes of all in the synagogue were fixed on him. Then he began to say to them, 'Today this scripture has been fulfilled in your hearing' (Luke 4.21).

This brief study of Luke's programmatic passage (4.16–21) demonstrates that Jesus saw his mission and ministry as the fulfilment of Isaiah's prophecy. By deliberately quoting the words of Isaiah (61.1–2 and 58.6), Jesus clearly identified himself as a prophet. Imbued with the Holy Spirit, Jesus announced good news to the poor and liberty to the oppressed. He plainly stated that what was spoken by Isaiah is actually 'being fulfilled' (Luke 4.21). Jesus' prophetic proclamation in the synagogue at Nazareth caused quite a commotion and eventually led to outright rejection when he compared his ministry to that of Elijah and Elisha. Identifying himself with the ancient prophets, Jesus said, 'Truly I tell you, no prophet is accepted in the prophet's hometown' (4.24; see also John 4.44). The story of Jesus' homecoming ends on a tragic note because his townsfolk became enraged, drove him out of town and tried to push him off a cliff.

Prophet Mighty in Words and Deeds

Luke does not just tell his readers that Jesus is a prophet; he also shows them that he is a prophet.[23] He heals people of their infirmities (Luke 4.31–37; 5.17–26), feeds those who are hungry (9.1–6, 10–17) and raises people back

---

21 David L. Tiede, *Luke*, Augsburg Commentary on the New Testament; Minneapolis: Augsburg Publishing House, 1988, 107.

22 Culpepper, 'The Gospel of Luke', 106.

23 In narrative criticism, scholars distinguish between the literary features of 'telling' (direct characterization) and 'showing' (indirect characterization). Characterization by means of 'showing' has a greater effect on the perception of the character by the readers. See van-Thanh Nguyen, *Peter and Cornelius: A Story of Conversion and Mission*, American Society of Missiological Monograph Series; Eugene, OR: Pickwick Publications, 2012, 107–32.

to life (7.11–17). When the disciples of John are sent to ask Jesus about his identity, he answers them, 'Go and tell John what you have seen and heard: the blind receive their sight, the lame walk, the lepers are cleansed, the deaf hear, the dead are raised, the poor have good news brought to them' (Luke 7.22). His actions fulfil exactly what he had promised to do in his inaugural speech in the synagogue at Nazareth. As a prophet, he performs miraculous deeds that are similar to those of Elijah and Elisha. As such, when Jesus raises the widow's son in Nain, everyone glorifies God and exclaims, 'A great prophet has risen among us!' and 'God has looked favourably on his people!' (Luke 7.16)

As a prophet, Jesus teaches with authority and power, revealing the mystery of the kingdom of God through parabolic images. To farmers he speaks in images of fields and wheat, to housewives in images of bread-making and housecleaning, to builders in images of stone and mortar, to fishermen in images of net and fishes, to merchants in images of pearls and treasures.[24] As a prophet, Jesus can foresee the future, as he makes three famous predictions of his suffering, death and resurrection (9.22, 43–44; 18.31–34). More importantly, Jesus sees his death in Jerusalem as the death of a prophet, 'because it is impossible for a prophet to be killed outside Jerusalem' (13.33). Like his predecessors, Jesus performs symbolic prophetic acts. Consequently, his triumphal entry into Jerusalem (19.29–40) and the cleansing of the Temple (19.45–48) draw too much attention and probably lead him to crucifixion.

One dominant motif Luke uses to characterize Jesus throughout the passion narrative is that of an innocent and righteous prophet. Jesus possesses prophetic knowledge to assist Peter and John to prepare the Passover meal (22.12–13). At the supper he tells the disciples that this will be the last meal he will eat and drink with them until the kingdom of God comes (22.16, 18). He foretells the identity of his betrayer (22.21–22) and predicts Peter's denial (22.34). He warns the disciples about future persecution (22.35–38). In his prayer for the removal of the cup Jesus knows exactly what will happen to him (22.42). Ironically, when he is mocked, beaten and blindfolded by his captors they command him to 'prophesy' (22.64), which actually fulfils what Jesus had already foretold in the third prediction (18.32). At the trial before the council Jesus prophesies that he 'will be seated at the right hand of the power of God' (22.69). Interestingly, Luke goes out of his way to show that Jesus is innocent of all charges raised against him. Three times Pilate declares Jesus' innocence (23.4, 14, 22). Herod too cannot find any charges against Jesus (23.15), so he sends him back to Pilate dressed in a 'white' robe (23.11), which symbolizes innocence or purity. The repentant criminal also asserts that Jesus 'has done nothing wrong' (23.41). Finally, the Roman centurion dramatically declares: 'Certainly this man was

---

24 vanThanh Nguyen, 'Speaking in Parables', *Give Us This Day*, July 2012, 240–1.

innocent' (NRSV) or 'just' (NIV) (23.47). The Greek word *dikaios* is more appropriately rendered as 'just' or 'righteous' (cf. 2.25; 23.50); Luke applies it to Jesus in Acts when he calls him the Righteous One (Acts 3.14; 7.52; 22.14). Consequently, it is being the righteous prophet who does God's will that brings him to the cross.[25]

Luke presents Jesus in ways that are parallel to ancient prophets.[26] People actually thought that he was John the Baptist or Elijah returned from the dead or some other prophet (8.27–28). He associates his mission with Isaiah's prophetic vision (4.16–21) and performs miraculous deeds that are similar to the works of Elijah and Elisha.[27] Jesus is also compared to the prophet Jonah. When asked for a sign, the sign of Jonah was the only one Jesus would give (11.29–30). For Luke, however, Jesus is most comparable with Moses the prophet par excellence of the Old Testament.[28] There are several notable references to Moses in both Luke's Gospel and the Acts of the Apostles. The most important references are found in the transfiguration story (9.28–36), Peter's kerygmatic speech (Acts 3.12–26) and Stephen's great speech (Acts 7.35–44). Luke clearly underscores the symmetry and parallelism between Moses and Jesus; furthermore, the risen Jesus fulfils the promise made by Moses himself, which is attested by Stephen saying: 'This is the Moses who said to the Israelites, "God will raise up a prophet for you from your own people as he raised me up"' (Acts 7.37; Deut. 18.15, 18).[29]

Lukan scholars have long noticed the parallelism between the Third Gospel and the Acts of the Apostles.[30] What is promised in Luke is fulfilled in Acts.[31] What Jesus does in the Gospel, the apostles also will do in

---

25 vanThanh Nguyen, 'Luke's Passion as Story of Good News', *The Bible Today* 48:2 (2010), 61–7 (64–5).

26 J. Serverino Croatto, 'Jesus, Prophet like Elijah, and Prophet–Teacher like Moses in Luke–Acts', *Journal of Biblical Literature* 124:3 (2005), 451–65. Croatto makes a strong case for Luke's construction of the figure of Jesus as a prophet. Moreover, de Jonge considered it highly probable that Jesus saw himself as a prophet; see H. J. de Jonge, 'The Historical Jesus' View of Himself and of His Mission', in Martinus C. de Boer (ed.), *From Jesus to John. Essays on Jesus and New Testament Christology in Honour of Marinus de Jonge*, Sheffield: Sheffield Academic Press, 1993, 21–37.

27 O'Toole correctly noted the parallelism between Elijah and Elisha and Jesus. These parallels are: the raising of the widow's son of Nain (Luke 7.11–17; 1 Kings 17); the cleansing of the leper (Luke 5.12–16; 2 Kings 5–19); the feeding of multitude (Luke 9.10–17; 2 Kings 4.42–44). For other allusions, see O'Toole, *Luke's Presentation*, 33–5.

28 The Moses typology is also very evident in the Gospel of Matthew.

29 For examples of parallelism between Moses and Jesus in Luke–Acts, see Croatto, 'Jesus', 462 and O'Toole, *Luke's Presentation*, 35–42.

30 William S. Kurz, *Reading Luke–Acts: Dynamics of Biblical Narrative*, Louisville, KY: Westminster John Knox Press, 1993, esp. 135–55; Tannehill, *The Narrative Unity of Luke–Acts*, vols 1 and 2.

31 The risen Jesus promised the gift of the Holy Spirit in Luke 24.49 and it is fulfilled at Pentecost in Acts 2.1–4.

Acts.[32] The fate of Jesus will also be the fate of his disciples.[33] Just as Jesus is presented as a prophet, the apostles and other leading disciples are also portrayed as prophets. Luke's major characters in Acts (for example, Peter, John, Philip, Stephen, Barnabas and Paul) are described in ways that clearly identify them as prophets. Luke Timothy Johnson notes:

> Each is 'filled with the Holy Spirit' (4.8; 5.32; 6.3; 7.55; 11.24; 13.9). Each is 'bold' in proclamation (4.13; 13.46; 28.31) of 'the good news' (5.42; 8.4, 12, 25, 40; 11.20; 13.32; 14.7; 15.35) or the 'word of God' (4.29; 8.14; 13.5). Each is a 'witness' (2.32; 10.41; 13.31; 22.20) who works 'signs and wonders' (4.30; 6.8; 14.3; 15.12) among the 'people' (*laos*), that is, the Jewish population considered as the people of God (3.12; 4.1; 6.8; 13.15). In the symbolic world of Torah, this composite of character-istics belongs unmistakably to the prophet.[34]

Having shown that Luke's characterization of the apostles in Acts is expli-citly connected to Moses and Jesus, Johnson confidently concludes by stating: 'The apostles are therefore portrayed as prophets like Jesus, and Jesus is portrayed as a prophet like Moses.'[35] The summary statement of the two disciples on the way home to Emmaus fully captures Jesus' authentic identity: 'Jesus of Nazareth ... was a prophet mighty in deed and word before God and all the people' (24.21). Consequently, Luke's presentation of Jesus as a 'prophet mighty in deed and word', who the apostles should imitate, is fundamentally Luke's Christology.

Christian Prophetic Mission Today

Jesus as prophet is a reliable portrait of Jesus since this is well attested in all four Gospels and throughout the New Testament.[36] Ben Witherington

---

32 Jesus performed miraculous deeds, so too did the apostles (Acts 3.1–10; 9.36–43; 14.1–7). Most notably, Jesus healed a lame man (Luke 5.17–26); Peter did likewise (Acts 3.1–10). Jesus raised a widow's son from death (Luke 7.11–17); Peter raised a widow from death (Luke 9.36–43).

33 Just as the religious leaders attacked Jesus (Luke 5.29—6.11), they also attacked the apostles (Acts 4.1—8.3). Just as Jesus was seized by an angry mob (Luke 22.54), so was Paul (Acts 21.30). Jesus was tried four times and declared innocent three times (Luke 22.66—23.13); Paul was also tried four times and declared innocent three times (Acts 23.1—26.32).

34 Luke Timothy Johnson, 'The Christology of Luke–Acts', in Mark A. Powell and David R. Bauer (eds), *Who Do You Say That I Am?: Essays on Christology*, Louisville, KY: West-minster John Knox Press, 1999, 49–63 (55).

35 Johnson, 'Christology of Luke–Acts', 55. For a more comprehensive treatment of how prophecy plays a key role in Luke's construction of his two-volume work, see Luke Timothy Johnson's latest book, *Prophetic Jesus, Prophetic Church: The Challenge of Luke–Acts to Con-temporary Christians*, Grand Rapids, MI: Eerdmans, 2011, especially chapter 2, pages 23–38.

36 Scholars have devised several criteria for determining which of the traditions that sur-vive in our ancient sources preserve historically reliable information about Jesus. The most

keenly notes, 'One of the most enduring images of Jesus in Christian history is that of Jesus as a prophet.'[37] R. David Kaylor effectively summarizes his investigation as follows:

> Above all else, he was a prophet, in word and deed. He did not curry favor with the wealthy and powerful in order to garner their support for his reform movement. Neither did he pander condescendingly to the poor in order to use them in his enterprise. Like true prophets of the past, he fearlessly proclaimed God's will as he saw it, letting offense or approval be the result of his message, not the shaper of it.[38]

Many scholarly investigations of the historical Jesus conclude that Jesus was a prophet. However, different scholars qualify him in distinct ways: as a 'Jewish eschatological'[39] prophet, as a 'social/political'[40] prophet, as a 'charismatic'[41] prophet or as a 'feminist'[42] prophet. While prophet is a limited term to fully capture the totality of Jesus, I believe that prophet

---

important criterion is called 'independent attestation'. The criterion of independent attestation maintains that traditions about Jesus preserved in more than one independent source are more likely to be historically accurate. These independent sources are: Mark, John, the Apostle Paul and the authors of *Quelle* or 'Q', special Matthew (M) and special Luke (L). It is important to note that Matthew and Luke are not necessarily independent sources since they relied on Mark as their primary source.

37 Ben Witherington III, *The Jesus Quest: The Third Search for the Jew of Nazareth*, New Expanded Edition, Downers Grove, IL: InterVarsity Press, 1997, 117. See also Ben Witherington III, *The Many Faces of the Christ: The Christologies of the New Testament and Beyond*, New York: Crossroad, 1998.

38 Kaylor, *Jesus the Prophet*, 211.

39 Many scholars consider Jesus as a Jewish eschatological prophet who was expecting God's imminent intervention in history to restore Israel and establish God's reign. Some most influential works are: Albert Schweitzer, *The Quest of the Historical Jesus: A Critical Study of Its Progress from Reimarus to Wrede*, revised edn; New York: Macmillan, 1968; E. P. Sanders, *The Historical Figure of Jesus*, London: Penguin, 1993; John P. Meier, *A Marginal Jew: Rethinking the Historical Jesus*, 4 vols, New York: Doubleday 1991, 1994, 2001, 2009; N. T. Wright, *Jesus and the Victory of God*, Minneapolis: Fortress, 1996.

40 Several scholars saw Jesus as a Jewish social prophet, promoting a peasant social revolution. See Richard Horsley, *Jesus and the Spiral of Violence*, San Francisco: HarperSanFrancisco, 1987; Kaylor, *Jesus the Prophet*; William R. Herzog II, *Jesus, Justice, and the Reign of God: A Ministry of Liberation*, Louisville, KY: Westminster/John Knox, 2000.

41 Several scholars consider Jesus as a charismatic Jewish mystic and spirit person, who was uniquely in touch with the divine and performed miraculous deeds. See Geza Vermes, *The Religion of Jesus the Jew*, Minneapolis: Augsburg Fortress, 1993; Marcus Borg, *Meeting Jesus Again for the First Time*, San Francisco: HarperSanFrancisco, 1994.

42 See Elizabeth Schüssler Fiorenza, *In Memory of Her: A Feminist Theological Reconstruction of Christian Origins*, New York: Crossroad, 1984 and *Jesus: Miriam's Child, Sophia's Prophet: Critical Issues in Feminist Christology*, New York: Continuum, 1994. According to Fiorenza, Jesus was a prophet of God who saw himself as Sophia or Wisdom and led a renewal movement that stood in continuity with an egalitarian tradition within Judaism that was critical of the dominant tradition of Jewish patriarchalism.

is most descriptive of Jesus and his mission, as well as of New Testament Christology.

We live in a time when prophetic activity is waning. The Church and our world desperately need radical prophets to challenge the social, political and economic injustices of our time.[43] Our planet earth and its ecosystem are rapidly deteriorating due to people's lack of care for and respect for God's creation. Our mother earth desperately needs prophets to champion her cause. Religious and well as civic leaders, whose fundamental character is being prophetic, have declined in their charisma.[44] We live in a time when prophetic activity is urgently needed. Consequently, promoting a prophetic Christology as a model for the Christian mission is very timely and suitable.

Christian mission as prophecy is not new of course! Michael Amaladoss argued that prophecy is the theological foundation of mission.[45] Stephen Bevans and Roger Schroeder too have been great champions of this aspect of mission. Moreover, they developed another step noting that Christian mission is not just prophetic but also dialogical. Bevans and Schroeder stress that Christian mission in the twenty-first century is best done in 'prophetic dialogue'.[46] Their writings and reflections have contributed to a fresh understanding of Christian mission today.

Prophetic Christology likewise underscores that Jesus the prophet constantly engaged in prophetic dialogue. Jesus spoke frankly, treated everyone respectfully and loved all unconditionally. Jesus excluded no one in his teaching and healing and included everyone in table fellowship. He moved among the poor and rich, the tax collectors and lepers, the scribes and Pharisees, Jews and Gentiles. He spoke boldly and acted prophetically. Jesus announced liberation regardless of nationality, gender or race and denounced all forms of injustice. Like Israel's ancient prophets, Jesus criticized the political and religious structures of his day and energized the people of his time to follow the will of God.[47] While Jesus is clearly prophetic, the Jesus of history was also dialogical in his prophetic engagement. There are numerous examples that illustrate Jesus' cross-cultural or (more appropriately) 'intercultural' dialogue that are themselves prophetic. These

---

43 Johnson poignantly points out that in this and every age, the Church desperately needs prophecy; furthermore, 'prophecy-as-a-way-of-being-in-the-world' is the challenge of the contemporary Church (*Prophetic Jesus, Prophetic Church*, 29 and 181–6).

44 For a description of the prophetic character of religious life, see vanThanh Nguyen, 'Biblical Foundations for Religious Life: A Prophetic Vision', *Verbum SVD* 53:2 (2012), 263–73.

45 Michael Amaladoss, 'Mission as Prophecy', in James A. Scherer and Stephen B. Bevans (eds), *New Directions in Mission and Evangelization 2: Theological Foundations*, Maryknoll, NY: Orbis, 1994, 64–72.

46 Stephen B. Bevans and Roger P. Schroeder, *Prophetic Dialogue: Reflections on Christian Mission Today*, Maryknoll, NY: Orbis, 2011, 38.

47 To criticize and energize are two important tasks of a prophet; see Nguyen, 'Biblical Foundations for Religious Life', 267–70. See also Walter Brueggemann, *The Prophetic Imagination*, 2nd edition, Minneapolis: Augsburg Fortress, 2001, 3–4.

encounters are considered 'dialogical' and 'prophetic' because both parties are mutually enriched and transformed in the interaction and exchange. One notable example that is uniquely found in the Gospel of Luke is the numerous occasions that Jesus participated in table fellowship. His inclusivity at the dinner table was a radical move, for people in Jesus' time did not eat with just anyone. To sit at table with someone was a sign of respect, trust and friendship. Jesus surprised everyone by sitting down to eat and carry on conversations with people of different backgrounds, status and gender. Moreover, Jesus offered his very self as food and drink for those who were hungry and thirsty for the kingdom of God. Many who came in contact with him were transformed, for example, Zacchaeus the tax collector (Luke 19.1–10), the sinful woman who anointed Jesus (7.36–50), the demonic possessed man (8.26–39), Martha and Mary (10.38–42) and the two disciples from Emmaus (24.13–35). Noticeably, Jesus did not just simply interact with people; rather he and those he encountered and conversed with were mutually enriched.[48] There are many other stories found in other Gospels that showed Jesus was dialogical in his prophetic engagement; two most notable examples are: the Syro-Phoenician woman (Mark 7.24–30) and the Samaritan woman (John 4.4–42).[49]

Accordingly, prophetic Christology provides a basic foundation for current mission theology. Drawing especially from the programmatic missionary passage of Luke 4.16–21, Christian prophetic mission today ought to imitate Jesus as prophet in three ways: (1) by being led by the Spirit; (2) by inaugurating the reign of God; and (3) by conveying the good news of hope and salvation to all.[50]

First and foremost, Christian prophetic mission must be led by the Spirit. The evangelist Luke asserts that Jesus' entire life was imbued with the Holy Spirit. From the moment of conception (1.35) to his last breath on the cross (23.47), Jesus was infused with the Holy Spirit. Likewise, Jesus entered into his ministry by the same 'power of the Spirit of God' (4.1–2, 14–15), which allowed him to teach, heal and drive out demons. Indeed, it was the power of the Spirit that directed Jesus' activity and therefore authorized him as the prophet of God mighty in words and deeds. Just as Jesus acted in the power of the Spirit, the early Church too was guided by the same Spirit. The Spirit enabled the apostles and disciples to be witnesses from Jerusalem to the ends

---

48 For more about Jesus' as an intercultural Jew, see vanThanh Nguyen SVD, 'Biblical Foundations for Interculturality', *Verbum SVD* 54:1 (2013), 35–46 (42).

49 For an interpretation that is both dialogical and prophetic, see Laurie Brink, 'In Search of the Biblical Foundations of Prophetic Dialogue: Engaging a Hermeneutics of Otherness', *Missiology: An International Review* 41:1 (2013), 9–21.

50 These three aspects of Christian prophetic mission are similar to the three strains of mission theology and practice developed by Bevans and Schroeder. The three threads are: 'mission as participation in the life and mission of the Trinity (*missio Dei*); mission as liberating service of the Reign of God; and, mission as proclamation of Jesus Christ as Universal Saviour' (*Prophetic Dialogue*, 111).

of the earth (Acts 1.8), expanding beyond its geographical boundaries and ethnic restrictions. For Christian mission to be genuine, it must be deeply connected with the Holy Spirit and serve to fulfil the will and purpose of the Spirit. In other words, the Church must humbly recognize that its mission is essentially God's mission or *Missio Dei* and not her own.

Second, Christian prophetic mission today must actively promote the reign or kingdom of God since this was the central message of Jesus' prophetic proclamation. For example, the Gospel of Mark introduces Jesus and his mission with these opening words: 'Now after John was arrested, Jesus came to Galilee, proclaiming the good news of God and saying, "The time is fulfilled, and the kingdom of God has come near; repent, and believe in the good news"' (1.14–15). Jesus' primary mission was to launch God's reign of justice. This was the heart of Jesus' purpose on earth, which he publicly proclaimed in his opening speech at the Nazareth synagogue. Likewise, the Church must also make the proclamation of the reign of God its central focus of mission. Furthermore, the Church must remember that she exists not for herself but for the reign of God.

Finally, today's mission must boldly convey the good news of hope and salvation to all. It is well known in the Gospel of Luke that Jesus offered special privileges to the insignificant and the poor. Jesus blessed them for being poor (6.20), and it was to them that the gospel was announced (4.18; 7.22). Jesus also showed special concern for women in his ministry (7.11–17; 8.1–3; 10.38; 18.1–8; 24.1–10). As Saviour of all, Jesus offered salvation to sinners (7.36–48; 19.1–10), his enemies (7.27; 22.51; 23.34), Samaritans (10.33; 17.16) and Gentiles (4.26–27; 7.2; 23.43). Clearly Jesus excluded no one! For the Church's mission to coincide with Jesus' mission, it too must be universally inclusive, having a preferential option for the poor and the insignificant.

Conclusion

The aim of this chapter is to establish a historical–Christological portrait of Jesus found in the New Testament. Since the Gospels are the most reliable and available sources to uncover who Jesus really was, I naturally relied on them for my investigation. I have pointed out that the Gospels are essentially Christological narratives depicting Jesus differently according to each evangelist's perspective or the community's profession of faith. Consequently, there are four Christological portraits of Jesus. For Mark, he was the Son of God (Mark 1.1); for Matthew, he was the unique and obedient Son of the Father (Matt. 11.26–27); for Luke, he was the universal Saviour and Lord of all (Luke 1.47; Acts 10.36). Finally, for John, he was the eternal Logos (John 1.1). These portraits of Jesus are basically expressions of the 'Christ of faith' and not necessarily representations of the 'Jesus of history'. To discover who Jesus really was, one needs literally to turn the stones upside down and exegetically sift through the multiple layers of the sources to reconstruct the real Jesus from the Christ of faith attested in the Gospels and throughout the entire New Testament. The task is not easy to say the least!

Due to the limited space of this chapter, I chose to examine Luke's presentation of Jesus. Both Luke's Gospel and the Acts of the Apostles portrayed Jesus as the 'messianic' (anointed) prophet. Luke did not just tell his readers that Jesus was a prophet; he also showed them that he was a prophet by words and deeds. Jesus' life and ministry parallel many of the ancient biblical prophets, especially Moses, Elijah and Elisha. The people or characters in the Gospels, and even his own disciples, identified Jesus as a great prophet who dwelt among them (Luke 7.6; 9.19) who was 'mighty in deed and word' (24.21). More importantly, Jesus saw himself as a Spirit-filled prophet whose mission was to bring about the reign of God here and now. The programmatic passage of Luke 4.16–21 provided the key for unlocking the door to understand Jesus' entire prophetic mission and ministry and concretized the framework for establishing a prophetic Christology in the New Testament. As I observe the current situation of our Church and our world, I cannot help but notice the waning of a prophetic spirit among the leaders in particular and people in general. More sadly still, the few prophets who have risen among us are often silenced. This reminds me of an incident in the book of Numbers where the Spirit was poured out on Eldad and Medad, and they prophesied in the camps of the Israelites. Fearful of what might happen, Joshua appealed to Moses to stop them, but Moses answered him saying, 'Are you jealous for my sake? Would that all the people of the LORD were prophets! Would that the LORD might bestow his spirit on them all!' (Num. 11.29) We live in a time when prophetic voices and actions are urgently needed. Consequently promoting a prophetic Christology as a model for the Christian mission is very timely and appropriate.

2

Christological Constants in Shifting Contexts: Jesus Christ, Prophetic Dialogue and the *Missio Spiritus* in a Pluralistic World

AMOS YONG

Recent developments in Christian theology of religions have included a turn to pneumatology.[1] Yet these developments have drawn forth various reservations regarding how to understand the relationship between the work of Christ and the Spirit in a pluralistic world, whether it is possible to bracket Christological commitments, however momentarily (as some have urged), in the interfaith dialogue and encounter and what the implications of such a pneumatological prioritization are for the Christian self-understanding.[2] Although various responses to these concerns have been articulated,[3]

---

1 I have been one at the forefront of this discussion, with a number of books on the topic, including 'Discerning the Spirit(s): A Pentecostal–Charismatic Contribution to Christian Theology of Religions', *Journal of Pentecostal Theology* Supplement Series 20, Sheffield: Sheffield Academic Press, 2000, and *Beyond the Impasse: Toward a Pneumatological Theology of Religions*, Grand Rapids, MI: Baker Academic, 2003.

2 These are the major questions posed by critics such as James R. A. Merrick, 'The Spirit of Truth as Agent in False Religions? A Critique of Amos Yong's Pneumatological Theology of Religions with Reference to Current Trends', *Trinity Journal* 29:1 (2008), 107–25; Todd Miles, *A God of Many Understandings? The Gospel and Theology of Religions*, Nashville: B & H Academic, 2010, chapter 6; and Keith E. Johnson, *Rethinking the Trinity and Religious Pluralism: An Augustinian Assessment*, Downers Grove: InterVarsity Press Academic, 2011, chapter 4.

3 See, for instance, Tony Richie, 'The Spirit of Truth as Guide into All Truth: A Response to R. A. James Merrick, "The Spirit of Truth as Agent in False Religions? A Critique of Amos Yong's Pneumatological Theology of Religions with Reference to Current Trends"', *Cyberjournal for Pentecostal–Charismatic Research* 19 (2010), http://pctii.org/cyberj/cyber19.html. My own responses include 'A P(new)matological Paradigm for Christian Mission in a Religiously Plural World', *Missiology: An International Review* 33:2 (2005), 175–91, and 'Jesus, Pentecostalism, and the Encounter with (Religious) Others: Pentecostal Christology and (the Wider) Ecumenism in North America', in Dale Coulter and Kenneth Archer (eds), *North American Pentecostalism*, Global Pentecostal & Charismatic Studies series, Leiden and Boston: Brill, forthcoming.

questions persist about how to understand the mission of and in the Holy Spirit (*missio Spiritus*) in a world of many faiths.[4]

This chapter pursues the Christological questions related to pneumatological theology of religions. It is motivated by the sense that Christological concerns in this area reflect anxieties about how to understand the fundamental reality of Christian faith and mission in a pluralistic world. Hence, I argue, two interrelated theses: that although there is one Christ, there are many understandings of that Christ and that these are intrinsically related to the contexts of Christian mission as well as to the encounter with those in other faiths that occurs in mission;[5] and that such a multifarious and dynamic Christology both presumes a robust pneumatology in general and is supported by pneumatological or Spirit-Christology in particular. While we will not, in what follows, engage at any length with the details of the interreligious encounter, the discussion is both informed by as well as undergirds an openness to those in other faiths that yet respects and honours the differences of their particularities.

The chapter is structured triadically according to three central and interrelated categories related to the work of Christ embedded deep within the Christian tradition: of Christ as king, prophet and priest.[6] Each section, however, will unfold the two mutual theses in two steps: by approaching each Christological theme from a pneumatological perspective and by following out the opportunities and challenges opened up by such a pneumatologically understood Christology for the interfaith encounter. The considerations of Christ as king and prophet will also trace out the pneumatological trajectories towards their eschatological horizons in relationship to this discussion. In the end, we shall see that such a pneumatological Christology empowers Christian mission not just of lips (and words) but of hands and hearts as well, and it may well be that the latter witnesses ultimately do more for Christian mission in a pluralistic world than might have been anticipated. More precisely, what emerges is a dialogical posture of openness to those in other faiths on the one hand and yet a prophetic stance towards engaging such others from out of a committed Christian identity on the other.

---

4 On the *missio Spiritus* idea, see my article, 'Primed for the Spirit: Creation, Redemption, and the *Missio Spiritus*', *International Review of Mission* 100:2 (2011), 355–66.

5 Here I am helped by Stephen B. Bevans and Roger P. Schroeder, *Constants in Context: A Theology of Mission for Today*, Maryknoll, NY: Orbis, 2004.

6 E.g. Robert Letham, *The Work of Christ*, Downers Grove, IL: InterVarsity Press, 1993 and Robert Sherman, *King, Priest, and Prophet: A Trinitarian Theology of Atonement*, New York: T & T Clark, 2004.

Christ the King: The Spirit Enables Proclamation and Confession of Jesus

The Philippian hymn indicates that Christ's kenosis or humiliation was precisely the reason for his subsequent ascension and exaltation. 'Therefore', Paul writes, 'God also highly exalted him and gave him the name that is above every name, / so that at the name of Jesus every knee should bend, in heaven and on earth and under the earth, / and every tongue should confess that Jesus Christ is Lord, to the glory of God the Father' (Phil. 2.9–11).[7] This image of Christ's enthronement is comprehensive, cosmic and eschatological. Christ's kingship is both already established but not yet actually fully realized by every knee and tongue.

And how shall this realization unfold? Historically, it has been believed, through Christian obedience to the Great Commission of going to the ends of the earth, bearing witness to Christ, and making disciples of all people (Matt. 28.19; Acts 1.8). Paul also indicated as such:

> But how are they to call on one in whom they have not believed? And how are they to believe in one of whom they have never heard? And how are they to hear without someone to proclaim him? And how are they to proclaim him unless they are sent? As it is written, 'How beautiful are the feet of those who bring good news!' But not all have obeyed the good news; for Isaiah says, 'Lord, who has believed our message?' So faith comes from what is heard, and what is heard comes through the word of Christ. (Rom. 10.14–17)

The logic of this regal Christology suggests that each person will either acknowledge Christ as king freely in response to the gospel message or that even those who do not do so in the present life will, regretfully, do so in the world to come. The implications for Christian mission and evangelism are clear: that followers of Christ ought to be motivated to proclaim him to all nations before the end arrives (cf. Matt. 24.14). Failure to do so will mean that there will be more who bend their knee and confess the name reluctantly (while in the process of being consigned to eternal damnation) than willingly (the prerequisite for their joyous acceptance into eternal bliss).

There are two further implications for the preceding with regard to Christian mission in a pluralistic world. First, people in other faiths bow to and worship other (false) deities. Hence, second, unless they are converted to Christ in this life, they will, belatedly and amid the suffering of everlasting retribution, acknowledge Christ as king. Such conclusions seem inexorable when considered within the logic of Christian faith understood in this

---

7 Unless otherwise noted, all Scripture quotations in this chapter derive from the New Revised Standard Version of the Bible.

way. They do not, however, take into account what religiosity involves for others, or consider how the faith without which 'it is impossible to please God' (Heb. 11.6) might be otherwise manifest or expressed.

Such a classical 'exclusivist' position, as it has come to be known – which basically insists that salvation in the world to come is found exclusively in bending the knee to and confessing Christ in the present life 'for there is no other name under heaven given among mortals by which we must be saved' (Acts 4.12)[8] – nevertheless founders on the question concerning the status of those who are unevangelized: is Christ's kingship eschatologically begrudging for those who have never heard the gospel? More pointedly, it overlooks that Scripture is basically silent about this issue. The famous John 3.16 text, for instance, is followed by the assertions that, 'God did not send the Son into the world to condemn the world, but in order that the world might be saved through him. Those who believe in him are not condemned; but those who do not believe are condemned already, because they have not believed in the name of the only Son of God' (John 3.17–18). Yet 'those who do not believe' are neither logically nor actually equivalent to those who have never heard the gospel.[9] The latter do not believe not because they have rejected the gospel but because they have never been in the position to believe and confess. In fact, this raises a series of questions: What does it mean to be adequately evangelized? At what point can Christian missionaries or evangelists be assured that what they have communicated to their audiences is sufficient for their believing? How do we know all of the factors on the recipients' side which may facilitate their believing unto redemption or hinder their unbelief unto damnation? What if, for instance, we spoke of God the Father who loves us all so that he sent the Son to die for us, and our hearers include those who have been abused by their fathers? How do we know that our message may actually inhibit reception of Christ?

Other questions persist. What if people are evangelized first by Oneness Pentecostals, Jehovah's Witnesses or Mormons, all of whom affirm Christ's substitutionary atonement but otherwise have a variant understanding of the person of Christ from that of classical Christianity? Or what if people are first witnessed to by, and accept the testimonies of, Nestorian or Apollinarian or Arian Christians, all of whose Christologies have been rejected by the mainstream of the Christian faith? Is their bended knee to and confession of

---

8 I use 'exclusivism' as a catch-all phrase since it is the more traditional designation for the position sketched here, even though 'particularism' has become more popular in recent times; see, e.g., R. Douglas Geivett and W. Gary Phillips, 'A Particularist View: An Evidentialist Approach', in Dennis L. Okholm and Timothy R. Phillips (eds), *More than One Way? Four Views on Salvation in a Pluralistic World*, Grand Rapids, MI: Zondervan, 1995, 211–45.

9 These are contested matters especially among evangelical Christians, e.g., Gabriel Fackre, Ronald H. Nash and John Sanders, *What about Those Who Have Never Heard? Three Views on the Destiny of the Unevangelized*, Downers Grove, IL: InterVarsity Press, 1995 and William V. Crockett and James G. Sigountos (eds), *Through no Fault of Their Own? The Fate of Those Who Have Never Heard*, Grand Rapids, MI: Baker, 1991.

the Arian, etc. Jesus valid in God's sight? Or when exactly did the Christian dispensation begin, in which salvation is bestowed according to knowledge and confession of Christ's name? On the Day of Pentecost? At the moment of Christ's ascension? His resurrection? His death? His baptism? His birth? Let us assume, for the moment, that the answer to this is Pentecost and it can be dated. Then another series of questions arise: Did this moment of 'before' and 'after' Christ apply to all who were alive during this period? Only to all who were born after this moment? Only to those who died before this moment? In other words, if a new soteriological dispensation was inaugurated at Pentecost so that salvation after this related to confession of Christ, then did this requirement apply only to all living at that moment? To only those born after that moment? Or to those 'evangelized' (which is not easily definable, per above) after that moment? Does 'before' or 'after' Christ apply to Christ's person and work apart from hearers or receivers of the gospel or does it apply only when the latter are evangelized?[10]

I think that these questions are basically unanswerable both scripturally and theologically, and that this is in part why many evangelicals have moved from an exclusivist position to a more inclusive one that does not minimize the kingship of Christ but is less dogmatic about how to understand the exaltation of Christ, now and eschatologically, among those who are (properly or not) evangelized. The exclusive position's strength is its emphasis on the cognitive content of knowing Christ, but this strength is also its weakness for the unevangelized, which include those unevangelizable (those who die as infants or those with severe and profound intellectual disabilities).[11]

My approach is to emphasize not only Christ as Logos, 'the way, and the truth, and the life' (John 14.6), but also the one whom God anointed 'with the Holy Spirit and with power' (Acts 10.38a). Such a Spirit-Christological perspective recognizes also that Christ is the 'true light, which enlightens everyone' (John 1.9) and that 'no one can say "Jesus is Lord" except by the Holy Spirit' (1 Cor. 12.3b). The cosmic Christ (of John's Prologue) is the anointed one of God's Spirit even as confession of Christ's lordship occurs under the work of the same Spirit. Normally this occurs through evangelism and conversion as classically conceived. However, due to inadequate or non-evangelization – whether due to constraints of space and time or due to inhibitions related to biology (i.e. cognitive disabilities), psychology (i.e. lack of capacity to adequately comprehend or translate the gospel), culture (i.e. a culture of shame rather than that of sin) or the political (i.e. in a Muslim country where it is illegal to convert to Christianity) – faith in

---

10 For elaboration of these difficult questions, see my article 'The Spirit, Christian Practices, and the Religions: Theology of Religions in Pentecostal and Pneumatological Perspective', *Asbury Journal* 62:2 (2007), 5–31, esp. 14–16.

11 I take up the theological questions related to intellectual disability in my book *Theology and Down Syndrome: Reimagining Disability in Late Modernity*, Waco, TX: Baylor University Press, 2007.

Christ can be pneumatologically generated even if not expressed according to traditional manifestations.

In a pluralistic world, such Christ-following can be genuinely enabled by the Holy Spirit but be covert rather than overt as in the various forms of hidden or cultural rather than ecclesial (as in Hindu Christians or Muslim followers of Isa) Christians. Alternatively, understandings of Christ can be mediated in different categories more relevant to diverse religious contexts (as in Christ the guru in South Asia, the awakened one in Buddhist environments, as ancestor in Africa, etc.). These are not to be considered statically or absolutistically. Rather, they reflect the dynamic horizons of mission and evangelism, simply recognizing that sometimes people come into relationship with Christ through certain pathways, but that neither ends nor precludes further Christological development.

This is in part because what people (of any other or no faith) encounter is not just a set of doctrines (the Nicene or Chalcedonian Christ, for instance, as important as these symbols are for Christian orthodox self-understanding), but the living Christ. Indeed, the Christ who came is also the Christ who is coming, who we 'now we see in a mirror, dimly, but then we will see face to face' (1 Cor. 13.12). And knowing this Christ is not just articulating a set of propositions but being transformed into his living image: 'we are God's children now; what we will be has not yet been revealed. What we do know is this: when he is revealed, we will be like him, for we will see him as he is. And all who have this hope in him purify themselves, just as he is pure' (1 John 3.2–3).

A Spirit-Christology neither denies nor displaces a Logos-Christology. Rather, a pneumatological approach recognizes that the eternal Son and Word of God nevertheless became flesh, thus taking on human form in all of its concreteness, contextuality and particularity, and hence that human beings encounter the living Word amid their historicity, sociality, linguisticality and even perhaps cultural-religiosity. None of this embraces the worlds of the religions as is or only on their own terms. It is to say that insofar as God is in the redemptive business and insofar as there are elements of truth, goodness and beauty in the cultural and religious traditions of the world, then for Christians, these anticipate and are finally and eschatologically fulfilled only in Christ.[12]

Christ the king, hence, rules not by lording it over the improperly, under- or un-evangelized. Rather, the king is also the servant who meets human beings in their own tongues, idioms and realities. Confession of Christ is not imposed but emerges out of a living testimony to personal relationship with Christ in the Holy Spirit. Discernment of Christ's enthronement in a pluralistic world can only be eschatological, but even such can be anticipated in

---

12 See Pentecostal and evangelical Indian theologian Ivan Satyavrata, *God Has Not Left Himself without Witness*, Oxford: Regnum International, 2011.

the present by hints in the lives of people of faith, however implicit these may be. How else then might we discern the presence of Christ through his Spirit in the world? Thus while there is kerygmatic proclamation in any authentically Christian approach to and interaction with those in other faiths, such ought to be carried out conversationally with humility as well, and herein we anticipate the prophetic and yet dialogical posture to be more clearly delineated below.

Prophetic Christ: The Spirit Empowers the Hands of the Body of Christ to Anticipate the Reign of God

The clearest way to discern the shape of Christ is to identify the works of Christ. Here, a Spirit-Christology also emerges to the fore, one which empowers the prophetic message and even prophetic actions. At the beginning of his ministry, Jesus said of his own vocation, drawing from the prophet Isaiah in a synagogue in Nazareth:

'The Spirit of the Lord is upon me,
   because he has anointed me
   to bring good news to the poor.
He has sent me to proclaim release to the captives
   and recovery of sight to the blind,
   to let the oppressed go free,
to proclaim the year of the Lord's favour.'
(Luke 4.18–19; cf. Isa. 61.1–2)

The rest of his life and ministry, as recorded in the Gospel of Luke, manifests this prophetic way of life under the charismatic anointing of the Spirit. The good news of the prophetic Christ resonates with the poor, is liberative for those oppressed and captive in whatever respects, includes the healing of those afflicted or impaired and involves proclamation of the Jubilee year of redemption.[13] Note then that the gospel comes not as a set of abstract proclamations but as engaging, remedying and transforming specific historical situations. These include the Holy Spirit empowering life amid poverty, bringing healing to human bodies and transforming socio-economic conditions. Yes, there is a spiritual and perhaps even psychological dimension to these works of Christ, but these are not merely to be spiritualized or psychologized. Rather, the word of Christ is good news precisely because it addresses not just human heads but lives in all their specificity and complexity.

The disciples seemed to have 'got it' in terms of living out the Spirit-filled

---

13 See Michael Prior, *Jesus the Liberator: Nazareth Liberation Theology (Luke 4.16–30)*, Sheffield: Sheffield Academic Press, 1995.

life in the footsteps of Jesus.[14] They did not shrink back from proclaiming the name of Christ (note Acts 4.12 cited above), yet did so not in the abstract but in the concreteness of daily life. For them, the Pentecostal baptism of the Spirit which empowered witness to the living Christ involved baptism into his name and embodiment of his way of life. So,

> All who believed were together and had all things in common; they would sell their possessions and goods and distribute the proceeds to all, as any had need. Day by day, as they spent much time together in the temple, they broke bread at home and ate their food with glad and generous hearts, praising God and having the goodwill of all the people. And day by day the Lord added to their number those who were being saved. (Acts 2.44–47)

Notice then that the confession of Christ involved acceptance of and obedience to his message. If Jesus proclaimed the Jubilee message of full human redemption, then apostolic preaching would also need to be confirmed by liberation according to the Jubilee paradigm. Hence confession of Christ's name brought with it acknowledgement of his lordship, even over their personal possessions. The boldness of life in the Spirit here enabled not only pronouncement of a prophetic message but also embodiment of a countercultural way of life. In fact, Christian witness to the unbelieving world is here seen to flow out of rather than being derivative from Christian community. The disciples did not make evangelism of those outside the community their priority; rather, they focused on living out the liberative dimensions of a prophetic life and 'day by day the Lord added to their number those who were being saved'!

My claim is that in a pluralistic world, actions speak louder than words. In fact, turning up the amplifier on traditional evangelistic activities without preceding or following with a holistic Christian witness is counterproductive. A prophetic message about Christ without a prophetic Spirit-empowered mode of community engagement and transformation undermines the Christian witness. In that sense, Jesus himself challenged the Jews to heed the prophetic parable of the Good Samaritan. Whereas the lawyer's self-concern for inheriting eternal life blinded him to the way of life manifest in the teacher he was addressing, the Samaritan's concern for others reflected the fruit of eternal life without knowledge of the 'Teacher'.[15] This is not to say that people – whether of other or no faith – are saved by works. It is to say that while works on their own are not salvific, the fruits

---

14 I elaborate on this claim and those of this paragraph in my book, *Who is the Holy Spirit? A Walk with the Apostles*, Brewster, MA: Paraclete Press, 2011; cf. Yong, *In the Days of Caesar: Pentecostalism and Political Theology*, Sacra Doctrina, Grand Rapids, MI: Eerdmans, 2010, chapter 3.

15 See further my discussion of this parable vis-à-vis the interfaith encounter in my *The Spirit Poured Out on All Flesh: Pentecostalism and the Possibility of Global Theology*, Grand Rapids, MI: Baker, 2005, 240–4.

of the Spirit are expressions of the work of the Spirit perhaps even where the name of Christ is either unknown or unconfessed.

It is here that I think Christ the prophet requires not merely a repetition of prophetic discourse but embodiment of the prophetic message of liberation for the poor, justice for the oppressed and deliverance of all in captivity. In part for this reason, theologians of the religions like Paul Knitter think it inconceivable that we focus only on what religions (including Christianity) teach and neglect what they may or may not do to inspire missionary collaboration towards making the world a better place.[16] Knitter's point is that any message that does not prophetically engage the destructive powers of this world is a pseudo-gospel and that Christians thus should look for opportunities to work with other religionists towards a more just world. For me, Christ the prophet thus challenges the conventions, systems and structures of the world, especially those which perpetuate the death and destruction brought on by the satan (cf. John 10.10). Towards this end, any Christian theology of religions or any evangelical approach to other faiths that does not encourage mutual social witness when possible fails to heed the prophetic message of Christ.[17] As such, then, the prophetic stance in the footsteps of Christ is relational – even dialogical (as will be explicated momentarily) – in interacting mutually with those of other religious paths.

In the end, Christ the prophet judges the world in accordance to whether they have embodied his prophetic way of life. While there is much debate about how to understand the parable of the sheep and the goats in Matthew 25 – with some arguing that those who are poor, naked, hungry, sick and in prison are not people in general but missionaries of the gospel more specifically[18] – sometimes I think that this amounts to Christians looking for excuses to focus only on their own rather than on the non-Christians around them. The fact of the matter is that the telling of this parable, unique to Matthew, is yet consistent with the telling of the parable of the Good Samaritan, unique to Luke. In both cases, the discussion is on attaining eternal life, and in each case, inheritors of such life are not those 'in the know' but those who live out the heart of the gospel, in particular its concerns for the poor, the hurting and the oppressed. In the case of the Good Samaritan, it is precisely those 'in the know' who are in most danger of forfeiting life everlasting, and this is consistent also with the Matthean warnings that:

'Not everyone who says to me, "Lord, Lord", will enter the kingdom of heaven, but only one who does the will of my Father in heaven. On that

---

16 See especially Paul F. Knitter, *One Earth Many Religions: Multifaith Dialogue and Global Responsibility*, Maryknoll, NY: Orbis, 1995, and *Jesus and the Other Names: Christian Mission and Global Responsibility*, Maryknoll, NY: Orbis, 1996.

17 I make this argument in my book, *Hospitality and the Other: Pentecost, Christian Practices, and the Neighbor*, Faith Meets Faith series, Maryknoll, NY: Orbis, 2008, esp. chapter 5.

18 See my discussion of this passage in *The Bible, Disability, and the Church: A New Vision of the People of God*, Grand Rapids, MI: Eerdmans, 2011, 136–41.

day many will say to me, "Lord, Lord, did we not prophesy in your name, and cast out demons in your name, and do many deeds of power in your name?" Then I will declare to them, "I never knew you; go away from me, you evildoers."' (Matt. 7.21–23)

In fact, how followers of Christ respond to the poor and hurting of the world can be considered as the fruit of their confession. Such 'work' will in the Day of Judgement 'be revealed with fire, and the fire will test what sort of work each has done. If what has been built on the foundation survives, the builder will receive a reward. If the work is burned, the builder will suffer loss; the builder will be saved, but only as through fire' (1 Cor. 3.13b–15). Human beings will eventually be judged according to what they have done (Rev. 20.12), and this includes how they have responded to the message and life of Christ the prophet. It is the work of the Spirit to enable not just a verbal confession of Christ but the sanctified and missional life on behalf of others that Christ exemplified.

In a pluralistic world, this dimension of Christ the prophet is important since it highlights that we have to be concerned not only with the teachings of the religions but also with their practices.[19] To the degree that other faiths inspire liberative actions by their adherents and urge initiatives of justice to address social, structural and systemic inequalities, to that same degree followers of Jesus as Messiah ought to partner with their co-religionists to address these latter realities that often can only be confronted with coalitions across ideological (and religious) lines. To the degree that other cultural and religious traditions perpetuate unjust practices, to that same degree, concomitantly, living out the prophetic message of Christ should urge Christian opposition to and confrontation of such as well as provision for an alternative Jubilee-type future.[20] Christ the Spirit-filled prophet hence becomes an exemplar for a Spirit-empowered prophetic mode of interaction with people in other faiths.

Christ the Priest: The Spirit Dialogically Engages Human Hearts and Lives with the Living Christ

Christ is, finally, also priest. As priest, Christ is the 'one mediator between God and humankind ... who gave himself a ransom for all' (1 Tim. 2.5–6). Christ's priesthood is often considered as central to the doctrine of the atonement of Christ, especially its substitutionary character, which, however many other (non-substitutionary) facets there are, should not be minimized.

---

19 See Yong, 'The Inviting Spirit: Pentecostal Beliefs and Practices regarding the Religions Today', in Steven Studebaker (ed.), *Defining Issues in Pentecostalism: Classical and Emergent*, Eugene, OR: Wipf & Stock, 2008, 29–44.

20 For more on prophetic mission, see also Stephen B. Bevans and Roger P. Schroeder, *Prophetic Dialogue: Reflections on Christian Mission Today*, Maryknoll, NY: Orbis, 2011.

Christ the mediator between deity and humanity includes his intercessorial work. In the exclusivist model, this means knowledge of Christ that confesses his having bridged the chasm between God and creation opened up by sin.

As mediator, however, I would like to suggest also Christ as a dialogical pathway between divinity and humanity. The Greek for 'mediator' is *mesites*, which means also 'go-between', analogous in many ways to the etymology of dialogue, or *dialogos*, as a between space enabling two (or more) to meet and converse. Paul himself, the model apostolic missionary, utilized dialogical approaches in his evangelistic work. At Thessalonica, Corinth and Ephesus it is said that he engaged in dialogue and in reasoned discussion (*dialegato*) on a regular basis (Acts 17.2; 18.4, 19). The dialogues at Athens, especially at the Areopagus (Acts 17.27–28), reflected Paul's engagement with and drawing upon pagan sources familiar to his audience to make his points.[21] In Lystra, earlier, Paul similarly resorted to what might be called natural theological arguments in urging that God 'has not left himself without a witness in doing good – giving you rains from heaven and fruitful seasons, and filling you with food and your hearts with joy' (Acts 14.17). Throughout, Paul showed himself to be the consummate missionary, always holding fast to his commitment to Christ but yet sensitive to his audience, appreciative of his status as guest in the presence of others[22] and alert to a more mediating mode of interacting with others. This is nowhere more palpably expressed when on the isle of Malta, amid 'barbarians' (*barbaroi* from Acts 28.2), we find Paul being the recipient of Maltese hospitality and yet also purveyor of divine generosity in healing the father of the islanders' chief official, all without any indication that kerygmatic proclamation was the modus operandi. This suggests that while the Christian encounter with those in other faiths can never defer indefinitely the evangelical moment of lifting up the name and person of Christ, this can also be done in other than verbal ways. Christ as mediator can be present by the power of the Spirit in many forms and interactions, each of which can be charismatic moments of significance in the interfaith encounter.

My claim is that a Spirit-Christology empowers witness to Christ in many tongues and according to many modes of receptivity, at least as forecast in the Day of Pentecost narrative. If the Pentecostal miracle was both that of speech (in unknown and even unlearned languages) and of hearing (as the

---

21 See Bertil E. Gärtner, *The Areopagus Speech and Natural Revelation*, Acta Seminarii Neotestamentici Upsaliensis 21, Uppsala and Lund: C. W. K. Gleerup, and Copenhagen: Ejnar Munksgaard, 1955.

22 The theme of being guests of religious others is a challenging but important one; I have addressed its implications variously, e.g., 'The Spirit of Hospitality: Pentecostal Perspectives toward a Performative Theology of the Interreligious Encounter', *Missiology: An International Review* 35:1 (2007), 55–73 and 'Guests, Hosts, and the Holy Ghost: Pneumatological Theology and Christian Practices in a World of Many Faiths', in David H. Jensen (ed.), *Lord and Giver of Life: Perspectives on Constructive Pneumatology*, Louisville, KY: John Knox Press, 2008, 71–86.

crowd in Jerusalem queried in surprise: 'how is it that we hear, each of us, in our own native language?'– Acts 2.8), then why ought not the Christian witness amid the interfaith encounter also be mediated by a multiplicity of modes of communication? More precisely, the Pentecost model suggests that every encounter involves a two-way dialogue between the evangelist and his or her audience, one mediated by the translatability of the gospel into a diversity of tongues or cultural-linguistic, if not also religiously refracted, forms.[23] This is because languages never exist only in the abstract but are always carried by cultural realities and the latter are also never absolutely separable from religious beliefs and practices.

Concretely, we can see how the Spirit inspires a dialogical witness to the living Christ in Peter's encounter with Cornelius.[24] There is no de-emphasizing the fact that Peter declares and proclaims 'Jesus Christ – he is Lord of all ... judge of the living and the dead' (Acts 10.36b, 42b) to Cornelius and his household. He is also clear about Jesus' death and resurrection (10.39–40), and that 'everyone who believes in him receives forgiveness of sins through his name' (10.43b). The result is that Cornelius and all who were with him received the Holy Spirit, began 'speaking in tongues and extolling God' (10.46) and were 'baptized in the name of Jesus Christ' (10.48).

On the other hand, it also ought not to be minimized that through his encounter with Cornelius, Peter himself was also transformed. Whereas previously he considered himself an observant Jewish worshipper of the one true God who separated himself from unclean Gentiles and pagans, this episode brought about a change of perspective: 'God has shown me that I should not call anyone profane or unclean' (10.28). More pointedly, Peter came to see that 'God shows no partiality, but in every nation anyone who fears him and does what is right is acceptable to him' (10.34–35). Thus was Cornelius characterized, even before his conversion, as a 'devout' (or 'godly', from the Greek *eusebes*), 'upright' (or 'righteous', from the Greek *dikaios*) and 'God-fearing man' (10.2, 22). Not only did Peter come to a new estimation of Gentiles like Cornelius, he also came to see that the way of Jesus was wider than previously understood: 'Can anyone withhold the water for baptizing these people who have received the Holy Spirit just as we have?' (10.47). Later Peter would become an apologist for accepting and receiving such unclean or profane people (10.14–15; 11.8–9) into baptismal faith to other Jews who questioned such activity: 'If then God gave them the same gift that he gave us when we believed in the Lord Jesus Christ, who was I that I could hinder God?' (11.17). My point is to highlight the dialogical nature of the encounter between Peter and Cornelius. Both were transformed as a result of meeting. We might say that while Cornelius was

---

23 I make this argument in many places, but most succinctly in my article 'A P(new)matological Paradigm', 175–91.

24 See Tony Richie, *Toward a Pentecostal Theology of Religions: Encountering Cornelius Today*, Cleveland, TN: CPT Press, 2013, esp. chapter 1.

converted to Christ, Peter was also converted in his relationship with the God of Jesus Christ. Herein we find Christ revealed through the Spirit not only as dialogical priest (enabling the mutual transformation of Cornelius and Peter) but also prophetic king (inviting the repentance of Cornelius towards a deeper commitment to the God of Jesus Christ).

We see such a dialogical – and yet prophetic and regal – model of encountering others also in the life and ministry of Jesus.[25] Matthew (15.21–28) and Mark (7.24–30) tell of Jesus' meeting with a Greek-speaking Canaanite (Matt.) or Syro-Phoenician (Mark) woman who wanted him to deliver her daughter from demonic oppression and possession. Matthew's account indicates that she was rebuffed thrice: first through Jesus ignoring her cries and pleas; second through affirming to his disciples, and to her through them, that 'I was sent only to the lost sheep of the house of Israel' (Matt. 15.24); and finally, directly to her, while she was kneeling before him: 'it is not fair to take the children's food [meant for the house of Israel] and throw it to the dogs [an accepted euphemism in first-century Palestine for Gentiles]' (15.26). Yet despite this triad of rejections, she persists, with this resulting: 'She said, "Yes, Lord, yet even the dogs eat the crumbs that fall from their masters' table." Then Jesus answered her, "Woman, great is your faith! Let it be done for you as you wish." And her daughter was healed instantly' (15.27–28). What seems clear especially in the Matthean telling is that this woman's perseverance and determination brought about a change in Jesus' intentions and actions. In a similar account regarding Jesus' interactions with a centurion who had a paralysed servant and came to Jesus for healing on behalf of the servant, Jesus not only performs the healing but also comes to an unexpected new awareness: 'When Jesus heard him, *he was amazed* and said to those who followed him, "Truly I tell you, *in no one in Israel have I found such faith*"' (Matt. 8.10, emphases added). In this case, the centurion finds confirmation in Jesus' healing and saving power even as Jesus comes to recognize that a greater measure of faith existed in this pagan centurion than could be found within the house of Israel. Here, as with the Canaanite/Syro-Phoenician woman, there is a dialogical mutuality: both Jesus and these Gentiles undergo transformation of belief and behaviour as a result of the encounter. Simultaneously, of course, these Gentiles both evince a deep faith in Christ as Lord (Matt. 8.8; 15.22). From a pneumatological perspective it might be said that the Spirit accomplishes dialogical interaction while prophetically and regally inviting acknowledgement of the lordship of Christ.

My claim is that a Spirit-Christology both emphasizes that Jesus accomplishes the will of God in the power of the Spirit even as it provides a

---

25 Pablo Alonso, *The Woman Who Changed Jesus: Crossing Boundaries in Mark 7.24–30*, Biblical Tools and Studies 11, Leuven: Peeters, 2011; cf. Glenna S. Jackson, '"Have Mercy on Me": The Story of the Canaanite Woman in Matthew 15.21–28', *Journal for the Study of the New Testament* Supplement series 228, London: Sheffield Academic Press, 2002.

window into how Jesus was also surely 'a man attested to you by God' (Acts 2.22). As divine, Jesus bears iconic witness to God's message, glory and being (Heb. 1.3), but as human, he does so in the relational mode within which human beings existing in the Trinitarian image of God participate. The Spirit who is the bond of love between the Father and the Son is also the matrix within which human beings interact and through which creatures relate to and with God.[26] Jesus himself becomes the paradigmatic exemplar of such dialogical relationality, and it is therefore not surprising to see the apostolic community also embodying such virtues.

In the interfaith encounter then, such a dialogical approach enables authentic exchange. Christians can testify out of the depths of their experience of the living Christ.[27] But as with any dialogical encounter, they ought also to be open to the religious lives of others. The challenge here is more existential than dogmatic or doctrinal since the latter only has meaning within communities of practice. It is therefore the case that any inter-religious dialogue is also an intra-religious dialogue, that is, a conversation taking place within believers as they wrestle with what it means to be people of faith bearing witness to others while simultaneously receiving the witness of others.[28] It is surely the case that sometimes, Christian conversion in the interfaith encounter will be towards other faith commitments; more often, however, through such relationships Christians will convert more deeply to the living God of Jesus Christ, as was the case with Peter in his encounter with Cornelius.

Conclusion: The Winds of the Spirit of Christ and the *Missio Spiritus* in a Pluralistic World

At one level, 'Jesus Christ is the same yesterday and today and forever' (Heb. 13.8). At another level, as the living Christ, no words can ever exhaust the reality of Christ. This does not mean that words are unimportant, but that coming to know Christ is not only a matter of the head but also of the hands and of the heart. Christ as king, prophet and priest is the constant amid history's shifting contexts but the communication of Christ will take on various forms – cognitive, missional and relational – depending on such contexts. Faith in Christ surely involves the intellect, but its full expression involves expression in human behaviours, practices and ways of life, and the heads and the hands can only be in sync if the heart is involved.

---

26 As I elaborate in my book *Spirit of Love: A Trinitarian Theology of Grace*, Waco, TX: Baylor University Press, 2012.

27 As argued by Tony Richie, *Speaking by the Spirit: A Pentecostal Model for Interreligious Dialogue*, Wilmore, KY: Emeth Press, 2011.

28 See Raimon Panikkar, *The Intra-Religious Dialogue*, revised edn, New York: Paulist Press, 1998.

Thus the interfaith encounter will feature, at its foundations, the encounter of human hearts with horizons of transcendence. Propositional apologetics should not be rejected wholesale, although their effectiveness will be muted apart from a holistic approach that involves hands and hearts. Purely social justice engagement is essential but will also be incomplete apart from heads introduced to the words of Christ and hearts directed towards his person. Last but not least, human hearts in all of their complexity – including human hopes, loves, aspirations, affections, etc. – ought to be engaged on the interfaith front. If religion does not concern our hearts, then they may be ideologies or philosophies but they are not matters of ultimate concern, as Paul Tillich suggested. But if they are matters of ultimate concern, then they have to be adjudicated at the existential depths of the human gut, which will include both heads and hands as well.

A pneumatological approach to the interfaith encounter can facilitate such dialogical and holistic interchange even while prophetically and regally lifting up Jesus as the Christ and Messiah.[29] If knowing Christ is not merely cognitive (urging recognition and acknowledgement of his kingship) but also practical (embodying his prophethood) and even affective (embodying his dialogical and mediating relationality), then what is helpful is a pneumatological Christology that insists we understand and discern not just the doctrines of other faiths but also their practices and even their aspirations. Learning about other religious traditions therefore will include becoming vulnerable as hosts to and guests of not only the ideas but also the practices at the heart of other faiths. From a Christ-centred point of view, this may open up to recognition, through the Holy Spirit who leads into all truth (not to mention goodness and beauty), of the 'seeds of the Logos' that are within other traditions. Such may be aspects of Christian faith that have been neglected or even which are complementary to the truth, goodness and beauty of Christ. However, they will not contradict the revelation of the triune God, even if sometimes their initial manifestation will lead to a period of (prolonged) discernment and also disputation (as the various conciliar processes in history well depict). Such is the nature of life in the Spirit, whose 'wind blows where it chooses, and you hear the sound of it, but you do not know where it comes from or where it goes' (John 3.8).[30]

---

29 For instance, as displayed in my *Pneumatology and the Christian–Buddhist Dialogue, Does the Spirit Blow through the Middle Way?*, Studies in Systematic Theology, Leiden and Boston: Brill, 2012.

30 The first version of this essay was presented as a plenary paper at the 2013 meeting of the Society for Vineyard Scholars. Thanks to Caleb Maskell for the invitation, to Jason Clark for his dialogical response and for the SVS members who engaged with my paper during the conference, asked helpful questions and made suggestive and encouraging comments. I appreciate also Vince Le, my former graduate assistant, for proofreading the article. Enoch Charles, my present graduate assistant, also proofread a revised version of the essay and produced the bibliography. Last but not least, I am grateful to Stephen B. Bevans and Cathy Ross for inviting my contribution to this volume and for their helpful editorial feedback.

3

Jesus, Mission and the Holy Spirit in Luke–Acts: Dialogue, Prophecy and Life

KIRSTEEN KIM

Jesus and the Spirit is a vast topic that is at the heart of Christian pneumatology and has been the subject of much scholarly discussion. Much contemporary debate has been stimulated by contributions from Pentecostal and charismatic theology and in particular by James Dunn's engagement with this.[1] This chapter limits the scope of the theme, first, by probing the relationship through the lens of mission and, second, by focusing biblical discussion on Luke–Acts.[2] But first, I lay the Old Testament ground with help and stimulus from the recent work of John Levison.[3] I argue that the Spirit, being on the one hand the Life-giver, the creative Spirit of the universe, provides the continuity between Jesus and his wider context and, being at the same time the *Holy* Spirit and uniquely manifested in Jesus Christ, is discontinuous with it. By drawing attention to this tension and holding both beliefs together, I wish to address from a pneumatological perspective the dichotomy that affects mission which is implied in the phrase that is the theme of this volume – 'prophetic dialogue'.

The Spirit, the Giver of Life

According to the Hebrew Scriptures, which Christians have incorporated as the Old Testament, God involves himself in the world by the Spirit. Over a broad collection of texts from different eras and hands and in interaction with many other societies and beliefs, it is difficult to discern a unified Old

---

1 See James Dunn, *Jesus and the Spirit: A Study of the Religious and Charismatic Experience of Jesus and the First Christians as Reflected in the New Testament*, London: SCM Press, 1975 and Graham N. Stanton, Bruce W. Longenecker and Stephen C. Barton (eds), *The Holy Spirit and Christian Origins: Essays in Honor of James Dunn*, Grand Rapids, MI: Eerdmans, 2004.

2 The choice of Luke–Acts is not merely a convenience or even because it combines the missions of Jesus and the early Church. It is mainly because it has been the focus of New Testament study both by liberation theologians in support of the 'good news to the poor' (Luke 4.18–20) and also, self-evidently, by Pentecostal theologians (Acts 2).

3 John R. Levison, *Filled with the Spirit*, Grand Rapids, MI: Eerdmans, 2009.

Testament pneumatology. As Levison observes, 'The original Hebrew and Greek words for "spirit" were used to convey concepts as diverse as a breath, a breeze, a powerful gale, an angel, a demon, the heart and soul of a human being, and the divine presence itself.'[4] The Hebrew Bible provides many different meanings and metaphors of spirit on which Christians have also drawn. Nevertheless, Levison finds some unity of meaning: 'life-principle and the spirit of God ... were understood to be one and the same'.[5] This is convincing insofar as wind or breath is the root meaning of 'spirit', *ruach* in the Hebrew Bible and breath signals life. From this root comes the association of the Spirit with vitality, quality of life and with human gifts is derivative of that.[6]

The Hebrew Bible places the Spirit at the very foundation of the world when God spoke and the Spirit hovered over the waters. The word translated 'spirit' (Hebrew: *ruach*) is literally a wind or breath of God which blew as the Father uttered the Word that gave birth to creation (Gen. 1.1–2; cf. Gen. 8.1; Amos 4.13; Ps. 104.4). In the next chapter of Genesis, the Spirit was given specifically as the life-breath of the first human being (Gen. 2.7).[7] This breath of God is creative of life (Ps. 33.6) and also destructive (Ex. 15.8; 2 Sam. 22.16; Job 4.9) and all the creatures of the world are contingent on it (Ps. 104.29–30; Job 34.14–15; cf. Eccles. 3.19). The Spirit appears as the source of life – and even material reality, of fertility and abundance.

As human beings communed with God, they nurtured a garden. Even after the fall, they continued to bring forth fruit from the earth and from their own bodies they bore children. Although their experience of the Spirit was marred by their sinfulness, they created societies and cultures by the wisdom imbued in them by the Spirit (Ex. 35.30–5) and they were moved by the Spirit (e.g. Job 32.18–20). By the Spirit, judges, kings and prophets arose who exhibited extraordinary power (e.g. Joshua in Deut. 34.9–12; Samson in Judg. 14.6, 19; 15.14–15), displayed unusual qualities of leadership (David in 1 Sam. 16.13), cleverly discerned the truth (Daniel in Dan. 5.13–14) and fearlessly spoke God's word (Micah 3.5–8; Neh. 9.30). In

---

4 John R Levison, '*Filled with the Spirit:* A Conversation with Pentecostal and Charismatic Scholars', *Journal of Pentecostal Theology* 20 (2011), 213–31 (221).

5 Levison, *Filled with the Spirit*, 12.

6 Levison, *Filled with the Spirit*, 14–105. Levison is arguing against scholarly attempts to distinguish sharply between the endowment of the spirit at birth and a later, superior charismatic gift (Levison, *Filled with the Spirit*, 12). The main weakness of Levison's approach in my view is that, in focusing on the continuity between divine and human spirit, the Holy Spirit is reduced to the human spirit rather than elevated to be the Creator Spirit. This is not unrelated to the fact that his book begins with Genesis 2.7, not Genesis 1.2. The question of whether to capitalize the word 'spirit' depends on the outcome, and Levison chooses not to do so at all. I retain a more traditional pattern of capitalizing when the reference is to the Spirit of God.

7 Although the term used here is not *ruach* but *neshama*, the result – life – is the same and elsewhere in the Hebrew canon *ruach* and *nephesh* (life of a living/breathing being) are synonymous (see, e.g., Gen. 6.17; Isa. 42.5; Job 33.4).

these narrative histories, the Spirit appears as strengthener of the human spirit, the source of superhuman capability, uncommon wisdom and fearless testimony. So the Spirit of Life is, by extension, the fount of creativity and inspiration.[8]

In the exilic period, in the face of betrayal and destruction, the Spirit appears again as the Spirit of Life itself in the form of the overcomer of death, the one who can reconstitute dry bones into life, change hearts and recreate God's people (Ezek. 37). The Spirit is the hope of a new creation, a reconstructed society and restored lives. The Spirit is a promised power, a new energy, a future agent of transformation (Joel 2.28–9; Isa. 11).[9] When God's Spirit is withdrawn, living things die and return to the dust from which they were made.[10] Although Levison's argument should be qualified in a number of instances because *ruach*, like many words, can carry several distinct meanings,[11] it still holds that in the Israelite literature, the Spirit as elemental force or biological life is not clearly distinguished from the human spirit and human qualities such as wisdom and creativity and capacity for kindness and love. Nor is it separated from the spiritual hope and national spirit of Israel to cultivate the Promised Land and create a new Eden. In the Bible 'spirit' is not a category that is better than 'material' but which encompasses material life since God created earth as well as heaven.[12]

Jesus as Receiver of the Spirit: Spirit-Christology

In this section we will set Jesus within the context of the work of the life-giving Spirit and develop a Spirit-Christology. We will consider what Jesus' understanding and awareness of the Spirit may have been and look at the association of Jesus with the Spirit as made by Luke in his Gospel.

Jesus' belief in the Spirit was informed by faith of the society into which he was born. In order to understand this, we need to look not only at the pneumatology of the Hebrew Scriptures on which he drew but also at that of the culture and religions of his time, several hundred years after the writings of the Old Testament.[13] Since the work of Hermann Gunkel, it is commonly asserted that in the Second Temple period the Spirit did not seem to be active in Israel and that since the last prophets Judaism had produced little in the way of 'pneumatic phenomena'.[14] The intertestamental

---

8 Levison, *Filled with the Spirit*, 34–86.

9 Levison sharply distinguishes this Jewish expectation for the restoration of Israel from the hope that Christians later believed (Levison, *Filled with the Spirit*, 102–3).

10 Levison, *Filled with the Spirit*, 87–103.

11 Max Turner, 'Levison's *Filled with the Spirit*: A Brief Appreciation and Response', *Journal of Pentecostal Theology* 20 (2011), 193–200 (196–7).

12 Justo L. Gonzales, *Acts: Gospel of the Spirit*, Maryknoll, NY: Orbis, 2001, 17.

13 Levison credits Hermann Gunkel, one of the leaders of the History of Religions school, with this development (Levison, *Filled with the Spirit*, 110–12).

14 See Hermann Gunkel, *The Influence of the Holy Spirit: The Popular View of the Apos-*

period was dismissed as an era devoid of the Spirit in which the ministry of John the Baptist appeared as the first prophet for several hundred years; a 'negative foil' against which the pneumatic events of Jesus' ministry shone more brightly.[15] More recently John Levison has debunked that portrayal and painted instead a picture of the Judaism into which John and Jesus were born as full of vitality and with a lively literature of theology of the Spirit, stimulated by interaction of Jewish tradition with Graeco-Roman pneumatology.[16]

In the Septuagint or Greek translation of the Hebrew Bible, the Greek word *pneuma* is almost always used as a translation and so takes a very similar range of meanings to *ruach*. The early Christian writers were therefore able to bring together all the varied nuances of *ruach*, together with the range of meanings of *pneuma*, to inform their understanding of the Spirit that they experienced. This means that it is important to examine what was available to them to understand better the meaning of the Spirit in the New. We first note Luke's use of 'Holy Spirit', which occurs rarely in the Hebrew Bible (Ps. 51.11; Isa. 63.10–11). Use of the term developed in the inter-testamental period when it was particularly associated with virtue and 'the spirit within' – the 'holy spirit' of a person, or their soul.[17] At Qumran, the phrase 'holy spirit' took on a communal sense such as is found in the New Testament.[18]

In the first century, Jesus, the human being, understood himself as a partaker of the same spirit and subject to the same (spiritual) forces as his contemporaries. This is the strongest reason for binding the Spirit of Life in the Old Testament and the Holy Spirit of the New together as one and the same. We find in Luke–Acts instances of general use of the word 'spirit' to mean human spirit or life. For example, John grows strong in spirit and, in a parallel reference, Jesus 'became strong, filled with wisdom' (Luke 1.80; 2.40).[19] When Jesus restores a little girl, her spirit returns (Luke 8.55). The use of the word 'spirit' in the story of Stephen is more ambiguous: Was Stephen 'a man full of faith and holy spirit' or 'faith and the Holy Spirit' (Acts 6.5; cf. Acts 6.10; 7.55, 59)?[20] However, in the context there is little at stake here.

Luke begins his Gospel with insight into the spiritual world of contemporary Judaism. Zechariah, a priest, is burning incense in the sanctuary while the people are outside at prayer when he sees a vision of the angel Gabriel who announces the imminent birth of his son John, who 'even before his

---

tolic Age and the Teaching of the Apostle Paul, Minneapolis: Fortress Press, 2008 [1888], 21. See also Levison, Filled with the Spirit, 112–16.

15 Levison, Filled with the Spirit, 116.
16 Levison, Filled with the Spirit, 109–17.
17 Levison, Filled with the Spirit, 220–1.
18 Levison, Filled with the Spirit, 202–17.
19 Levison, Filled with the Spirit, 241.
20 Levison, Filled with the Spirit, 242–5.

birth ... will be filled with the Holy Spirit' (Luke 1.15).[21] When John is born, Zechariah is filled with the Spirit and prophesies about the role his son will play in preparing the way of the Lord, and John the Baptist fulfils these expectations. Luke portrays Jesus initially as a recipient, not a giver of the Spirit,[22] although it also becomes clear that Jesus is not merely filled with or even possessed by the Spirit but is constituted by the Spirit and is the Spirit's very embodiment. Gabriel's message to the unmarried Mary is that Jesus will be conceived by the Holy Spirit and this – rather than his pre-existence – is given as the reason that he will be holy, the Son of God (1.35).[23] When the two relatives meet, Elizabeth knows by the Spirit that Mary is more highly favoured, but both babies are being born due to the agency of the Holy Spirit as already known by the Jewish people. Jesus' birth and his presentation at the Temple are all in the context of spiritual energy – angels, visions, worship, sacrifice and prophecy – and his childhood is full of wisdom and grace (Luke 2.40–52).

That Jesus' spiritual experience was continuous with those of his fellow countrymen is shown clearly at his baptism by John in the Jordan, along with many others who were preparing themselves for the coming of the Messiah and the hoped-for baptism with the Holy Spirit and with fire (Luke 3.1–18, 21). At his baptism Jesus was singled out by the Spirit as the Son of God (Luke 3.22). The growing self-consciousness of Jesus himself of his unique relationship with God was sealed in a vision at his baptism and a conviction that the Spirit descended on him there.[24] Although there may be an allusion to the adoption of the king as God's son (in the shape of a reference to Psalm 2.7) and it may have been the result of a special petition of Jesus to the Father in heaven (Luke 11.13), there is no reason to suppose that this marked the beginning of Jesus' awareness of sonship or of his unique anointing by the Spirit.[25] It was rather the culmination of a growing conviction which the Church came later to believe (Acts 2.33), that Jesus was at one and the same time the incarnate Son of God and the one who uniquely received the Spirit.[26] The fact that the Holy Spirit visibly descended on Jesus as a dove does not mean that the Holy Spirit was absent from the rest of those who gathered by the river – at the very least, the Spirit was with John. As the recipient of the Spirit, Jesus shows the openness to a context,

---

21 Biblical quotations are from the New Revised Standard Version (NRSV).

22 See Alasdair I. C. Heron, *The Holy Spirit: The Holy Spirit in the Bible, in the History of Christian Thought, and in Recent Theology*, London: Marshall Morgan & Scott, 1983, 127.

23 Cf. Yves Congar, *I Believe in the Holy Spirit*, trans. David Smith, New York: Crossroad, 1983, 16.

24 Dunn, *Jesus and the Spirit*, 62–7.

25 Such an adoptionist view has been taken by pneumatologists such as Roger Haight and G. W. H. Lampe. Adoptionism is encouraged by the tendency among modern scholars to disregard the birth narratives in Luke on the grounds that they are a later addition or from less reliable historical sources than the rest of the gospel.

26 Dunn, *Jesus and the Spirit*, 65–6.

learning from the context, bonding with the context that is characteristic of dialogue.[27] Jesus was a man of the people, who lived with others and learned from his mother and father, dialogued with religious leaders and submitted to his older cousin John.

Jesus was baptized in the Jordan of Judaic religion, as he was to be later crucified at the Calvary of the oppression and poverty of Judaea.[28] His baptism was a sign of his coming suffering (Luke 12.50).[29] Jesus' self-belief was soon tested in the wilderness, where it was by the fullness of the Spirit that he was able to withstand the devil's tests of his sonship (Luke 4.1–13). This testing and the sustaining power of the Spirit continued throughout Jesus' ministry, especially in his life of prayer (Luke 5.16; 6.12; 9.28; 11.1). It enabled him to demonstrate the power of God over demons and other evil spirits that troubled the people. The presence of the Spirit in him gave him joy and a perception of God's working that was hidden from the wise and learned, although visible also 'to little children' (Luke 10.21) and evident not only in his own ministry but also in that of the Twelve and the Seventy-Two (9.1–6; 10.1–24). His claim to be the true leader of the people, backed up by his fearless demonstration of the word of God in terms of good news to the poor, excited the opposition of the religious leaders who, in Luke's account, engineered Jesus' crucifixion. On the cross, uniquely in Luke's account, Jesus cried 'Father, into your hands I commend my spirit' (Luke 23.46; Ps. 31.5) as he laid down his life in the expectation of rescue from death and resurrection life.[30] At Pentecost, Peter repeatedly asserted that God raised Jesus up by a greater power than death (Acts 2.24, 32–33). This resurrection life which raised Jesus from the grave was understood as the Holy Spirit now poured out on the people (2.33).

Jesus as Giver of the Spirit: Christian Pneumatology

Attention only to dialogue and the cultural continuity of Jesus' experience of the Spirit may lead to neglect of the countercultural and eschatological nature of Jesus' ministry. Jesus was not only a receiver, he was also a giver of the Spirit. He meted out, spoke out, gave out and poured out the Spirit he received from the Father. Not only was the Spirit perceived to be acting in and through him but he was the interpreter of the Spirit's will and, for the early Christians, he came to define the Spirit. The Spirit was 'the Spirit

---

27 Stephen B, Bevans and Roger P. Schroeder, *Prophetic Dialogue: Reflections on Christian Mission Today*, Maryknoll, NY: Orbis, 2011, 19–39.

28 Aloysius Pieris, *An Asian Theology of Liberation*, Faith Meets Faith Series, Maryknoll, NY: Orbis, 1988, 45–8.

29 Congar, *I Believe in the Holy Spirit*, 19.

30 Robert C. Tannehill, *Luke*, Abingdon New Testament Commentaries, Nashville, TN: Abingdon Press, 1996, 345–6.

of Jesus' (Acts 16.7). In this way a distinctively Christian pneumatology emerged.

Jesus was not only a man of dialogue, he – like John – was recognized as a prophet. He was witnessing to the vitality of the gospel as well as to its countercultural nature, committed to speaking forth the gospel boldly and clearly and speaking against any injustice, oppression or death-dealing elements in a context.[31] Jesus was seen as a prophet in the style of Elijah. He was 'proclaiming a message from the covenant God, and living it out with symbolic actions', such as driving out the sellers in the Temple and breaking bread and sharing wine at the Last Supper. 'He was confronting people with the folly of their ways, summoning them to a different way, and expecting to take the consequences of doing so.'[32]

According to Luke, Jesus' status as a prophet is first made clear in his appearance at the synagogue in Nazareth, where he declared the fulfilment of the Scripture from Isaiah in terms of 'good news to the poor', 'release to the captives', 'recovery of sight to the blind' and freedom to the oppressed (Luke 4.18–19). In Luke's presentation, at Nazareth, Jesus announced that the source of his prophetic ministry was the Holy Spirit who had anointed him for this purpose (4.18). In doing so, he drew on the prophecy of Isaiah (61.1) and thus identified himself with the Coming One, the Messiah, who would liberate the poor and bring about the kingdom.[33] Jesus' claim to messiahship and his message, at least the part in which he expressed his willingness to recognize the working of the Spirit of God beyond the people of Israel, set him at odds with many in his own home town in Nazareth (4.22–30).[34]

Jesus' prophecy was not just in words but also in deeds; he brought healing and salvation. Like the prophets of old, in his ministry, he brought about many of the changes he proclaimed and had an effect on crowds, individuals and even the elements that was widely reported (Luke 6.20–6; 7.18–23). The apocalyptic dimension of Jesus' message is evident especially in his proclamation of a future kingdom. The kerygma of Jesus was not only a logical deduction from Hebrew prophecy but also a result of Jesus' own consciousness of the power of God's Spirit breaking through in his own ministry and bringing in the end times.[35] Jesus' 'awareness of being uniquely possessed and used by divine Spirit was the mainspring of his mission and the key to its effectiveness'.[36] This self-consciousness was especially evident in Jesus' practice of exorcism and healing, which was particularly controversial. But it was taken by Luke and the early Church as a sign that Jesus

31 Bevans and Schroeder, *Prophetic Dialogue*, 40–55.
32 N. T. Wright, *Jesus and the Victory of God*, London: SPCK, 1996, 167–8.
33 Dunn, *Jesus and the Spirit*, 53–62.
34 Tannehill, *Luke*, 93–4.
35 Cf. Dunn, *Jesus and the Spirit*, 41–3.
36 Dunn, *Jesus and the Spirit*, 54.

was confronting evil in the form of Satan or Beelzebub; that Jesus' action was by the finger of God; that the spirit or power which was in Jesus was greater than that of other strong men and that this power was the Holy Spirit (Luke 11.15–23; 12.10; Acts 10.38).[37]

Unlike John, who baptized only with water, the Messiah was expected to baptize 'with the Holy Spirit and with fire' (Luke 3.16). However, Jesus is not recorded as baptizing during his lifetime. We have to wait until after the resurrection and the beginning of Luke's second volume for this special baptism on the people, the outpouring of the Spirit as wind and fire at Pentecost. Luke identifies this with a particular historical moment on the feast of Pentecost, a specific experience of Jesus that in his account is invested with epochal significance as the occasion of the outpouring and gift of the Spirit of God on all.[38] Pentecost was not only the fulfilment of the expectation of the disciples, based on Hebrew prophecy (particularly Joel, see Acts 2.17–21), Judaic expectation of the kingdom and the words of Jesus himself about the coming 'power from on high' (Luke 24.49; Acts 1.1–8), the early Church saw the event as directly dependent on Jesus himself as the ascended and son of God (Acts 2.33).[39] For John and the people, it was a given that the Messiah, the one anointed by the Spirit, would bring about the giving of the Spirit to the people as part of the renewal and transformation that would restore Israel (cf. Acts 1.6). So although the Spirit was poured out from the Father, the Spirit was recognized as the Spirit that was in Christ (Acts 2.33).

Jesus as Giver and Receiver of the Spirit: Prophetic Dialogue and Fullness of Life

In their post-Pentecost ministries, the apostles prophesied and performed many similar acts to those Jesus had done in the power of the Spirit that demonstrated the arrival of the kingdom and fulfilled expectations of the last days. Although they understood themselves to have a direct experience of the eschatological Spirit, the apostles took their authority from Jesus, preached that their actions were derived from Jesus and dependent on his death and resurrection and called others to repentance and faith in him.[40] In both chapters 2 and 19 of Acts, 'there is a very close association between having the Spirit and being able to confess fully who Jesus is' so that 'Without the Holy Spirit, it is impossible to be a Christian' and 'What the Spirit will teach is not revelation beyond that which Jesus brought; it is the same as Jesus brought.'[41] In Acts 19.1–7, Paul tells the 12 disciples of Apollos

---

37 Dunn, *Jesus and the Spirit*, 44–53.
38 Dunn, *Jesus and the Spirit*, 135–56.
39 Dunn, *Jesus and the Spirit*, 194–5.
40 Dunn, *Jesus and the Spirit*, 157–96.
41 Gonzales, *Acts*, 220, 16, 17.

both about Jesus the Christ (19.4) and also about the Holy Spirit (19.2, 6). So although by common consensus the Holy Spirit, rather than Christ, becomes the major actor in Acts, the Spirit is so closely associated with testimony about Jesus and witness to salvation in Christ that there is little discernible difference between actions in the name of Jesus and by the Spirit.

This bond between Jesus and the Spirit is especially important in view of the complexity of the spirit-world in Luke's writing[42] – a complexity which is surely partly signalled by Luke's use of the qualification *Holy* Spirit rather than just 'Spirit or spirit', which might be confused with other notions of spirit. The complexity of the Lukan Spirit-world is partly a question about the characteristics of filling with this 'Holy Spirit'. In Acts 2 Luke brings together aspects of spirituality that in modern theology have been forced apart by debates since Gunkel: doctrinal authority and illumination of Scripture on the one hand and ecstatic behaviour and glossolalia on the other.[43] Also in view in Acts are links of spirit-possession with wisdom, signs and wonders, angels and exorcism, although drunkenness (Acts 2.15) and magic (8.9–13) are rejected as manifestations of the Holy Spirit.[44] Furthermore, the apostles in Acts are part of a spiritual power encounter at many different levels. Luke–Acts begins and ends with political power. The advent of the Lord is in the context of Jewish and Roman power (Luke 1.5; 2.1–2) and in conclusion, Paul is a prisoner in Rome on account of the actions of certain Jewish leaders.[45] If, as most commentators suppose, Luke–Acts was written after the Roman destruction of Jerusalem, then it was addressing a key question of his contemporaries about whether the Spirit of God was more powerful than the gods of Rome and he depicts the God of the Jews 'as being in process of accomplishing an almighty and universal victory'.[46] However, the means of this victory is not a military one like Rome's but the spread, by the Spirit, of a message, by a reordering of values and a new form of community that was 'turning the world upside-down' (Acts 17.6) and bringing about the kingdom – or empire – of God. There are other powers in view as well in Acts: temptations to pride (Acts 3), fear (Acts 4), greed (Acts 5), communalism (Acts 6), conformity (Acts 8), prejudice (Acts 10) and so on. Throughout the book, the human actors are faced with questions

---

42 Cf. John R. Levison, 'A Stubborn Missionary, a Slave Girl, and a Scholar: The Ambiguity of Inspiration in the Book of Acts', in Amos Yong, Kirsteen Kim and Veli-Matti Kärkkäinen (eds), *Interdisciplinary and Religio-cultural Discourses on a Spirit-filled World: Loosing the Spirits*, New York: Palgrave Macmillan, 2013, 15–27.

43 Cf. the emotional and intellectual response of the disciples on the road to Emmaus, Luke 24.32.

44 Cf. Levison, *Filled with the Spirit*, 317–65.

45 Gonzales, *Acts*, 279.

46 Bruce W. Longenecker, 'Rome's Victory and God's Honour: The Jerusalem Temple and the Spirit of God in Lukan Theodicy', in Graham N. Stanton, Bruce W. Longenecker and Stephen C. Barton (eds), *The Holy Spirit and Christian Origins: Essays in Honor of James Dunn*, Grand Rapids, MI: Eerdmans, 2004, 90–102 (92, 99).

about 'under whose power they reside, which Lord they obey'.[47] Under the guidance of the Holy Spirit, they test the spirits – both affirming the Spirit in others (Acts 17.22–8) and discerning which spirits or powers are on the side of the Holy Spirit and which are against the Spirit they know in Christ (cf. Luke 11.14–23; 12.4–12).

For some commentators, the power and activity of the Spirit is exclusively, or mainly, prophetic in the social justice sense[48] or in the sense of missionary proclamation.[49] Levison tends to agree in that he regards the New Testament as Hellenized and neglectful of its Jewish roots. But, having shown the extent to which Jesus is depicted as the receiver of the Spirit, mission as 'prophetic dialogue' would seem to make better sense of Luke–Acts. It also allows us to consider under mission other roles of the apostles in Acts that are equally inspired and transformational, such as community leadership (e.g. Acts 6.3), ethical renewal (e.g. 10.9–23) and spiritual discernment (e.g. 13.1).[50]

Nevertheless, although mission as 'prophetic dialogue' well describes a theology of Christian mission for today, exegesis of Luke–Acts shows that the unique mission of Jesus Christ cannot be encompassed by this phrase (or for that matter by any phrase in English or any other language). This is for two main reasons. First, we cannot say that Jesus' relationship to the Spirit, according to Luke–Acts, is 'archetypal of Christian relationship to the Spirit' as some have done.[51] This is (a) because the prophets were not ordinary believers, they had a particular, God-given gift and role. It is (b) because, as we have seen in the birth narrative, Jesus is not simply filled with the Spirit but uniquely born by the Spirit (Luke 1.35) so that 'Luke does not think of the chrism on Jesus as the organ of revelation to him' (at least not primarily) 'but as the power by which his words and actions bring salvation to others';[52] (c) the role of the Messiah, for which Jesus is anointed, although having much in common with the prophets, is also a unique one.[53] Jesus was not just a believer, nor only prophet. If John the Baptist was perceived as 'more than a prophet' (Luke 7.26), how much more than a prophet must Jesus have appeared?[54] The people of Palestine were constantly questioning

---

47 Beverly Roberts Gaventa, 'Initiatives Divine and Human in the Lukan Story World', in Graham N. Stanton, Bruce W. Longenecker and Stephen C. Barton (eds), *The Holy Spirit and Christian Origins, Essays in Honor of James Dunn*, Grand Rapids, MI: Eerdmans, 2004, 79–89 (88–9).

48 E.g. Gonzales, *Acts*.

49 E.g. R. P. Menzies, *Empowered for Witness: The Spirit in Luke–Acts*, London: T & T Clark, 2004.

50 Cf. Max Turner, 1996, *Power from on High: The Spirit in Israel's Restoration and Witness in Luke–Acts*, Sheffield: Sheffield Academic Press, 1996, 78–9, 119–37.

51 Max Turner, 'Jesus and the Spirit in Lucan Perspective', *Tyndale Bulletin* 32 (1981), 3–42 (3), where he names L. S. Thornton, J. D. G. Dunn, T. S. Smail and G. W. H. Lampe.

52 Turner, 'Jesus and the Spirit', 41.

53 Turner, 'Jesus and the Spirit', 41–2.

54 Wright, *Jesus and the Victory of God*, 197.

Jesus' identity and searching for new titles to apply to him. While Jesus is presented as a prophet in Luke and the disciples emulate his ministry, the Gospel also attributes other titles to him, and arguably the term 'Saviour' is the one that most clearly captures the way Jesus blends together the stories of Israel and the world.[55] Furthermore, the early Christians and Jesus himself understood he was the Son of God and (d) he therefore possessed a unique relationship with God and the world God created. As if to emphasize this further, in Luke's account, the apostles' experience of the Spirit is further distinguished from that of Christ by a complete disregard of sonship as a dimension of it. 'God is never addressed as "Father" in Acts; and on the only occasions in which he is spoken of as "the Father" it is always in immediate relation to Jesus (1.4, 7; 2.33).'[56]

So the second reason that 'prophetic dialogue' is limited as a description of the mission of Jesus Christ is that, as we showed at the beginning, the Spirit who empowers that mission is the Spirit of creation, life and vitality.[57] Pentecost is therefore not only an empowerment of the disciples for mission but also an integral part of their salvation that affects every aspect of their lives.[58] In the book of Acts we read not only about prophecy and dialogue but about the shared life of the Christian community and the transformation of the lives of individuals within it to be Christlike. A prime example is Stephen, who, 'full of faith and holy spirit' waited on tables (6.2) as well as doing wonders and signs (6.8) and speaking wisdom (6.10) until he was called on to follow his master in making the ultimate sacrifice. It is Luke's project to demonstrate that everything that Christ came to do is continued by the Spirit working through the disciples.[59] He shows 'the holistic (multidimensional), transformative, dynamic and eschatological dimensions of what it means to be the people being saved by God'.[60] As well as prophecy, teaching, doing signs and wonders, these included learning, fellowship, breaking bread, prayers, sharing of material wealth and testifying (Acts 2.42–47; 4.32–37). The moral lives and ethics of the community are affected as well as their confidence as they engage in bold witness and successful debate and grow in numbers. James takes all these as a sign that the restoration of

---

55 N. T. Wright, *The New Testament and the People of God*, London: SPCK, 1992, 378–84.

56 Dunn, *Jesus and the Spirit*, 191.

57 The re-expression of mission as joining in with the Spirit of Life informs the 2012 World Council of Churches statement 'Together towards Life: Mission and Evangelism in Changing Landscapes'.

58 Cf. Congar, *I Believe in the Holy Spirit*, 46. For the longstanding discussion on this question, see Turner, *Power from On High*, 20–79, and on the debate between Dunn and Robert P. Menzies, see Turner, 'The Spirit and Salvation in Luke–Acts', in G. N. Stanton, B. W. Longenecker and S. C. Barton (eds), The Holy Spirit and Christian Origins: Essays in honor of James Dunn, Grand Rapids, MI: Eerdmans, 2004, 103–16.

59 Congar, *I Believe in the Holy Spirit*, 44–7.

60 Amos Yong, *The Spirit Poured Out on All Flesh: Pentecostalism and the Possibility of Global Theology*, Grand Rapids, MI: Baker, 2005, 166.

Israel, for which the prophets looked and the disciples hoped, is underway and this why the Gentiles are flocking to it (Acts 15.13–18).[61]

Although, as we have shown, Jesus in Luke receives the Spirit already known from the Hebrew and Judaic tradition, some Christian theologians have insisted on a radical discontinuity between the spirit in the Old Testament and the Spirit in the New on biblical grounds.[62] Despite recent attempts to reconnect the Creator Spirit with the Spirit of Pentecost in Christian theology[63] Turner insists that, according to Luke–Acts, 'The gift of the Spirit is not some intensification and re-direction of God's s/Spirit in all humanity. Those who have not received the gift of the Spirit simply do not have God's Spirit *at all'*[64] and Levison would agree with him, although where Turner seems to regard this as a strength, Levison sees it as a weakness.[65] However, if this were the case, Acts would be inconsistent with Luke's Gospel, which sets Jesus in his Hebrew–Judaic context. Jesus Christ both confirmed and redirected his pneumatological inheritance. What Luke proclaimed was not a new spirit but that the already-known Holy Spirit was manifested and experienced uniquely in Jesus Christ. In the early Church, the Spirit of God became identified with the Spirit of Jesus (e.g. Acts 19.5–6). The identification of the Spirit as the creative Spirit of the universe was retained but the understanding of the life brought about by that Spirit was Christianized. That is it was shaped by the living example of holiness in Jesus and by his teaching on justice, mercy and love.

The strongest evidence for this process is that Christian theology early on discerned life to be the overriding characteristic of the Spirit. The Nicene-Constantinopolitan Creed declares that the Holy Spirit is 'the Lord, the Giver of Life'. As in the Hebrew Bible, the theme of life is continued through to the end of the Nicene Creed in an extended sense. The Creed goes on to attribute to the Holy Spirit the word of justice and peace spoken through the prophets and then to link the Spirit with the life in community and mission ('one holy catholic and apostolic Church') as well as with restoration ('one baptism for the forgiveness of sins'), with 'the resurrection of the dead and the life of the world to come' (English Language Liturgical

---

61 Cf. Turner, 'The Spirit and Salvation in Luke–Acts', 108.

62 Eduard Schweizer, 'On Distinguishing Between Spirits', *Ecumenical Review* 41:3 (1989), 406–15; Levison, *Filled with the Spirit*.

63 Notably Jürgen Moltmann, *The Spirit of Life: A Universal Affirmation*, trans. Margaret Kohl, London: SCM, 1992.

64 Turner, Levison's *Filled with the Spirit*, 199.

65 Levison regards the early Church as having a Hellenized understanding of Spirit. For a criticism of this reading on biblical grounds see the following reviews: George Montague, 'Review of J. R. Levison, *Filled with the Spirit*', *Catholic Biblical Quarterly* 72 (2010), 831–2; Blaine Charette, '"And Now for Something Completely Different": A "Pythonic" Reading of Pentecost?', *Pneuma* 33 (2011), 59–62; and James Shelton, 'Delphi and Jerusalem: Two Spirits or Holy Spirit? A Review of John R. Levison's *Filled with the Spirit*', *Pneuma* 33 (2011), 47–58.

Consultation translation). The Creed both preserves the Hebrew sense of the Spirit of Life in its material, biological and cultural senses while also linking the Spirit to the Church and its mission. The third and final paragraph of the Creed, which includes another 'believe', is constructed to express both continuity and discontinuity between the Spirit as Creator as Recreator in the life of the Church.[66] The relationship between Old and New Testaments is captured here: Christians believe in both the Spirit of creation and the prophets and also the Spirit of Pentecost and the new age.

However, the Church has not always maintained the link between the Spirit in creation and re-creation that is inherent in the Creed. The Eastern Churches have criticized the Western Church for narrowly defining the Spirit through its insistence on the inclusion of the phrase *filioque* in the Latin version of the Creed to read: 'We believe in the Holy Spirit ... who proceeds from the Father *and the Son*', where the original creed concluded with 'from the Father'. They argue that this subordinated the Spirit to Christ, reduced theology to Christology and confined the work of the Spirit within the Church.[67] It is noticeable that Yves Congar's digest of the pneumatology of the Second Vatican Council, although focused on the Holy Spirit, did limit the Spirit's work to matters affecting the Church and believers.[68] Nevertheless, the Second Vatican Council clarified that the Spirit is present and active beyond the Church in other people and communities. Drawing on the documents of the Council,[69] the 1991 document *Dialogue and Proclamation* makes clear that 'that the Council has openly acknowledged the presence of positive values not only in the religious life of individual believers of other religious traditions, but also in the religious traditions to which they belong. It attributed these values to the active presence of God through his Word, pointing also to the universal action of the Spirit.'[70] In so doing, the Council paved the way for dialogue with people of other faiths and for a dialogical approach in human interaction more generally, which seeks to learn as well as teach, receive as well as give. This development was paralleled in the World Council of Churches which established its theology of dialogue on a pneumatological foundation.[71]

Not only is the confession that the Holy Spirit is both the Spirit of life and also the Spirit of Christ established by the links Luke makes between Jesus

---

66 Kirsteen Kim, *The Holy Spirit in the World: A Global Conversation*, Maryknoll, NY: Orbis, 2007, 45–52.

67 For this debate, see D. Ritschl, 'Historical Development and Implications of the Filioque Controversy', in L. Vischer (ed.), *Spirit of God, Spirit of Christ: Ecumenical Reflection on the Filioque Controversy*, Geneva: World Council of Churches, 1981, 46–65.

68 Congar, *I Believe in the Holy Spirit*, see e.g., the contents of vol. 2.

69 *Ad Gentes* (4), *Lumen Gentium* (16), *Nostra Aetate* (2) and *Gaudium et Spes* (92–3).

70 Pontifical Council for Inter-Religious Dialogue and the Congregation for the Evangelization of Peoples, *Dialogue and Proclamation: Reflection and Orientations on Interreligious Dialogue and the Proclamation of the Gospel of Jesus Christ*, Rome: Holy See, 1991, para 17.

71 Kim, *The Holy Spirit*, 67–102.

and the Hebrew and Judaic traditions, this is also signalled by the progress of the narrative in the book of Acts. Luke makes the feast of Pentecost the paradigmatic bestowal of the Spirit on the community but, as commentators have pointed out,[72] there are repeated 'Pentecosts' in Acts: the Spirit comes upon Samaritans (8.14–17); on Cornelius and his party of Gentiles (10.44–48; 11.15–17); and on the disciples of Apollos, who had hitherto only experienced the baptism of John (19.1–6).[73] The key message of the book of Acts is the universal offer of this gift – especially to Gentiles as well as Jews – and the open-endedness of its spread.[74] At the beginning of the book Jesus tells his disciples they will be witnesses 'to the ends of the earth' (Acts 1.8). At the end Paul has reached as far as Rome. Since this is the centre of a great empire, the stage is set for a great expansion but the story is far from over. The invitation goes out to join oneself to the Holy Spirit, the living power of the universe, through repentance and faith in Jesus Christ until the kingdom comes. There is an indication too, in the key quotation from the prophet Joel (Acts 2.19–20) and in the references to Jesus' ascension into heaven in Acts 1 and 2, that the coming of the kingdom is not only an event in human society but also a material and cosmic transformation.

Although there are many spirits abroad, there is only one who proceeds from God the Father as the wind or breath of God in the world. Since the incarnation of God in Jesus, Christians have identified this Spirit with the Life working in and through him. This Spirit continues to blow in the world and it is the Christian confession that the Life-Giver is uniquely available to all through union with Jesus Christ. The Church is sent into the world to proclaim Christ so that all may be filled and be saved.

---

72 Congar, *I Believe in the Holy Spirit*, 45.

73 Dunn, *Jesus and the Spirit*, 62–7.

74 Cf. John Christopher Thomas, *The Spirit of the New Testament*, Leiden: Deo Publishing, 2005, 223–32.

PART 2

Ecclesiology: The Mission of the Church as Prophetic Dialogue

4

Mission, Ecclesiology and Migration

EMMA WILD-WOOD

Christians cannot be distinguished from the rest of the human race by country or language or customs. They do not live in cities of their own; they do not use a peculiar form of speech ... Yet, although they live in Greek and barbarian cities alike ... and follow the customs of the country in clothing and food and other matters of daily living, at the same time they give proof of the remarkable and admittedly extraordinary constitution of their own commonwealth. They live in their own countries, but only as aliens. They have a share in everything as citizens, and endure everything as foreigners. Every foreign land is their fatherland, and yet for them every fatherland is a foreign land ... They busy themselves on earth, but their citizenship is in heaven. They obey the established laws, but in their own lives they go far beyond what the laws require. (*Epistle to Diognetus* 5.1–10, second century)

Introduction

Migration is as old as humanity and has influenced the Christian Church since its inception. The twentieth century and early twenty-first century have seen mass movements of populations across the globe that show little sign of abating. Sociologists of religion have charted the contemporary rise of migrant churches and the particularities of the various trajectories of migration.[1] Missiologists are now reflecting on the mass movement of peoples. The reasons for migration, the experience of migration, the place of origin and location necessitate a careful contextual response to a complex and ever-changing situation. This chapter explores the prophetic-dialogue mission spirituality in the context of global migration by noting how the Christian Church is being reshaped and sketching an intercultural ecclesiology in the light of migration and its societal effects. It asks what questions and opportunities does the global phenomenon of migration present to the witness of the Church in the world.

The chapter assumes that migration as a social reality influences our understanding of God's mission in the world and of the nature of humanity

---

1 See for example the work of Gerri ter Haar, *Halfway to Paradise: African Christians in Europe*, Cardiff, Cardiff Academic Press, 1998 and Afe Adogame, *The African Christian Diaspora: new currents and emerging trends in world Christianity*, London: Bloomsbury Academic, 2013.

and the Church. Therefore, it notes certain trends as important to consider in forming ecclesiology. In 2010, 859 million people, 12.5 per cent of the world's population, were living outside their nation-state of origin.[2] Migration is global; it is influenced by political, economic and technological forces whose impact is abbreviated in the word 'globalization'. International trade agreements and political alliances disproportionately benefit some parts of the globe and some groups within nation-states. The reduction in the effort and time to communicate and to travel provides opportunities for increased mobility. Migration also takes on regional and local characteristics: the policies of governments influence who emigrates and who is permitted to immigrate; extreme weather and natural disasters make living in some states precarious; educational policies and labour-markets also impact on how and why individuals migrate. Some migrants settle permanently, others return to their country of origin, others move to another location. In 2010 Mexico, Bangladesh and Argentina were the top 'sending' countries.[3] Some migrants take advantage of the rapidity of travel and communication to improve their educational or economic status. Others bear the brunt of political and economic inequalities and increasingly the effects of changes to the world's climate and weather systems. Migration is also significantly Christian: those concerned about social cohesion in the growing plurality of Europe and the USA have focused on the extremely valuable response of interreligious dialogue.[4] Yet 47.4 per cent of migrants are Christians, compared with 25.4 per cent migrants who are Muslim.[5] Immigrant religious beliefs and practices shape religion in destination societies. The way in which migrant and non-migrant Christians relate to each other has consequences for the Christian Church in each place.

While there are many references to migration in the biblical texts – expulsion, nomadism, exodus, exile, return, missionary journeys, disciples as strangers[6] – this chapter provides short reflections on two passages: the vision of Revelation 7.9–end in which 'a great multitude that no one could count, from every nation, from all tribes and peoples and languages' worship God in the presence of the Lamb, and the community ethic of 1 Peter 2, which revolves around a corporate identity as 'resident aliens'. These passages are helpful in developing an ecclesiology that takes seriously the processes of migration and their culturally plural consequences. The conclusion points towards a mission-focused intercultural ecclesiology. The word

---

2 Centre for the Study of Global Christianity, *Christianity in its Global Context, 1970–2020, Society, Religion, and Mission*, South Hamilton, MA: CSGC, 2013, 82, wwwgordonconwell.com/netcommunity/CSGCResources/ChristianityinitsGlobalContext.pdf.

3 Centre for the Study of Global Christianity, *Christianity in its Global Context*, 82.

4 See for example, Andrew Holden, *Religious Cohesion in Times of Conflict: Christian–Muslim Relations in Segregated Towns*, London: Continuum, 2009.

5 Centre for the Study of Global Christianity, *Christianity in its Global Context*, 82.

6 Tim Naish, 'Mission, Migration and the Stranger in our Midst', in Stephen Spencer (ed.), *Mission and Migration*, Calver: Cliff College, 2008, 7–30.

'intercultural' is used for the sharing of difference and the mutual sifting of identities, beliefs and practices to discern the work of the Spirit.[7] 'Multicultural' indicates many cultures tolerating the existence of others. The use of 'intercultural' is an attempt to move from a mere tolerance of difference to explore a mutuality and a 'being together' in Christ. It demands deep listening and compassion as part of being Church. When societal fissures form along racial and linguistic lines, when problems can be blamed on the most recent arrivals, intercultural worship and service of God can be a powerful witness to the Lamb who was slain.

Compassion for Migrants, Solidarity with Migrants, Power to Migrants

Mission in contexts affected by migration is influenced by different migrant experiences of dislocation, the interpretation of those experiences and varying theological comprehensions of suffering and power. This in turn influences assumptions about church life. In theological writing a strong ethical focus on care and justice for the most vulnerable migrants has been more prominent than an ecclesiology informed by migration.

I was an eyewitness to the migration of Rwandans into Congo after the genocide in 1994. The political effects of the sudden movement of over a million people precipitated a series of conflicts in Congo which still continue. This has eclipsed the immediate hospitality shown by the Congolese to their Rwandan neighbours. Rwandans in their thousands streamed over the border day after day in buses, cars, on foot, carrying mattresses, clothes and food on their heads. Many settled at the side of the road, others approached local people for shelter, many arrived at church compounds seeking aid. Churches allowed refugees to settle on their land and in their buildings, clergy facilitated the organization and distribution of aid, and ordinary people accepted Rwandans into their homes at some considerable cost to themselves. The majority of citizens of Bukavu and Goma were generous in a situation that was beyond their control. Congolese compassion arose from an empathy with vulnerability and a recognition that their lives were also precarious and were subject to displacement. Christian charities responded to the plight of refugees and asylum seekers in the Great Lakes region and across the globe, providing aid and succour, advocating for their rights, working with legal systems and challenging government policy. The genocide called forth huge international efforts of aid, but churches in Eastern Congo were the first port of call for refugees and they remain at the forefront of care for those who are internationally or internally displaced. Poverty

---

7 See Gemma Cruz, *An Intercultural Theology of Migration*, Leiden: Brill, 2010 and Peter Phan, 'The Experience of Migration as a Source of Intercultural Theology', in Elaine Padilla and Peter C. Phan (eds), *Contemporary Issues of Migration and Theology*, New York: Palgrave Macmillan, 2013, 179–210.

and political instability in Latin America, for example, or the political convulsions in North Africa and the Middle East from 2011 have resulted in many economic migrants and refugees. Far from the gaze of the international media, other movements of people occur, like those from North Korea into China.[8] The plight of migrants at these and many other places pricks the conscience of the Christian Church and pushes it to respond in missional acts of justice and of loving service. Many theological and ethical reflections on migration arise from a concern to speak and act compassionately in these situations.[9]

Some sites of migration have become particularly resonant of the struggles of globalization: the Sonoran desert traversed by the US–Mexican border, for example, or the island of Lampedusa in the Mediterranean, a European toehold for African migrants seeking a new life. The tragedies of death by dehydration or drowning present in stark relief the human aspiration and suffering behind complex systems of inequality, injustice, corruption, xenophobia and control. Pope Francis, the first Latin American to hold the See of Rome, held a Mass on Lampedusa soon after his consecration.[10] He spoke to both the long-term residents of Lampedusa and the migrants for whom it provides access to Europe, conscious of those who had lost their lives reaching the island. He called for 'solidarity' with migrants and a sense of 'fraternal responsibility' that challenged the 'globalization of indifference'.[11] It was an act of dialogue, in that Pope Francis entered a particular context, one iconic of other contexts and came alongside those living there, yet he was also witnessing to the vitality of the gospel to speak prophetically against systems of global inequality and injustice. Pope Francis's particular engagement is honed by the priority given to social justice by liberation theology: a theological tradition that abhors the gross inequalities between rich and poor and declares God's preference for the marginalized, the vulnerable and the impoverished, calling on all Christian people to act in solidarity with them. This theology has infused ethical and missional thinking on responses to migrants. As Catholic theologian Peter Phan says, 'A theology out of the context of migration must begin with personal solidarity with the victims of this abject condition of human, often innocent, suffering.'[12] For Phan it is the experience of profound dislocation[13] which informs theology. Such theological reflection promotes compassion and care and, in order to seek

---

8 Hiroyuki Tanaka, 'North Korea: Understanding Migration to and from a Closed Country', http://migrationinformation.org/Profiles/display.cfm?ID=668.

9 For example, Daniel G. Groody and Gioacchino Campese (eds), *A Promised Land, A Perilous Journey: Theological Perspectives on Migration*, Notre Dame, IN: University of Notre Dame Press, 2008.

10 www.bbc.co.uk/news/world-europe-23224010.

11 http://en.radiovaticana.va/news 2013/07/08/ppe.

12 Phan, 'The Experience of Migration', 198.

13 I use 'dislocation' to indicate a variety of feelings evoked by the migrant experience of relocating, from significant suffering and trauma to mild perturbation at new cultural norms.

justice and reconciliation for the marginalized, it encourages the exploration of thorny issues such as questions about rights and duties, of autonomy and integration, the balancing of claims to land, the significance of the foreign and the native. Solidarity with vulnerable migrants is part of a process of healing and reconciliation.[14]

The narrative of the impoverished, the fearful or the highly motivated risking all to cross borders is one facet of migration. Another is corporate relocation, the deliberate recruitment of workers, or the successful application for study or employment. The Indian subcontinent, for example, provides the British National Health Service with medical staff and the Gulf States with construction workers. A large number of Africans are studying in Chinese universities.[15] Some migrants, rather than consider themselves to be at the mercy of globalizing forces, engage with them to maximize opportunities. This includes, for some, the opportunity of cross-cultural mission activity. The rapidity of communication and travel is understood to open new possibilities and permit access. The establishment of Christian communities can be part of the migrant toolkit in adapting to new surroundings. Churches provide a space to assess how to live well in new surroundings. Like other migrant associations, churches offer mutual support, succour and familiar language and culture in the new location. Some form new churches,[16] others take their religious traditions with them. India and China experience the growth of Christian congregations of migrant workers. Some of these are return-migrants who, during time away from their country of origin, have become Christians or deepened their faith, and they go home to spread the gospel and plant churches.

There is another theological tradition emerging, one that is often associated with the Pentecostal movement.[17] It is suspicious of a *focus* on suffering and less interested in critiquing socio-economic structures. It places greater emphasis on the power of God and empowerment by the Spirit in the amelioration of suffering. For some a theological appreciation of prosperity as a sign of God's blessing as found in some Old Testament writings has become a focus of their expectations. The desire for an improved lifestyle is a theological reason for some Christians to migrate: God's blessing is made manifest in gaining a place to study or obtaining a visa. If the destination country proves not to be the Promised Land flowing with milk and honey,

---

14 Robert Schreiter 'Migrants and the Ministry of Reconciliation', in P. G. Groody and G. Campese (eds), *A Promised Land, A Perilous Journey: Theological Perspectives on Migration*, Notre Dame, IN: University of Notre Dame Press, 2008, 107–23.

15 Simon Allison, 'Fixing China's Image in Africa one Student at a Time', theguardian.com, 5 July 2013, www.theguardian.com/world/2013/jul/31/china-africa-students-scholarship-programme.

16 Jehu J. Hanciles, *Beyond Christendom: Globalization, African Migration and the Transformation of the West*, Maryknoll, NY: Orbis, 2008, 328–49.

17 See for example, Allan Anderson, *An Introduction to Pentecostalism*, Cambridge: Cambridge University Press, 2004.

but the Babylon or Egypt of societal marginalization, stressful working conditions or different cultural values, God has greater opportunities for acting in power. The sense of dislocation may also encourage strong cohesion with other migrants and the establishment of flourishing Christian communities. Furthermore, some have critiqued attitudes of Western Christians towards migrants in their countries. They suggest that Western Christians may be hostile or uninterested, but more insidious, in focusing attention on the most vulnerable, they may perceive migrants only as victims who require help.[18] Migrants and their communities are actors in the process of reconciliation. Victims are never simply victims, and empowerment permits healing to take place.

The virtues of compassion, solidarity and empowerment are not mutually exclusive but the trends mentioned here may pull in different directions. A focus on service and justice must never become a form of patronage and power. Nor should certain parts of the Christian Church perceive themselves as being the only ones who host or serve or who are able to resolve situations. Likewise a focus on empowerment should not lead to condemnation of those who remain vulnerable.

Church and Migration

In order to move towards a missional ecclesiology shaped by migration two very broad groupings of Christian congregation influenced by migration – single/similar culture congregations and multicultural congregations – and the ways in which they are prophetic and dialogical will be examined.[19] Both kinds of congregations can develop an intercultural missiology, as outlined at the end of the chapter, but they will do so from different points on the prophetic-dialogue continuum.

The terms 'single' and 'multi' and 'cultural' are both useful and dangerous. A small town I lived in had a single church building used by a Protestant (Anglican, Baptist, Methodist and United Reformed) congregation and a Catholic congregation both of whom had around 20 per cent of their members who were first generation immigrants to the UK and came from all (humanly inhabited) continents.[20] Worship was largely in English. These congregations were occasionally attended by migrants who preferred to travel to single-culture congregations. The building was also used by a

---

18 Claudia Wahrish-Oblau, *The Missionary Self-Perception of Pentecostal/Charismatic Church Leaders from the Global South in Europe: Bringing Back the Gospel*, Leiden: Brill, 2009, 314–17.

19 For the purposes of this chapter the single-culture churches of destination societies are not discussed.

20 Emma Wild-Wood, 'The Experience of Migrants in a Native British Church: Towards Mission Together', in H. Im Chandler and Amos Yong (eds), *Global Diasporas and Mission*, Oxford: Regnum Books International, 2014, 175–90.

third congregation, a Syrian Orthodox church from India, whose worshippers came from Kerala and whose liturgy was in Malayalam. The first two congregations were partially multicultural but the third congregation was certainly monocultural. The terms are also slippery because outsiders may perceive a congregation as one thing while the insiders might understand it quite differently. For example, an outsider may perceive a black congregation as monoculturally African, but the members understand themselves as multicultural or 'international', because they come from a variety of different African cultures and countries and some are from the Caribbean. The differences between cultures may be acute internally, nevertheless cultural similarities that emerged when faced with the destination culture sometimes brought the members together, often in the face of hostility from the destination society.[21] Likewise, multicultural congregations comprising people from all over the globe may have a cosmopolitan, professional culture or a shared loyalty to a particular denomination that binds its members together. Furthermore, 'culture' cannot be understood as a bounded or static entity; cultures are fluid and transmuting – no more so than when people move. Such nuances need to be borne in mind when reflecting on any particular congregations. The ecclesiological approach taken here assumes attention to social realities and cultural perceptions and as such it can only be properly developed in particular situations.

Nicholas Healey has developed a practical–prophetic ecclesiology that critiques theological 'blueprints' considering that they do not sufficiently deal with divine action or the messy contingency of the temporal Church. Models or guiding ideas may inspire, but they encourage confusion when they are understood *not* as 'what God's people are inspired by the Spirit to become' but *rather* as 'what the Church actually *is* ...' People of God, body of Christ and sacrament are inspiring images but when they provide the principle for a systematic ecclesiology they are unlikely to engage with real communities that aim to follow and witness to Jesus Christ. The sociocultural fluidity of migrations makes systematizing ecclesiology particularly problematic. 'The practice of ecclesiology arises out of ecclesial practices, and is ordered directly towards them', says Healey, Ecclesiologists, he continues, 'assess the church's witness and pastoral care in the light of Scripture and in relation to a theological analysis of the contemporary ecclesiological context. They propose changes in the Church's concrete identity that will conserve, reform or more radically restructure it, in order to help it embody its witness more truthfully.'[22] Practical–prophetic ecclesiology, like prophetic-dialogue missiology, provides an encapsulating idea, but one which is presented as an axis along which context-appropriate responses,

---

21 For an example, see Dominic Pasura, 'Modes of Incorporation and Transnational Zimbabwean migration to Britain', *Ethnic and Racial Studies* 36:1 (2013), 199–218.

22 Nicholas M. Healy, *Church, World and the Christian Life: Practical–Prophetic Ecclesiology*, Cambridge: Cambridge University Press, 2000, 46.

guided by the Trinity, tradition and Scripture, can flourish. It is rooted in attending to the lived experience of the Church and also raising the vision of the Church beyond its present reality so it may live out the values of God's reign. The broad descriptions below of trends in church development as a result of migration are an attempt to sketch some 'ecclesial practices' and note acts of prophecy and dialogue that can already be observed. The biblical and theological reflections that follow are intended to provide some first steps towards an intercultural ecclesiology which further integrates the experience of migration into the life and witness of the Church.

Single or Similar Culture Congregations

Single/similar culture congregations may have a number of charisms. Homogeneity, as proponents of the McGavran and Wagner models of church growth appreciate,[23] allows for easy bonding and greater community cohesion. For those who are dealing with dislocation through migration homogeneous churches can offer a caring, pastoral space. The Orthodox congregation from Kerala mentioned above, for example, prioritizes the preservation of tradition for the sustenance of a faith-filled life in a new situation; drawing deep upon that tradition it re-forms community in the worship of God. It offers understanding and support to those who come from Kerala, by fellow Keralans who empathize with the transition from one culture to another. Single/similar culture congregations often act as a refuge from a hostile or bewildering environment, providing a place to be oneself, to learn news from home or send remittances to family members. Gender and generational expectations, which may be inverted by new work patterns, can resume a familiar pattern in the church. Members can give and receive advice on the destination culture: for those migrating from the Global South to the North this might include how to deal with an individualistic ethos when one is accustomed to family- or community-centred ethics, how to use technological advancements, or adapt to a market economy, or comprehend the competing claims of freedoms and rights. Single/similar culture congregations often offer the particular charism of comprehension, succour and support. The healing of dislocation may take place within a congregation where affirmation of one's cultural identity is significant. Those worshipping in similar culture churches often perceive the need for adaptations. The Keralan congregation, for example, is visited only once a month by a priest, so it has developed a prominent lay leadership, which organize Bible studies, social events and local representation. It is concerned about the second generation: the children growing up in the church who speak English with greater ease than Malayalam and whose upbringing distances them from

---

23 See Donald McGavran *How Churches Grow*, London: World Dominion Press, 1959 and editions of *Understanding Church Growth*, Grand Rapids, MI: Eerdmans, 1970, 1990, etc.

the role the Church played in Keralan life. They recognize that the culture of their children is different to that of the parents. Indeed, the processes of migration demonstrate just how malleable is any 'culture', as a set of attitudes, customs, beliefs and language constantly mutating in response to external factors. Children are often able to make the most of their hybrid identity but may be ambivalent about retaining forms of Christian worship that are very specific to their parents' culture of origin.

The attention to the worship of God in familiar forms and the pastoral care of those who live in two cultural milieus, can be understood as a form of dialogue, a 'ministry of presence, of respect',[24] which offers migrants a place of safety and love. It is precisely in places of comfort that some find healing and reconciliation from the dislocation and trauma of the migrant experience. These churches maintain identity and enable adaptation to a new environment. There is evidence that single/similar cultural congregations serve and evangelize their own people deliberately and with success.[25] People become Christians or renew their Christian commitment as a result of their migration. The inculturated, pastoral care engenders renewed comprehension of the gospel in this scenario, as Bevans and Schroeder suggest, the dialogical approach of pastoral care is intertwined with the prophetic approach of evangelism. Furthermore, a number of international churches established by migrants are intentionally missional. They wish to see the 'dark continent' of Europe respond to the gospel, and they understand themselves as 'reverse' missionaries. Yet they bemoan the lack of interest by white Europeans. The Embassy of God in Kiev, Ukraine, is a famous exception to the rule of largely black membership, for a church initiated by Africans in Europe.[26] Some thinkers have questioned whether they suffer from a 'cultural captivity' and require more work to understand the destination culture because the inculturated nature of church life prevents evangelism beyond the cultures represented within it.[27] Yet this reason cannot be held entirely responsible for such lack of interest; white Europeans do not go to church at all – on the whole. Nevertheless the realities sketched here suggest different forms of dialogue from those of Bevans and Schroeder and their missionary order, the Society of the Divine Word.

Bevans and Schroeder describe the process of dialogue as first to '*leave* our homelands or our places of comfort' (something members of the congregations described above manifestly have done) 'and *pass over* into people's cultures, languages, economic standards'. Migrants often learn a new

---

24 S. B. Bevans and R. P. Schroeder, *Constants in Context: A Theology of Mission for Today*, Maryknoll, NY: Orbis, 2004, 59.

25 Hanciles, *Beyond Christendom*, 346–9.

26 Afe Adogame, 'Up, Up, Jesus! Down, Satan! African Religiosity in the Former Soviet Bloc: The Embassy of the Blessed Kingdom of God for All Nations', *Exchange* 37:3 (2008), 310–36.

27 Babatunde Adedibu, *Coat of Many Colours: The Origin, Growth, Distinctiveness and Contributions of Black Majority Churches to British Christianity*, Gloucester: Wisdom Summit, 2012, 239, 247.

language and adapt to new political and economic standards. However, the creation of associations and churches that resonate with the cultural norms they have left behind suggests that *passing over* into people's cultures may not be a priority or attempts may have been met by rejection. The development of similar culture migrant churches suggests that assumptions about mission, which have emerged through the modern missionary movement and are predicated on a model of missionary-as-migrant crossing geographical and cultural boundaries, may require re-examination.

Western career missionaries may have been challenged to divest themselves of trappings of power and influence in order to attempt to engage in the cultures of the peoples among whom they serve. Yet the dynamics of power often work differently for those who find themselves marginalized in the host society and who develop a mission focus as a result of their migration. Passing over into another culture remains an important element of dialogical mission but an awareness of the ways in which varying access to resources and influence might impact intercultural engagement is vital in order that we recognize forms of dialogue that may appear different to the one sketched by Bevans and Schoeder. It may enable an appreciation of wider charisms of single/similar culture congregations.

The gifts of these congregations are not limited to internal benefits. They may offer fresh insights to their destination society and its churches, and they have the potential to offer a prophetic critique. The liturgy of the Keralan congregation links the small English town in which it worships to the very early Syriac Church. Long, incense-filled services, with frequent 'kyries' and recitation of early Church fathers are a reminder that people have been worshipping God sincerely and faithfully for centuries, in many different ways and across the globe. The inculturated ethics or forms of spirituality of a particular group of migrant Christians, has the potential offer a prophetic challenge to the Church in the destination country which may not be easy to receive. Yet an openness to these charisms may enrich church life. A sharing of such gifts requires, however, a 'passing-over' into the lives of others and an ecumenical engagement between congregations.

Multicultural Congregations

Congregations who have members from a number of different cultures have developed in many forms. Some arise because of denominational loyalty, language preference or cultural heritage. Scottish Presbyterian churches or English Anglican churches in large cities around the globe, for example, draw a cosmopolitan membership for whom one or all three elements is significant. Others may have membership drawn from one or two cultures, like Methodist churches in London who may have white-British members and members originally from Ghana or Zimbabwe. The African members may also organize themselves in fellowship groups with a national or linguistic focus. Some congregations are thoroughly multicultural. Others have a majority membership from the destination country and a smaller number of migrants from a variety of locations across the globe. Migrants in these latter congregations often show a generosity of spirit in accepting a form or language of worship that is different from the one with which they are familiar. They are adapting not only to the society of the destination country but also to one part of its cultural expression.

Multi-ethnic congregations have the potential to play a prophetic role in society. They may offer a model of reconciled diversity, of fruitful boundary crossing, inhabiting the universality of the Church. Yet the place of culture and the migrant experience varies greatly in these congregations. A profoundly prophetic element is only possible once a dialogical attitude is present which takes cognizance not only of the variety of cultures but also of the migrant experience. Some congregations may strongly emphasize a common Christian identity, claiming a colour, class and gender blindness interprets 'there is no Jew nor Gentile, slave, free ... all are one in Christ Jesus' as a command to ignore difference.[28] Usually this results in silencing minority ethnicities in favour of the majority and becomes a form of power perpetuation. This approach shows a limited social understanding of migrant experiences and cultural divisions and is ineffectual in approaching them.[29] Other multicultural congregations may attempt to include those who adapt to the dominant way of doing things, who attend services in a form or language that is different to their own, who accept the ignorance of native Christians towards other cultures or the dislocation of migration. Such congregations make small concessions to the presence of migrants. Diversity in this scenario may lead to assimilation, certain forms of which are desirable for some migrants. Other migrants, particularly those with strong communitarian expectations, may be willing to concede to assimilation. Other multicultural congregations may recognize the enrichment of insights into God's work in the world from other cultures and experiences and attempt to make these public through leadership and worship. Yet it may be easier for these congregations to be intentionally inclusive by celebrating the plurality of cultures than to address the tensions provided by such differences and by the dislocation often felt in migration processes. It is in addressing issues of healing and reconciliation as well as in bringing cultural insights to bear on church life and worship that an intercultural ecclesiology will emerge which may balance the missional demands of prophetic dialogue.

In multicultural congregations there are greater challenges of hospitality (the subject of another chapter). The language of host and guest requires careful thought. Using this language may anticipate shared expectations about how to behave towards one another. However, those native to the

---

28 Kathleen Garces-Foley, *Crossing the Ethnic Divide: the Multi-ethnic Church on a Mission*, New York: Oxford University Press, 2007, 13.

29 Garces-Foley, *Crossing the Ethnic Divide*, 44.

destination country may be unaware of other traditions of hospitality; they may be racist, they may also be unaware that assumptions of 'common courtesies' are often culturally bound and may not be shared at all. Such a situation requires careful dialogue of attentive listening to each other and the passing over into each other's experience before it can be prophetic and attend to issues of reconciliation.

Practical–prophetic ecclesiology moves from describing the cultural relationships within the body of Christ as a result of social change to developing new ways of understanding itself as a sacred community. Having sketched the contemporary global and fluid phenomenon of migration and having highlighted Christian responses to various forms of migration we now turn to biblical reflections and practical steps towards an intercultural ecclesiology that may allow us to travel together, to discern what may inspire us to live interculturally as Church and engage with the world around us. How far the conclusions drawn here will be pertinent to every situation will be for others to decide.

Biblical Reflections towards an Intercultural Ecclesiology

The vision in Revelation 7 describes the worship of 'a great multitude that no one could count, from every nation, from all tribes and peoples and languages'. These countless people have particular origins, sets of relationships and ways of speaking. They lift their voices in one song of praise to God Almighty, adoring the one who created and saved them. The worshippers are the suffering witnesses to Christ, they include Jews and Gentiles from across the globe. This is an extraordinary vision in the first century: the small scattered, harassed Christian groups emerging in the Roman Empire are imagined as a great multitude of global diversity with a single common cause – the unceasing worship of God. And yet, perhaps the writer of Revelation had glimpsed something of the reality of that unity (if not the scope) in his experience beyond his visions. The island of Patmos, the location of his visions, was close to the great port of Ephesus, the third largest city of the Empire. It had a church since the earliest days of Christianity, which, as the letter to the Ephesians suggests, drew people from many nations, tribes and languages.[30] Christian worship with people from many nations was not simply a future eschatological vision, it was a fragmentary reality. The imperial forces, critiqued so severely elsewhere in the book of Revelation, are responsible for drawing together those who wish to take advantage of what the Empire offered and those who suffered under the structure of Empire. The song sung by the multicultural crowd is a song that emerges from suffering: the suffering of Jesus and of Christians. The reference to

---

30 Andrew Walls, *The Cross-cultural Process in Church History*, Maryknoll, NY: Orbis, 2002, 79.

hunger, thirst, lack of shelter and sorrow suggests that some ordeals were difficulties felt by many in the world. In a book that has lent the name of its genre, 'apocalypse', to descriptions of catastrophe that often cause forced migration, this chapter sings of the hope that is the ultimate purpose of John's visions. This vision of adoration is an inspiration for mission. The purpose of God's sending forth and of humanity's participation in God's mission is that we are ultimately drawn into the worship of the Godhead. The vision is intercultural: it brings people together while acknowledging their differences and their sufferings. How may we shape ourselves as Church in order to live out such a vision? The first letter of Peter provides some suggestions.

In an age of large-scale migration the call of 1 Peter to community living and corporate witness may read differently from interpretations that encourage a quietist, otherworldly spirituality. The letter is addressed to 'the elect strangers (those passing through) of the Diaspora, scattered throughout Pontus, Galatia, Cappadocia, Asia and Bithynia'.[31] The identification of stranger is used positively, in a call to holiness, 'conduct yourselves with reverence through the time of your residence as aliens' (1.17) and exemplary behaviour to witness to the pagans 'as resident aliens and visiting strangers in the world' (2.11). The church in Asia Minor may have been composed of those whose legal identity was 'resident alien', they expected to pay taxes to the state but they could also anticipate harsh treatment from the state. The epistle draws upon social realities in order to form Christian identity and Christian responses to the situation in which households of Christians lived. The scattered, marginal nature of first-century Christian communities is considered a virtue, one which allows them to live as witnesses to Christ; their distinct modes of conduct should not only silence detractors but convert them. The epistle encourages the 'elect strangers' to consider the hostile treatment they receive not as shame but as partaking in Christ's suffering and glory. Through the experience of dislocation the resident alien Christians have a new place of belonging in the household of God. First Peter honours a historic form of migrant experience not as some accident of relocation but as an insight into the Christian life. The alienation of homelessness, or being far from home, may indicate the tenor of Christian communities. A settled state is not necessarily desirable. Because our citizenship is in heaven, we may inhabit the whole earth: 'every foreign land is their fatherland' says the *Epistle to Diognetus*. Taking a cue from 1 Peter, it can be said that the experience of displacement is itself a resource for constructing intercultural theology.

---

31 Translation and commentary from John H. Elliott, *1 Peter*, New Haven, CT: Yale University Press, 2000, esp. 90–107 and 115–18.

Steps towards an Intercultural Ecclesiology

Resident-Alien Spirituality

The term 'resident alien' in 1 Peter denoted a particular civic status in ancient Asia Minor, yet, as explored in the epistle, it reveals possibilities of corporate Christian identity in a time of mass migration. As translated into English, its binary construction is also resonant of the terms 'prophetic-dialogue' mission and practical-prophetic ecclesiology: the terms call for a spirituality that expects a way of being Christian that prayerfully weighs up the contemporary context with Scripture and tradition, discerning where and how God is at work and how we might participate. Being resident alien may demand a resident/dialogical approach in some circumstances and an alien/prophetic approach in others. Being resident aliens, as Church, unsettles the comfortable and makes welcome the stranger, it provides a community and assumes a journey.

A spirituality of displacement allows those of different cultures to listen and learn from one another and permit appreciation of diverse comprehensions of God's relations with humanity. Exploring the idea that we are strangers together in the world, however short or long we may have lived in a particular nation, may allow us to think beyond the categories of migrant, native, guest, host with which we often live. Similar culture congregations that have developed as a direct result of migration or migrants in mixed congregations may provide particular insights into being resident aliens from which those of the destination society, who often consider themselves to be hosts, at home, could learn. This may turn the tables on our dominant experiences. Reflection on what it is to be a stranger can best be done in the company of those who have experienced alienation and marginality. It opens us to finding God in marginal places, to learning from those that dominant society may overlook or disparage. A resident-alien spirituality expects change in ecclesial practice. Such a spirituality requires that migrant experiences are heard and appreciated, it permits migrants' popular practices of the Christian faith to find accommodation within the life of the Church in destination countries.

Resident-Alien Ecclesial Practice

Healey insists that the people of God, in seeking 'the truth revealed in the person and work of Jesus Christ', need to 'construct and reconstruct' ecclesial cultural identity 'by experimentation, by bricolage and by retrieval of earlier forms'.[32] He recognizes that such a process means different congregational configurations within common Christian practice. For a church

---

32 Healey, *Church, World*, 175.

responding to Christ in its particular migration situation those configurations may be many and varied.

Those congregations that, for the purposes of this chapter, we have described as migrant similar culture congregations offer insights into living as communities of resident aliens which they may offer to similar culture congregations of the destination society. Congregations of the destination society may also share what it is to be resident while learning how to be alien. Inviting others into our space, accepting the invitation to visit others in order to learn the charisms and commitments of the congregation, participating in the life and worship of each others' congregations can develop new forms of ecumenical relations which enrich the life of the Church while maintaining distinct cultural groups.

In mixed culture congregations resident-alien spirituality will encourage experiences of migration to redefine religious expressions and sites of worship. The language, music, liturgy and song of Christian worship will reflect a variety of cultures. Migrants will be visible in church leadership. The organization of social events will take into consideration different customs and a variety of food. There would be a careful and intentional working to hear all voices. In taking such an approach, the congregation would embody the global within the local and vice versa. This gives opportunity to celebrate a realized vision of Revelation 7, worshipping God together in our variety and difference.

Resident-alien spirituality and ecclesial practice also calls for developing relationships that allow for lament and the sharing pain as well as celebrating common life. As in Revelation 7, worship of God is born out of suffering, ushered in by the Lamb who was slain. It requires of all parties a gracious comprehension of different life-experiences which they may not immediately understand. It takes time to listen to the experiences of others and to pray together for God's healing and reconciliation of traumatic experiences.

One denomination has called for 'an intercultural habit' that 'is grounded on mutuality in giving and sharing: where we are all in need; where we all must be mutually inconvenienced for the sake of the other and the gospel'.[33] A practice of mutual inconvenience acknowledges that the development of intercultural theology can be slow and discomforting. Yet a worshipful community of Christians of different cultures living in dialogue is a prophetic witness to Christ in a world where social divisions often fall along ethnic lines.

---

33 Michael Jagessar, *URC Mission Council Report*, London: United Reformed Church, 2011, 5.

Resident-Alien Mission

First Peter expects the resident-alien behaviour of Christians to attract others to Christ. Developing a spirituality and ecclesial practice that offers sympathetic comprehensions of trajectories of migration and a place of reconciliation and celebration in Christ between peoples of different origins will permeate relations beyond our Christian community. Our witness to Christ may take place together; our compassion and solidarity with and empowerment of refugees and other marginalized people may take place together. Together we may tackle xenophobia. Together we may be open to other differences, of age, class and gender.

Furthermore, it has been suggested that the hybridity which develops through migration and continues into the second and third generations provides exactly the kind of insight that the Church needs as it renews itself in every generation.[34] Particularly in the Western world where many are disaffected by the traditional forms of Christian faith but have little understanding of its message the hybridization of faith, the crossing of boundaries, the double vision provided by migrants may help a new form of inculturation. The social realities of the migrant experience may provide missiological insight. The hybrid holding together of resident and alien provides a way of being always attentive to the context while measuring it by the values of God's reign.

Conclusion

Mass migration around the globe permits Christians to encounter one another as never before. Migration provides us with insights into who we are as the people of God borne out of engagement in the world. In a context of migration, rapid cultural change prevents the reification of any particular cultural form while allowing appreciation of the richness of the world we inhabit as resident aliens. It allows celebration of diversity within a search for common identity in Christ. An intercultural ecclesiology within and between congregations presents us with a new form of ecumenism, a recognition of difference and a sharing of life in common. It also presents a mission of migrants and non-migrants who together have a profound sense of the movement of God's people. It requires passing over into the experiences of others, to develop a spirituality that is in evidence beyond the Church. There is nothing romantic or easy about intercultural church. It requires constant negotiation and renegotiation. Yet it also brings great joy. We may rejoice in the opportunities to worship as many nations, peoples and languages, witnessing together to the Lamb who was slain. We may learn anew what it is to be resident aliens called to transform the communities around us.

---

34 Julius-Kei Kato, *How Immigrant Christians Living in Mixed Cultures Interpret their Religion*, New York: Lewiston, 2012, 298–319.

5

Hospitality:
The Church as 'A Mother
with an Open Heart'

CATHY ROSS

Introduction

What is the Church? How do we describe the Church, which is divinely instituted but humanly organized with all our frailties and failings? My favourite biblical metaphor is the Church as the household of God (Eph. 2.22) with Jesus as the cornerstone. This is a metaphor we can all relate to – we have all experienced a household, a dwelling place in some form or other. At its best, a household or dwelling place evokes stability, warmth, safety, relationships with people who care about us, home. The Church as the household of God is where God is, where we can find God, where we can live with God. Pope Francis speaks of the Church as 'a mother with an open heart ... whose doors are open'. He expands this picture by adding that 'The Church is called to be the house of the Father, with doors always wide open ... where there is a place for everyone, with all their problems.'[1] This is a powerful and beautiful picture of the Church as a place where our Mother/Father God is ready to welcome all. This metaphor resonates with the theme of hospitality for surely the Church, as the household of God and the body of Christ is the institution par excellence which exemplifies and lives out hospitality as its mission and its purpose.

Hospitality is a rich seam to mine when we consider the Church. It is a word redolent with meanings and ideas we would wish to associate with the Church. In this chapter we will consider some such as welcome of all especially the stranger, nourishment, seeing and listening, risk, marginality and spaciousness. Hospitality is also a theme that resonates and meshes with the concept of 'prophetic dialogue'. Hospitality is in itself a prophetic practice as it crosses boundaries, welcomes all and involves taking risks. It is

---

1 Apostolic Exhortation, *Evangelii Gaudium* of the Holy Father Francis to the Bishops, Clergy, Consecrated Persons and the Lay Faithful on the Proclamation of the Gospel in Today's World, 46, 47. www.vatican.va/holy_father/francesco/apost_exhortations/documents/papa-francesco_esortazione-ap_20131124_evangelii-gaudium_en.html.

also dialogical as it requires listening and learning. It practises attentiveness and encourages spaciousness. Hospitality cannot be practised as a monologue. It requires relationship, receiving, community and change. Our God embodies hospitality in the Trinity. Hospitality is at the heart of God's reign and is essential for the practice and meaning of the kerygma. Hospitality is an ongoing practice that will be modified and negotiated as we interact and engage with one another – all this is implied by the concept of 'prophetic dialogue'. Moreover, Bevans and Schroeder claim that the art of prophetic dialogue functions more as a spirituality rather than a strategy, a way of being that we inhabit rather than a schema. So 'prophetic dialogue' with its allusions to community and conversation is indeed an appropriate and helpful frame to guide our reflection on hospitality as the mission of the Church.

Hospitality as Welcome of the Stranger

Hospitality is a fertile concept, full of potential and part of a rich biblical tradition echoing through the ages. Most of the ancient world regarded hospitality as a fundamental virtue and practice, as do many cultures still in our world today. In the Ancient Near East there was a sacred bond between guest and host and when guest or host violated their responsibility to each other, the world was shaken. The offering and receiving of hospitality was holy ground.

Israel experienced God as a God of hospitality. Stories of hospitality are foundational to their very existence and identity. These stories of hospitality contain themes and tensions that resonate through the centuries – stories of hospitality received and hospitality abused. The well-known story of Abraham and Sarah welcoming three strangers brought them good news and bad in the context of their hospitality. The guests confirmed they would have a son in their old age, but they also warned Abraham of the impending destruction of Sodom and Gomorrah. Hospitality was considered an important duty and often we see the hosts becoming beneficiaries of their guests and strangers. So Abraham and Sarah entertained angels in Genesis 18, the widow of Zarephath benefited from Elijah's visit (1 Kings 17) and Rahab and her family were saved from death by welcoming Joshua's spies (Josh. 2). Pohl remarks in her superb book on hospitality, *Making Room: Recovering Hospitality as a Christian Tradition*, 'The first formative story of the biblical tradition on hospitality is unambiguously positive about welcoming strangers.'[2]

The very etymology of the word, hospitality, is illuminating. In Latin the word that signifies host is *hospes* and the word for enemy is *hostis*, from which we derive hostile. So this suggests ambiguity and tension around the

---

2 C. Pohl, *Making Room: Recovering Hospitality as a Christian Tradition*, Grand Rapids, MI: Eerdmans, 1999, 24.

concept of hospitality. However, the derivation from the Greek offers us something slightly different. There is an interesting and intriguing conundrum around the Greek word *xenos*, which denotes simultaneously guest, host or stranger. The Greek word for hospitality in the New Testament, *philoxenia,* refers not so much to love of strangers but to a delight in the whole guest–host relationship and in the surprises that may occur. Jesus is portrayed as a gracious host, welcoming children, tax collectors, prostitutes and sinners into his presence and therefore offending those who would prefer such guests not to be at his gatherings. But Jesus is also portrayed as vulnerable guest and needy stranger who came to his own but his own did not receive him (John 1.11). Pohl comments that this 'intermingling of guest and host roles in the person of Jesus is part of what makes the story of hospitality so compelling for Christians'.[3] Think of Jesus on the Emmaus Road as travelling pilgrim and stranger, recognized as host and who he was in the breaking of bread during a meal involving an act of hospitality. Or think of the Peter and Cornelius story (interestingly, another story involving varieties of food) – who is the host and who is the guest? Both offer and receive, both listen and learn, both are challenged and changed by the hospitality of the other. So we can see the importance of not only the ambiguity but also the fluidity of the host/guest conundrum. We offer and receive as both guest or stranger and host.

This intermingling and fluidity is vital for us to understand and appropriate. Jesus modelled powerlessness and vulnerability by being a guest in our world, by letting go and being among us in our place and space. This radically changes the power dynamics. So often in mission, the receiving person or culture is seen as needy, vulnerable, in need of help. We have to turn this on its head. We need to be in relationship with them and learn to see the resources and spirituality inherent in that community and context. Jean Vanier reminds us of this. He writes, 'it will take decades to see all the consequences of listening to the least powerful among us and allowing ourselves to be led by them'.[4] This also reminds us that the Church, as a household, may need to be part of someone else's household – that we too are needy ones who crave transformation and healing. Vanier again,

> Befriending a person with a disability or alcoholism isn't going to provide an instant solution to their difficulties. But this friendship can lead to a mutual transformation by touching the place where God lives in each one of us. We can then begin to work *with* people who are fragile instead of simply *for* them.[5]

---

3 Pohl, *Making Room*, 17.

4 J. Vanier, *Signs of the Times: Seven Paths of Hope for a Troubled World*, London: Darton, Longman & Todd, 2013, 10.

5 Vanier, *Signs of the Times*, 119.

Then there will be a mutually transformative encounter where hospitality is offered and received in a reciprocal manner. This may be challenging for the confident and self-assured, the strong and secure but in fact enables the strong and secure to discover their own vulnerability. This is indeed prophetic dialogue – an understanding and living out of hospitality that challenges our normal assumptions.

And so we need the stranger as strangers may actually enhance our well-being rather than diminish it. The three major festivals of the Church – Christmas, Easter and Pentecost – all have to do with the advent of a divine stranger. In each case this stranger – a baby, a resurrected Christ and the wind of the Holy Spirit – all meet us as mysterious or strange visitors, breaking into our world, challenging our worldviews and systems and welcoming us to new worlds.[6]

However, we do not just welcome the stranger because of the biblical examples of hospitality – important and vital though they are. We need the stranger. We need the stranger to challenge us, to help us see ourselves as others see us, to call us out of our complacencies and Christian ghettos, to offer us new worlds, to break us out of our cosy domesticities. By practising hospitality we may think we are engaging in 'prophetic dialogue' – in fact, the stranger can bring that gift to us. Newlands and Smith cite an example of a congregation that took the risk of practising intentional hospitality:

A vague notion that hospitality to strangers was a decent Christian virtue became something we began to see as one of the healthy marks of a congregation ... Hospitality involves taking the risk of sacrificing our own status and becoming genuinely humble and vulnerable ... That is the strange and difficult work of hospitality that Christ invites us to share in and that is freighted with promise and blessing.[7]

So the tables are turned as we experience the gift of reversal and the prophetic rebounds back on us as our egos are broken open and we come to know our weaknesses, vulnerabilities and gifts.

Quaker scholar and educationalist, Parker Palmer reminds us, in his intriguing book *The Company of Strangers: Christians and the Renewal of America's Public Life* of the importance of the stranger. Our spiritual pilgrimage is a quest, a venture into the unknown, away from safety and security into strange places for if we remain where we are, we have no need of faith. The visitors to Abraham and Sarah, the stranger on the Emmaus Road brought new truths to their lives. According to Palmer, we need the stranger. In his view, 'the stranger is not simply one who needs us. We need

6 See J. Koenig, *New Testament Hospitality: Partnership with Strangers as Promise of Mission*, Eugene, OR: Wipf and Stock, 2001, 5.

7 Quoted in G. Newlands and A. Smith, *Hospitable God: The Transformative Dream*, Farnham: Ashgate, 2010, 127.

the stranger. We need the stranger if we are to know Christ and serve God, in truth and in love.'[8] For him, 'hospitality to the stranger gives us a chance to see our own lives afresh, through different eyes'.[9] So the stranger, the other, becomes a person of promise. The stranger may be unsettling; the stranger may challenge or provoke us; the stranger may provide a wider perspective. Remember the injunction from the book of Hebrews, 'Let mutual love continue. Do not neglect to show hospitality to strangers, for by doing that some have entertained angels without knowing it' (Heb. 13.1–2). Strangers save us from cosy, domesticated hospitality and force us out of our comfort zones. Strangers may transform us and challenge us. Strangers may embody and offer the gift of prophetic dialogue.

Ultimately Israel's obligation to care for the stranger is because of her experience as a stranger and alien. God instructs them to care for the alien and stranger as they themselves were aliens in the land of Egypt. Just as God created them as a nation, delivered them from slavery in Egypt and fed them in the wilderness, so their hospitality in turn serves as a reminder of and witness to God's hospitality towards them. And always they have the stories in their tradition that guests and strangers might be angels, bringing divine promises and provision. In the early Church hospitality was an important discipline. Offering care to strangers was one of the distinctive features of being a Christian. Steve Summers in his book on friendship claims that 'hospitality to the stranger is what the Incarnation *exemplifies, offers and requests*'.[10]

To love our neighbour, to enter into the presence of another human being is to enter into the presence of God. In Genesis we are reminded that all human beings are created in the image and likeness of God (Gen. 1.26–27; 5.1–3; 9.6; 1 Cor. 11.7; James 3.9). This is a profound way of speaking about human nature. This provides our starting point for relating to the stranger. As John Taylor reminds us in his book *The Go-Between God: The Holy Spirit and the Christian Mission*, 'If one is closed up against being hurt, or blind towards one's fellow-men, [sic] one is inevitably shut off from God also. One cannot choose to be open in one direction and closed in another.'[11]

This understanding of the image of God is integrally related to the Trinity which means it is not primarily an individualistic understanding but a relational one. This can help us in our relating to the stranger. Paul Fiddes, in his book *Participating in God: A Pastoral Doctrine of the Trinity*, urges us

---

8 P. Palmer, *The Company of Strangers: Christians and the Renewal of America's Public Life*, New York: Crossroad, 1986, 131.

9 Palmer, *Company of Strangers*, 132.

10 S. Summers, *Friendship: Exploring its Implications for the Church in Postmodernity*, London: T&T Clark, 2009, 173. Italics in original.

11 J. V. Taylor, *The Go-Between God: The Holy Spirit and the Christian Mission*, London: SCM Press, 1972, 19.

to do more than just imitate the triune God by actually participating in the Trinity. He claims that this participation then enables us to truly appreciate the other because of our engagement with the other. Engagement in the life of God means an experience of otherness – the otherness of God from humanity, the otherness of the Creator from the created. He writes:

> Nothing in the world can prepare us for this gulf of otherness in a God who abides in the unity of love. ... Because it is an otherness which arises in participation within God, it can only be known *through* participation. To engage in the relationships in God means that we are brought up against the challenge of the alien, the radically different, the unlike; but at the same time we have the security of experiencing a fellowship more intimate than anything we can otherwise know.[12]

Our ego is broken open by encountering the Thou in the other, and through the Thou of other people we can meet the transcendent Thou, God. So again, we need the stranger to break us open, to enlarge our private (and inner) space and to meet God in a new way. Kosuke Koyama defines mission as 'extending hospitality to strangers'.[13]

Hospitality is subversive because it undermines and challenges existing power structures and restores human dignity and respect. Moreover, the practice of hospitality protects us from the danger of abusing ownership and possession. Hospitality to the stranger is, in fact, a statement about how we perceive ownership and possession. In God's new kingdom, we sit lightly to ownership and possessions because the call to follow Christ means that we are willing to give up everything to belong to his family. Jesus reinforces this in the two great texts of Luke 14 and Matthew 25 where he distinguishes between conventional and Christian hospitality. In Luke 14 Jesus says,

> 'When you give a luncheon or a dinner, do not invite your friends or your brothers or your relatives or rich neighbours, in case they may invite you in return, and you would be repaid. But when you give a banquet, invite the poor, the crippled, the lame, the blind. And you will be blessed, because they cannot repay you.' (Luke 14.12–14)

This is, of course, the prelude to the parable of the Great Banquet, a powerful metaphor for the kingdom of God, where all are universally welcomed. When the expected guests turn down the invitation to the banquet; the same four groups are to be invited, 'the poor, the maimed, the lame, the blind' and then everyone else from the highways and byways. And in Matthew

---

12 P. Fiddes, *Participating in God, A Pastoral Doctrine of the Trinity*, London: Darton, Longman & Todd, 2000, 5.

13 K. Koyama, '"Extend Hospitality to Strangers" – A Missiology of Theologia Crucis', *International Review of Mission* 83:327 (1993), 283–95 (285).

25 Jesus explicitly identifies himself with the stranger. Here, God's invitation into the kingdom of God is clearly linked to Christian hospitality in this life. This has been a key passage in the entire Christian tradition of hospitality. Dorothy Day, one of the founders of the Catholic Worker Movement explained the significance of this passage for her life of hospitality to destitute people:

> There He was, homeless. Would a church take Him in today – feed Him, clothe Him, offer Him a bed? I hope I ask myself that question on the last day of my life. I once prayed and prayed to God that He never, ever let me forget to ask that question.[14]

It is becoming clear that welcoming the stranger is a fundamental requirement of being a Christian and being a part of the Church. We can see here very clearly how hospitality as welcome of the stranger is not only an exercise in prophetic dialogue but also a gift to the Church to challenge and unsettle us.

The four classic marks of the Church are one, holy, catholic and apostolic. Drawing on work from *Mission-Shaped Church,* Mike Moynagh has reworked these classic marks into four sets of relationships described as:

> UP relationships through participating in the life of the Trinity;
> IN relationships through fellowship within the gathering;
> OUT relationships in love for, and service of the world;
> OF relationships, as part *of* the whole body, through connections with the wider church.[15]

The appeal of this approach is that it enables us to focus on the Church as relationships expressed through practices, of which hospitality is a key practice and virtue. Church or community is sustained by a way of life that acknowledges our lives and our ways of knowing are inherently relational, enhanced by our life together. Jean Vanier acknowledged this as a result of his experience of founding the l'Arche communities. He writes, 'In years to come we are going to need many small communities which will welcome lost and lonely people, offering them a new form of family and sense of belonging.'[16] Following the trajectory of the Old Testament to care for the stranger and the example of Jesus' openness and universal welcome, the Church is where we welcome the stranger with doors wide open where there is a place for everyone.

---

14 Quoted in C. Pohl, *Making Room*, 22. See also Sara Miles, *Take This Bread: A Radical Conversion*, New York: Ballantine, 2007.

15 M. Moynagh, *Church for Every Context: An Introduction to Theology and Practice*, London: SCM Press, 2012, 107.

16 J. Vanier, *Community and Growth*, New York: Paulist Press, 1989, 283.

Hospitality as Seeing the Other

Pope Francis, in his apostolic exhortation, *Evangelii Gaudium,* claims that a Church that goes forth

> does not mean rushing out aimlessly into the world. Often it is better simply to slow down, to put aside our eagerness in order to see and listen to others, to stop rushing from one thing to another and to remain with someone who has faltered along the way. At times we have to be like the father of the prodigal son, who always keeps his door open so that when the son returns, he can readily pass through it.[17]

We are to be like this father – watching, waiting, looking out for our son. So we need the gift of sight, which is a gift of the Holy Spirit as John Taylor reminds us. The Holy Spirit is the Go-Between who opens our inward eyes and makes us aware of the other. 'The Holy Spirit is that power which opens eyes that are closed, hearts that are unaware and minds that shrink from too much reality.'[18]

The concept of sight and recognition of the other are clear in the parable in Matthew 25 when the righteous say to Jesus, 'Lord when was it that we *saw* you hungry and gave you food, or thirsty and gave you something to drink? And when was it that we *saw* you a stranger and welcomed you, or naked and gave you clothing? And when was it that we *saw* you sick or in prison and visited you?' (Matt. 25.37–39, italics mine) And we all know Jesus' answer. Here again we experience the subversive dimension of hospitality. When we do what Jesus commended in Matthew 25 – visit those in prison, feed the hungry, clothe the naked, entertain the stranger – we are living out a very different set of values and relationships. We are according dignity to others, we are breaking social boundaries, we are including those who are so often excluded; we are engaged in transformation. It begins with seeing the other person; the act of recognition – a powerful act indeed. Looking the other in the eye – the establishment of the 'I–Thou' relationship is a fundamental act of hospitality because it acknowledges people's humanity, accords them dignity and denies their invisibility. As Pohl says, 'Hospitality resists boundaries that endanger persons by denying their humanness. It saves others from the invisibility that comes from social abandonment. Sometimes, by the very act of welcome, a vision for a whole society is offered, a small evidence that transformed relations are possible.'[19] This is indeed a prophetic act. Think of the Good Samaritan who refused to pass by or pretend that he had not *seen* the wounded man. His act of hospitality crossed ethnic boundaries, caused him personal cost and inconvenience and

---

17 *Evangelii Gaudium,* 46.
18 Taylor, *The Go-Between God,* 19.
19 Pohl, *Making Room,* 64.

saved a life. When we see the other person, we see the image of God, as well as our common humanity, which establishes a fundamental dignity, respect and common bond. The parable in Matthew 25 reminds us that we can *see* Christ in every guest and stranger.

Hospitality means a new way of seeing – seeing with expectancy, seeing with love, seeing prophetically, seeing the other as a human being. Failure to do this can eventuate in the most terrible atrocities, and I think here of one of Fergal Keane's moving reflections on the genocide in Rwanda – 'A Letter from Africa'. On seeing a macheted baby trapped between rocks in a river, he asks himself the question: 'What kind of man would kill a baby? What kind of man?' He concluded after having experienced the hatred, the evil and the lack of recognition of the other's right to exist, 'What kind of man can kill a child? A man not born to hate but who has learned hatred. A man like you or me.'[20]

Seeing otherwise goes against the grain. But this is what Jesus offers us: an alternative reality, a remedial perspective, the gift of reversal, as we live out this spirituality of 'prophetic dialogue' in the Church, the household of God. The parables of the Prodigal Son, the Great Banquet and the Sheep and the Goats do indeed mean a reconstruction of reality. God's universal welcome is displayed and as we see the other, we are welcoming Jesus. This is indeed a new way of seeing and reminds me of one of the Occupy slogans: 'Another world is possible'.[21]

Hospitality as Nourishing the Other

Pohl reminds us that we need to eat together to sustain our identity. Think how important it is to eat together as a family and the same applies to the household of the Church. She writes, 'the table is central to the practice of hospitality in home and church – the nourishment we gain there is physical, spiritual and social'.[22] Offering food and drink to guests is central to almost every act of hospitality. This takes time. It requires attention to the other, it requires an effort. It requires us to stop and focus. As a Benedictine monk once observed, 'In a fast food culture, you have to remind yourself that some things cannot be done quickly. Hospitality takes time.'[23] This is a challenge in our time-starved culture. Hospitality emerges from a willingness to create time and space.

The theme of banqueting, of food and drink is central in the ministry of Jesus. Was he not accused of being a glutton and a drunkard and of eating with sinners? Jesus was celebrating the messianic banquet but with all the

---

20 F. Keane, 'A Letter from Africa', *Letter to Daniel*, London: Penguin, 1996, 232.

21 Occupy London was part of a worldwide protest movement against corporate greed. It set up camp outside St Paul's Cathedral in October 2011.

22 Pohl, *Making Room*, 158.

23 Pohl, *Making Room*, 178.

wrong people! Bretherton even goes so far as to state that 'This table fellow-ship with sinners, and the reconfiguring of Israel's purity boundaries which this hospitality represents signifies the heart of Jesus' mission.'[24] Jesus and his followers here are also celebrating the abundance of God – think of all the stories of food and drink overflowing, of parties enjoyed, of the feeding of the five thousand. God's household is a household of superabundance, of extravagant hospitality, where food and wine is generously shared and the divine welcome universally offered. Jesus' rejection of social and religious categories of inclusion and exclusion was offensive to the authorities. As one theologian expressed it, 'Jesus got himself crucified by the way he ate.'[25]

Shared meals are therefore central to hospitality and to mission. Michele Hershberger claims that when we eat together we are 'playing out the drama of life'[26] as we begin to share stories, let down our guard and wel-come strangers. Alongside the sharing of food is the sharing of stories. Revd Rebecca Nyegenye, chaplain at Uganda Christian University, told me that in Uganda hospitality goes with both elaborate meals and listening to the visitor. Ugandans believe that for any relationship to be strong, food and intentional listening must be shared. Listening is an important part of honouring the guest – in both hospitality and mission, listening to the other is the beginning of understanding and of entering the other's world.

Eating together is a great leveller. It is something that we all must do so it has a profoundly egalitarian dimension. Jean Vanier, of l'Arche commu-nity, confessed that when he started to share meals with men of serious mental disabilities, 'Sitting down at the same table meant becoming friends with them, creating a family. It was a way of life absolutely opposed to the values of a competitive, hierarchical society in which the weak are pushed aside.'[27] When we eat together, as we let down our guard and share stories, we begin to create relationship and this is at the heart of mission – our relationship with God and neighbour. In a unique moment in the book of Ephesians, we see Jews and Gentiles coming together. The test of their com-ing together in the Church, the household of God was the meal table – the institution that once symbolized ethnic and cultural division now became a symbol of Christian living. It is this experience that was reproduced at Antioch, Jerusalem and other places as 'one of the most noticeable features of life in the Jesus community', for 'the followers of Jesus took every oppor-tunity to eat together'.[28] Eating together locates us in the *missio Dei*. So

24 L. Bretherton, *Hospitality as Holiness: Christian Witness amid Moral Diversity*, Farnham: Ashgate, 2006, 128.

25 Robert J. Karris, *Luke: Artist and Theologian*, New York: Paulist Press, 1985, 47.

26 M. Hershberger, *A Christian View of Hospitality: Expecting Surprises*, Scottdale, PA: Herald Press, 1999, 104.

27 Pohl, *Making Room*, 74.

28 E. Katangole, 'Mission and the Ephesian Moment of World Christianity: Pilgrimages of Pain and Hope and the Economics of Eating Together', *Mission Studies* 29:2 (2012), 183–200 (189).

not only eating together but also with whom we eat is an expression of 'prophetic dialogue'. This brings together the prophetic as we learn and converse together, the dialogical as we listen, and breaking boundaries by eating together.

This is perhaps most powerfully expressed in the Eucharist, where this ritualized eating and drinking together re-enacts the crux of the gospel. As we remember what it cost Jesus to welcome us into relationship with God, we remember with sorrow the agony and the pain but at the same time we rejoice and celebrate our reconciliation and this new relationship made possible because of Christ's sacrifice and supreme act of hospitality. We rejoice in our new relationship with God, made possible through the cross and we rejoice as we partake of this meal together in community. When we share in the Eucharist, we are not only foreshadowing the great heavenly banquet to come but we are also nourished on our journey towards God's banquet table. Jesus is, quite literally, the host as we partake of his body and blood and we are the guests as we feed on him by faith with thanksgiving. In this way, the Eucharist connects hospitality at a very basic level with God and with the *missio Dei* as it anticipates and reveals God's heavenly table and the coming kingdom.[29] This is beautifully expressed in one of the Eucharistic Prayers from the *New Zealand Prayerbook*:

Most merciful Lord,
Your love compels us to come in.
Our hands were unclean
Our hearts were unprepared; we were not fit
Even to eat the crumbs from under your table.
But you, Lord, are the God of our salvation,
and share your bread with sinners.
So cleanse and feed us
With the precious body and blood of your Son,
That He may live in us and we in Him;
And that we, with the whole company of Christ,
May sit and eat in your kingdom.[30]

Vanier claims that as we eat together we become friends – no longer guest nor stranger. Indeed, we were all strangers until God welcomed us into his household by grace to be his friends – the supreme act of God's hospitality. Timothy Gorringe makes the point that there is a continuation of shared table fellowship after Jesus' resurrection, particularly in the Emmaus Road encounter. He suggests that Emmaus is as much a forerunner to the Eucharist as the meal in the Upper Room with its celebratory dimension linking

29 See Hershberger, *A Christian View*, 228–9 for further discussion on this.

30 *A New Zealand Prayer Book, He Karakia Mihinare o Aotearoa*, Auckland: William Collins, 1989, 425.

this to Jesus' open table fellowship with friends prior to his arrest and crucifixion where these meals were open to all. As already suggested, this radical
inclusiveness may have led to his crucifixion.[31] Friendship is a powerful
force for good; friendship moves us towards wholeness. Jesus offered his
disciples friendship rather than servanthood (John 15.15) and this is what
the Eucharist offers us – an invitation to friendship, community and family.
As Summers writes, 'To be friends in this context means to be friends of
God, friends of Christ, and friends with each other.'[32] In the Western context where family breakdown and loneliness are on the increase and where
'ready meals for one' fill the supermarket shelves, the simple act of eating
together and thereby signalling friendship and community is indeed an act
of prophetic dialogue foreshadowed in both the Last Supper and Emmaus
Road encounters.

Hospitality from the Margins

Pohl contends that the 'periods in church history when hospitality has been
most vibrantly practised have been times when the hosts were themselves
marginal to their larger society'.[33] This may be because they were a persecuted minority, hidden away in convents, or poorer sectors of society such
as the early Methodists.[34] So it is important to note that hospitality does not
need lavish or elaborate resources to flourish.

Poverty may be a good place to start with hospitality. Poverty of heart
and mind creates space for the other. Poverty makes a good host – poverty
of mind, heart and even resources where one is not constrained by one's
possessions but is able to give freely. Hospitality from the margins reminds
us of the paradoxical power of vulnerability and the importance of compassion. Pohl cites the example of a friend of hers who directs a home for
homeless people and who, every year takes a few days to live on the streets.
By doing this, he experiences in a small way what it means to be marginal
and invisible. He describes the impact of this: 'What I experience in these
journeys is replenishing the reservoir of compassion. I tend not to realize
how hardened I've become until I get out there. And when I see someone
mistreating the homeless – a professional – it's a prophetic voice. It's the
most effective teaching method for me.'[35]

Pope Francis reminds us of the responsibility of the missionary impulse of
the whole Church. He also reminds us of the indissoluble link between the
good news and the poor:

---

31 See Summers, *Friendship*, 166–72.

32 Summers, *Friendship*, 171.

33 Pohl, *Making Room*, 106.

34 The persecuted recipients of the book of Hebrews were reminded to keep on practising
hospitality (Heb. 13.2).

35 Pohl, *Making Room*, 123.

If the whole Church takes up this missionary impulse, she has to go forth to everyone without exception. But to whom should she go first? When we read the Gospel we find a clear indication: not so much our friends and wealthy neighbours, but above all the poor and the sick, those who are usually despised and overlooked, 'those who cannot repay you' (Luke 14.14). There can be no room for doubt or for explanations which weaken so clear a message. Today and always, 'the poor are the privileged recipients of the Gospel', and the fact that it is freely preached to them is a sign of the kingdom that Jesus came to establish. We have to state, without mincing words, that there is an inseparable bond between our faith and the poor. May we never abandon them.[36]

To make oneself vulnerable reminds us that both hospitality and engagement in mission require authentic compassion and genuine love. Somehow these are more freely expressed and experienced from a context of poverty – poverty both within and without. Poverty of heart and mind reminds us that we are the needy ones, that our hands were empty before God filled them, that we are in need of grace, forgiveness, healing and newness of life. Then genuine hospitality as well as genuine engagement in mission can begin as we realize our own emptiness and our own need for God. As we experience the divine welcome born out of divine compassion, so then we can share this grace and hospitality with others.

Hospitality and Migration

We are undeniably living in an age of migration. The International Organization for Migration estimates the global migrant population to be 214 million and that one out of every 33 persons is a migrant.[37] Groody and others[38] claim that we need a theology of migration as we reflect on migration today. He reminds us that migration shaped Jesus' own self-understanding as God crossed boundaries to enter the human race, 'a place of "otherness"'[39] expressed in the incarnation. Groody explains that many migrants and refugees make sense of their journey in light of Jesus' journey – leaving their home, sometimes undertaking dangerous journeys and possibly leaving everything behind without any assurance of a stable future. By reminding us that the incarnation is a border-crossing event of self-giving

---

36 *Evangelii Gaudium*, 48.

37 www.iom.int/cms/en/sites/iom/home/about-migration/facts-figures1-.html.

38 See J. Hanciles, *Beyond Christendom: Globalisation, African Migration and the Transformation of the West*, Maryknoll, NY: Orbis, 2008; D. Groody and G. Campese (eds), *A Promised Land, A Perilous Journey: Theological Perspectives on Migration*, Notre Dame, IN: University of Notre Dame, 2008; S. Snyder, *Asylum-Seeking, Migration and Church*, Farnham: Ashgate, 2012.

39 Daniel Groody, *Crossing the Divide: Foundations of a Theology of Migration and Refugees*, Oxford: Crowther Centre Monographs, 2010, 16.

love, Groody claims that this gives us a different framework by which to evaluate migration and to engage with migrants. This takes us beyond the rhetoric that fuels fear about migrants coming to take jobs from locals, abuse benefit systems and compete for scarce resources. Migrants are seen as other, the stranger and a threat. In a recent book on migration, Snyder writes, 'Whatever the reality, and although people may not articulate the sense of threat as a challenge to citizenship and sovereignty, there is a widespread feeling that national identity and British culture are under threat.'[40] Sadly British Christians, according to Snyder, were more likely to think that immigration should be reduced than other religious groups or groups with no religious affiliation. This is exactly why we need a theology of migration to remind us of the importance of hospitality towards the stranger.

Themes of exodus, exile, diaspora are biblical themes. Care for the alien and stranger, widow and orphan are ancient Christian virtues. The recognition that the alien and stranger, the migrant as not just a recipient but also a gospel-bearer is embedded in our scriptural tradition – think of Ruth, the Syro-Phoenician woman and the injunction in Hebrews 13.2. Hospitality towards the migrant is a fundamental part of the mission of the Church in her attempts to welcome the stranger and promote human dignity and flourishing. Groody writes movingly that if we limit compassion (we could say hospitality) to the borders of our own nation or family, then this is 'a migration toward disintegration'.[41] The gospel is an invitation towards wholeness and integration and this is what the practice of hospitality embodies.

Hospitality and Risk

If hospitality is to be genuinely open and free, then there is certainly an element of risk. As Derrida asks bluntly, 'How do we distinguish between a guest and a parasite?'[42] And there is also a tension as the host may be in a position of power over the guest so hospitality offered may imply a sense of ownership and control on the part of the host. Derrida maintains that this therefore requires moment by moment negotiation.

> That's why it has to be negotiated at every instant, and the decision for hospitality, the best rule for this negotiation, has to be invented at every second with all the risks involved, and it is very risky. Hospitality, and hospitality is a very general name for all our relations to the Other, has to be re-invented at every second, it is something without a pre-given rule.[43]

40 Snyder, *Asylum-Seeking*, 92.

41 Groody, *Crossing*, 34.

42 J. Derrida, *Of Hospitality: Anne Dufourmantelle invites Jacques Derrida to respond*, Stanford, CA: Stanford University Press, 2000, 59.

43 G. Bennington and J. Derrida, 'Politics and Friendship, A Discussion with Jacques

There will always be an element of risk in the practice of hospitality. A theology of hospitality is a theology of risk but this should not surprise us as God is a God who delights in taking risks. The Bible narrates a long lineage of risk takers such as Abraham, Joshua, Deborah, Ruth, Esther, Daniel, Nehemiah, Mary, Elizabeth, Paul, Peter, Jairus, the unnamed bleeding woman to name but a few.

I am involved in pioneer mission leadership training at the Church Mission Society in Oxford. One of its aims is:

> to equip and train pioneer ministers, lay and ordained in prophetic mission to initiate and grow sustainable mission projects and Christian communities that have a transforming impact on church and society in contexts that are currently challenging to our faith and to existing patterns of Christian community.[44]

I have learned much from the students on this programme especially around risk, ways of seeing (the gift of sight), marginality and imagination – all constituent parts of prophetic dialogue. Jonny Baker, director of the programme writes:

> I didn't expect that we would talk so much about seeing and about imagination. This seeing involves grief over the way things are and where we have got stuck, and dreaming of new worlds and communities that are possible. It says 'why not?' and 'what if?' rather than 'why?' and 'what for?'[45]

Dreaming, risk-taking, seeing and imagining, marginality and liminality are all vital components of hospitality and of a church whose doors are to be always open. Again these seem to be further components of a prophetic dialogue spirituality that is able to take risks, sit lightly, breathe freely and imagine other worlds.

Hospitality as Creating Space

Finally let us consider hospitality as creating space. The very act of creation is an act of creating space. Originally 'the earth was a formless void and darkness covered the face of the deep' (Gen. 1.2) and gradually God created until 'the heavens and the earth', as well as humanity, 'were finished, and all their multitude' (Gen. 2.1). God is the Creator God, the Creator of space – both literally and metaphorically. And furthermore, in the divine act of the

---

Derrida', Centre for Modern French Thought, University of Sussex, 1 December 1997, http://hydra.humanities.uci.edu/derrida/pol+fr.html.

44 http://pioneer.cms-uk.org/about-2/aim/.

45 J. Baker, 'Five Things I've Learned', www.freshexpressions.org.uk/views/five-things.

creation of humanity, this marvellous act of generosity, we have the privilege of participating in this divine nature – this nature that created space and allows for spaciousness. And of course, the divine nature is Trinitarian. God is not a monad – God is a community of three divine persons. God is also one God. These realities allow not only for relationship but also for unity and diversity. This Trinitarian understanding of God, expressed so beautifully in Rublev's famous icon, means that we experience God in relationship with the other within community. The concept of the Trinity allows space for the created individual, but only in relationship to the other. So each person of the Trinity has their own divine nature, expressed in relation to the other persons of the Trinity. There is the space to be each divine person, as each person relates to the other. They cannot each exist without this relationship. This icon picks up many themes of hospitality here – of welcome, of the home or the Church as the household of God as the place for hospitality, of relationship, of nourishment, of seeing the other. Catherine LaCugna, comments on this icon:

> How fitting indeed that hospitality, and the quite ordinary setting of a household, should have emerged as the inspiration for this icon and so many other artistic interpretations of the Trinity. In Rublev's icon, the temple in the background is the transformation of Abraham's and Sarah's house. The oak tree stands for the Tree of Life. And the position of the three figures is suggestive. Although they are arranged in a circle, the circle is not closed. One has the distinct sensation when meditating on the icon that one is not only invited into this communion but, indeed, one already is part of it. A self-contained God, a closed divine society, would hardly be a fitting archetype for hospitality. We should not miss the significance of the Eucharistic cup in the centre, which is, of course, the sacramental sign of our communion with God and one another.[46]

This is not a closed society but rather an open circle, an open community where there is always space. There is space for each divine person; there is space for the other and so there is space for us, created in the divine image to be who we were created to be.

Henri Nouwen's definition of hospitality picks up this idea of spaciousness. 'Hospitality ... means primarily the creation of a free space where the stranger can enter and become a friend instead of an enemy. Hospitality is not to change people, but to offer them space where change can take place.'[47] Creating space does not mean that there is no room for dialogue, nor for disagreement. Rather creating space means allowing for a spaciousness in

---

46 C. LaCugna, *Freeing Theology: The Essentials of Theology in Feminist Perspective*, San Francisco: Harper Collins, 1993, 84.

47 H. Nouwen, *Reaching Out: The Three Movements of the Spiritual Life*, Glasgow: William Collins, 1976, 68–9.

all our encounters. Ultimately mission really is about creating space – after all, there is a wideness in God's mercy. There is space for all to come in, the divine invitation is that whoever believes may have eternal life. This reminds us of the theme of the Great Banquet where all are invited, all may come in and where, ultimately, we may be surprised at who is feasting at God's table and who is part of God's household. God is indeed a God of spaciousness. We see this as we marvel at the wonderful diversity and beauty of God's creation – there is space and room for all in God's family; there is space and room for all in the heart and mind of God; there is space and room for all in the home and hearth of God. There is space to be free to be who we are created to be – and to welcome others into that spaciousness also.

Conclusion

The Church, the household of God, is where we can live with God. God is a God of hospitality who welcomes all and invites everyone in. The Church, the household of God, where the stranger (and migrant) is graciously welcomed, where we are lovingly seen and recognized, where we are generously nourished, where marginality and risk-taking are regular postures and space abounds. This is indeed a picture of a mother with an open heart – welcoming, nourishing, noticing those on the margins, taking risks to defend and bring in her own. A church that warms hearts, take risks and brings people home to Jesus lives out an ecclesiology of hospitality and a spirituality of prophetic dialogue. This is beautifully expressed in this ancient Celtic prayer:

> I saw a stranger last night. I put food in the eating place, drink in the drinking place, music in the listening place, and in the sacred name of the Triune, he blessed myself and my house and my cattle and my dear ones. And the lark said in her song, 'Often, often, often goes the Christ in the stranger's guise.'[48]

---

48 www.bbc.co.uk/programmes/b01ph59z.

PART 3

Eschatology: Our Future in the Light of the Planet

6

The Church's Mission of Ecojustice: A Prophetic Dialogue Approach

DAWN NOTHWEHR

Introduction

Herman Daly's Story[1]

World renowned environmental economist, Herman Daly was hired by the World Bank (1988–94) for the purpose of bringing greater environmental sophistication to that institution's economic analysis. Daly's contribution to one issue of that agency's *World Development Report* included a graphic depicting the world's economy. He purposefully placed the graphic within a rectangle labelled 'biosphere', indicating that every economic action takes place within the limits of the natural world. Prior to publication, Daly's boss edited out his rectangle and label, arguing that the 'biosphere' was about conservation – not economics! After much thought and discussion, Daly returned his final draft with only the rectangle and not the 'biosphere' label. Sadly – the published report featured the graphic – but no rectangle and no label! Like gods, humans have presumed we are all-powerful, and increasingly we have edited considerations of the natural world off the pages of our consciousness. Even more deplorable is the reality that Christians and Christian missionaries have frequently been complicit in such idolatry.

God and Anthropocentrism

Today, environmentally literate and well-intentioned theologians sometimes come dangerously close to continuing the complicity. For example: one US theologian states, 'What Jesus reveals "is a God who is *anthropocentric*. God's cause is the cause of human existence. God is a God for humanity, as creator and thus one who is intrinsically interested in what God creates."'[2]

---

1 Daniel K. Finn, 'Theology and Sustainable Economics', in Richard W. Miller (ed.), *God, Creation, and Climate Change: A Catholic Response to the Environmental Crisis*, Maryknoll, NY: Orbis, 2010, 95–111 (95–6).

2 Stephen B. Bevans and Roger P. Schroeder, *Prophetic Dialogue: Reflections on Christian Mission Today*, Maryknoll, NY: Orbis, 2011, 45 cite Roger Haight, *Jesus, Symbol of God*, Maryknoll, NY: Orbis, 1999, 16. Emphasis added.

Though the intent of that statement certainly is to stress the intimate God–human relationship, the use of the term *anthropocentric*, is unfortunate. It begs the question: Is God interested *only* in humankind, or in *all* of 'what God creates?'[3] Not infrequently, theologians and church leaders fail to place humans in their actual interdependent relationship with the cosmos or neglect the topic completely.[4] Such silence effectively blesses the presumption that humans always trump other creatures and can thrive *independent* of other earth creatures, elements or ecosystems. Thus many Christians never learn or understand the ecological and ontological reality that everything is connected and *interdependent* nor – more urgently – that the irreparable harm, resulting from living in such a false reality, is *morally* significant! The Church's ecojustice mission urgently requires a renewed understanding of the relationship between the doctrines of creation, redemption and incarnation.[5] Fortunately, new attention to the complementary covenantal and sacramental traditions of Christianity has again sparked interest in the Church's ecojustice mission.

Foundations for Ecojustice: Covenantal and Sacramental Traditions

The Covenantal Tradition

The covenant (*berit*, Gen. 6.18) relationship of God with the universe as the divine intent, actually begins with the moment of creation as God's self-expression.[6] The Hebrew Testament overflows with accounts of God's delightful and animated relationship with *all* creation.[7] Animals share in the Noahic covenant (Gen. 8.20—9.17). Nature's *mitzvah* (commandment) is to praise God (Ps. 148.3–4, 7–10).

---

3 Bevans and Schroeder make clear God's care for all creation (Gen. 8.20—9.17).

4 Seán McDonagh, 'Trees and "God Talks"', *SEDOS Bulletin* 43:7–8 (2011), 208–21.

5 I use 'ecojustice' because today's ecological crisis and the ongoing human devastation of the planet colours any discussion of the doctrine of creation and the environment. It would be inadequate to treat those topics without giving priority to their ethical and moral dimensions. Darren Stanley and Kelly Young, 'Conceptualizing Complexities of Curriculum Developing a Lexicon for Ecojustice and the Transdisciplinarity of Bodies', *Journal of Curriculum Theorizing* 27:1 (2011), 35–47, journal.jctonline.org/index.php/jct/article/view/306. See *World Council of Churches, Ecumenical Dictionary*, D. Preman Nile SV, 'Justice, Peace and the Integrity of Creation', November 2003, www.wcc-coe.org/wcc/who/dictionary-article11.html. Ours is the Anthropocene era – 'the age of humans' – because we are actually rearranging the major systems of the planet causing unprecedented and irreversible harm. See Branden Allenby, 'The Industrial Ecology of Emerging Technologies: Complexity and Reconstruction of the World', *Journal of Industrial Ecology* 13:2 (2009), 168–83.

6 Walbert Bühlmann, *The Chosen People*, Slough: St. Paul Publications, 1982. See Pss. 33.1–7; 104.1–5.

7 Pss. 104.10–18, 24–8; 148.3–4, 7–10; 19.1–6.

God, humans and otherkind also have a moral relationship.[8] Creatures are *nefesh chayah* (living souls, Gen. 1.20; Ps. 42.2–3) and all life is animated by God's *ruach* (breath – Gen. 1.24–26; Eccl. 3.19, 21). All creation participates in the Mosaic covenant as witnesses to Israel's fulfilment of *mitzvoth* (Deut. 30.10). For example, when floods or other natural forces destroy the fruits of human labour, God is judging human infidelity. God *likewise* responds to human repentance and fidelity, restoring justice, and bringing harmony between humans and animals, the heavens and the earth (Isa. 35.1–2). Animals will participate in the new covenant, no longer fearing destruction (Isa. 11.6–9; 65.25; Hos. 2.20).

The tenets of right relation between and among God, humans and otherkind were formalized in the 'Holiness Code' (Lev. 17—27).[9] God works *and* rests, setting a wholesome pattern for human relations with each other, the land and animals as the creation covenant (Gen. 1.1–31; 2.1–3). That pattern is mandated as the Sabbath day, Sabbath year and Jubilee year (Ex. 23.10–11; Deut. 15.1–2). On the seventh day of each week, the farmer and the workforce – including animals – must rest (Ex. 23.12). In the seventh year, rights are restored to the poor, wild animals; the land renewed; slaves set free and labourers rest (Ex. 23.10–11; Lev. 27.1–7; Ex. 21.2). In the Jubilee year, the fiftieth year, there must be a great restoration of all relationships (Lev. 25.8–17). The theocentric focus (Lev. 25.23) shows that ecological well-being of the land is intimately tied to the spiritual and material well-being of the people of Israel. God who owns the land requires restoration for the poor and rest for the land. When heeded, the laws of holiness bring wholeness to people and all of creation.[10]

In Luke 4.18–19, Jesus linked the Jubilee year with his mission to bring about the reign of God. In the synagogue in Nazareth, he read Isaiah 61.1–2 (Isa. 58) and subsequently linked his ministry and teaching about the reign of God with the ideals of holiness. His teaching reckons back to the great prophetic promises and talk of the new covenant (Jer. 31.31–34), the resurrection (Ezek. 37.1–4) and the new creation (Isa. 65.17–25).

---

8 Jeanne Kay, 'Concepts of Nature in the Hebrew Bible', in Dawn M. Nothwehr (ed.), *Franciscan Theology of the Environment: An Introductory Reader*, Quincy, IL: Franciscan Press, 2002, 23–45.

9 Dianne Bergant and Dawn M. Nothwehr, 'The Earth Is the Lord's and All It Holds (Psalm 24:1)', *The Bible Today* 47:1 (2009), 185–91. See Dawn M. Nothwehr, *Ecological Footprints: An Essential Franciscan Guide for Sustainable Living*, Collegeville, MN: Liturgical Press, 2012, 244–8.

10 Covenantal values undergird subsequent developments: natural rights arguments for constitutional governance, abolition of slavery, extension of the franchise, protection of endangered species and ecosystems, e.g. 1982 UN World Charter for Nature, 1989 Montreal Protocol on Restoration of the Ozone Layer, and international climate change agreements.

The Sacramental Tradition

The sacramental approach to Christian ecological theology is rooted in the Wisdom literature of Hellenistic Judaism.[11] Lady Wisdom (Heb. *Hôkmah*; Gk *Sophia*) is the secondary manifestation of God and as God's mediator, creates, sustains and brings *all things* into a harmonious unity in God. Biblical wisdom literature ties the themes of creation and redemption together. Today Scripture scholars understand that wisdom theology is creation theology. Wisdom represents the human effort to relate to creation as God has intended. The theme of redemption is closely intertwined with creation because people always struggle with the forces of chaos in their lives.

In the New Testament Christians identify this cosmogonic Wisdom of God with Christ. Jesus as the Christ incarnates the cosmogonic principle through which the cosmos is created, sustained, redeemed and reconciled with God. The cosmic Christ is the beginning and end of all things (John 1.1–14; Heb. 1; Col 1.5–20; Eph. 1.2–10).

Irenaeus of Lyons' (AD 175–85) Christology links Christ to the origins of creation and how that plays out in the redemption of the world (*Against Heresies*, V:18.1–3).[12] The Word and Spirit are God's 'two hands' used to create the world and the ground and principle of being of the cosmos.[13] Irenaeus influenced Bonaventure of Bagnoregio (1217–74), who in his *Intinerarium Mentis in Deum* shows how the cosmic presence of God lovingly transforms people, drawing them into union with God.[14] In their teaching, the Victorine theologians correlated the sacraments of the Church with the sacramentality of creation; the entire cosmos is in a sense sacramental.[15] Over the centuries, various forms of dualism and materialism displaced the integrated notions of the sacramental universe, but yet this tradition has survived in various forms of European philosophy, theology, poetry and art; especially in the Franciscan theological and ethical traditions.[16]

In the end, for Christians, the God of the covenant is the God of Jesus Christ. And Jesus Christ is the eternal Word, Holy Wisdom, the cosmic Christ. The covenantal and the sacramental traditions taken together reveal a radically relational triune God – creator and redeemer – who has come to us as the Incarnate One and who draws us into discipleship and mission

---

11 See Wisdom 7.24—8.1. Also Nothwehr, *Ecological Footprints*, 16–30.

12 Irenaeus of Lyons, *Against Heresies*, Book V, www.earlychristianwritings.com/text/irenaeus-book5.html.

13 Irenaeus, *Against Heresies*, V.2.2 and 36.3.

14 Nothwehr, *Ecological Footprints*, esp. chapter 2.

15 Nothwehr, *Ecological Footprints*, 38–9, 108–9. Also Kenan B. Osborne, *Christian Sacraments in a Postmodern World: A Theology for the Third Millennium*, New York: Paulist Press, 1999.

16 Nothwehr, *Ecological Footprints*, 64–5, 11–112. Also David Toolan, *At Home in the Cosmos*, Maryknoll, NY: Orbis, 2001, 64–7. Toolan discusses 'imperial ecology' and 'Arcadian ecology'.

for the sake of the entire cosmos. Together these traditions serve up ample material in support of the ecojustice mission of the Church. It is to that mission we now turn.

The Ecojustice Mission of the Church as Prophetic Dialogue

Bevans and Schroeder proffer a concept of mission that engages both *dialogue* – openness to a context, learning from the context, bonding with the context – and *prophecy* – witnessing to the vitality of the gospel as well as to its countercultural nature, commitment to 'speaking forth' the gospel boldly and clearly and 'speaking against' any injustice, oppression, or death-dealing elements in a context.[17] Bevans holds that working out of an adequate contextual theology 'depends on the context'.[18] Exactly when mission needs to be 'dialogical' or 'prophetic' is the result of profound and prayerful discernment.

The Ecojustice Mission and Context

Ecology and other sciences show us that, quite literally, everything is connected to everything else.[19] Thus, the context for the ecojustice mission of the Church is actually the entire cosmos! Practically, Christians need to be aware of the variety of their relationships: the limits of their particular bioregion *to* and *within* other bioregions and earth systems; and how the actions of each human person has a cumulative effect on the well-being and common good of their immediate physical place, and ultimately, the entire planet – human and otherkind, alike. Today in the Anthropocene era, the highest priority is to remain conscious of the *utter fragility and irreplaceable nature* of these interdependent planetary and cosmic contexts.

Following Ernest Haeckel's 1866 formulation, 'ecology' was soon understood as the unity of three ecologies.[20] *Environmental ecology* examines the relationships various societies and individual human beings have with the natural environment. *Social ecology* explores the reality that humans are both earth creatures and social beings. How humans organize themselves enables exploitation or collaboration, respect and reverence for the natural world. 'Hence social justice, the right relationship with persons, roles and institutions, implies some achievement of ecological justice, which is the

---

17 See Bevans and Schroeder, *Prophetic Dialogue*, chapters 2 and 3.

18 Stephen B. Bevans, *Models of Contextual Theology*, revised and expanded edn, Maryknoll, NY: Orbis, 2002.

19 Frank B. Golley, *A Primer for Environmental Literacy*, New Haven, CT: Yale University Press, 1998. Also Fritjof Capra, *The Web of Life: A New Scientific Understanding of Living Systems*, New York: Doubleday, 1996, 36–50. Also 'Chaos Theory and Butterfly Effect', www.dnatube.com/video/29086/Chaos-Theory-and-Butterfly-Effect.

20 F. Guattari, *As Três Ecologias*, Campinas, Brazil: Papirus, 1988.

right relationship with nature, easy access to its resources, and assurance of quality of life.'[21] *Mental ecology* starts from the recognition that nature is *within* human beings – in their minds, in the form of psychic energy, symbols, archetypes and behaviour patterns that embody attitudes of aggression or of respect and acceptance of nature. Thus, human persons live in multiple contexts internal and external that affect their very being, and in turn, human actions – for good or for ill – shape the well-being of the cosmos.

As classical liberation theologies claim, people stand in need of a threefold liberation: first, as an integral human person; second, as a social being who participates in political, economic and social relations; and third, as a spiritual person in need of redemption from sin.[22] Notice how the three levels of liberation align well with the three ecologies. People thrive when they are at home, at peace, in right relationship with God and neighbour and respectful of the integrity of creation. Leonardo Boff rightly contends that when any of these relationships are broken, dehumanizing poverty, oppression and injustice of all sorts *also* emerge.[23]

The Franciscan Tradition: A Vital Resource for the Church's Ecojustice Mission

I suggest that fitting and important correlatives to the related threefold understandings of ecology and liberation are found in the spirituality and ethics rooted in the vernacular theology of Francis of Assisi and his threefold praxis – penance, poverty and prayer.[24] The resulting integration of spirituality, theology and ethics makes the Franciscan tradition a vital resource for shaping the Church's ecojustice mission as prophetic dialogue. That tradition is the formal integrated expression of a profound Christian spirituality deeply rooted in the Christian doctrines of the Trinity and the incarnation.[25]

---

21 Leonardo Boff, *Cry of the Earth, Cry of the Poor*, Maryknoll, NY: Orbis, 1997, 105.

22 See Gustavo Gutierrez, *A Theology of Liberation: History, Politics, and Salvation*, trans. and ed. Caridad Inda and John Eagleson, revised edn, Maryknoll, NY: Orbis, 1988, xxxvii–xi, 83–105, especially 86–91 and 101–2.

23 Leonardo Boff, *Cry of the Earth*, 63–85.

24 See Regis J. Armstrong, 'Francis of Assisi and the Prisms of Theologizing', *Greyfriars Review* 10/2 (1996); 179–206. Francis's theological authority originated in the gift of grace of his experience of God (*ex beneficio*), not *ex officio*. See Bernard McGinn, *Meister Eckhart and the Beguine Mystics*, New York, Continuum, 1983, 6–7, and his *The Flowering of Mysticism: Men and Women in the New Mysticism, 1200–1350*, New York: Crossroad, 1998, 21. Three themes in Francis's vernacular theology irrevocably link Franciscan spirituality, theology and ethics: the humanity of Christ, the mystery of God as generous love and the sense of creation as family. See John 14.6–9 and St Francis, *Admonition* I, 1–4, in Regis Armstrong and Ignatius Brady (eds), *Francis and Clare*, Mahwah, NJ: Paulist Press, 1982, 25–6.

25 Nothwehr (ed.), *Franciscan Theology of the Environment*. Also Nothwehr, *Ecological Footprints*, especially Parts 2–4. See Keith Douglas Warner, 'Franciscan Environmental Ethics: Imagining Creation as a Community of Care', *Journal of the Society of Christian Ethics* 31:1 (2011), 143–60.

It is not without reason that on 29 November 1979 the late John Paul II proclaimed Francis of Assisi 'the Patron of Ecologists'.[26] The tradition that evolved from the life and praxis of St Francis is ecumenical in that the focus is the *full* gospel and its central theological formulations took shape prior to the embattled sixteenth-century Reformation era. Its major concerns for the poor, the care for creation, peace-building and dialogue are central for interfaith relations – all necessary for implementation of the Church's ecojustice mission. Its method utilizes a variety of ways of knowing familiar to a wide array of cultures to formulate a creation theology and an ethics of care for creation. The transformative power of the Franciscan tradition is held in its utter, but profound, simplicity rooted in the vernacular theology of Francis.[27]

The Franciscan tradition grounds the Church's ecojustice mission, clearly articulating how all creation is theologically and morally significant. Creation has a religious purpose: it bears God; it communicates God; it prompts human beings to journey into God; it praises God independently of human beings. Once Christians (and others) understand that creation bears religious meaning, its moral connotation readily follows. Unique among many others, the Franciscan ethical tradition relies on a wide range of biblical 'creation texts' beyond Genesis, thus avoiding the harmful exclusively anthropocentric reading that undergirds claims of sharp ontological division between humanity and the rest of creation assumed by many. Central to the Franciscan ethics tradition is Bonaventure's *agapic* virtue ethics (the *Imitatio Christi*) that holds in high relief the virtues visible in the Trinity and given Christocentric expression in the incarnation. Space here allows only a sampling of the Franciscan tradition.

The Franciscan Tradition and Ecojustice Mission as Dialogue

Francis of Assisi: Kinship of Creation

Genuine dialogue must be grounded in respectful and trusting relationships. A dialogical and relational dynamic among God, humans and otherkind is a hallmark of the more than 28 texts that expose the spirituality, theology and ethics of Francis.[28] These passages show how the incarnation

---

26 See Pope John Paul II, Apostolic Letter *Inter Sanctos: Franciscus Assisiensis Caelestis Patronus Oecologiae Cultorum Eligitur*, www.vatican.va/holy_father/john_paul_ii/apost_letters/1979/documents/hf_jp-ii_apl_19791129_inter-sanctos_lt.html.

27 Fidel Aizpurua, OFM Capuchin, 'Following Francis: A Catechism of Franciscan Spirituality', *Greyfriars Review* 17, supplement (2003), 3–102.

28 The critical edition of Franciscan sources: trans. and ed. Regis J. Armstrong, J. A. Wayne Hellmann, William J. Short, New York: New City Press: *Francis of Assisi: Early Documents*, vol. 1, *The Saint* (1999); *Francis of Assisi: Early Documents*, vol. 2, *The Founder* (2000); *Francis of Assisi: Early Documents*, vol. 3, *The Prophet* (2001) (hereafter cited as FAED, volume number, text, page numbers). See The Franciscan Intellectual Tradition, www.franciscantradition.

indelibly formed his worldview and moral vision.[29] Because Christ became human, part of the material world, everything and everyone – even the enemy,[30] indeed the entire 'creation manifests Christ'.[31] Francis brilliantly expresses this relational, dialogical interdependence in his 'Canticle of the Creatures'; a kinship of creation united by love in Jesus Christ, that praises and reverences God.[32] What Francis knew cointuitively,[33] theologians today, understand as 'deep incarnation'.[34] The Greek term *sarx* (John 1.14), often translated as 'flesh', also points beyond the humanity of Jesus and us to the world of biological life, and it calls forth the entire interwoven web of life that God sustains and embraces in divine love. As we reverence Christ, so too we must respect creation.

Bonaventure of Bagnoregio: Trinitarian Creation Theology

Bonaventure's theology of creation derives from his understanding of the Trinity, which stressed the relations of the three persons.[35] God is the perfect good (Mark 10.18; Luke 18.19), and goodness is 'self-diffusive'. Therefore, God is *necessarily* uniquely *relational*. God also *chooses* to love, and thus God is: the perfectly gratuitous love (Father), absolute love (Spirit) and both gratuitous and receptive love (Son).

---

org/. Also Franciscan Intellectual Tradition Heritage Series: www.franciscanpublications.com ?page_id=554.

29 Giovanni Iammerrone, 'Franciscan Theology Today: Its Possibility, Necessity, and Values', *Greyfriars Review* 8.1 (1994): 103–26. Pierre Brunette OFM, *Francis of Assisi and His Conversions*, trans. Paul La Chance OFM and Kathryn Krug, Quincy, IL: Franciscan Press, 1997.

30 Thomas of Celano, *The Life of Saint Francis*, (1228–9), Book I 20: 55–56, in FAED, vol. I, *The Saint*, 229–30. Kathleen A. Warren, *Daring to Cross the Threshold: Francis of Assisi Encounters Sultan Malek al-Kamil*, Rochester, MN: Sisters of St. Francis, 2003, 32–3.

31 Thomas of Celano, *The Life of Saint Francis*, Book I 28: 77, in FAED, vol. I, *The Saint*, 248. See John 1.14; 2 Cor. 8.9; Phil. 2.6–8. Francis of Assisi, 'The Latter Admonition and Exhortation' (1220), 4–6, in FAED, vol. I, *The Saint*, 46. See Francis of Assisi, *Undated Writings*, 'The Admonitions' I: 15–18, in, FAED, vol. I, *The Saint*, 129. Also Ewert H. Cousins, 'Francis of Assisi and Bonaventure: Mysticism and Theological Interpretation', in Peter Berger (ed.), *The Other Side of God: A Polarity in World Religion*, Garden City, NY: Anchor Press, 1981, 74–103 (79).

32 FAED, vol. I, *The Saint*, 113–14.

33 Bonaventure of Bagnoregio, *The Major Legend of Saint Francis* (1260–3), Chapter IX: 1, in FAED, vol. II, *The Founder*, 596–7.

34 See 'deep incarnation': Duncan Reid, 'Enfleshing the Human', in Denis Edwards (ed.), *Earth Revealing – Earth Healing: Ecology and Christian Theology*, Collegeville, MN: Liturgical Press, 2000, 69–83. Neil Darragh, *At Home in the Earth*, Auckland: Accent Publications, 2000, 124. See Neils Henrick Gregersen, 'The Cross of Christ in an Evolutionary World', *Dialog: A Journal of Theology* 40 (2001), 197–207 (205).

35 Ilia Delio, *Simply Bonaventure: An Introduction to His Life, Thought, and Writings*, Hyde Park, NY: New City Press, 2001, 39–67. Catherine Mowry LaCugna, *God for Us: The Trinity and Christian Life*, New York: HarperCollins Publications, 1991, 53–81.

God is the personal, self-communicating, generous, overflowing goodness and source of all reality who expresses the divine self *ad intra* and *ad extra* (outward in the created universe). The Trinity is our radically relational God who created a universe that is related to its core! The divine persons are interdependent, as are the Godhead and creation.[36] Humans (material and spiritual beings) stand between God and otherkind as the guardians of creation; and otherkind inspires humans to praise God.

John Duns Scotus: Haecceitas *and Mutual Relations*

Any dialogical relationship requires genuine integral partners. Thus, concerning the Church's ecojustice mission as dialogue, Scotus's most important philosophical concept is *haecceitas* or 'thisness'. In order for one subject to be related to another, it must first be known for what it is in itself. *Haecceitas*[37] provides the philosophical foundation for all created reality being specified; it makes a singular thing what it is and differentiates it from all other things (of common nature) to which it may be compared (because of its commonality).[38]

Further, *haecceitas* is important for ecojustice because it exposes *mutuality* as the ontological relationship between and among distinct beings.[39] *Each* cosmic element is sacred, and that affects how one understands contingent reality. Not only is each element of the cosmos different in its accidental characteristics, each is distinct in its very essence.

Through the incarnation humans can partner with God in the ongoing co-creation and co-redemption of the world. Christ is the very person in whom the human and divine achieve mutuality.[40] Because the entire cosmos in some way resembles Christ, the 'first born of all creation', we must cherish creation as we reverence Christ.

---

36 Elizabeth A. Johnson, *She Who Is: The Mystery of God in Feminist Discourse*, New York: Crossroad, 1992, 232.

37 'Glossary', in John Duns Scotus, *God and Creatures: The Quodlibetal Questions*, trans. Felix Alluntis and Allan B. Wolter, Washington, DC: Catholic University of America Press, 1981, 511.

38 Eric Doyle, 'Duns Scotus and Ecumenism', in C. Berubé (ed.), *De Doctrina I. Duns Scoti*, vol. III, Acta Congressus Scotistici Internationalis Oxonii et Edimburgi, 11–17 September 1966 celebrati, Roma: Cura Commissionis Scotisticae, 1968, 633–52 (640): 'The uniqueness, the unrepeatable something of all things, is what gives them their intrinsic and eternal value. There is about everything, every person, an originality that gives new insight into reality, another aspect that has never been seen before. Each person enters into a new enriching relationship of knowledge and love with every new person met, with every new thing encountered.'

39 Mary Elizabeth Ingham, 'Integrated Vision', in Kenan B. Osborne (ed.), *The History of Franciscan Theology*, St. Bonaventure, NY: The Franciscan Institute, 1994, 185–230 (210).

40 Ingham, 'Integrated Vision', 222. See John 1.1–15; 1 John 1.1–3; Col. 1.15–20; Eph. 1.3–14; 1 Cor. 8.6; and Heb. 1.2–14. Also John Duns Scotus, *Ordinatio* III.7.q.3, trans. Allan B. Wolter, 'John Duns Scotus on the Primacy and Personality of Christ', in Damian McElrath (ed.), *Franciscan Christology: Selected Texts: Translations and Essays*, Franciscan Sources No. 1, St. Bonaventure, NY: The Franciscan Institute, 1980, 138–82 (151).

Ecojustice: Mission as Dialogue

Bevans and Schroeder rightly ground the dialogical nature of mission in the life of the Trinity *ad intra*.[41] Indeed, the Church

> called into being by that mission must be a community that not only gives of itself in service to the world and to the peoples of the world's cultures but learns from its involvement and expands its imagination to the depths of God's unfathomable riches ... Mission, as participation in the mission of the triune God, can only proceed in dialogue and can only be carried out in humility.[42]

More explicitly, the Church's mission for ecojustice finds support in the very nature of God as the standard for radical inclusivity in relationship and the fabric of interdependencies that is the universe. Just as any artist reveals her/himself in their creations, so too a radically relational God is perceptible through the deep ecological relations of the cosmos. 'Together with unity (one cosmos, one planet Earth, one human species) reigns also a diversity (galactic clusters; solar systems; biodiversity; a multiplicity of races, cultures and individual persons). This coexistence between unity and diversity opens a space to situate a trinitarian and communal understanding of God.'[43] Trinitarian *perichoresis* reveals the characteristics that are necessary in just societies and an ecologically sustainable world – intrinsic value and mutual respect for each creature and earth element; freedom, interdependence, justice and love.[44]

Understanding God as Trinity, taken together with the biblical witnesses of the intrinsic value for all elements of creation found in the covenantal and sacramental approaches to mission, provide a compelling mandate for the Church's ecojustice mission as dialogue. But beyond that, the Trinity as three distinct persons in mutual relationship also grounds mutuality as a formal moral norm of Christian ethics that functions together with love and justice to frame the ethical dimension of mission as prophecy.[45]

---

41 Stephen B. Bevans and Roger P. Schroeder, *Constants in Context: A Theology of Mission for Today*, Maryknoll, NY: Orbis, 2009, 348.

42 Bevans and Schroeder, *Constants in Context*, 348.

43 Mark Hathaway and Leonardo Boff, *The Tao of Liberation: Exploring the Ecology of Transformation*, Maryknoll, NY: Orbis, 2009, 326.

44 See Leonardo Boff, *Trinity and Society*, trans. Paul Burns, Maryknoll, NY: Orbis, 1988, 215–24.

45 Dawn M. Nothwehr, *Mutuality: A Formal Norm for Christian Social Ethics*, San Francisco: Catholic Scholars Press, 1998; repr., Eugene, OR: Wipf & Stock Publishers, 2005. Dawn M. Nothwehr, 'Mutuality and Mission: A "No Other" Way', *Mission Studies* 21:2 (2004), 249–70.

The Franciscan Tradition and Ecojustice Mission as Prophecy

Ecojustice: Mission as Prophecy

Trinitarian communion, as well as the covenantal and sacramental traditions of Christianity opposes atomistic individualism, isolationism and asocial personhood. Yet today dominant social, political, economic and cultural systems continue to promote, support or impose such harmful relationships. The four most critical ecological issues for the twenty-first century – human induced global climate change, world potable water crisis, crisis in food security[46] and crisis of sustainable energy[47] – glaringly illustrate the results of ignoring the common good and ontological interdependence. Space here permits review of only two issues.

Human-Induced Global Climate Change[48]

Unequivocally, global warming, largely caused by human activities is taking place.[49] The main culprit is greenhouse gases from fossil fuels, which trap solar heat in the oceans and atmosphere, warming the earth's surface. Climate change is already visible in sea-level rise, loss of alpine glaciers and snow cover, shrinking Arctic summer sea ice, thawing permafrost and poleward migration of many animals and plants towards cooler habitats. Between 20 and 30 per cent of plant and animal species are threatened with extinction if average global temperatures increase by 1.5–2.5°C (2.7–4.5°F) compared to the average temperature during the two last decades of the twentieth century.

This irretrievable damage to God's creation has a human face – the egregious suffering of those already the poorest. Millions are left desperate; for example, droughts in Malawi;[50] stronger hurricanes in the Mekong Delta[51] or super Typhoon Haiyan in the Philippines.[52]

---

46 Nothwehr, *Ecological Footprints*, 225–74.

47 Nothwehr, *Ecological Footprints*, 275–323.

48 Nothwehr, *Ecological Footprints*, 155–86 used data from the IPCC's 4th *Assessment Report*. For updates see the three-part IPCC 5th *Assessment Report*, www.ipcc.ch/.

49 IPCC, *Climate Change 2007: Synthesis Report Summary for Policymakers*, www.ipcc. ch/publications and_data/ar4/syr/en/spm.html. See Berkeley Earth Surface Temperature Project, http://berkeleyearth. org/resources.php. Also Pontifical Academy of Sciences report 'Fate of Mountain Glaciers in the Anthropocene', 11 May 2011, www.vatican.va/roman_ curia/ pontifical_academies/acdscien/2011/PAS_ Glacier_110511_ final.pdf.

50 Judd Birdsall, 'In Malawi, Evangelicals Don't Doubt Climate Change', *The Blog*, posted 28 May 2013 5.19 p.m. EDT, www.huffingtonpost.com/judd-birdsall/in-malawi-evangelicals-do_b_3345490.html.

51 'Climate Change and the Shifting Mekong Delta', *Planet Action*, www.planet-action.org/web/139-climate-change-and-the-shifting-mekong-delta.php.

52 John Vidal, 'Typhoon Haiyan: What Really Alarms Filipinos is the Rich World Ignoring Climate Change', The Guardian.com, 8 November 2013 09.31 EST, www.theguardian.com/commentisfree/2013/nov/08/typhoon-haiyan-rich-ignore-climate-change. Haiyan was one of

Meanwhile, Europeans and North Americans have been able to ignore climate change and the *real impact* that *their* greenhouse gas pollution (since the 1850s) is causing, affecting lives across the globe. Technological adaptation has allowed lifestyles to remain relatively untouched! Hurricane Katrina, Super-storm Sandy, wildfires or dust storms give the USA and Europe only a wee taste of the perils of unchecked climate change.

But globally, the size and scale of storms, droughts, floods, fires and other 'natural' disasters are encroaching on the coping capacity of even the most technologically sophisticated nations. In such conditions people justly assert their human right to survive; but when 'help' is impossible, desperate people readily become vicious and violent.[53] Climate refugees add pressure on the availability of resources in host locales.[54] These are *preventable* moral matters of justice requiring the Church's prophetic denunciation and confrontation at all levels. Indeed, these are spiritual matters for Christians that affect our journey towards salvation (see Matt. 25.31–46). Here the Church's ecological mission is to use its resources in every way possible to act out of love for the poor and for the preservation of God's planet by pre-empting additional human caused global warming.[55]

World Crisis of Potable Water[56]

For basic dignity and health each person needs 13 US gallons of water per day. The average US person uses 65–100 gallons of water per day; the average African uses only 12 gallons! Consider the current reality:[57] one billion people worldwide do not have *any* water within a 15-minute walk of their homes. There is no more water on the earth than there was 2,000 years ago when the world population was about *200 million*; today, people number nearly *seven billion*! The western United States, northern China, northern and western India, and northern and western Africa consume ground water faster than aquifers can be replenished. One-third of US rivers, one-half of US estuaries and more than one-half of US lakes are unfit for fishing, swimming or drinking. Nearly 40 per cent of the world's

---

the most powerful ever recorded anywhere: 25 miles (40 km) wide and reaching astonishing speeds of possibly 200 mph (322 km/h).

53 See Elizabeth Landau, 'Climate Change May Increase Violence, Study Shows', CNN, updated 6.41 a.m. EDT, 2 August 2013, www.cnn.com/2013/08/01/us/climate-change-violence/index.html.

54 The vast needs of 'climate refugees' or 'environmentally displaced persons' are not included in the 1951 United Nations Convention Relating to the Status of Refugees.

55 Catholic Relief Services – How We Serve, www.catholicrelief.org/how/. Also Lutheran World Relief – Our Work, http://lwr.org/ourwork.

56 Nothwehr, *Ecological Footprints*, 187–224.

57 *National Geographic*, special issue, 'Water: Our Thirsty World' (April 2010), 112–13 and passim.

populations live alongside international rivers. Two billion people depend on international cooperation to ensure an adequate water supply.[58]

As the Pontifical Justice and Peace Council asserted in its 2003 statement, 'Water is an essential element for life.'[59] Defence of water as a human right is an essential part of the prophetic ecojustice mission of the Church.[60] Christians must denounce and act to reverse behaviours, strategies or policies that ignore the fundamental interrelatedness of our entire world, particularly the hydrological cycle.[61] The tides, currents and weather patterns that sustain the water supply are globally intimately interconnected with the quality of the air, soils and water. Water is often wasted, in a world where the human population continues to soar.[62]

Bonaventure's Virtue Ethics and Ecojustice Mission as Prophecy

Many experts in science and religion have long held that the environmental crisis that now imminently threatens human extinction is the result of a deep spiritual malaise.[63] Bonaventure's *imitatio Christi* has both an internal and external dimension useful for anyone engaging the Church's ecojustice mission.

As spiritual beings, humans, seek union with God while on a journey in the brilliant context of the *created world* that *expresses* God's self-revelation. Bonaventure also asserted that the whole life of Jesus Christ is instructive for the moral life.[64] But 'following Christ' moves beyond merely mimicking

---

58 Ahmed Abukhater, *Water as a Catalyst for Peace: Transboundary Water Management and Conflict Resolution*, Earthscan Studies in Water Resource Management, New York: Routledge, 2013.

59 Pontifical Council for Justice and Peace, 'Water: An Essential Element for Life', www.vatican.va/roman_curia/pontifical_councils/justpeace/documents/rc_pc_justpeace_doc_20030322_kyoto-water_en.html. Also World Council of Churches, 'Statement on Water for Life', adopted at Porto Alegre, 2006, www.oikoumene.org/en/resources/documents/assembly/2006-porto-alegre/1-statements-documents-adopted/international-affairs/report-from-the-public-issues-committee/water-for-life?set_language=en.

60 See National Catholic Rural Life Conference, 'Pure Water: A Sacramental Commons for All', www.ncrlc.com/page.aspx?ID=80.

61 United Nations General Assembly, Resolution 64/292, 'The Human Right to Water and Sanitation' (28 July 2010), www.un.org/ga/search/view_doc.asp?symbol=A/RES/64/292. Also John H. Knox, *Report of the Independent Expert on the Issue of Human Rights Obligations Relating to the Enjoyment of a Safe, Clean, Healthy and Sustainable Environment*, http://ap.ohchr.org/documents/dpage_e.aspx?m=199.

62 For examples, see USEPA, WaterSense: Fix a Leak Week, www.epa.gov/WaterSense/pubs/fixleak.html.

63 National Religious Partnership for the Environment, 'The Joint Appeal in Religion and Science: Statement by Religious Leaders at the Summit on Environment', 3 June 1991, in New York City, http://fore.research.yale.edu/publications/statements/joint_appeal.html.

64 Zachary Hayes, *The Hidden Center: Spirituality and Speculative Christology in St. Bonaventure*, Franciscan Pathways, St. Bonaventure, NY: The Franciscan Institute, 1992, 27.

Jesus' activity, to the transformation of an individual's interior disposition, grounded in a loving relationship with God.

Transformation requires a constant interplay between the ethical (external) and the spiritual (internal) that is illuminated by God's grace and through which people are made whole and holy ('rendered deiform').[65] Christ mediates this deification by forgiving sin, his example and teaching, pardoning punishment and conferring grace and glory. All the elements of the cosmos are deified in their unique ways. But the spiritual life directs the Christian moral life through the virtues of humility, poverty, obedience and love.[66]

Humility

'Humility' comes from the Latin word for 'earth', *humus*. God, in the incarnation, entered our reality, choosing an intimate relationship with us *earth creatures*.[67] Today Christians must reclaim their *creaturely* identity and use our considerable, though limited, scientific and technological prowess to care for one another and the planet.[68] Humility is vital when contemplating massive and destructive projects such as tar sands extractions, huge dams, or vast deforestation:

> Embracing doubt, a signature of strength of science, is an essential core component of an ignorance-based world view (IBWV) that assumes the areas of certainty are small and relative. The contrasting knowledge-based world view (KBWV) assumes small and mostly insignificant knowledge gaps exist. When the KBWV is combined with a sense of urgency to 'do something,' then the intellectual landscape is flattened, the introduction of

---

See Bonaventure, *IV Sent.* d.3, p.2, a.3, q.1, ad3 (IV, 84). All references to the primary works of St Bonaventure of Bagnoregio are to *Opera Omnia: Doctoris Seraphici S. Bonaventurae opera omnia*, 10 vols (Quaracchi: Collegium S.Bonaventurae, 1882–1902). Volume number is indicated by Roman numerals in parentheses, and is followed by the page reference in Arabic numerals. I, II, III, IV *Sent.* is for I, II, III, IV *Commentaria in Quatuor Libros Sententiarum. Hex.* is for *Collationes in Hexaemeron. Sermo.* is for *Sermones. Dom.* is for *Dominicales*. Since Bonaventure's sermons are also found in J. G. Bougerol (ed.), *Sancti Bonaventurae Sermones Dominicales, Bibliotheca Franciscana Scholastica Medii Aevi*, 27, Rome: Grottaferrata, 1977, both sources are cited, indicating Bougerol as needed.

65 Hayes, *The Hidden Center*, 42.

66 Hayes, *The Hidden Center*, 44–5. Hayes cites *Dom. III, Adv. I* (IX, 58); Bougerol, *Sermo* 4, 159–60. See Denis Edwards, 'Final Fulfillment – The Deification of Creation', *SEDOS Bulletin* 41:7–8 (2009), www.sedosmission.org/web/en/sedos-bulletin/cat_view/93-bulletin/253-sedos-bulletin-2009/283-july-august-2009-seminar.

67 Bonaventure, *Sermon on the Nativity* (IX, 106) cited by Hayes, *The Hidden Center*, 42. See Matt. 18.4.

68 Leonard J. Bowman, 'The Cosmic Exemplarism of Bonaventure', *The Journal of Religion* 55 (1985), 181–98 (187).

new ideas is impeded, monitoring and adaptive management is marginalized, risky behaviors continue, and social learning is restricted.[69]

Christian environmental ethics is normatively rooted in values that strongly embrace prudence and the precautionary principle when dealing with great complexity, the unknown, or the unknowable. Thus, the virtue of humility clearly directs the Church's ecojustice mission to an IBWV approach to action and policy advocacy.[70]

Poverty

Bonaventure holds that material poverty (Christian simplicity) must accompany humility. Often materially wealthy people suffer from the illusion of never having enough; this is *spiritual* poverty. Today people must choose to live with what is sufficient for a life of dignity and ecologically sustainable! Key to the virtue of poverty is being confident in God's generosity and openness to others in need (Matt. 10.8). Today this means eliminating unsustainable human consumption of goods and developing renewable sources and ways of living.

Obedience

'Obedience' comes from the Latin *oboedire*, 'to pay attention' or 'to hear'. Jesus Christ modelled this virtue by listening to his Father's will (Heb. 10.7, 9; John 14.31; 5.30) and by caring for the needs of people and nonhuman others.[71] Christians must be attentive to the poor and what makes people poor – especially environmental degradation (Matt. 25). Today Christians must heed the groaning of the suffering earth, become ecologically literate, engage in prayerful discernment and then act to halt environmental destruction.

Love

Having first received God's love, Christians then share it with human and otherkind (John 13.34–35).[72] Christians must love all of their 'ecological neighbours', as themselves and *as* God loves. Christ is the ultimate norm

---

69 R. Eugene Turner, 'Doubt and the Values of an Ignorance-Based World View for Restoration: Coastal Louisiana Wetlands', *Estuaries and Coasts* 32 (2009), 1054–68 (1054).

70 See COMEST and UNESCO, *The Precautionary Principle*, http://unesdoc.unesco.org/images/0013/001395/139578e.pdf. See also COMECE, 'A Christian View on Climate Change: The Implications of Climate Change for Lifestyles and EU Policies', Brussels: COMECE, 2008, 17.

71 Hayes, *The Hidden Center*, 37. Bonaventure's commentary on Luke stresses Jesus' obedience to people.

72 Hayes, *The Hidden Center*, 38–9. In Bonaventure's speculative theology and spirituality, love drives the Christ mystery.

and negotiator of justice (love).[73] Today the Church's ecojustice mission must advocate and enforce policies and laws that keep air, water and soils pure; that sharply restrict the plundering and warming of the planet; and that support the restoration of environmental damage.[74]

Christ: Paradigm and Norm

The Christian life is a journey deeper into the ontological realities of the world.[75] Understanding those realities also shapes Christian ethics that must inform the Church's ecojustice mission. Jesus' life, ministry and teaching is radically relational and intimately connected with the earth.[76] Beginning with his inaugural sermon (Luke 4.16–22) he sustained the vital theo-logical and ecological bond between care for the earth and care for the poor (Lev. 25) – debt forgiveness, return to one's homeland, liberation of slaves (economics), as well as rest for the land and animals (ecology). These values, virtues and vision need to be reflected in the Church's ecojustice mission.

Conclusion: Ecojustice Mission as Prophetic Dialogue

Creation care has been a Christian concern through the centuries.[77] Simi-larly, major Christian denominations have responded to recent ecological crises: Pan-Orthodox Conference (1986); The World Council of Churches (1989); Evangelical Leaders – Sandy Cove, Maryland (2004); and Lausanne III and Edinburgh (2010).[78] Beginning with Pope Paul VI, Catholic social teaching has increasingly emphasized the moral obligation to care for the earth.[79]

---

73 Hayes, *The Hidden Center*, 202–3. Hayes cites *Hex.* 1, 31–3 (V, 334); Aristotle, *II Ethics*, c. 6; and *Hex.*1, 34–6 (V, 335).

74 Jeanne Kay Guelke, 'Looking for Jesus in Christian Environmental Ethics', *Environmental Ethics* 26/2 (2004), 115–34 (123).

75 Hayes, *The Hidden Center*, 39: 'To perceive the life of Christ as a paradigm is to accept its fundamental values as normative for human life. The fundamental attitude and values of Christ must be so personalized in one's life that they truly define one's relationship to reality.'

76 Elizabeth A. Johnson, 'An Earthy Christology: "For God So Loved the Cosmos"', *America* 2000 12, whole no. 4852 (2009), 27–30 (28).

77 Dana L. Roberts, 'Historical Trends in Missions and Earth Care', *International Bulletin of Missionary Research* 35:3 (2011), 123–8.

78 *World Council of Churches, Ecumenical Dictionary*, D. Preman Nile SV, 'Justice, Peace and the Integrity of Creation', November 2003, www.wcc-coe.org/wcc/who/dictionary-article11.html. Allan Effa, 'The Greening of Mission', *International Bulletin of Missionary Research* 32 (2008), 171–6.

79 Some examples: Pope Paul VI, 'A Hospitable Earth for Future Generations', Address at the Stockholm Conference on Human Environment, Conservation Catholic, http://conservation. catholic.org/pope_paul_vi.htm. Pope John Paul I, General Audience, 20 September 1978, www.vatican.va/holy_father/john_paul_i/audiences/documents/hf_jp-i_aud_20091978_ en.html. Pope John Paul II, *Inter Sanctos: Franciscus Assisiensis Caelestis Patronus Oecologiae Cultorum Eligitur*, www.vatican.va/holy_father/john_paul_ii/apost_letters/1979/

Common Biblical and Doctrinal Themes

The Christian churches have been remarkably unified, grounding their teaching in common biblical and doctrinal themes especially creation, salvation and eschatology.[80]

Creation

Creation is God's masterpiece, a witness to divine presence and power. Humans (*imago Dei*) along with all other cosmic elements are part of the divine self-expression, each uniquely declaring God's glory. Ethically, humans must acknowledge the intrinsic value of each creature and element, while exercising sustainable and limited use and enjoyment of them. Humans relate to creation primarily as caretakers and guardians.

Salvation

The Johannine and Pauline witnesses of the cosmic Christ, who renews and brings 'all things' to fulfilment proclaims God's redemptive plan is about the *entire* cosmos, not only *human* destiny. Jesus' death and resurrection brings 'all things' including humans into a state of reconciliation with God. Jesus' ascension serves as evidence that not only is he the exalted Lord, who transforms human life, but also of 'all things' – renewing and healing – bringing *all* to fulfilment.

Eschatology

The Bible provides a 'grand *inclusio*' (Gen. 1—3 and Rev. 20—22) that not only shows the unity of the two testaments, but that also shapes Christian understanding of both.[81] Sin, the fall and the cosmic embodied redemption provide convincing evidence supporting Christian expectations that Christ's offer of redemption necessitates a transformation of the physical

---

documents/hf_jp-ii_apl_19791129_inter-sanctos_lt.html. Pope Francis, World Day of Peace Message, 1 January 2014, www.vatican.va/holy_father/francesco/messages/peace/documents/ papa-francesco_20131208_messaggio-xlvii-giornata-mondiale-pace-2014_en.html. Pontifical Council for Justice and Peace, *Compendium of the Social Doctrine of the Church*, www.vatican.va/roman_curia/pontifical_councils/justpeace/documents/rc_pc_justpeace_ doc_20060526_compendio-dott-soc_en.html. USCCB, *Renewing the Earth:* An Invitation to Reflection and Action on Environment in Light of Catholic Social Teaching, www.usccb. org/ issues-and-action/human-life-and-dignity/environment/renewing-the-earth.cfm. USCCB, *Global Climate Change A Plea for Dialogue Prudence and the Common Good* www.usccb. org/issues-and-action/human-life-and-dignity/environment/global-climate-change-a-plea-for-dialogue-prudence-and-the-common-good.cfm.

80 The National Religious Partnership for the Environment, www.nrpe.org/.

81 Ronald Manahan, 'Christ as Second Adam', in Calvin DeWitt (ed.), *The Environment and the Christian: What Does the New Testament Say about the Environment?*, Grand Rapids, MI: Baker House, 1991, 46.

and material universe. The New Testament shows God's plan for creation in history. Human fulfilment is intimately intertwined with that of creation. Precisely how that will happen is unclear, but Christians are people of hope, based on 'the character of God' revealed in the Christ event.[82]

Practical Strategies for Ecojustice Mission as Prophetic Dialogue

Ongoing Theological Reflection

Bevans and Schroeder claim the Christian ecojustice mission must be the subject of constant discernment, continued scrutiny of the signs of the times and of the context. Issues of public policy, the discoveries of science and methods of caretaking must be evaluated and practised in light of the best scholarship, Christian theology and spiritual wisdom. What does salvation and liberation mean in the context of this time, place and ecosystem; within this culture; among these people? How does the development of technology support or hinder the 'fullness of life' (John 10.10)? What are the occasions of grace and 'ecological offences' (sinfulness) that require proclamation or denunciation?

Interreligious Cooperation

The very global nature of the context of the Church's ecojustice mission requires an interreligious dialogue about thorough and consistent cooperation in earth care. Major world religious groups hold that environmental activism requires interfaith cooperation and are well organized across the globe for such purposes. The United Nations Environment Programme, Interfaith Partnership for the Environment has become a major clearinghouse for bringing religious and spiritual wisdom to all dimensions of creation care.[83] The Yale Forum on Religion and Ecology is outstanding for gathering theologians, practitioners and environmentalists to a wide-ranging interreligious environmental dialogue, considering the implications of their work.[84]

Training and Professional Expertise

The ecojustice mission of the Church requires personnel who can integrate Christian theology and ethics with the necessary scientific and technical expertise to care for the environment in their particular region of the world. Curricula of Christian educational institutions need to support this

---

82 Elizabeth A. Johnson, *Friends of God and Prophets: A Feminist Reading of the Communion of Saints*, London: SCM Press, 1998, 201. Denis Edwards, 'Final Fulfillment: The Deification of Creation', *SEDOS Bulletin*, 43:7–8 (2011), 181–94.

83 United Nations Environment Programme, Interfaith Partnership for the Environment, www.unep.org/newyork/interfaithpartnershipfortheenvironment/tabid/56210/default.aspx.

84 See http://fore.research.yale.edu.

need, offering training and knowledge necessary for intercultural dialogue; comprehension of social, political and economic impacts of environmental interventions; and strategies for challenging unjust and harmful policies and practices. Changing people's relationship to the land is both a deeply spiritual and a practical form of intervention into traditional worldviews. Ecojustice ministers always need to discern with others the right course of action for the common good of humans and otherkind.

God's Work: The Church's Ecojustice Mission

Fundamental for the Church's ecojustice mission is humble faith that humans are creatures within God's creation and that we must relate to it *all* as God relates to us with great reverence, love and respect.[85] By virtue of baptism, the same Spirit animates the faith of all Christians building communion and giving life to all of creation (Wisd. 11.24—12.1).[86] The Trinitarian relations (equal persons in mutual relationship) are the model for all social and ecological relations. Mutuality is 'power-*with*' others and *for* others engaging their participation and consent.[87] Christian conversion does not require modernization by Western standards; only, seeking best practices for the common good. Christian ecojustice mission requires that missionaries act as guardians of creation for the good of all (Gen. 2.16–17). But most importantly, the ecojustice mission is God's work, and it is accomplished in many ways in many cultures.

---

85 Raymond Finch, MM, 'Missionaries Today', *Origins* 30/21 (2000), 327–32 (329).

86 Dennis Edwards, *Breath of Life: A Theology of the Creator Spirit*, Maryknoll, NY: Orbis, 2004.

87 Nothwehr, *Mutuality*, 12–13, 92–3.

7

'Continents of moil and misery': Mission, Justice and Prophetic Dialogue

TIM NAISH

Introduction

These days it is easy to picture the earth as a whole. Through the human exploration of space we have become familiar with visual images encompassing continents, even the entire earth. Some of us are old enough to remember the excited astonishment when these began to appear. For the first time one could take in photographically the nature of it all, whether the patterns of land masses and oceans known from our maps, but now dotted with real clouds, or the myriad paths of human activity revealed by our unnatural lights. Since then developments have been so rapid that now using Google or other Internet maps one can zoom in and out over any part of the globe.

Before all this one had to use one's imagination. However, there is one very rare moment when the natural order offers us its own vestigial picture of the whole planet: as its shadow is cast on the moon by the sun at an eclipse. Such a sign stimulated Thomas Hardy to write this poem:

> Thy shadow, Earth, from Pole to Central Sea,
> Now steals along upon the Moon's meek shine
> In even monochrome and curving line
> Of imperturbable serenity.
>
> How shall I link such sun-cast symmetry
> With the torn troubled form I know as thine,
> That profile, placid as a brow divine,
> With continents of moil and misery?
>
> And can immense Mortality but throw
> So small a shade, and Heaven's high human scheme
> Be hemmed within the coasts yon arc implies?

Is such the stellar gauge of earthly show,
Nation at war with nation, brains that teem,
Heroes, and women fairer than the skies?[1]

Here is a serious eschatological challenge to Christian faith and mission. Hardy asks us as human beings whether the claims we make for significance can have any credence in the light of a broader perspective; his gloomy outlook is not so much on evil and darkness as on meaninglessness and futility. One might argue that our ever-increasing knowledge of the universe of which we are part only serves to intensify his vision. The psalmist's cry 'What are human beings, that you are mindful of them?' is turned on its head to become not an expression of wonder, but a lament. What feel and seem to us to be deeply significant human affairs, the result of our teeming brains, are revealed by the wider universal perspective as fleeting shadow.

The demands and hopes of those who work for justice in our world can easily seem to be overwhelmed not just by the reality of evil but also by the absence of meaning and purpose. This is perhaps the most acute issue facing the agents of God's mission who see in Jesus Christ a promise that 'brains that teem, heroes, and women fairer than the skies' – human creativity, courage and beauty – do have an ultimate value and a goal; and who moreover believe that even the ugly truth of the apparently endless repetition of 'nation at war with nation' can be overcome and incorporated into a greater peace.

In our era the pictures of the earth sent from space generate a similar sense of challenge. There is something startlingly poignant in having it all before us in one image. We desire to affirm that the beauty, courage and creativity that we do indeed see around us are not inconsequential happy accidents but are signs of something made 'very good' and pointing to the defeat both of evil and of meaninglessness. We have to be painfully honest about the 'moil[2] and misery', both within human degradation and also in the natural order, while asserting that they are not the end.

Hardy's intention is surely to expose as illusory the 'beauty' that he sees cast by the sun on the moon's face: serenity, symmetry, all placid and imperturbable. It is mere shadow, mirage. Christian eschatology on the other hand confesses that that kind of imagery *is* actually a valid picture of what the world is, what life is. Hence the goal of the Christian mission is to work towards it; because this is understood to be *God*'s mission, God's good purpose for God's good creation.

---

1 Thomas Hardy, *The Complete Poems*, New Wessex edn, ed. J. Gibson, London: Macmillan, 1976, 116.

2 The archaic word *moil* lies at the root of 'turmoil', with much the same meaning.

Justice, Justification and Prophetic Dialogue

Over the last 60 years or so, the conjunction of the rediscovery of the *missio Dei* with that of long-overlooked aspects of the doctrine of the Trinity has taken theology and the Church towards a more thoroughly relational understanding of mission. In the light of God's being in 'incomparable mutual hospitality',[3] God's desire for right relationship in every aspect of creation comes better into focus. God's mission is one which embraces the setting free of the whole creation which has been groaning in labour pains, in the bondage of decay, until now. It encompasses 'all things' – a favourite phrase of the Pauline letters.[4]

So the moil and misery of the continents are the concern of the divine mission. Heroic courage and intense beauty are to be celebrated, as nations at war with nations are to be enabled to beat their swords into the pruning hooks that will bring the earth's bounty to all; and brains that teem are in the midst, capable both of heroism and beauty and also of hatred and violence.

The righting of wronged relationships is one way of putting what we describe by the word 'justice'. It is the justice of God, who is Trinity, which requires the peaceful and fair ordering of all things. One of the acknowledged sadnesses of Christian mission in recent decades has been the dividing up of this justice of God into components and fighting over their relative importance. It is good that this dividing and fighting is now in many places less prevalent than it was, but there is still a need to underline the holistic nature of God's longing for reconciliation at every level. The most common articulation of the battleground has been in terms of 'mission as evangelism' versus 'mission as social justice', or something similar. It is important to see how a holistic vision of God's justice must incorporate both into one reconciliatory practice and way of being.

One factor which has been influential here is the rendering of 'justice' in English translations of the Bible. The key words in the original languages are *tsedaqah* in Hebrew and *dikaiosynē* in Greek and their cognate forms.[5] In English there are two quite different words (also with their cognate forms) often used as alternative ways of translating these two words from

---

3 A version of Daniel Migliore's phrase attempting to encapsulate something of the meaning of God's being in Trinity and of the word *perichoresis*, the rediscovery and elaboration of which has been one feature of the explosion of Trinitarian theology over the last 60 years or so. Migliore, *Faith Seeking Understanding*, 2nd edition, Grand Rapids, MI: Eerdmans, 2004, 79.

4 E.g. 1 Cor. 15.26f.; Eph. 1.10, 22f.; Col. 1.20 – cf. 'the whole creation' in Rom. 8.22.

5 *Dikaiosynē* is one of several important words sharing the stem *dik-* in the NT; the comments I am about to make on their translation refers to all of these forms from the basic root. The verb *dikaioō* and adjective *dikaios* are the most frequently used, and serve well to make my point: *dikaioō* is usually translated 'justify' and *dikaios* as 'righteous', thoroughly disguising the fact that they are two forms of the same stem in the original Greek.

the Old and New Testaments: 'justice' and 'righteousness'.[6] Each word has tended to be associated with one of the two divisions of mission suggested in the last paragraph, exacerbating the unfortunate separation: 'righteousness' and its cognates have been used with regard to God's longing for right relations at the personal level, while 'justice' with regard to that same longing as it applies to wider dimensions of relating, including those which we often intend by the adjective 'social'. This has taken place despite the fact that the absence of a simple verb derived from the 'right/righteousness' stem has meant that 'justify' is most often used to translate the verb *dikaioō*. It is probably true that most English-speaking Christians, even those who are fairly committed and biblically literate, are unaware how often in the New Testament words like 'justify', 'righteous', 'justice' are usually all translating the same root word in the original Greek.

So the strong linguistic connections between right relationship between human beings and God and right interrelationships among human beings have not been sufficiently integrated. The former have tended to be a matter of 'righteousness' and the latter a matter of 'justice' without awareness that in New Testament terms these might be referred to by the same language.[7] Understandings of mission in terms primarily of working towards personal 'righteousness' in restored right relationship to God through Jesus Christ have been set against understandings primarily in terms of working towards social 'justice' in restored right relationship within God's whole creation.

A unified vision of the centrality of the *tsedaqah/dikaiosynē* of God is needed if we are to develop an appropriate understanding and practice of missional justice. This is not the place even to begin on this large task. In this context we can merely point to the kind of resources on which we can draw. I summon two of the most renowned contemporary biblical scholars, one for each Testament.

In the Hebrew Bible, *tsedaqah* is one of the foundational attributes of Yahweh, and my claim that it is fundamentally to do with right relationship is borne out by Walter Brueggemann, who at a pivotal juncture of his Old

---

6 As Richard Hays puts it, 'Both in the OT and the NT the terms "just, justification, justify" usually translate exactly the same linguistic stock represented elsewhere in English translation by "righteous, righteousness." The English language regrettably lacks a verb etymologically akin to "righteousness" ... Consequently, English translations of the Bible are generally unable to convey the close linguistic linkage between "the righteousness of God" and the justification of persons.' (Anchor Bible Dictionary III, 1129 – article on *'Justification'*) The ways that different English translations render the seven occurrences of *dikaiosynē/dikaios/dikaioō* in Romans 3.21–26 serve as a good example here.

7 Daniel Groody uses the distinction between 'internal' and 'external' justice, to describe them: 'Internal justice deals with one's experience of justification or being put in right relationship with God through the saving work of Jesus Christ. External justice deals with the promotion of good works. Internal justice refers to God's activity within a person; external justice refers to one's response to God's grace.' *Globalization, Spirituality and Justice*, Maryknoll, NY: Orbis, 2007, 26–7.

Testament theology identifies as central to its portrayal of Yahweh a critical tension between his self-regard or sovereignty and his commitment to Israel or solidarity; and he finds a proximate resolution to this tension in the assertion of Yahweh's *righteousness*:

> The substance of that righteousness is the well-being of the world, so that when Yahweh's righteousness (Yahweh's governance) is fully established in the world, the results are fruitfulness, prosperity, freedom, justice, peace, security and well-being (*shalom*). Because Yahweh in righteousness wills good for creation, there is a complete convergence of Yahweh's self-regard and Yahweh's commitment to Israel and to creation.[8]

The most nearly corresponding quality attributed to God in the New Testament is *dikaiosynē*; while of course the uses of this word in Greek prior to the New Testament have also to be taken into account), the New Testament writers have been deeply influenced by *tsedaqah* in using it to identify a central attribute of the God revealed in Christ. So N. T. Wright in an illuminating and missionally fruitful account of righteousness in Pauline thought, in the latest volume of his magnum opus, writes regularly of '*tsedaqah/dikaiosynē*'. For example:

> The word *tsedaqah/dikaiosynē* and its cognates in the Israelite Scriptures seem to have the primary meaning of 'right behaviour'. But the emphasis is not merely on implicit conformity to a law or abstract standard, though that may be involved as well, but to the question of being in right *relation* with others.[9]

He moves towards a conclusion of his analysis of the word with a recognition of the difficulty of finding an adequate English (or French or German) translation, regretting that we do not have

> a word or even a single phrase that can sum up the broad ethical and 'relational' sense, add to it the overtones of the law court, give it the extra dimensions of the divine covenant with Israel and set it within a world-view-narrative that looked ahead to a final judgement in which the creator would set all things right at last.[10]

---

8 W. Brueggemann, *Theology of the Old Testament* (Minneapolis: Fortress, 1997), 303. Cf. also: '[... *tsedaqah*] belongs to the terminology of relationship. He is just who does justice to the claims made upon him in the name of a relationship. Thus God's righteousness is manifested first in that he rules according to the covenant in fellowship with his people.' G. Quell and G. Schrenk, *Righteousness*, London: A & C Black, 1951, 29.

9 N. T. Wright, *Paul and the Faithfulness of God*, London: SPCK, 2013, 796.

10 Wright, *Paul and the Faithfulness of God*, 801. Here he is referring to aspects of *dikaiosynē* identified in his intervening analysis.

He suggests that if we took the notions of 'God's restorative justice' and 'God's covenant faithfulness' as two points of a triangle then *tsedaqah/dikaiosynē* at the third point might link them in a 'fresh, combined sense'.[11] This is one pointer to what I called above a unified vision of the centrality of the justice of God which might enable a more holistic practice of mission. Wright is not everyone's favourite New Testament scholar, and there are other directions in which one might move towards such a vision. However one construes it though, the justice or righteousness of God embraces the right relationship of all things in Christ and underlies the Church's participation in the *missio Dei*.

It is regrettable though not surprising that the word 'justice' became linked particularly with one half of the false dichotomy we have been considering; if the Church had been able to work in the categories of New Testament Greek, a missional vision based on the *dikaiosynē* of God[12] might have had the capacity to hold together participation in God's work to heal the broken relationship between humanity and God with participation in God's work to heal other broken dimensions of relationship, especially between human beings. And we might have been better able to act according to the principle that most Christians acknowledge, that love of God and love of neighbour cannot be separated, that the love of God which freely opens for humanity a way of justification in Jesus Christ is the same love that holds out in Jesus Christ a pattern for the reconciliation of all things in the justice of *shalōm*.

Both the missional emphasis on 'righteousness' and the one on 'justice' in their own ways and in the sphere of their own priorities recognize the importance of what one could call prophetic challenge. They both affirm the keynote call of Jesus as Mark's Gospel programmatically has it: '*metanoiete*' – repentance,[13] a change of direction. The sadness is that in the prophetic tradition of the Hebrew Bible, the Old Testament, turning back in recognition of covenant to a right relationship with Yahweh cannot be held apart from turning to one's neighbour in fairness and care, especially for those especially vulnerable, the alien and the poor, the orphan and the widow.

Arguably, what has in some parts of the Church helped towards a greater rapprochement between these two missional traditions in more recent decades has been a growing awareness of the need for a dialogical dimension alongside the prophetic. One aspect of this has been the rapidly expanding realization of the importance of *context* and of listening to it. For example,

---

11 Wright, *Paul and the Faithfulness of God*.

12 The phrase 'the righteousness of God' is of course one that has been very much debated in both New Testament and theological scholarship over the years; these debates while sometimes having connections to the point I have been making do not on the whole bear centrally upon it. Mark Seifrid, *Christ, Our Righteousness*, Leicester: Apollos, 2000 gives a good idea of the debates to which it contributes.

13 It is regrettable that the English words 'repentance' and 'conversion' often used to translate *metanoia* have come to have narrow 'religious' connotations rather than a more broad and life-affirming range of 'changes of direction'.

from the perspective of my viewpoint in Britain, the dominant model across much of the Church for engaging the neighbour with the message of God's justifying love has shifted from one of which Billy Graham was the primary example to one of which the Alpha Course is the prime example.[14] A second aspect has been the increasing formation of partnerships with diverse bodies – within and outside the Church – to work for greater justice, both in terms of campaigning and in practical action to alleviate poverty. This has often been true both at the grassroots level, where parishes and congregations have learned better to engage with community action and local government and services and on the larger scale of regional, national and international efforts to create a more just world.

Every understanding of the kind of restored relationship that God's reconciling love ushers in, every vision of missional justice, needs both to be prophetic in its challenge to the broken relationships that it encounters and to respond with sensitive wisdom to the realities that have contributed to their existence and growth. The balance of the prophecy and dialogue will vary in each situation of mission, and of course they cannot be neatly separated or measured, and the danger of speaking thus is that it can make missional engagement sound like a clinical assessment – a great danger in the contemporary West given that this is the tendency of our cultures.[15] But, for example, in a context of ethnic cleansing, gross oppression or conspicuous inequality, the prophetic dimensions of Christian speech and action are likely to be more to the fore, whereas in getting alongside a family in which relationships are strained to breaking point because of incompatibilities and complicated personal histories, skills in dialogue will be in evidence as Christians look for ways of being that are as just as possible for all involved. Or (for it is as possible for the prophetic challenge to be necessary on the smaller scale and dialogical listening at the larger), domestic violence may need to be forcefully confronted with a demand for justice for the vulnerable while peacemaking in areas of deep-rooted regional or tribal hostility and violence may require acute attention to historical and contemporary contexts and years of dialogue.[16]

In a parallel manner, within these and in every dynamic of Christian loving of the neighbour, the speaking of the name of Jesus and our perception of our graceful demand for justice as a bearing of witness to him will also sometimes suggest to us the uttering of a prophetic word and sometimes a patient process of dialogue and often will involve speech and action

---

14 I apologize for the element of caricature in choosing these big names – there are of course many other varieties both of 'proclamation evangelism' and of 'process evangelism'.

15 On this, see powerfully if provocatively, B. Thorne, *Infinitely Beloved*, London: Darton, Longman & Todd, 2003, 37ff., where (41) he inveighs against the language of 'standards', which brings with it 'a whole new army of evaluators, inspectors, surveillance monitors, appraisers, quality-control experts, thought police'.

16 None of this is intended to imply that mission is only reactive, though it might be read thus.

which cannot be neatly packaged out in this way. Almost all Christians will have experienced the tensions of knowing how and when to speak of their faith and of Jesus as Lord in ways which are honest, bold, open, friendly, appropriate – one could extend a list of adjectives. This is an *art*, as also is every part of our lives as a step towards justice in our relationships and our world and towards the *dikaiosynē* of God.

Taken as heuristic and not as programmatic, a construal of mission as prophetic dialogue is a useful guide to help Christians, agents of God's mission, to weigh their creative engagement with the world's injustice, with its fractures, its brokenness, its evil. Where our horror at depravity and the darkest recesses of human wickedness rightly calls out of us the most forceful protest and condemnation, the reminder that we remain fundamentally also in a place of dialogue, even if that be temporarily occluded, is important. And when are trying patiently to understand as fully as we can the complex roots of pain in a community large or small, or are rejoicing in the astounding resilience and courage of some who are living on the edge, we have at the same time to be aware of the potential prophetic challenge that may emerge for our giving of attention.

Prophetic Dialogue and the Nature of Justice

Up to this point I have argued that a prophetic and dialogical model of mission can help us in broadening the scope of our ultimate vision of God's justice and of reconciled relationship, which much recent theology of mission agrees needs to be holistic and wide-ranging. Without losing that more extensive viewpoint, there is a further need to establish in the context of today's debates what the nature of 'justice' is; this is the case within the Church, but if our missional being is to be effective, Christian voices have also to be part of the debate within contemporary society.

How do we begin to establish what 'justice' is? What vision, what principles, what sources, guide our life towards what our culture might call rightly ordered life in society, or we within the Church might call God's perfection of relationship? This fundamental basis for our pursuit of justice – being able to name or envision in some fashion what is the goal of human and created life – is itself conflicted territory; therefore to understand some of the tensions and factors involved through a lens of prophetic dialogue helps us in our work.

The most obvious place for the Christian to start is from the roots of our faith and its traditions – in Scripture and the rich deposit of reflection upon it. In the previous section we have already taken this for granted in commenting upon the righteousness/justice of God. In virtually every part of the Bible there is reflection in one way or another on this aspect of the character of God and its implications for life: in the narrative parts of the Old Testament, in its psalmody, in the prophetic writings and the wisdom literature, in the Gospel accounts of Jesus' life and teaching, in Paul's and others' letters, in what we learn of the embryonic Church from them and from the Acts of the Apostles and the Revelation of John. A construal of justice along these lines is necessary and important for the practice of Christian mission, but is not a task to be undertaken here.[17]

Another place of beginning is in the understandings and practices of justice that predominate in the societies where we are actually living. While in the West this has itself been deeply influenced by the same Christian sources as we acknowledge, there have from early days been other channels also. Much serious discussion of the nature of justice, for example, begins with Aristotle, and while his significant contribution was for centuries in many ways absorbed into Christian theology, it stands in its own right and has since the Enlightenment come into its own again as an independent voice. From that time, and with rapidly growing speed in the nineteenth and twentieth centuries, the discourse of justice, whether in philosophical or in legal quarters, has like other areas of life together separated itself from any theological roots and become a 'secular' narrative. So the discussion of the nature of justice can start from a wrestling with the kind of debates that one may find among philosophers, or politicians, or social scientists, or the more serious journalists.

A dip into theological and missional writing on the subject of justice reveals that different Christians do indeed approach the subjects from these varied starting places. Daniel Groody explores the biblical roots of justice and develops a passionate spiritual and missional critique of the earth's and humanity's predicament on the foundation of his reading of Scripture and of the inherited reflection upon it – in his case primarily the rich resources of Catholic social teaching and liberation theology.[18] Nicholas Sagovsky, on the other hand, offers a wider spectrum of the totality of reflection on justice.[19] Chapters on the Old Testament and on Jesus, on Augustine and Aquinas are preceded by one on the Greeks and followed by one on the twentieth-century American philosopher John Rawls whose work on the theory of justice has been the major influence in this area of thought since it appeared in 1971. The subsequent discussion across four chapters, while thoroughly informed by his serious commitment to the Christian tradition – which he is trying to enunciate afresh for his day and place – is principally conducted in debate with Rawls and others who have critically engaged with him. A final chapter on the Eucharist and justice seeks to bring that extended debate back to the Church's ground.

---

17 It leads into contested territory of course: to give just a couple of examples, the weight to be given to such a notion as a divine 'bias to the poor' and to liberationist praxis, and (thinking of texts like Isaiah 58 and the book of James), the integration of the practice of justice into other dimensions of the religious life.

18 Groody, *Globalization*.

19 Nicholas Sagovsky, *Christian Tradition and the Practice of Justice*, London: SPCK, 2008.

Within a framework of prophetic dialogue it would not be entirely unfair, though obviously a generalizing simplification, to characterize Groody as speaking from a prophetic tradition and Sagovsky from within a dialogical tradition. Both of them are without doubt Christian and missional in intent; while like most Christians I might have my preferences (which in this chapter I am trying to hide as far as possible), more strongly I would want to argue for the legitimacy and the necessity of both approaches. The Church has to hold out with great boldness and confidence its distinctive vision of the truth of things, rooted in God the Trinity as we find God revealed to us in Jesus Christ. We have a prophetic duty to speak the truth as we see it and to live as best we can in accordance with that vision. At the same time the Church has to engage with the world as it is, listening with great care to its complexities, addressing what we find, taking it seriously in love, recognizing that the Holy Spirit works well beyond the boundaries we are tempted to draw. We have a duty to be in dialogue, to temper our boldness with humility[20] in an openness to find God's truth in surprising places.

The search for justice therefore, from within the contemporary Church in its longing (in which it hopes to identify with God's longing) for the world's reconciliation, has to have this constant holding together of the prophetic and the dialogical. There has to be both idealism and realism. This is not so much a balancing act, as a lived paradox, parallel to Jesus' statement that we are in the world but not of the world. It is in the world and for the world that we seek justice, and therefore we have to be passionately engaged with it. But engagement happens both to lovers, in the act of betrothal, and to enemies, in the act of battle. We get engaged to the beloved, we engage the enemy in warfare.

A third recent Christian discussion of the nature of justice is found in the writings of Stanley Hauerwas, who in typically provocative manner suggests that 'justice is a bad idea for Christians'. He argues that debates about the meaning of the term setting out from within the range of current options in the academy or in its practice are, for the Church, an abdication of its calling. 'So in the interests of working for justice, contemporary Christians allow their imaginations to be captured by the concepts of justice determined by the presuppositions of liberal societies.'[21] A particular target of his suspicion is not surprisingly the same John Rawls whose *Theory of Justice* Sagovsky has used by no means uncritically but also with considerable approval. Although Hauerwas might appear more strikingly prophetic than dialogical – and inimitably challenging to certain kinds of dialogue

---

20 'a bold humility – or a humble boldness' is a phrase of David Bosch's (*Transforming Mission*, Maryknoll, NY: Orbis, 1991, 489), originally in the context of interfaith dialogue, that has struck a chord with many; see W. Saayman and K. Kritzinger (eds), *Mission in Bold Humility: David Bosch's Work Considered*, Maryknoll, NY: Orbis, 1996.

21 Stanley Hauerwas, 'The Politics of Justice: Why Justice is a Bad Idea for Christians' in *After Christendom*, Nashville, TN: Abingdon, 1991, 63.

– actually as in much of his writing the stirring of the waters is conducted through a kind of dialogue.

A fourth recent theological commentator on justice is Duncan Forrester.[22] At the end of the first part of his book, on the nature of justice, he cites Hauerwas with approval:

> 'As Christians', writes Stanley Hauerwas, 'we will speak more truthfully to our society and be of greater service by refusing to continue the illusion that the larger social order knows what it is talking about when it calls for justice. But we also have to clarify the account of justice which lies at the heart of Christian faith and experience and see whether it may be constructively employed in relation to tricky issues of public policy, which have such deep impact on human flourishing.'[23]

This suggests that Forrester's book is more in a dialogical vein than a prophetic, but a reading of the whole perhaps points out the dangers inherent in my attempt to analyse in these terms. The final section of the book, four chapters of 'Theological Fragments'[24] are a powerful attempt to bring Christian theology and tradition to bear on the injustices of our world and might arguably be held out as a model of holding together prophecy and dialogue.

However, granting this danger, if we pursue these distinctions, it is noteworthy that Sagovsky himself points in this direction. He writes of 'another account of justice' from his own kind of conversation: one which 'would have embraced communitarian and socialist thinkers with very different priorities', 'would have stressed equality before it stressed opportunity', and

> would have put more stress upon the Christian community as one in which the eschatological values of the Kingdom are realized here and now, so that it presents to society the clear vision of justice, equality and hope – rather than the liberal gradualism which characterizes the account in this book.[25]

His own conversation engages most substantially, as we have seen, with Rawls and with other contemporaries such as Amartya Sen, whereas he recognizes that the other kind would have pursued the discussion with Rousseau, Hegel, Marx and Habermas – and among theologians he specific-

22 Duncan Forrester, *Christian Justice and Public Policy*, Cambridge: Cambridge University Press, 1997.

23 Forrester, *Christian Justice and Public Policy*, 60. A further major contribution deserving attention here had space permitted is the work of Alasdair MacIntyre, esp. *Whose Justice? Which Rationality?*, London: Duckworth/UNDP, 1988. The footnote comes here as MacIntyre especially dwells on the notion of competing justices implied in the citation from Hauerwas.

24 Forrester, *Christian Justice and Public Policy*, 193–259.

25 All citations from Sagovsky, *Christian Tradition and the Practice of Justice*, xix.

ally cites Hauerwas. He goes on to imply that this other tradition, directly related to Catholic social teaching, has more to say about social and structural transformation, which he wants to hold onto alongside (what one infers is his own emphasis) 'work towards the social consent that will bring about structural change'. While he does not use the word, he is acknowledging here his own desire to be dialogical. Sagovsky is clear enough that although he is, in terms of his own work on justice, engaging primarily with one trajectory, the other is a necessary 'partner', in the sense of both helpmeet and of sparring partner; each hones its own ways of being by virtue both of its opposition to, but also its necessary counterbalancing by, the other.

It is worth picking up in our own context of the practice of prophetic dialogue his phrase 'two kinds of conversation'. This can perhaps shed light on the model: it suggests that each stream, the prophetic and the dialogical, tends towards its own set of discussion partners, within history and in contemporary debate and practice, but that each also needs the other as both friend and foe, as complement and contrary. So in relation to the pursuit of justice, more prophetic, countercultural, and thus perhaps confrontational missional ways of being, speaking and acting should be practised alongside more dialogical, consensual and attentive missional ways of being, speaking and acting.

Thus while it is most natural to assign 'justice' to the 'prophetic' dimension of mission,[26] Sagovsky offers a model for a 'dialogical' approach to the theology of justice. This needs to be respected even by those who find it difficult.[27] It is likely that the Church will always have its 'denouncers' and its 'seekers of consensus', and that there will always be disagreement between them. These differences can have manifold roots: some are genuinely theological, some are contextual, some are temperamental, and some are based on experience (which one might regard as the intersection of context and temperament). As we pursue justice for God's sake and for the sake of our neighbour, we need to weigh these differences, especially when we find fellow Christians' views or practices very hard to fathom. This is not to rule out the rejection in the end of their views or their practices; but this

26 As Bevans and Schroeder themselves do: 'The second way that mission is prophecy is, in the spirit of the Old Testament prophets like Amos, Hosea, and Isaiah, its clear critique and exposure of any kind of injustice in the world ... working for justice is a *constitutive part* of the prophetic preaching of the gospel.' *Prophetic Dialogue: Reflection on Christian Mission Today*, Maryknoll, NY: Orbis, 2011, 60.

27 If anyone were to make the charge that such approaches will always lead to ineffective missional practice in terms of addressing injustice, Sagovsky has also within the UK context set an interesting example of bold witness – that might be best construed as both prophetic and dialogical – in an area in which he has become deeply involved, around policy and practice with regard to immigration and asylum. See for example *Fit for Purpose Yet?* the report of the Independent Asylum Commission of which he was co-author: www.citizensforsanctuary. org.uk/pages/reports/InterimFindings.pdf.

must be done with care. We can be angry, but we must also be loving. And this is a way of being that a recognition of mission as prophetic dialogue can help us achieve.

Justice and Prophetic Dialogue: an Example

At this point it will help to give some kind of example of the application of a prophetic dialogical missional approach to justice in practice. Hardy writes of the 'torn, troubled form' of the world he knows, of 'continents of moil and misery'. One major justice issue facing the world and therefore the Church in our time, and quite clearly involving the misery of the continents, is the matter of migration, of inequalities between different parts of the earth leading many to move in the hope of better life, greater security, prosperity, peace – a wide variety of mixed motives.

In Britain, and this is largely true of many other so-called 'developed' countries – ironically one might ask whether the attitudes in question justify the label – attitudes towards immigrants are often hostile, and thus there is a temptation for parties seeking democratic election to government to outdo one another in seeking popularity through putting forward the toughest policies. Finding policies that are fair to the incomer, the stranger and also to the indigenous population, and then implementing them justly, is inevitably contested territory.

For the past six and a half years I have worked one morning a week as an assistant chaplain at one of the UK's 'Immigration Removal Centres', places in which foreign nationals whom the government believes have no legal right to remain in the country are held pending legal and practical arrangements for their removal. The questions of justice around these men's[28] detention are manifold and conflicted. While the details will be different in other nations, similar questions of what is just with regard to immigration policy and practice are widely debated at many levels in countries across the globe – for the nature of the crisis is that it is worldwide. Indeed the nature of what is at stake, the freedom or otherwise of people to travel across the world, usually to escape deprivation of some kind, makes it hard to think of another set of justice questions that is more truly global, except that of climate and the physical future of the planet.[29]

My purpose here is not to enter into the resolution of these questions of justice, either in general global terms or in relation to the specifics of the British system. Rather, through pointing to some of the complexities involved and clarifying that these are undoubtedly missional matters, we may recommend the benefit of Christian approaches that may fairly be described as following a path of prophetic dialogue.

---

28 In the centre where I work only men are detained.

29 Nuclear questions of course affect all, but rarely affect the residents of poorer countries as directly as do matters of migration.

We can identify a range of overlapping matters of justice that impact upon migration and the policing of it. There are manifold issues of economic and trade justice influencing people's desire to be here, there or elsewhere. Immigration cannot be held entirely separate from these issues which deeply affect it. The wealth of the Christian tradition's reflection upon and teaching about poverty and fairness in trading needs to be brought to bear on these issues, as happens widely through the relevant arms of the various churches and through para-church Christian agencies and campaign groups. At the same time, this goes on alongside listening with understanding to the claims and responses of governments, companies and other players in establishing the economic and trading environment. Within these processes the effects upon the lives of those who might end up as migrants are significant. Factors such as the substantial biblical and Christian commitment to those with little or no status, the 'lowly' and 'hungry' of Luke 2, over against the 'proud', 'powerful' and 'rich', have to be carefully weighed as they are brought into the discussion.

The controlling of borders, the criteria for granting and refusing visas (and their application) and the handling of claims for asylum are clearly important matters of justice which generate powerful emotions and arguments. The compassion of the Jewish and Christian stories to the resident alien has to be clearly expressed and heard; so too do arguments, in the UK context, with regard to the size of our islands and the density of population. These will be assessed in diverse ways by prophets and those who seek dialogue – and many people will be in both categories.[30] There is a fairly constant need to be asking both of oneself and of others where selfish or prejudiced motivation is interfering with what might genuinely be the demands of justice.

What is a just response to foreigners who commit crimes? In some countries these are people who, once the penalty for the crime has been paid according to the law, are detained pending their enforced return to their country of origin. Is this second penalty just for them and for our society? Does the breaching of the country's immigration laws ever justify the breaking up of a family in order to return one parent to another country? What, if any, are the appropriate restrictions for those who have broken immigration laws, and how might that change if one questions the justice of the laws themselves? Wrestling with such questions and putting forward arguments for what we understand as just in the light of our theology, our prayer and our humanity in Christ is part of the Church's missional calling. Not every Christian or every congregation – far from it – will be heavily involved in this aspect of mission; but some need to be on behalf of the whole, and among them are needed both those whose outlook is primarily prophetic and those

---

30 My argument entails that the Church as a whole *must* be in both categories.

whose outlook is primarily dialogical – and those whom we cannot so easily pigeonhole in this way.

Alongside these larger structural matters, in my own involvement I face daily decisions about how to relate to detainees and officers inside the centre. Listening to detainees, often across language barriers, and explaining that I am not a lawyer, handling my doubts and frustrations, sifting what I hear, offering encouragement and hope that is not just religious platitudes, respecting officers doing good work and showing care in difficult circum-stances and attending to their own dilemmas, discerning where something needs taking further within the structures of the institution, or where to challenge those structures when I question them, in the knowledge that my presence requires of me a large measure of acceptance of them. Within these and many other questions of engagement I find helpful, at the practical level and not just the theological, a viewpoint that makes sense of the balancing acts required; though I often prefer to think of them not so much as balanc-ing acts as the holding onto both parts of a paradox. I may not always or even often articulate it in terms of 'prophetic dialogue', but when I reflect on the experience of offering this presence as a whole, such an articulation feels right.

Conclusion

This is just one example of the many hotly contested areas of justice with which Christian mission has to engage. Christians do so believing that there is lasting significance in longing and working for relationships that reflect as well as we can possibly imagine the peace that exists between Father, Son and Spirit. We reject Hardy's vision of the sadness of human endeavour as a pale and profitless shadow. But to make 'sense' of our engagement we need ways of envisaging and embodying our task that hold together in creative tension the goals that we perceive as God's and the realities of the lives of our neighbours near and far. In the pursuit of justice, a model of prophetic dialogue offers an effective structure for being and working amid the moil and misery, beauty and brokenness of our world within the conviction of its and our ultimate reconciliation.

PART 4

Soteriology: Salvation as Prophetic Dialogue

8

Reconciliation and Prophetic Dialogue

ROBERT SCHREITER

Introduction

Reconciliation began to emerge as a significant theme in the public forum with the political upheavals of the 1990s, following upon the end of the Cold War. There was a twofold concern at the time that prompted interest in reconciliation. On the one hand, the need for the reconstruction of authoritarian societies was much in evidence as the Soviet Union's empire crumbled. A whole range of societies needed to find ways out of an authoritarian grip, come to terms with their histories and find ways to build a culture of trust that could be the basis for civil society. On the other hand, numerous armed conflicts that were raging within countries – rather than between countries – made creating an environment of healing and renewal imperative if these countries were to survive and flourish. Events in the 1990s themselves, such as the United Nations' commemoration in 1992 of indigenous peoples, the Rwandan genocide of 1994 and the fall of apartheid in South Africa, called for a healing of memories, the pursuit of justice and the building of something new that would foreclose a return to the violence of the past.

The theme of reconciliation had of course its precedents, both in a long history and with more recent events. As to the latter, one may recall the appeal for racial reconciliation that had been set forth in the United States in the wake of the Civil Rights movement of the 1970s,[1] and appeals to look ahead to the end of apartheid in South Africa in the 1980s.[2] There were also misuses of the idea of reconciliation, as it was denounced in Argentina after the 'dirty war' there (1979–83) and in the *Kairos* document in South Africa (1985). In both of these cases, reconciliation was being presented as 'leaving the past behind us and going into the future together'. In effect, this amounted to forgetting the suffering of victims and forgoing any seeking of justice for victims – essentially impunity for the perpetrators.

---

1 J. Deotis Roberts, *Liberation and Reconciliation: A Black Theology*, Philadelphia: Westminster Press, 1971.

2 See especially the account in J. N. J. Kritzinger, 'Black Theology: Challenge to Mission', unpublished DTh dissertation, University of South Africa, Pretoria.

Why the sudden interest in reconciliation in those two decades? Reconciliation is admittedly an ancient theme. It finds ritual expression in small-scale societies around the world, where enmities cannot be permitted to smoulder indefinitely, lest the interdependence that those small-scale societies need to survive be threatened. Some opined that reconciliation became an attractive theme precisely in the two final decades of the twentieth century because the utopian themes that had dominated so much of the nineteenth and twentieth centuries had exhausted themselves. Something was needed to deal with a past that continued to have a stranglehold on the present and was precluding a different kind of future. Moreover, strategies for seeking justice and bringing about positive change in society were found to be much more complex than some of the prescriptions presented earlier had supposed. In its own way, reconciliation was a more modest approach to bringing about change and improvement in the lives of those who had suffered.

Changes in the understanding of Christian mission intersected with these larger movements in societies around the world. Since the late 1970s mission was being re-envisioned in conciliar Protestant and Roman Catholic settings. This re-envisioning had happened in the wake of the end of colonialism and the acknowledgement of Christian mission's deep implication with this ideology. What emerged were two important shifts in the understanding of mission. First of all, mission was now being seen not only from the perspective of the missionary, but also from the perspective of the interaction between the missionary and the communities where mission was taking place. This shift recognized the mutuality (as well as the asymmetries of power) that was at play in missionary activity. Second, there was a move away from thinking about mission solely from a priori concepts of mission towards much more contextual ones. Thus, mission was not just about saving souls and planting churches (although these themes remained), but also about concrete venues of the quest for salvation. Among those that came to be so defined were inculturation, interreligious dialogue, the pursuit of justice and an option for the poor. Both of these changes – greater mutuality and commitment to the concrete demands of context – were viewed theologically in a distinctive way; namely what was God's action in the world, and was accompanied by a commitment to the incarnation as a guiding principle for the conduct of mission.

These changed attitudes towards mission then provided a ready entry for mission into the discourses of reconciliation. A concern for relationships that needed to be healed and restored, as well as engaging the concrete needs of communities and larger societies for a new wholeness and integrity, were a good fit for the renewed soteriological shapes that mission was taking. In the 1990s, mission and reconciliation came together, with the Christian understanding of reconciliation providing a fruitful theological framework for this encounter.

This chapter begins by looking at the Christian understanding of reconciliation as it frames an approach to mission today. It offers a theology of reconciliation that can support mission and then turns to the practices of reconciliation that constitute its engagement with situations in need of reconciliation. In a second part, it turns to engaging in a twofold manner this understanding of reconciliation with the theme of mission as prophetic dialogue: (1) how mission as reconciliation embodies the perspectives of mission as prophetic dialogue, and (2) what mission as reconciliation and mission as prophetic dialogue have to say to each other, at the present time. Does mission as reconciliation give us a deeper insight into mission as prophetic dialogue? Does mission as prophetic dialogue present challenges to mission as reconciliation?

Reconciliation as Mission: Its Theology

The theme of reconciliation is prominent in the Scriptures, even though it is generally not spoken about directly. The word 'reconciliation' does not appear in the Hebrew Scriptures, although we find there powerful stories of reconciliation, such as that of Esau and Jacob and of Joseph and his brothers. Forms of the word 'reconciliation' occur only 14 times in the New Testament, with all but two of them being in the Pauline corpus. Paul's message has been called a 'gospel of reconciliation' inasmuch as he had experienced being reconciled to God and the followers of Jesus by a gracious act on the part of God and not due to anything that he himself had done.

The key passage for understanding God's reconciling the world to God's own self is in Romans 5.1–11. There God's reconciling action is presented as God's free gift to a sinful humanity through the death of Jesus Christ and the outpouring of the Holy Spirit: while we were still sinners, Christ died for us.

God's reconciling act through the death and resurrection of Christ is not only the central exposition of the Christian understanding of reconciliation. It is embedded in the central narrative of Christianity itself: of God creating the world, humankind's fall from grace, God's sending the Son into the world and how the passion and death of the Son restores humanity to God's friendship. Within that narrative, themes of alienation, suffering, healing, justice and forgiveness find concrete form and their relationship to one another. It is this narrative of reconciliation that forms what theologians call 'vertical reconciliation'; that is, our being reconciled to God by God's gracious action, not by any merit of our own. This vertical reconciliation is celebrated and re-enacted in the liturgy of the Church through its sacraments.

Christians believe that 'horizontal reconciliation' – reconciliation between human beings, societies and with the earth itself – is possible because of vertical reconciliation. It makes possible a 'new creation' as is spoken of in

2 Corinthians 5.17–20. Indeed, that same passage speaks of a message and ministry of reconciliation being entrusted to us by God. The message is that reconciliation is indeed possible, and it is a duty of Christians to bring this reconciliation to a world much in need of healing and forgiveness. Other passages in the New Testament speak of this message and ministry, most notably Ephesians 2.12–20, where reconciliation between Jew and Gentile is made possible in the household of God.

Theologically, these biblical passages can be elaborated upon and focused with five headings. They are presented here, along with some of the implications they have for mission. First of all, reconciliation is the work of God, who makes it a gift to us. In turn, we are called to cooperate in God's reconciling activity. Only God can bring about reconciliation; that is the message of Romans 5.1–11. While the ministry of reconciliation is entrusted to us, it remains dependent upon God's action.

What are some of the consequences of this principle for mission? First of all, true reconciliation does not come about because of what we do. Our effectiveness as messengers and ministers of reconciliation arises out of our cooperation with God. Anyone who has worked for reconciliation, especially social reconciliation, knows how difficult and frustrating it can be. There are usually more failures than successes, and even those successes are usually only partial ones. We are at best mediators of God's work. Now such an attitude is not a warrant for passivity in the face of alienation, suffering and injustice. It is but a sober recognition of the dynamics of reconciliation and the challenging contexts in which it takes place.

A corollary to this principle is that our effectiveness as mediators, as ministers of reconciliation will depend upon the quality of our communion with God. In other words, it is our deepening communion with God that makes us worthy and effective 'ambassadors of Christ' (cf. 2 Cor. 5.19). We need to seek out spiritual disciplines that will facilitate and sustain a deepening communion. One such set of spiritual disciplines can be found in the mystical and contemplative traditions of the Church, where our intentions and outlook are gradually purified as we learn how to wait upon God and listen for God's speaking. Rather than our speaking to God in praise, thanksgiving and intercession, we learn to wait for God to speak. Besides deepening our communion with God, such contemplative waiting also helps us attend more closely to the settings where reconciliation is most desperately needed.

Seen from this perspective, it can be said that reconciliation is more a spirituality than a strategy. Strategies and techniques are important and necessary tools, but every situation calling for reconciliation is different – in its history, its actors and its sought-after outcomes. A spirituality of communion with God provides a framing of the situation so that God's action within the situation might be discerned, and what our experience and knowledge have taught us can be brought to bear in the best way possible.

Moreover, such a spirituality helps us care better for ourselves and those around us in the trying circumstances of work for reconciliation.

A second principle is that God begins the reconciling process with the healing of the victim. Most people envision reconciliation as happening when wrongdoers show remorse for what they have done and then apologize and seek the forgiveness of the victim. If the victim can accept the apology and extend forgiveness, then reconciliation can happen. This is indeed an acceptable framework for understanding and working towards reconciliation. But quite often the wrongdoers do not apologize and seek forgiveness; they may even believe that there is nothing to be sorry for. Or in the case of massive wrongdoing, we may not even know who they are. And if the wrongdoing took place in a distant past, the wrongdoers may be dead and so cannot apologize. Where do all of these scenarios leave the victim? Is the victim to be held hostage to past events because no one apologizes? We know of circumstances in which victims can come to healing and sometimes even to forgiveness without the wrongdoers' change of mind. How is this possible? Christians believe this can happen because God begins the healing process in the lives of victims, by restoring their humanity and human dignity that were wrested away from them by the harmful things done against them. Christians believe that we are made in the image and likeness of God (Gen. 1.26–27), and healing can be understood as restoring us to that image and to the agency it implies. That God should begin with the victim is not surprising. It is borne out in a consistent picture of God as caring for the orphan and the widow, the stranger and the prisoner. The option for the poor, a central tenet of Catholic social teaching, expresses that same insight in a yet broader way.

What this implies for a ministry of reconciliation is that special attention is given to victims. Work with wrongdoers remains important and imperative, but special attention is given to victims who have been alienated and marginalized by their suffering. What Latin American theologians have called 'accompaniment' is a practical consequence of this insight. To be sure, not every victim will experience healing in this way, and to try to force this trajectory on victims can victimize them once again. What is meant here is that healing and even forgiveness cannot be blocked by intransigent or absent wrongdoers; God has a way of acting apart from them.

A third principle is that the healing process in reconciliation makes of the victim (and the healed wrongdoer) a 'new creation' (cf. 2 Cor. 5.17). This means that the healing process does not return victims to a status quo ante, but rather takes them to a new place. This new place is often one that they would not have anticipated or imagined. The experience of that new, unexpected place is often one of grace, of something having been freely given to them.

A consequence of this experience of being brought to a new place sometimes (not always) awakens within the healed victim a call or vocation.

Often that call is to help others who have gone through the same experience of loss and harm; at other times, it becomes a commitment to work with wrongdoers and help them along the road to healing. One can thus become aware of a call to become a minister of reconciliation out of the experience of having experienced reconciliation.

A fourth principle has to do with coming to terms with suffering. Suffering in and of itself is not redemptive. On the contrary, it can be isolating and destructive of relationships and of one's own self. A path towards reconciliation requires finding a way to cope with suffering. A way this is frequently done is by connecting one's own narrative of suffering to a larger, redemptive narrative. Christians frequently do this by connecting their suffering to the story of the suffering and death of Christ. In so doing, they hope to find in that larger narrative, central to Christianity's own self-understanding, redemption of their own suffering. By placing their suffering in Christ's own suffering, they hope to discover a way out of suffering that not only does not destroy them, but brings them into deeper communion with a reconciling God.

Participating in the suffering of Christ has long been seen as part of Christian discipleship. By patterning our suffering onto the suffering of Christ, we hope too to come to know the power of the resurrection (Phil. 3.10–11). This does not glorify or commend suffering. What it does is allow suffering to become a spiritual discipline that brings us into deeper communion with a God who alone can overcome all forms of suffering. Thus, suffering can become a kind of 'school' that tutors us deeper into the mystery of the reality in which we find ourselves. It can also help us see more clearly the challenges of a ministry of reconciliation.

The fifth and final principle is that reconciliation will only be complete when God has reconciled the whole universe in Christ (Eph. 1.10), when God will be 'all in all' (1 Cor. 15.28). Even with our best efforts at reconciliation, we come to realize that what we achieve is always incomplete. This arises out of the complexity of situations calling out for reconciliation (both in their current extent and past development), as well as our incapacity to effect completely what we set out to do. We are again reminded that God is the author of all reconciliation: our effectiveness as ministers of reconciliation depends on the quality of our communion with God.

A consequence of this principle is that our ministries of reconciliation must find ways to engender and sustain hope as we struggle towards greater reconciliation. Christians see hope not as an estimate of what we ourselves can achieve, but as a gift from God. Again, a dimension of the spirituality of reconciliation is the capacity to hope. We learn and discover hope in many different ways. One such way is a capacity to see and celebrate the small victories that portend a greater reconciliation. These small victories (in anticipation of larger ones) are for us moments of grace where we see God at work.

With this capacity for hope, we see reconciliation as the work of God coming full circle: God is both the author and the end of reconciliation. It is our participation in this action of God – another way of seeing the *missio Dei* or the Trinitarian God's activity in the world – that makes reconciliation possible.

Reconciliation as Mission: Its Practices

How then does a theology of reconciliation shape the practices of reconciliation as a form of mission? We need to begin with some aspects of how reconciliation itself is to be understood. Two preliminary considerations need to be made before turning to that question.

First of all, reconciliation is both a process and a final goal. Too often people want to jump immediately to the end point, when reconciliation has been achieved by overcoming past enmity and alienation. Such a move fails to recognize the complexity of reconciliation and the many dimensions that need to be taken into consideration. Moreover, if reconciliation is really about becoming a 'new creation', then that end point can only be partially imagined at the beginning: what will count ultimately as reconciliation may be beyond the hopes and expectations at an earlier stage. Reconciliation is both a process and an end goal. The process is not simply a means to an end; it is part of the transformative nature of reconciliation itself. Hence it becomes important to attend as much to the process as to its final point.

Second, the process of reconciliation is seldom a linear one. The frustrations, disappointments and setbacks one experiences in reconciliation are well known to anyone who has tried to engage in practices of reconciliation. The process often uncovers unsuspected and unknown dimensions that need to be healed. One has to be prepared to double back at times as these elements present themselves.

Having stated these two caveats, one can now ask: just what is reconciliation? The simple answer is that reconciliation is about healing the past and building a different kind of future, such that the painful experiences in the past cannot be repeated. Healing the past, building the future: this is the challenge of reconciliation. Put another way, it is about restoring trust and rebuilding relationships.

What then are the principal practices that constitute a ministry of reconciliation? Four of them need to be named here.

The first is *healing* in its multiple dimensions – the healing of memories, the healing of victims and the healing of wrongdoers. The healing of memories has to do with healing our relationship to past wrongdoing. Memory is not a direct record of the past; rather, it must be seen as our relationship in the present to the past. Memory is the narrative that tries to capture the meaning of the past for our present situation. In the healing of memories, memory is not dismissed or denied. It is allowed to change so that it does not unduly restrict present or future possibilities. Roman Catholic Church documents often speak of the 'purification' of memory, an attempt to capture this transformation of memory. The narrative of memory changes as the healing process takes place, draining memory of much of its toxic character and establishes as best it can patterns of meaning that can shape and orient future thought and action. Some of what this entails will be seen shortly in the second practice of reconciliation, which is truth-telling. What is evident already in the practices of healing memories is the importance of narrative or story as the carrier of meaning that helps reposition actors in their relations with self, others, the world and God.

The healing of victims is a dimension of the healing process. As was noted in the theological principles of reconciliation, the healing of victims is about the restoration of their dignity as being made in the image and likeness of God and their regaining agency to act out of that dignity. Accompaniment of victims in the healing process is one of the most important dimensions of the ministry of reconciliation. That process entails creating safe and hospitable spaces where victims can examine their wounds and come to terms with the loss and change of direction that is entailed. This involves too coming clear of the stranglehold that past wrongdoing can have over their lives.

Also important is a third dimension of healing, the healing of wrongdoers. This is often made difficult by the wrongdoers themselves, who may deny or underestimate the harm that they have done. Here the ancient penitential practices of the Church provide an outline of the practices needed: acknowledgement of wrongdoing, remorse, seeking forgiveness, amendment of life and accepting punishment for the wrongdoing. Separation from the community may also be required as part of the process.[3] A healing of wrongdoers so that they may be reintegrated into the community is something that not always can be achieved.

A second principal practice of reconciliation is *truth-telling*. Situations that need to be addressed in reconciliation have often been distorted by lies told about the victims and the wrongdoers and by a pall of silence thrown over the wrongdoing to hide or disguise it and its effects. Part of rebuilding the narrative and of restoring the agency of victims involves speaking the truth about what has happened. It is upon such actions of truth that a future can be built that overcomes the suffering of the past.

The work of numerous Truth and Reconciliation Commissions that have been implemented since 1970 has helped us see the importance of truth-telling, but also the complexity and difficulty of speaking the truth even with the best of intentions and efforts. The Truth and Reconciliation Commission that worked in South Africa after the end of apartheid there, has provided one of the most useful classifications of the kinds of truth that need to be sought. They note four types: (1) objective or forensic truth – the 'who,

---

3 For a contemporary use of these rituals, see Jay Carney, 'Roads to Reconciliation: An Emerging Paradigm of African Theology', *Modern Theology* 26 (2010), 549–59.

what, when and where' of past events; (2) personal or existential truth – the 'why' of past events; (3) dialogical truth – a truthful narrative in which both sides can recognize themselves; and (4) moral truth – what can be learned from past events for the sake of a better future.[4] All of these forms of truth need to be sought after and engaged. The capacity to acknowledge and to articulate the truth about past events is an important part of victims' gaining agency in the transformation of their own experience of the past.

A third principal practice is the *pursuit of justice*. Pursuing justice is an important consequence of having sought the truth. It should be noted that seeking out the truth is something that needs to be done before undertaking the pursuit of justice. Otherwise, the justice sought and meted out risks becoming 'victors' justice' – retaliation or revenge against the wrongdoers. Such justice will typically continue the cycles of violence.

Like truth, justice admits of multiple dimensions. Most often, three forms of justice need to be pursued. The first is *punitive justice*, whereby wrong-doers are identified, the wrongdoing is examined and punishment for the wrongdoing is meted out. It is important that punitive justice be done in an orderly way that respects human rights; in so doing, it becomes a model for dealing with injustice in the future. Consequently, proper persons and structures must be used, such as juridical and legal institutions of a society. Not to do so perpetuates a climate of wrongdoing.

The second is *restorative justice*. If punitive justice is aimed at wrong-doers, restorative justice is directed towards victims. It involves restoring to them their dignity and anything that rightfully belongs to them. While punitive justice is provided for by a legal system, channels of restorative justice often arise in civil society and through social institutions. In speaking of reconciliation as a form of mission, it is especially bringing about restorative justice that is the arena for mission activity.

The third is *structural justice*. Structural justice aims at changing structures in a society in such a way that the wrongdoing of the past will have less chance of being repeated. It may involve too supporting structures that will reduce violence in a society, such as guaranteeing access for all citizens to a better life through education and employment. As a form of mission, it involves working with a society to get laws and structures in place that will achieve these ends.

Pursuing justice is an essential part of reconciliation as a form of mission. Without greater measures of justice, social reconciliation will not be possible. At the same time, however, it is important to recognize that we cannot expect full justice to be achieved (see the fifth theological principle above). Hence to think that nothing can be done towards reconciliation until there is full justice forgets that reconciliation is both a process and

---

4 John W. de Gruchy, *Reconciliation: Restoring Justice*, Minneapolis: Fortress Press, 2002, chapters 5 and 6, provides a good account of this.

a final goal. Such an attitude can end up paralysing or even occluding the reconciliation process.

The fourth practice is *forgiveness*. Like reconciliation itself, forgiveness is both a process and a final goal. It is something that comes out of the restored agency of victims, in either personal or social forgiveness. It typically comes later in processes of reconciliation, after healing, truth-telling and some measure of justice have been achieved. A danger in reconciliation as a form of mission is to try to introduce forgiveness too early in a process. Christians have a tendency to do this because of Jesus' own mandates to forgive. Conditions for forgiveness need to mature before an appeal for forgiveness can be genuinely heard and embraced.

Nonetheless, forgiveness is something that cannot be ignored. If no measure of forgiveness can be extended, then victims remain in the thrall of the wrongdoing of the past – it continues to shape their view of the world and of themselves.[5] It forecloses a different kind of future. Forgiving does not condone past wrongdoing: what was wrong remains wrong. Nor does forgiving mean that we forgo punishment. Punishment may be necessary for a variety of reasons, both personal and social.

Christians believe forgiveness is possible because it is rooted in the forgiveness and mercy of God. When we forgive, we participate in God's mercy. And it is out of the strength of God's grace that we are able to forgive.

This brief overview of the practices of reconciliation as mission cannot capture all the forms involved. It does, however, give the basic architecture of reconciliation as a form of mission. It is now time to turn to the relation of reconciliation as a form of mission to prophetic dialogue.

Reconciliation as Prophetic Dialogue

What can be said of mission as reconciliation as a form of prophetic dialogue? Mission as reconciliation, as we have seen, is an expression of a Christian view of soteriology, closely linked to the central Christian narrative itself about the *missio Dei* in the world. It rests upon the account of that narrative in Romans 5.1–11. In this section, how the theology and practices of reconciliation as a form of mission conforms to prophetic dialogue will be explored: first as a form of *dialogue* and then as a form of *prophecy*.[6]

The discussions of the dialogue dimension of prophetic dialogue have focused on the Trinitarian dialogue – both in its immanent and its economic forms – and dialogue as a form of spirituality. The dialogue among the

---

5 This idea is captured in the title of Archbishop Desmond Tutu's memoir of his leadership of the Truth and Reconciliation Commission in South Africa: *No Future without Forgiveness*, New York: Doubleday, 1999.

6 Of the various accounts of prophetic dialogue that have been presented by Stephen Bevans and Roger Schroeder, I will be drawing principally upon the one in their *Prophetic Dialogue: Reflections on Christian Mission Today*, Maryknoll, NY: Orbis, 2011.

persons of the Trinity and the communion that it connotes is coextensive with the dialogue the persons of the Trinity engage in the world. In turn, this dialogue becomes the prototype of all the forms of dialogue with which the Church engages the world. It is not simply communication for the sake of communication; it has a strong soteriological dimension. The communion into which the world is drawn is salvific for the world.

The same can be said for reconciliation. It is an embodiment of this communication with the world, creating deeper communion as well as healing and restoring relationships. One could indeed say that reconciliation as a form of mission is one of the prime sorts of the divine dialogue with the world, since its intentions of healing, restoring and sustaining relationships are its primary goal. One might even go so far as to call it the prototype of this prototype.

The driving force of this dialogue cannot be reduced to an instrumentalist vision of achieving an end once and for all. Rather dialogue has value for its own sake. It is for this reason, I believe, the Bevans and Schroeder consider it a spirituality – a way of living in the circle of the triune God. As was noted in the first section of this chapter, reconciliation is in many ways more a spirituality than a strategy. While strategies remain important and necessary, they are never in themselves sufficient. The spirituality of an ever deepening communion with God is at the very heart of reconciliation.

One trajectory of this ever deepening communion is to be found in the practices of healing that constitute a fundamental dimension of reconciliation. Healing is aimed at the conditions of possibility for greater communion: a developing sense of trust, a restoration of broken relationships, an openness to a 'new creation'. It interweaves the countless narratives of human beings as individuals and as societies with the soteriological narrative of the *missio Dei*. And we are increasingly aware of its interweaving of the planetary and cosmic narrative as well.

But it is more than practices of healing that constitute this dialogue. It is also evident in what John Paul Lederach has called the 'moral imagination', that is, the capacity to see the world as more than the sum of its polarities as well as the capacity to imagine something very different.[7] This 'capacity building' (to use the language of development) is part of the work of reconciliation – not only to meet the needs of the current situation but also to have the possibility of addressing challenges yet unseen. The moral imagination, in other words, is a more secular way of speaking about significant dimensions of spirituality.

Finally, dialogue enters one of its more daunting risks in acts of forgiveness. Forgiveness is the forging of a new relationship with a wrongdoer, even when the wrongdoer has not changed stance. It is not a condoning of the wrongful act, but is a leap beyond this to a vision of the wrongdoer as

---

7 John Paul Lederach, *The Moral Imagination: The Art and Soul of Building Peace*, New York: Oxford University Press, 2005.

part of God's creation. It is often a hope in the conversion of the wrongdoer rather than an affirmation of a conversion that has already taken place. Such risk-taking can teach us much about faith, about trust and about commitments to communication that are not yet visible. It is why forgiveness can be so difficult and at times seem impossible. It is why forgiveness most often happens in what might be seen as the final stages of a reconciliation process. It is caught in the poignant phrase of the letter to the Romans of the meaning of reconciliation: 'God proves his love for us because while we were still sinners, Christ died for us' (Rom. 5.8).

As prophecy, prophetic dialogue speaks out, speaks on behalf of God. Prophecy is also a constitutive dimension of reconciliation. It is most evident in practices of truth-telling and the pursuit of justice. As we have seen, truth-telling is the bold attempt to undo cultures of lies and cultures of silence. It reflects the empowerment of the healing process, whereby victims reclaim their dignity and exercise their agency to speak and to take action against the lies and the wrongdoing that have been perpetrated against them. Like biblical prophecy, it is a mysterious energy that emerges out of the victim to be more than a victim, to be more than someone beholden to the wrongdoing of the past. Truth-telling exposes lies and oppressive silence for what they are: against God's will for the world. The pursuit of justice, in all its liberative power, is the sheer energy of God at work in restoring the world and reconciling all things in Christ. It is the foretaste of that 'new creation' coming about with the reign of God.

Forgiveness is both a risk of communication as well as a word of prophecy. In forgiving, a future is announced that may be hard to discern in a still ambivalent present. Forgiveness is indeed a portal into that future where God will be 'all in all'.

In the concept of 'prophetic dialogue', 'dialogue' is the substantive and 'prophetic' the modifier, signifying perhaps a modality of dialogue. While it may be asserted that dialogue and prophecy are of equal importance, such a position does little to further our understanding of how the two work together. I think that it is appropriate that their relationship as substantive and modifier is so construed. 'Dialogue' is of the essence of which we are trying to speak here – both in its Trinitarian and its God-and-world dimensions. 'Prophetic' points to necessary elements that must be brought forward again and again for soteriological reasons. The world, good as it is, remains a fallen one. To be sure, objective redemption has been achieved through the suffering, death and resurrection of Jesus Christ. But the full restoration of the dialogue of communion between God and creation needs constantly to be called upon in a prophetic voice to keep the trajectory of reconciliation on track, as it were, until all things are restored in Christ. So the relation between dialogue and prophecy is not an utterly symmetrical one. Rather, the modifier reveals and reminds us of dimensions of the substantive that at times escape our awareness or exceed our capacity to hope.

Prophetic Dialogue: A Mystagogy for Reconciliation as Mission?

I conclude here with a suggestion about how the more general idea of mission as prophetic dialogue might contribute to or enhance reconciliation as a form of mission. Following upon what has just been said, prophetic dialogue as a call and a pathway into ever deeper communion with the Trinitarian God might provide a mystagogy for reconciliation as a spirituality. By this I mean that prophetic dialogue, in its revealing to us the *perichoresis* or inner movement of communion among the persons of the Trinity, can help chart the way into a greater contemplative union with God that is an essential part of a ministry of reconciliation. As expressed in the first theological principle above, it is this movement into deeper union with God that is the heart of a spirituality of reconciliation. Mystagogy, as opposed to pedagogy, is an initiation into the divine mysteries already presented. To understand the salvific movements that reconciliation bespeaks, one has to enlarge one's understandings of evil, sin, grace, mercy, truth, justice and forgiveness. The prophetic edge of this mystagogical movement reminds us constantly that God's ways are not always our ways, that God's grace is enough for us, and in our weakness we are made strong (2 Cor. 12.9–10). The trajectories of prophetic dialogue might provide the pathways for that deeper entry into reconciliation itself.

Much more might be said about the relation of prophetic dialogue to reconciliation. What should be evident here, however, is how much the two perspectives on mission share common territory and how reconciliation might be considered one of the foremost enactments of prophetic dialogue.

9

Wounded Communion:
Prophetic Dialogue and Salvation in
Trinitarian Perspective

S. MARK HEIM

Christians have generally treated salvation as the single, universally desired religious end. Particularly in the context of religious diversity, this assumption led theologians to focus on the question of how many might succeed in accessing that end and the question of what kinds of relation with Christ's redeeming work were necessary to produce that result.[1] I have come to think instead of salvation as a distinctively Christian end, sought by some though open to all. That particularity goes hand in hand with understanding salvation as Trinitarian in its very nature. This shift in understanding is relevant to the topic of this volume not just because it throws new light on mission and prophetic dialogue. More to the point, the shift is for me actually a result of prophetic dialogue as the editors of this volume understand it.

In one sense a Trinitarian view of salvation is nothing but standard Christian tradition. But in my own case, both its application to religious diversity and my grasp of its essential character were developed in dialogue, through the prophetic witness of other religious traditions to their own truth. I knew the basic Christian teachings in regard to the Trinity, but their contemporary significance was largely hidden from me. That situation changed as a result of my own immersion in interreligious relations. That dialogue taught me that most in other traditions did not seek salvation as Christians understood it. The Jewish rabbi who said that 'Jesus is the answer to a question I have never asked', expressed this succinctly. But the more I learned of Buddhism, for instance, the more clearly the same conclusion emerged.

Salvation is a relation of communion (*koinonia*) with God and other creatures in Christ. Properly, it is the fullness of such communion, but it is no less real in its partial and anticipatory forms. The definition is in one sense extremely general. There is space within it for all the traditional differences

---

1 This assumption undergirds the common typology of theological views of religious diversity (exclusivist–inclusivist–pluralist), presumed no less by 'pluralists' than exclusivists. See Paul Knitter, *Introducing Theologies of Religion*, Maryknoll, NY: Orbis, 2002.

among Christians over issues of *theosis,* justification, sanctification and the resurrection life. This *koinonia* dimension of salvation is of special importance in terms of the distinctive character of the Christian gospel, a constant feature of the pilgrim faith in its different contexts.[2] Virtually every word in that short sentence distinguishes salvation from ultimate ends valued in alternative religious visions. 'God' of course distinguishes it from non-theistic traditions, but the word 'relation' is equally significant, marking divergence with traditions of full monism or radical emptiness. In connection with paths that also aim at relation with God, the words 'communion' and 'Christ' add something distinctive. Salvation is not a generic aspiration and its particularity needs explanation. The specific character of the fulfilment that is salvation depends very much on the special characteristics of the God who is party to that fulfilment. The Trinitarian nature of God is a kind of watermark in the nature of salvation, which is a relation of communion with a God whose nature is communion. The religions that led me to understand salvation afresh also made me grasp Trinity anew.

This also meant that I had to consider the religious ends in other religious paths that were not salvation but were, I came to believe, actual attainments and real goods. As such, I believed that they must involve some real relation with God. But how could there be diverse actual contacts with God? Only if God's character itself is complex. Trinity was thus the lesson about Christianity that other religions retaught me, and it was at the same time the Christian lens for understanding other religions in their integrity and uniqueness. Trinity is a key both to Christian openness to other faiths and to its witness among them.

Salvation as Communion

No individual alone can or could approximate the fullness of relation with God in all of its possible dimensions. But one can approach that fullness through *koinonia* with other persons, each of whom in their relations with God and with others fills out aspects that would be lacking for any single person. The communion of saints is not an assembly of individuals who each repeat an identical unity and reconciliation with God. It is a living exchange in which one person's participation in God is enriched by the distinctive quality of another's. This is why the concrete body of the Church has been regarded as fundamental to the Christian life, even to salvation itself. The way that we can most deeply participate in a divine fullness that literally overflows our finite capacities is through mutual indwelling with other persons. Speaking of the communion of the Trinity, we may say seriously that the divine nature is so great that even God cannot encompass it

2 See a discussion of constants in the Christian mission in chapter 2 in Stephen B. Bevans and Roger Schroeder, *Constants in Context: A Theology of Mission for Today*, Maryknoll, NY: Orbis, 2004.American Society of Missiology Series (Maryknoll, N.Y.: Orbis Books, 2004).

except through sharing. *Koinonia* with each other is the condition of our participation in the divine life. Our finite receptions of the triune self-giving multiply each other, in a kind of spiritual calculus that deepens each one's participation in the triune life itself.

The divine nature is a communion-in-difference, and creation is an overflow of the divine nature. It is an act of sharing. The patristic maxim on the incarnation stated that God became as we are so that we might become as God is. The maxim is premised on a view of creation in which God made us as we are so that we might share in the communion that God is. The meaning of our existence then is to share proportionally in the divine life through our unity with other creatures. This is summed up in the scriptural statement of the two great commandments to love God and to love our neighbours.

Miroslav Volf points out that the dominant self-designations used by early Christians to describe their connection to others in the Church were 'sisters/brothers' and 'friends'.[3] Their *koinonia* or mutual participation in one another was described with sibling language (as something constituted by a prior, given relation) and with friendship language (pointing to a voluntary, associative freedom). God makes creatures with freedom to choose, to condition their own intimacies. Yet God makes us with intrinsically relational natures, creatures who cannot be 'ourselves' alone. Through the incarnation of the Word, the inner *koinonia* of the Trinity has been shared with a human being. Through our human *koinonia* with that crucified and risen one we partake in that sharing to the limits of our individual created natures. And through our communion with each other in the body of Christ we are able to share ever more of the fullness of God. Like a series of Russian dolls nested inside each other, we might say that the Christian understanding of salvation is communion all the way down – it is communion with a God whose nature is communion, by means of communion with other persons and with Christ, whose nature is the mutual indwelling of human and divine.

Communion is the substance of salvation, but also the path that leads to it. This provides the ultimate context for both prophecy and dialogue. Dialogue is an instrument that knits together those who do not yet share deeper levels of *koinonia*. It is a conduit by which we can come to indwell each other more fully. Prophecy can be the telling forth of the truth of the distinctive knowledge or experience of God from one part of the body to another. It can also be a witness to the brokenness of the body, to the ways in which communion is blocked. Both dialogue and prophecy may have instrumental uses, for overcoming estrangements and misunderstandings. But they both have a permanent significance, as part of the relation that is salvation.

---

3 Miroslav Volf, *After Our Likeness: The Church as the Image of the Trinity*, Sacra Doctrina, Grand Rapids, MI: Eerdmans, 1998, 180.

Dimensions of Communion: Dialogue and Prophecy in Relation to the Religions

Christians understand God's nature to be complex, because Trinitarian. If the divine is intrinsically complex, this necessarily suggests that there can be various dimensions of relation with God which are authentically grounded in the divine nature. For instance, within the Trinity there is a communion of persons, in which each one makes space for the immanence of others, in which each one encounters the other *as* a true other and in which all are truly one by virtue of their mutual indwelling. There are thus three dimensions of the *koinonia* within the Trinitarian life and these three are reflected both in the economy of God's relation with the world and in corresponding human analogies.[4]

The first dimension is characterized by the interplay of emptiness and immanence. Thus, humans can experience a dimension of God's relation to the world by encountering God's absence as a being alongside or over other beings, the gracious emptiness of a 'withdrawal' in which God makes way for creation and human selves to have their own reality. The same can be said of encounter with God's immanent presence 'in, with and under' all that is, the creative word without which nothing can be upheld. These relations with creation are rooted in the divine nature itself, where they are already exemplified. God practises an active absence and an anonymous identity in creation. If we look for analogies for this in relations between humans, we tend to draw on non-personal examples. We can think of immanence as similar to physiological indwelling, a blood transfusion from one person to another, or the near identity of the genetic codes shared by humans. We can think of emptiness in terms of the physics of our material world, which leads at the subatomic level to an ever more ephemeral and paradoxical description of the 'matter' that we are.

In a second dimension of *koinonia* within the Trinity, each of the three persons encounters the others in freedom, with its own unique character. The relations are asymmetrical, because each has its own identity and is no copy of another. In human beings we see a likeness to this in the dimension of direct personal encounter, in which we meet as distinctive others, honouring and enacting our identities in exchange. We do this face to face or through a medium like writing or art. Humans can likewise experience God's relation to the world in this mode, as one who acts and speaks within the history and nature that are otherwise marked by the 'non-personal' relations just described. This is a God known in epiphany and revelation.

The third dimension refers to communion. The divine persons do not only share one divine life process. They do not only encounter each other's uniqueness. They also indwell each other *as* different persons. The incarnation is a

---

4 For a fuller development of these ideas, see S. Mark Heim, *The Depth of the Riches: A Trinitarian Theology of Religious Ends*, Sacra Doctrina, Grand Rapids, MI: Eerdmans, 2001.

window into this Trinitarian communion and the path that opens our way to participate in it. We know some shadow of this in our human relations when empathy and intimacy with someone gives rise to a vicarious capacity for us to share his or her inner life. His or her characteristic responses and feelings begin to arise in us also, as a kind of second nature. They arise not instead of our own reactions, but *as* our own, yet inexplicable apart from the indwelling of the loved one in us. This is not an abstract process, in which, for instance, a parent rationally infers what her child would like. It is a profoundly incarnational one, in which a mother encountering or contemplating a certain experience feels the delight or fear the child would feel. Relations of deep love or friendship are marked by this dynamic. But it is manifest above all for us in our incorporation into Christ by faith through the indwelling of the Holy Spirit.

In God's relation with creation, God manifests in a proportionate way the same three dimensions of relation present in the divine life itself. What does this imply about the dimensions of relation with God found in the religions? Communion is not an identity of contradiction. Because they are rooted in the divine nature itself, each of these dimensions of relation is authentic and insofar as they realize these dimensions, so are religions. The uniqueness of communion in Christ is not the addition of a relation with God that replaces all others. The apophatic mystery of the divine emptiness, the unitive mystery of the divine immanence, the majesty of the divine law, the love and mercy of personal encounter with the divine – each of these has an irreducible character, for they are dimensions of salvation itself. If this is true, then there is a prophetic quality in the witness of the religions, one to which Christians need to attend. That prophetic quality is perhaps most pronounced precisely where other traditions affirm their distinctive testimony.

For instance, in relation to the first dimension we discussed, if creation is examined rigorously on the apophatic frequency – through meditation or science – searchers may legitimately find impermanence or emptiness at its base. All enduring, distinct identities are found without substance. This conclusion and the rigorous practice based on it, are characteristic of the Theravadan Buddhist understanding of *nirvana*. Insight into this dimension is far more developed in Buddhism than in any facet of Christian tradition. To realize such emptiness is to cling to nothing, not even one's own identity and so surely to be delivered from all suffering, estrangement and relationship. The practice of compassion, mindfulness and insight on the Theravadan Buddhist way, for instance, do offer a path to unconditioned reality and release from suffering. And this way is based in a real dimension of apophatic mystery in God's relation with the world. What makes the Buddhist witness unique is both the depth of the grasp on this dimension and the power of the affirmation of its ultimate exclusivity. In this concrete respect the end in view is an actual aspect of the salvation for which

Christians hope. But realization of this condition alone would relinquish a whole range of other possible relations with God and with others (not least of all with Christ). And the presence of these relations is integral to the communion of salvation. In that respect the Buddhist ideal is similar to what Christians mean by loss. Therefore Christians cannot fail to offer their own witness in distinction from the Buddhist one, even though that witness need not involve denial of the reality and value of the Buddhist aim.

We noted that there was an alternative way to apprehend this same dimension. If creation is examined rigorously on the immanence frequency – through meditation or science – searchers look deeply into ourselves and nature and legitimately find oneness and eternal being at its base. Here what is most profoundly grasped is not God's withdrawal, but God's sustaining presence in all that is made. The constant dynamism of the divine life which upholds the world is taken as the substratum of one great self whose body is the world. Every individual part may change and pass away, like cells in a body, but the one self goes on. The *advaita Vedanta* tradition of Hinduism expresses this perception powerfully. *Brahman*, the one unshakable reality, sustains all things by pervading all things. If pursued intensely and separately, this insight suggests an end in which the small 'I' of the particular creature resolves into a perfect identity with the one absolute being. The creature can realize the impersonal immanence of the divine as their sole being and yield back all unique identity and relations. Here is an end distinct from the Buddhist one, but also constituted by limitation and intensification within a particular dimension of the Trinitarian life.

Either of the insights I have described can lead reasonably to the conclusion 'I am that'. All things are empty, or all things are literally divine, including me. The conviction that *samsara* is *nirvana*, or that *atman* is *Brahman* are two distinctive religious conclusions born of such wisdom. The purity of the wisdom behind these conclusions is developed more profoundly within Buddhism and Hinduism than in Christianity. That wisdom serves the attainment of the religious ends which each of these traditions affirm. Christians, Buddhists and Hindus diverge over which religious end is most encompassing and ultimate. But this wisdom is prophetic witness to Christians, for it is right to honour God's universal presence and to realize our complete dependence on God.

God's relation with the world in the dimension just described is the presupposition for another dimension of relation. The background of God's universal 'withdrawal' and immanence sets the stage for a free and historical encounter of humans with God as a single 'Thou' on the stage of creation. We may call this the personal dimension of God's relation with the world. It also has two sides. Under the influence of the biblical tradition, we tend to think of this dimension in terms of encounter with God as *a* person, even if the focus sometimes falls on law or Scripture as a crystallization of God's will and purpose. Obviously, this is a vision Christianity shares with

Judaism and Islam. This is the God of the biblical and Qur'anic traditions, an agent, who speaks and acts with humanity. But it is possible to conceive a specific transcendent order without any personal being who expresses it, a divine will without a God whose will it is, so to speak. The *Tao* of Taoism or the *logos* in Stoicism or the Kantian moral law would be examples. Thus at one end of the range there is revelation of a transcendent, ideal order and at the other end there is the personal God who is both subject of loving encounter and source of law and guidance.

The key point that distinguishes this dimension as a whole from the first dimension we discussed is that it allows for, indeed requires, contrast and tension. Specific, historical revelation marks the divine, and relationship with it, off from other possibilities. Divine word or image testifies that the sole truth about transcendent reality is not that it is empty nor that all being is already in perfect identity with it. There is a distance between us and God that must be travelled by moral and spiritual transformation. Revelation bridges the gap between God and us, pointing the way for change. The motto is not 'thou art that', but 'become what you are called/structured to be'. A Trinitarian perspective suggests that what is apprehended in these cases is the external unity of the Trinity, God's personal will for the good of creation. Human reception may focus on the content of that divine order, or also on the personal character of the one who wills it. In either case, faithful response to the revelation of God is an authentic personal relation to God. Here the idea of prophecy takes on a very concrete form. For in the traditions of Judaism and Islam literal prophets, stirred by the Holy Spirit, have risen as messengers to humanity. God is not left without personal witness to any nation. Christians already attend to such prophets in adopting the text of Hebrew Scriptures as their own. The challenge is to continue to hear prophetic testimony in the living Jewish and Muslim traditions. Dialogue becomes very much the medium for this prophecy, in which the distinctive relations with God that these faiths manifest are shared with Christians.

Christian faith presupposes the dimensions we have described. Christian faith extends the personal dimension of relation with two decisive steps. The first is the conviction that the decisive revelation of the personal God is itself a living person: Jesus Christ. The second is the confession of God as Trinity, which finds this single divine 'I' grounded in a communion of persons. This is what impels Christians to confess that God relates with creation in the dimension of *koinonia* or communion, and salvation is the fulfilment of relation in this dimension. This dimension of relation with God is defined by the fact that we can only have it by sharing it with others. We can have *koinonia* with God only through *koinonia* with others. A typical feature of our communion with Christ is that we discover a new openness and love towards neighbours and enemies, a response that we can hardly credit as coming solely from us, except by virtue of Christ's dwelling in us. The effect of communion is openness to communion.

Phenomenal experiences of these various dimensions of relation are themselves recognized in most major religious traditions.[5] However, each interprets some of these dimensions in terms of others that are thought or experienced to be more fundamental to the divine and hence to final human realization. Personal qualities, for instance, may be interpreted as heuristic constructs attributed to the divine for instrumental spiritual purposes by those at a less developed level of insight, without any actual ground in the divine itself. Christians are formally no different, as they also regard one of these dimensions as key to understanding the others. They take communion as the most fundamental character of the divine and of relation with God. Communion cannot function effectively as an identity of replacement. If the communion dimension is given priority in interpreting the others, this means that those dimensions can only be affirmed *as* the distinctive others they are, in a coequal and eternal pattern.

It is impossible then to believe in the Trinity *instead* of the distinctive religious claims of all other religions. The Trinity is a map that finds room for, indeed requires, concrete truth in other religions. On this map, in other words, there is room for affirmation of the other and for witness as well. From this perspective we can understand how to hold together two things that seem contradictory to many. On one hand, there is the firm conviction that there is no salvation apart from Christ and that Christians have a vocation to witness for Christ in every context. On the other hand, there is the firm conviction that there is authentic connection to God in other religions and that Christians have something to learn from them, even from what is contrastingly different in them. It is a benefit of this approach that it allows us to take the distinctive testimony and practices of various religions on their own terms. They are not reduced either to anonymous Christianity or to a shapeless cosmic convergence. They can be taken with full seriousness as real alternatives which judge Christianity as penultimate or distorted from their perspectives. And with equal seriousness a Christian inclusivist hope may view them as contributory strands in the texture of salvation. In other words, the dialogue among religions has a place for a prophetic word that passes between Christianity and religions in both directions.

I believe this perspective offers grounds for a theology of Christian mission that can adequately engage mature religious traditions at their best. It also illuminates actual missionary experience. There are times when Christian faith is received as deliverance from a demonic condition, from a present and future of raw negation of God's goodness. For there are people, whatever their nominal religious label (including a Christian one), who find themselves precisely in such situations. In this case deliverance can rightly evoke the relief of a Gadarene demoniac, who comes out from his chained prison among the tombs. Left behind is only loss and evil. Christian witness

---

5 See a much fuller discussion of this in Heim, *Depth of the Riches*, 216 ff.

to the same salvation can take a different flavour in relation to people of religious devotion. In that case, it may elicit something more like the leaping hearts of those who responded to Jesus' words in the Sermon on the Mount, 'Do not think that I have come to abolish the law or the prophets; I have not come to abolish but to fulfil' (Matt. 5.17). We are adequately equipped to understand these cases. But what of the much more usual instance where Christian witness is not accepted by conversion but remains alongside the witness of another religious tradition, whose adherents reject or subsume the Christian end as subordinate to the overwhelming goodness and power of its own? And what of the cases where Christians themselves convert to the truth and the aim of another religious path?

Christians have traditionally been able to extend only the most limited respect to the rejection of the gospel message, by reference to defects in its presentation (it has not been truthfully explained or it has been associated with the sins of its proponents) or limitations of its hearers (an 'invincible ignorance' born of cultural barriers or presuppositions). Missionary failures could legitimately be seen as a prophetic message to the Church about its own profound failings (as for instance its failure to achieve the unity in its own house for which Christ prayed, 'so that the world may believe'). But I believe that most missionaries (and many Christians) in fact know a more positive quality to be found in the adherence of other believers to their traditions, a connection to God that merits respect and humble attention. Missionaries frequently manifest in practice a respect for and a humble apprenticeship to the religious other that this theology reveals as consistent with the heart of Christian faith, not a mere instrumental or personal strategy. The Trinitarian perspective I have outlined goes a long way to make sense of this and to ground a more positive attitude towards the vitality of other faiths.

In this perspective, the religions play a truly providential role. God's activity in the world is not confined to a narrow salvation history. God's grace enfolds the world and touches it in many dimensions. The religions reflect the fact that every human response to any dimension of God's manifestation and revelation meets only God's 'yes' of grace in return. Every relation with God that proceeds on the basis of some dimension of God's self-giving to us meets a fulfilment for which it aims and hopes and opens towards the full *koinonia* of the divine life. The Christian universal witness is that to each of these cases, the knowledge and love of Christ bring yet another dimension, one that knits these all together in communion and so constitutes salvation.

Wounded Communion: Prophecy and Dialogue in Relation to Justice

I have spent most of this chapter indicating the way prophecy and dialogue are built into Christian relation with the religions. But this is only one important example of the way that our understanding of salvation calls for prophecy and dialogue. We are made in the image of God and so in each other's. Just as God's being is communion, so we in our analogous ways are constituted by our relations with others. The image of God makes us not so much individuals as 'interviduals'. This has a simple and profound implication. Every injustice and oppression is a tear in the fabric that connects us with each other and a wound in the communion that can unite us more fully with God. As relation with God is integral to salvation, so is relation with other persons and creatures.

Christian tradition sees human being arising at the intersection of three types of relation: our relation with God, with other persons and with the rest of creation (or nature). This created nature is the mirror of our eschatological end in which all these relational dimensions will be filled through communion. Three profound types of brokenness lie in the disruption of these three axes of relation, estrangements we call sin, evil and death. Sin is not only the act of violating God's will, but the rupture in faith and unity with God. Evil is not only outward harm and hurt to our neighbours but also the poisoning of the channels of empathy between us with the seeds of envy or malice. Death is not only the dissolution of our bodily natures (through disease, injury and pain), but the hopelessness that grasps for permanency through dominance over the rest of nature.

Here, in terms of what we are saved from, there are additional channels for dialogue and prophecy. Advocacy and activism for social development and justice are intrinsic to Christian life, for even where these look no further than basic human welfare they serve the substance of salvation. Where oppression and inhumanity characterize human relations they destroy communion or its possibility, and thus we might say that the world's 'wiring' for salvation is short-circuited. Justice and liberation are preconditions for our eschatological hope, the healing of the web that is the very texture of salvation. This actually understates the point. For the one through whom Christians seek saving *koinonia* is precisely the crucified one. For those who would have communion with Christ, there is a priority on communion with those who are in the place of Christ, the place of victims and the marginalized.[6] Therefore, those who force us to face these concerns are witnesses to call us to conversion to the Christ outside our walls, hidden from us by the blindness of our own sin and scapegoating.

---

6 See S. Mark Heim, *Saved from Sacrifice: A Theology of the Cross*, Grand Rapids, MI: Eerdmans, 2006.

We have seen the way the Christian understanding of salvation can be contextualized in the setting of the religions. In that setting we are dealing with varied visions of religious ends and the dimensions of God's relation with the world. The context of human need is a distinct setting, with its own imperative for dialogue. In this dialogue, we are dealing with the raw material of salvation. A number of authors have sought to ground a common approach to human suffering in what they call 'pre-moral goods'.[7] These are goods that are not viewed as moral or religious in themselves, but as the prerequisites of human flourishing in the sense that no matter which ideal state is sought, some measure of these goods is needed to pursue that aim, and some respect for other humans' need for these goods is entailed in that pursuit. Such goods would include life, bodily health and integrity, food, education and free agency. These are conditions or capabilities necessary for achievements that do have moral and spiritual value. To say that they are pre-moral or pre-religious also means that they can, in certain cases, be subordinate to the moral and the religious in terms of value: one need not and should not put one's own life or health ahead of every other consideration. But even to exercise that choice requires some measure of those goods. From a Christian point of view, such an approach is congenial because our understanding of creation views these capacities not only as good in themselves, but as actually participating in or underlying salvation.

If we refer back to the three dimensions of relation with God that I described earlier (the non-personal, the personal and the communion dimensions), we note that we find analogies for these in dimensions of relation between human persons. And each of these human relations has what we may call pre-moral (or pre-religious) features. For instance, in our bodily natures there are basic goods like a functioning immune system or normal blood chemistry that make healing possible. These goods are non-personal, though they can feature in moral and personal acts (as our chosen behaviours can harm our bodies or as a blood transfusion can be an act of love between persons). Our personhood rests on pre-moral goods such as the capacities for language and self-consciousness. These are necessary for our own identities and for relation with others. They come to us as prior gifts, outside our control, though by our own agency we can deform or expand these qualities and put them to destructive or positive uses. And in our communion nature, there are also pre-moral goods, such as the natural familial indwelling of parents and children, our empathetic capacities to read each other's hearts and minds. Without such pre-moral goods, the image of God in us would be distorted and the path to interpersonal communion obscured, though

---

7 See for instance William Schweiker, *Responsibility and Christian Ethics*, New Studies in Christian Ethics, Cambridge and New York: Cambridge University Press, 1995; Don S. Browning and Terry D. Cooper, *Religious Thought and the Modern Psychologies*, 2nd edition, Minneapolis: Fortress Press, 2004; Martha C. Nussbaum, 'Women and Cultural Universals', in *Sex and Social Justice*, New York: Oxford University Press, 1999, 29–54.

in our freedom we can turn away from communion or turn these means of empathy into instruments of manipulation. The religions have common cause in seeking to assure these goods for all persons. In this respect, salvation and other religious ends overlap. Thus all need to be open to the prophetic challenge that comes from those denied these goods, particularly through poverty or oppression. It is not only individuals that need to be saved, but structures, for those structures condition the relations that constitute salvation.

Each tradition has characteristic visions of human flourishing that go far beyond these basic goods and that in their diversity widen the scope of human transformation. From a Christian perspective, there is bodily disease that robs us of a basic good of health, but there is also death itself, which threatens relation and which is overcome with the hope of eternal life. There is intrinsic suffering for a person cast into human society without the full means of communication in language or the full development of their capacities. Christians see a distinct additional reality of evil, when this disadvantage is imposed by some on others, as by violence or the suppression of cultures. Such evil needs to be transformed by regeneration of our wills and reform of society. There is an intrinsic suffering that stems from a loss of the tools for communion (as for instance the deprivation of human nurture or family life, the lack of models for empathy). Christians see a further dimension and cause for the poisoning of our openness to each other's minds and hearts, which we call sin, the disruption of our communion with God.

In this respect, religious diversity helps reveal the full range of brokenness in our human condition. At the same time, it points towards a fuller grasp of the breadth of salvation. Taken in isolation, as ultimates, some religious ends exclude each other. But in the formulation and pursuit of these ends, various aspects of the human condition are plumbed with unique power. Thus in our efforts to overcome sin, evil and death, let alone to provide the basic goods of human life, we need the dialogue of prophetic partnership with our religious neighbours to open new insight and possibilities.

Some brief examples may illustrate what I mean. Christian salvation revolves around communion. One reflection of this is the particular Christian interest in forgiveness. This is an emphasis that is puzzling or offensive from some religious perspectives. Forgiveness presupposes repentant action to reverse or ameliorate the effects of the action in question. But its significance in Christianity carries even further to refer to the image of another, the disposition towards another, that is maintained within me (or the image of me maintained within another). In very simple terms, we may say that an act of forgiveness between two persons changes nothing except the reality of the way in which each one continues to indwell the other. The act between them remains, but their communion changes. The anguish of an unforgiven one includes the fact that the past act cannot be undone, but also the present reality that the presence of that act in the mind of the victim cannot be changed and that the offender's permanent dwelling in that victim's consciousness is as a source of pain and anger. Forgiveness counts as a good grace in correlation with an understanding of persons as profoundly mutually constitutive. Along these lines, the Christian tradition offers a distinctive insight into the understanding and healing of certain kinds of human suffering.

The various traditions of Buddhism offer wisdom about a dimension of suffering less well explored in Christian history. I am thinking particularly of Buddhist analysis of suffering in terms of its container, the mind. Since suffering is registered and experienced in consciousness, Buddhism pursues an intense exploration of suffering as a product of mind. The resulting analysis uncovers the ephemeral and empty nature of all phenomena when considered strictly in themselves. When applied to our consciousness, this insight discovers that we grant great reality to the products of our own mental activities and that our attachments to these products of mind produce needless suffering in our minds themselves (and the minds of others). Buddhist practice then prescribes a very sophisticated therapy in which the mind, which is the source of suffering, is trained to distance itself from its own products and so become free of their effects. In this way, Buddhism offers a crucial perspective on suffering and its alleviation that will not be found in the same way in other sources.

The love and forgiveness in communion and the compassion and wisdom in mindfulness might be parsed as nothing but opposing elements in incommensurate ultimate systems. But they can also be seen and experienced to intertwine, with the truth of one expanding the truth of the other, though the expansion remains recognizably Christian in one case and Buddhist in the other. The Trinitarian view we have outlined grounds the second approach. Beyond this one example, it offers a supple spiritual and intellectual framework for the many depth encounters we find in the growing interreligious engagement around us.

Salvation is a particular Christian aim distinguished from others. Yet its nature draws us towards others (religious others and social others) and their witness and experience. We cannot seek salvation apart from healing the broken relations and structures that connect persons. The Trinitarian communion which is source and end for the Christian path is not an identity of isolation or contradiction, but of reconciliation. This is the deep grammar by which prophecy and dialogue are necessarily written into the Christian mission.

PART 5

Anthropology: Mission as What it Means to be Human

10

Contemporary Women's Contributions to Prophetic Dialogue as Mission

FRANCES S. ADENEY

Introduction

Previous chapters of this book have taken the reader on a journey that shows the theological and practical usefulness of using prophetic dialogue as a model for mission. Here we ask the question, how do contemporary women missiologists contribute to this framework? Characteristics of prophetic dialogue as mission include on the dialogue side an openness to leaving our comfort zones and passing over into the world of the stranger. Missionaries do this. Prophetic dialogue as mission also includes listening deeply with a presence and respect that honours others and a humility that learns from them.[1] On the prophetic side, Christian mission includes a telling forth of the good news, a liberating practice and an attention to context that determines how we go about mission. Here we have a critique of injustice alongside work for justice.[2] Linking those characteristics of dialogue and prophecy result in a complex view of mission that is both relevant and useful in many global contexts.

Once the idea of prophetic dialogue as mission catches hold, one can see it in many places. Women's mission theologies include many aspects of prophetic dialogue. To be prophetic means to speak into the future. Contemporary Christian theological reflection can become prophetic as dialogue among theologians incorporates all of the current voices speaking to the complex issues of Christian mission around the world. No one voice contains all of the wisdom needed to speak to the future. No one perspective is right. Rather each perspective speaking in its particular context adds texture and value to the global discussion. The idea of prophetic dialogue as mission recognizes those complexities.

Kirsteen Kim's theology of the Holy Spirit contrasts views of spirit across cultures. Studying at Fuller Seminary, teaching missiology in India and living in Korea led her to the view that missiology is a global conversation

---

1 S. Bevans and R. Schroeder, *Prophetic Dialogue: Reflections on Christian Mission Today*, Maryknoll, NY: Orbis, 2011, 50.

2 Bevans and Schroeder, *Prophetic Dialogue*, 60.

among contextual theologies. Different theologies are compared across contexts. To do that, Western systematic theology must take its place alongside other theologies. Rather than the standard for theological enquiry, systematic theology must be seen as one view among many.

As that happens, comparisons of theologies become easier. Gender becomes important to that discussion. Mission theologies of women are sometimes neglected in the theological discourse. Dialogue with women's theologies of mission brings perspectives that can balance dominant male voices in contemporary missiology.

Consequently, this chapter presents diverging theologies of women doing mission theology and finds common threads among them. The thought of contemporary missiologists from three groups are analysed: World Evangelical Alliance, Roman Catholic women and theologians from the American Society of Missiology. Historical theologies and methodologies of women in mission in the West since World War Two set their thinking in the global context of today. We see how women's mission theologies from those sources both connect with traditions in mission theology and display divergences from mainstream Western missiology. We find antecedents of prophetic dialogue among their theologies.

Changes in Women's Mission Theology since World War Two

Let me begin with a story, told to me by Revd Carol Chamberlain Rose Ikler. She was 92 years old in 2012, the first woman to be ordained by the Presbytery of Philadelphia of the Presbyterian Church (USA) in 1958. Her life illustrates the changes for women doing mission theology since World War Two. She lived through those changes.

Born into a family of four generations of ministers, Carol's youth was marked by the hospitality of parents deeply involved with social issues of the day. Her father, a Congregational minister, did inner city ministry in the slums of New York City, and her mother led the choir at Riverside Church. As a young person, the influences of Walter Rauschenbusch and Harry Emerson Fosdick shaped her theology of mission.

During her college years Carol spent summers doing mission work. She cared for patients in a mental hospital in Europe, worked with Japanese children in internment camps in the United States and gave children made homeless by the war opportunities to do outdoor camping in the mountains of Switzerland. Graduating in 1942 from Mount Holyoke College, Carol went on to study at Union Theological Seminary in New York and Columbia University in a joint programme. She then went to Hawaii where she spent eight years working with a Congregational church as director of children's ministry.

On her return, a crisis of faith led her to Yale Divinity School, where she studied with Reinhold and H. Richard Niebuhr and other prominent theologians. Her professors helped her to solidify her progressive theology and she went on to become one of the editors of the Faith and Life Curriculum for the Presbyterian Church. 'H. Richard Niebuhr came nearer to being Jesus to us than any other professor' she said frankly.[3]

Carol Ikler's journey illustrates the changes in women doing mission theology since World War Two. Both the ecumenical movement and the women's movement in the Church were vibrant during the 1940s. Her time at Union and Columbia coincided with the birth of the World Council of Churches. Carol said it was a time of great excitement and expansion in the intellectual and practical worlds of theology. Prophetic witness that spoke to justice issues expanded as did a focus on dialogue that served reconciliation among churches. Those changes created opportunities for women. Women students were welcomed at Union Seminary. Ordination for women started to be considered as talents of women began to be recognized and utilized by the Church. Women found opportunities to do mission work that was usually the work of men.

Studies at Yale continued to open paths for Carol Ikler and other women to do serious work in theology. In 2011 Yale celebrated '70 years of women at Yale'. Carol was one of the pioneers of women doing mission theology. She looked back at the changes with humility, grateful for the opportunities she was able to pursue. She spoke of theology as a practice, something she did every day. Grappling with theological ideas, studying the works of others and reformulating her own thoughts in light of Scripture formed an important part of Ikler's spirituality. She credited the Holy Spirit for direction in those endeavours and the Church for nurturing them. 'Young women today', she said, 'seem surprised that there was ever a time when women were not ordained, were not leaders in the church, were not doing theology.' For that we can be grateful to women like Carol Rose Ikler.[4]

Social changes in the United States and around the world since World War Two make finding theologies of Christian mission by women much easier. World War Two itself laid the groundwork for women in the United States to participate more fully in the workplace. A wave of feminism in the 1970s furthered that freedom. Academic positions began opening up for women, and Protestant churches began to ordain women, recognizing their leadership capabilities. Women's independence on the mission field also increased as para-church organizations developed in the second half of the twentieth century. Immigration from Africa and Asia and the proliferation of world religions in the USA brought the mission field home, giving women

---

3 Interview 26 April 2012, for forthcoming book *Women and Christian Mission*, Louisville Presbyterian Seminary.

4 Carol Ikler died in 2013, a loss to the Presbyterian Church and Louisville Seminary where she had remained active until her death. She organized a monthly Presbyterian Book Review meeting, inviting faculty from the seminary to present books they had recently read or published.

more opportunities to work and reflect on mission and Christianity. Finally prominent Christian women such as Frances Willard, Eleanor Roosevelt, Mary McCleod Bethune, Dorothy Day and Mother Theresa provided role models for women called into mission service. Their work prefigured the holistic emphasis that prophetic dialogue as mission now emphasizes: listening, respect, learning and discernment combined with the need to speak out.[5]

Evangelical Women's Mission Theologies

Evangelical women participating in the World Evangelical Alliance provide insights into the content and methods of evangelical women's mission theologies. In 1999 the Iguassu Missiological Consultation brought together 160 missiologists in Brazil. The publication of the papers from that consultation along with 'The Iguassu Affirmation' outlined the mission theology of the World Evangelical Alliance (then known as the World Evangelical Fellowship) at that time. It also included 35 articles by men and 5 articles by women. One article was co-authored by seven men and one woman. Additional articles by Samuel Escobar and Christopher Wright were added before publication.

The Iguassu Affirmation provides a baseline of evangelical mission theology. It was crafted by World Evangelical Fellowship Missions Commission leadership David Tai-Woong Lee and Jim Stamoolis, revised by a team of seven theologians from various continents and discussed in groups at the meeting itself.[6] The Affirmation includes 14 declarations of evangelical mission theology that stress the foundations in the authority of Scripture, the saving work of Jesus Christ, the Trinitarian basis for mission and the importance of the Church in fulfilling God's plan for the world.[7]

The articles by women reveal a number of theological themes and emphases that differ from the text of the Affirmation developed by their male colleagues and reflect an approach of prophetic dialogue. It is those views that we wish to explore here.

Antonia Leonora van der Meer's article stresses the missionary's ongoing relationship with God and the calling from God that drives the work of mission. She uses the Scriptures to emphasize the unity of the human race and the love of Jesus for all nations – a love that broke through the disciple's prejudices, preparing them for a worldwide ministry.[8] She relies on the mission theology of David Bosch, drawing out the thread of God's

---

5 Bevans and Schroeder, *Prophetic Dialogue*, 63.

6 William D. Taylor (ed.), *Global Missiology for the 21st Century: The Iguassu Dialogue*, Grand Rapids, MI: Baker, 2000, 2.

7 Taylor, *Global Missiology*, 17–21.

8 A. L. Van der Meer, 'The Scriptures, the Church, and Humanity: Who Should Do Mission and Why?', in Taylor, *Global Missiology*, 149–62 (151).

relationship of love as a basis for mission.[9] Mission, according to van der Meer is 'the fruit of the love of God'.[10] It is 'caring for whole human beings with the compassionate love of God'.[11] Van der Meer brings her emotions into her theology. 'When Christians and even missiologists call Africa "the cursed continent," call African culture "demonic," and look down upon our African brothers and sisters, I become very angry.'[12] Here is the 'fierce challenge' spoken of by Stephen Bevans and Roger Schroeder when they relate mission to prophecy.[13] Van der Meer shows empathy for the suffering of extreme poverty many faced in Angola and declares that 'in response to my caring, many believed'.[14] She stresses enabling the local people to do the work of mission, not rejecting some groups as heretics but treating all as those who have the right to learn and understand what Jesus commanded us in Matthew 28.20.[15] In those and other ways, van der Meer changes the tone of evangelical mission theology from one of authority and effectiveness to one of respect, compassion and whole engagement of the mind and the emotions in the work of mission. She demonstrates the veracity of Bevans and Schroeder's statement that 'Christians cannot engage in mission that is not contextual'.[16]

Miriam Adeney's essay centres on the theme of unity-in-diversity, couching respect for American subcultures in the language of Ephesians 1.9 – the mysterious plan of God to bring all things together in Christ. She advocates seeing the subcultures of the United States as unique and precious particularities to be explored and embraced. 'This means teaching unity at every opportunity', she declares.[17] It is in Adeney's essay that we hear the condemnation of racism and classism, ideas that seem distant from the formal Affirmations of the consultation. Fostering such unity demands a reconciling spiritual practice as outlined by Robert Schreiter in *Prophetic Dialogue*, a spirituality that 'facilitates the recognition of God's gracious working in the midst of so much violence and tragedy'.[18] Adeney connects her anthropological insights and social analysis about American compartmentalization with her convictions about the respect and unity that

---

9 Van der Meer, 'The Scriptures, the Church, and Humanity', 153.

10 Van der Meer, 'The Scriptures, the Church, and Humanity', 153.

11 Van der Meer, 'The Scriptures, the Church, and Humanity', 154.

12 Van der Meer, 'The Scriptures, the Church, and Humanity', 154. Here we see a direct link to both the prophetic tradition of the Old Testament and the explanation made by Bevans and Schroeder of mission as prophecy that 'calls people back to the right direction'. *Prophetic Dialogue*, 51.

13 Bevans and Schroeder, *Prophetic Dialogue*, 51.

14 Van der Meer, 'The Scriptures, the Church, and Humanity', 155.

15 Van der Meer, 'The Scriptures, the Church, and Humanity', 157.

16 Bevans and Schroeder, *Prophetic Dialogue*, 63.

17 Miriam Adeney, 'Telling Stories: Contextualization and American Missiology', in Taylor, *Global Missiology*, 377–88 (385).

18 Bevans and Schroeder, *Prophetic Dialogue*, 70ff.

American Christians must foster in order to tell the story of how God in Christ brings together all things.

Rose Dowsett's essay gives an overview of problems in the West, an analysis possibly sourced in Os Guinness's work. The creative part of her theology appears somewhere in the middle of her discourse when she introduces the topic of listening. She calls upon Christians to listen, not only to the Word, but also to non-Western churches. She describes the preferred attitude of that listening as humility.[19] Dowsett argues that critical contextualization begins with humility and continues as a practice. Rather than a thought process, she describes contextualization as something the missionary *does* – 'a living out of biblical truth in the here-and-now'.[20] Here, as in van der Meer's essay, Dowsett brings emotions into her theology. She says, 'The Western church must listen with tears and pain and penitence.'[21] Here we see a call for a genuine practice of *kenosis* as described by Yves Raguin in *Prophetic Dialogue*.[22]

Paula Harris's article on the Nestorian Church brings up the question of women's influence in earlier times. She wonders what influence clergy wives had on the Church through their husbands. She speculates that queens and mothers of queens could have affected the course of Christian history in that part of the world. These wonderings show a keen interest in women's mission theologies and the desire to recover women's voices. Although she does express unity as a theological concept, Harris admires the Nestorian communities for their ability to display unity in the face of diversity.[23]

Cathy Ross's reflections on the Iguassu Affirmation lament the lack of women's voices at the consultation. Here again, emotions are not ruled out as part of theological reflection as Ross says she is 'shocked and disappointed' that women's perspectives are not heard.[24] She brings out that although women represent two-thirds of missionaries worldwide, only 19 out of 160 delegates were women. She speaks of the need for evangelicals to address women's issues as a response to the injustices that women suffer.[25] Finally she stresses the importance of developing partnerships of equals in mission and advocates for humility in the process of interacting with

---

19 Rose Dowsett, 'Dry Bones in the West', in Taylor, *Global Missiology*, 447–62 (454).

20 Dowsett, 'Dry Bones', 455.

21 Dowsett, 'Dry Bones', 456.

22 Bevans and Schroeder refer to Yves Raguin's *I am Sending you: Spirituality and the Missioner* (Manila: East Asian Pastoral Institute, 1973) as an example of *kenosis* as a missionary virtue (*Prophetic Dialogue*, 169, n. 8).

23 Paula Harris, 'Nestorian Community, Spirituality, and Mission', in Taylor, *Global Missiology*, 497. Stephen B. Bevans and Roger P. Schroeder also note this trait of the East Syrian Churches who saw themselves more as a diaspora community than as an institution. *Constants in Context: A Theology of Mission for Today*, Maryknoll, NY: Orbis, 2004, 133.

24 Cathy Ross et al., 'The Iguassu Affirmation: A Commentary by Eight Reflective Practitioners', in Taylor, *Global Missiology*, 521.

25 Ross et al., 'The Iguassu Affirmation', 530.

Christians from other cultures and contexts.[26] Here Ross brings together critical aspects of prophetic dialogue as prophecy, a critique of the injustice of inequality and the importance of an attitude of humility, salient features of prophetic dialogue as mission.

The common themes and their relation to prophetic dialogue as mission in these articles are not difficult to find. Unity-in-diversity, the need for women's voices to be heard, careful listening, critical practices of contextualization and compassion, emotional expression and humility are stressed in these articles. The Iguassu Affirmation might read differently if those themes were added to the evangelical mission theology already present in the document. Its tone would change – perhaps to a more fierce yet more friendly theology of mission for the twenty-first century.

Roman Catholic Women's Mission Theologies

Women's Roman Catholic mission theology has gone through major changes since World War Two. In her book *The Missionary Movement in American Catholic History*, missiologist Angelyn Dries OSF describes World War Two itself as an important marker for Catholic mission theology. Between 1946 and 1959, Maryknoll founder John Considine developed a broad vision to frame human societies into a Christian social order. Women in mission took on the fourfold goals of 'world Christianity': regard, love for and knowledge of all cultures; promotion of the welfare of all; justice according to Christian ideals; and the transmission of Christ's teaching to non-Catholics and non-Christians.[27] The women religious who developed the US Catholic school curriculum of this era focused on those goals, thus having a profound impact on future leaders of the Church. The curriculum emphasized the evils of racism and attitudes of superiority towards others, themes not dissimilar from some of the voices we heard by women in the World Evangelical Alliance.[28] The 'trail guides' in Bevans and Schroeder's *Prophetic Dialogue* move in a similar direction. 'He or she has been given the gift of being able to read the signs of impending storms, how to stay the course on a path that keeps on forking, and to offer words of caution or warning in the face of potential danger.'[29]

By the 1960s mission to Latin America involved women in both pastoral ministry and education for women's leadership. The Sisters of St Joseph brought a theology of the mystical body to Peru in 1965. They stressed the importance of living with the same privations as the people they were serving, becoming willing to receive gifts of religion and social warmth from the

26 Ross et al., 'The Iguassu Affirmation', 536.

27 Angelyn Dries, *The Missionary Movement in American Catholic History*, Maryknoll, NY: Orbis, 1998, 168.

28 Dries, *Missionary Movement*, 269.

29 Bevans and Schroeder, *Prophetic Dialogue*, 50f.

people.[30] Mary McCormick, a widow and lay volunteer demonstrated that theology spending 27 years in Colombia. She organized a nutrition and milk programme for young mothers, started a day-care centre and managed a loan programme focused on housing. In addition she organized a four-week 'conscientization' programme for North Americans so they could live with local families in Bogota and assist her in her work in the barrio.[31]

Two-thirds of the Papal Volunteers for Latin America (PAVLA) during that time were single women.[32] Those women had the opportunity to practise the Latin American liberation theology that was being developed by Gustavo Gutierrez and others. Many women missionaries focused on education with a two-level approach. Educating the elite was crucial for the growth of the Church, but women missionaries also emphasized educating the poor, grooming them for a way out of poverty and demonstrating the love of Christ at the same time.[33] Here we see prophetic dialogue in action, a praxis of dialogue and prophecy melded into a contextual theology.

In the area of pastoral formation, Gretchen Berg, a Franciscan from Rochester MN, started Regina Mundi, a two-year programme that prepared Peruvian women to enter university. Through weekly seminars on liturgy, ecclesiology, Scripture and the Church in the modern world, the sisters learned and discussed the latest theology. Conferences were sponsored that brought rich and poor congregations together for the first time.[34] Although conflict between rich and poor communities ended this effort in 1967, the women educators were at the forefront of practising a theology that would significantly influence the Catholic mission theology in the coming decades.[35]

An important aspect of that theological vision for mission had to do with method. Mary Xavier O'Donnell MM, stressed a new approach to evangelization of Hispanic groups in Chicago. In teaching the catechism of the Family of God, she affirmed the traditional family values that the people embraced, using what they already knew as a basis for understanding God in their lives. The emphasis was on hearing the Word of God in experience and community which then led to action.[36] That liberation theology praxis model was used in women's groups: observe, judge, act.[37]

During this time, women religious moved from educational institutions into more pastoral work.[38] The formation of communities of the Word, an emphasis on team ministry and the development of lay leadership provided

---

30 Dries, *Missionary Movement*, 185.
31 Dries, *Missionary Movement*, 195.
32 Dries, *Missionary Movement*, 196.
33 Dries, *Missionary Movement*, 225.
34 Dries, *Missionary Movement*, 207.
35 Dries, *Missionary Movement*, 213.
36 Dries, *Missionary Movement*, 218f.
37 Dries, *Missionary Movement*, 225.
38 Dries, *Missionary Movement*, 243.

important trajectories for the new ecclesiology that the Church was embracing at the time of Vatican II. Women were at the forefront of implementing an ecclesial model that challenged the passivity and dependence that had marred the experience of many people in Latin America. Dries describes that ecclesial model as one that 'emphasized the sacramentality of human beings, promoted cohesiveness and collective experiential knowledge, and brought the Word of God to bear on daily life'.[39] As missionaries listened to people telling the stories of their own experiences, a spirit of humility developed among pastoral ministers.[40] Claude Marie Barbour's 'mission in reverse' emphasizes that attitude.[41] 'There is a real need today to recognize that mission should be done in vulnerability, in humility, and with a sense of being open to be evangelized by those whom we are evangelizing – a kind of "mission in reverse."'[42]

Another important theme of women's Catholic mission theology since World War Two is the theme of self-sacrifice. Living with the poor, seeing God's face in their visage and being willing to do whatever it takes to follow the mission call cost a number of Latin American missionaries their lives. Maura Clarke MM and Maureen Courtney CSA are only two of the women that gave their lives working among the poor in Latin America. Their contributions left us an unforgettable legacy.

Although the number of Catholic missionaries has decreased since the 1970s, the gains made through use of new educational and pastoral care methods are still with us. Women's influence on educational programmes that included anti-racism and equality dimensions, their pastoral work in empowering local communities and their dedication to the mission task provide cogent tools for mission theology today.

Although gender roles were at issue in many communities and women's ideas were sometimes not celebrated by the establishment, women's mission theologies moved ahead in educational and pastoral formation forums. Before 1960, a theology of the mystical body was emphasized, along with an emphasis on world Christianity as it was then defined. Developing curricula that emphasized equality of all peoples had great influence on future Catholic leaders. During the 1960s a horizontal ecclesiology and an option for the poor were at the forefront of women's educational efforts and mission practices. Those contributions by Catholic women to mission theology and methodology stand out as salient as we reflect on mission theology since the middle of the twentieth century.

As we move into an era of mission as prophetic dialogue we see its characteristics reflected in both the evangelical women missiologists and themes emerging in Roman Catholic women's mission theologies. Parallels

39 Dries, *Missionary Movement*, 244.
40 Dries, *Missionary Movement*, 244.
41 Bevans and Schroeder, *Prophetic Dialogue*, 22 and note 17, 160.
42 Bevans and Schroeder, *Prophetic Dialogue*, 22.

between Christian unity and a theology of the mystical body are clear. An emphasis on anti-racism and equality among all peoples can also be traced in both streams of theological reflection as can promotion of an attitude of humility and a goal of shared leadership. An emphasis on contextualization also runs through both evangelical and Catholic women's mission theologies.

A major difference can be seen in the Catholic women theologians' use of a liberation theology methodology that focuses on experience as a field for hearing God's word in community. Evangelical missiologists tend to emphasize the Word first and then the hearing of the Word in community rather than starting with experience and seeing God's word primarily through that lens.

American Society of Missiology's Women Missiologists

American Society of Missiologists' (ASM) women are recovering the history of women in mission in both Protestant and Catholic traditions, analysing theological streams and critiquing mission methods, making theological contributions to the academy and the Church and utilizing insights from social science for mission. Their focus on context and the needs of local settings dovetail with the model of mission as prophetic dialogue.

Beginning historically, significant mission history has been done by Sister Angelyn Dries OSF and Dana Robert. Much of that work reclaims the history of women in mission in both Protestant and Catholic realms. We have just explored some of the theological themes that Angelyn Dries recounts of Roman Catholic women's mission theology and methods.

On the Protestant side, significant historical recovery of women's theologies of mission has been captured in Dana Robert's *American Women in Mission: A Social History of Their Thought and Practice*. She documents the rise and fall of the women's missionary movement, highlighting theologies that emphasized the personal and ethical dimensions of mission work, ecumenical cooperation, women's missionary work with women and children and issues of women's leadership.[43] Unfortunately, in mainline denominations, that movement was quelled after World War Two, which Robert notes marked 'a prelude to foreign missions becoming a lower priority for the [mainline] churches'.[44] Looking more broadly at mission history, Robert outlines the major themes of women in mission as service, healing, teaching and hospitality.[45] She notes that because they were barred from ministerial roles, women missionaries became educators, establishing schools and

43 Dana Robert, *American Women in Mission: A Social History of Their Thought and Practice*, Macon, GA: Mercer University Press, 1997, 409–16.

44 Robert, *American Women in Mission*, 306f.

45 Dana Robert, *Christian Mission: How Christianity Became a World Religion*, Chichester: Wiley-Blackwell, 2009, 141.

training girls and women as well as boys and young men who would later become denominational leaders. In so doing, women have left a legacy of educated women and efforts to claim human rights for women all over the world. She describes women's mission method as one of building relationships, a method that not only allowed women access to women of other cultures but kept them from charges of cultural imperialism as they partnered with local and national leaders to establish hospitals, work for human rights and educate women for leadership.

With such a legacy, Robert asserts, 'The history of mission must focus on women for the majority of the Christians in the world are women.'[46] Looking at recent decades, we find that the decline of mission efforts in the mainline Protestant churches of the United States after World War Two is not reflected in the Catholic, Pentecostal and conservative Protestant traditions. Catholic women in Latin America implemented new forms of mission theology. Conservative Protestant women developed specialized forms of mission, producing Bible translations, gospel recordings and the training of indigenous pastors.[47] Pentecostalism grew exponentially after the 1960s spawning interest of women in mission in Central and South America. Protestant models of family life brought many into the churches in Latin America and in Africa, views of the missionary as mother played a central role in the spread of the gospel.[48] The contextualization process in those efforts led to expansion and indigenization of Christianity.

Another scholar who has reclaimed part of women's theological work in mission is Bonnie Sue Lewis. In *Creating Christian Indians: Native Clergy in the Presbyterian Church*, Lewis highlights the productive relationships women missionaries developed with Native American pastors. Despite frequent conflict, women missionaries educated and empowered the elders of Native American congregations to take leadership. Missionary Kate McBeth saw the wisdom of the Nez Perces' desire to establish their own churches with Native leadership.[49] Part of the appeal of the Christian gospel for Native Americans was its call to the weak and impoverished. Women missionaries reached out to the poor and lowly, practising hospitality and honouring Native American leaders who had to depend on persuasion to get support for their decisions. Because of their vulnerability and attitude of humility, women could more easily affirm male leadership among the Nez Perces than could male missionary leaders. Between 1874 and 1932, 18 men became ordained Presbyterian ministers under the training of women missionaries.[50]

---

46 Robert, *Christian Mission*, 141.

47 Robert, *American Women in Mission*, xxii.

48 Robert, *Christian Mission*, 130f.

49 Bonnie Sue Lewis, *Creating Christian Indians: Native Clergy in the Presbyterian Church*, Norman, OK: University of Oklahoma Press, 2003, 119.

50 Lewis, *Creating Christian Indians*, 121.

Besides reclaiming histories of women in mission, missiologists are re-orienting mission theology to benefit from women's experiences and theologies. Robert notes that the majority of Christian missionaries have been women and the majority of Christians in the world today are women.[51] Mission theology by women provides a tremendous resource developing a fitting response to those facts.

Sherron George's theology of mission provides one resource for that reorientation. Post-colonial critiques have shown the necessity of working in partnerships with the people that North American missionaries serve. George's *Called as Partners in Christ's Service: The Practice of God's Mission* describes how to develop those partnerships with the 70 per cent of Christians in the Two-Thirds World.

George focuses her theology on the mission of God, a Trinitarian mission that is part of redemption. She first describes God's mission of love and light to the world as portrayed in the Gospel of John. Turning to contemporary missionaries, George stresses attitudes and practices that give Christianity the appeal that inheres in it – compassion, respect for others, humility and the ability to receive as well as give.[52]

As she tells her own story, Sherron George traces a movement that reflects important changes in her mission theology.[53] Mutuality was her paradigm for mission in the 1970s. She immersed herself in the life and culture of rural congregations in south-west Brazil.[54] During the 1980s she gained a new perspective from her doctoral project – an understanding of solidarity as a missional stance.[55] In the 1990s, George was called to teach at the IPB Seminary of the South in Campinas. As the first ordained woman to teach at this oldest and largest Presbyterian seminary in Brazil, George felt herself moving into marginality as a new identity.[56] George was transformed by 'mission in reverse' during her 23 years in Brazil. From there she could move to a new attitude, a 'bold humility'. In that attitude she crafted a new definition of mission: 'Mission is everything the local-global church is sent into the world to be and do as a participant in God's mission and every person and gift the local-global church receives in Christ's name and way.'[57]

The work of Marsha Snulligan Haney provides insights into evangelism and Afrocentric approaches to Christian ministry. Standing in the prophetic tradition of the Black Church, Haney sees God as a liberating relational

---

51 Robert, *Christian Mission*, 141.

52 Sherron George, *Called as Partners in Christ's Service: The Practice of God's Mission*, Louisville, KY: Geneva Press, 2004, 60.

53 Sherron George, 'From Missionary to Missiologist at the Margins: Three Decades of Transforming Mission', in Patricia Lloyd-Sidle and Bonnie Sue Lewis (eds), *Teaching Mission in a Global Context*, Louisville, KY: Geneva Press, 2001, 40–53.

54 George, 'From Missionary to Missiologist', 43.

55 George, 'From Missionary to Missiologist', 45.

56 George, 'From Missionary to Missiologist', 51.

57 George, 'From Missionary to Missiologist', 52.

God interested in all peoples. Firmly rooted in biblical texts, Haney stresses the importance of addressing contextual challenges in diverse urban settings. That concern has taken her into studies of Protestant–Islamic relations and African American Presbyterians who work in a pluralistic denomination. From the Afrocentric perspective, Haney says 'there is no validity to our spirituality if it does not result in social action'.[58] Here again we are reminded of the focus on spirituality, prophecy and contextualization provided by the prophetic dialogue mission model explored in this book.

Unpacking Haney's substantive mission theology takes us into the middle of urban, pluralistic and post-colonial contemporary contexts. In telling her own story, Haney speaks of listening, seeking peace and staying connected to a missionary liberating God.[59] Using a pilgrim metaphor for missional identity allows Haney to focus both on the meaning of faith for the individual as well as the structures and systems that need the transforming power of the gospel.[60] Unwilling to leave her theology at the level of generalizations, Haney goes on to describe six steps for changing the 'traditional, convenient, and familiar patterns of mission defined by paternalism, exclusion, and elitism' into a new paradigm that responds to 'the *missio Dei* from the *ecclesia* of every nation, language, and people group'.[61] Those include understanding the relative nature of truth, centring on ways of being in the context of relationships and affirming diversity in a way that appreciates the gifts of others.[62] Haney's thinking and her process in developing a new mission identity offer crucial guideposts to missiologists as women and men formulate theologies in a fast-paced world of diversity.

Miriam Adeney, whose work was cited earlier in this chapter, brings anthropological insights into play in her theology of mission. Her work is both global and focused on issues in North American contexts. According to Adeney, reaching across cultural boundaries happens everywhere and has always been the Christian's call.[63] Adeney puts action behind her words by modelling a cross-cultural mission in her practice of teaching writing skills to Christians all over the world. Her stress on unity-in-diversity colours her work with both ecclesiological and egalitarian overtones, which she displays in her work on Muslim women. 'Can a single woman who follows

---

58 Marsha Snulligan Haney, 'Afrocentricity: A Missiological Pathway toward Christian Transformation', in Marsha Snulligan Haney and Ronald Edward Peters (eds), *Afrocentric Approaches to Christian Ministry: Strengthening Urban Congregations in African America Communities*, Lanham, MD: University Press of America, 2006, 151–65 (162).

59 Marsha Snulligan Haney, 'Toward the Development of a New Christian Missiological Identity', in Lloyd-Sidle and Lewis, *Teaching Mission*, 79–92 (79f.).

60 Haney, 'Development', 89.

61 Haney, 'Development', 91.

62 Haney, 'Development', 91.

63 Miriam Adeney, *Kingdom without Borders: The Untold Story of Global Christianity*, Downers Grove, IL: InterVarsity Press, 2009, 33.

Jesus thrive in the Muslim world?' she asks.[64] Adeney also contributes to the conversations among missiologists with her cogent critique of the compartmentalization in the academic field of missiology as well as in American life.[65]

ASM women missiologists have made significant contributions to reclaiming the history of women in mission as well as helping us to reorient our current understandings of mission theologies and methods. A striking congruence with prophetic dialogue as a mission model runs through their theologies.

Salient Themes and Questions

This whirlwind tour of women's mission theologies barely scratches the surface of the work that women have done and continue to do in mission theology, education and practice. Identifying a few salient themes provides us with questions and directions for theological reflection and links to the prophetic dialogue model.

First, the theme of God's relationality and the claim that places on Christian missioners to work in love with others stands out across all of the theologies observed in this chapter. It was also a strong theme in my own study of Christian women in Indonesia. Women there sought to sustain relationships with women and honour leaders even as they pursued theological education and leadership in the Church.[66] This is not a theme unique to women missiologists, however. But it does demand more study of women's interpretations of relationships with God and others. How are those views unique and how are they influenced by gender considerations – sociological, ecclesiological and biological? How might they fit in with a prophetic dialogue model of Christian mission?

Second, the themes of unity, of God's love for all humanity and of the importance of treating others with respect comes through strongly in much of the women's work in theology we have looked at. Whether couched in terms of compassion, justice or unity, the focus is on the mission of God in the world as a mission for all peoples, to be carried out through work that shows honour and love to all. As Christian communities reach out to those of other religions, respect becomes a baseline practice for interacting with others in our pluralistic world.[67] How can missiologists tie together

---

64 Miriam Adeney, *Daughters of Islam: Building Bridges with Muslim Women*, Downers Grove, IL: InterVarsity Press, 2002, 110.

65 Adeney, 'Telling Stories', 384f.

66 Frances S. Adeney, *Christian Women in Indonesia: A Narrative Study of Gender and Religion*, Syracuse, NY: Syracuse University Press, 2003, 113f.

67 Terry Muck and Frances S. Adeney, *Christianity Encountering World Religions: The Practice of Mission in the Twenty-first Century*, Grand Rapids, MI: Baker Academic, 2009, 174.

unity-in-diversity, liberating justice for marginalized people and ecclesial practices of worship and welcome together? Women's concern for those themes puts women missiologists in a position to expand and nuance the model of mission as prophetic dialogue.

Third, the emphasis on Christian values, particularly attitudes of humility and willingness to receive from others as an incarnational witness run through many of the studies. A further emphasis on family values was stressed in some of the work. The questions arising from this focus include parameters of family values as societies change, how humility presents itself in different cultures and how to become receptive to the gifts that others have to offer. Some of those questions are tackled by George and Haney. They are wrestled with in earlier chapters of this book. I also deal with them in my work on giftive mission and graceful evangelism.[68] But there is much more to be done.

A willingness to express emotions in doing scholarly work presents itself in some of the essays. How much does that willingness relate to social status in the Church and academy as women are 'given permission' in many societies to express emotion in ways that are discouraged for men? Should women lead in helping missionaries and missiologists to become more willing to engage in dialogue that includes expressions of disappointment and anger as well as joy and celebration? As women missiologists and mission workers practise legitimating emotions in their theological work, it may make a significant impact on theologies of mission and their prophetic usefulness to the churches.

Listening is another thread that runs through the work of women theologians in this chapter. Listening to the Third World majority, listening to the marginalized, listening with the intent to respond in love, listening to learn, listening to honour others different from ourselves. Becoming open enough to actually listen to someone who has radically different views from one's own is a task that takes conscious effort to achieve.[69] So here we confront a final question that is not only a research question but also a personal one; not only a prophetic issue but a gender issue.

I began this chapter with a story of Carol Rose Ikler, and I would like to close with a reference to her. Doing theology was an everyday practice for Ikler. She could not imagine going a day without reflecting on the work of God in the world and how Christians can be involved in it. Doing this in an academic setting was a new adventure for women in the 1950s and 1960s. Today it is commonplace. Can we utilize that practice of women seminarians, pastors, counsellors and missiologists to a better end than we have in the past? Through that intentional and intense listening we can become part of the prophetic dialogue of mission in our world.

68 Chapter 15 'Radical Habits', in Frances S. Adeney, *Graceful Evangelism: Christian Witness in a Complex World*, Grand Rapids, MI: Baker Academic, 2010.

69 Adeney, *Kingdom without Borders*, 166.

11

An Anthropology of Prophetic Dialogue: Rooted in Hope

MARIA CIMPERMAN

Introduction

What kind of person can not only do but live prophetic dialogue? What attributes, or even more, what virtues, are needed to live prophetic dialogue? What, in other words, grounds an anthropology of prophetic dialogue? These questions were part of my wonderings as I looked at the world around me this year, a year in which we mark a MOOC[1] course in Arabic from a university in Israel; efforts by Roman Catholic bishops in the Congo to galvanize people against a referendum to change the Constitution which currently mandates term limits for the highest political office; Olympic Games in Sochi, Russia, where politics for a few moments are forgotten as many watch athletes excel in beauty, speed and grace; a new Pope's words, actions and dispositions begin to shift polemic rhetoric in the US church and politics to communal attentiveness of persons made economically poor and marginalized; where ever more medical school students in Venezuela are trained through a community health model which quickly brings them to learning about and responding to needs of those often removed from help; a billionaire is planning a $100 million ad campaign during the 2014 US elections to push leaders to take action on climate change, this in the wake of a devastating November 2013 super typhoon and worldwide efforts to offer aid in the Philippines.

It is this same world which marks violent political upheaval in the Ukraine; continuing devastation and slaughter upon the citizens of Syria; protests in Brazil about the money spent on World Cup 2014 and the 2016 Summer Olympics preparations when there are great needs for education and civic infrastructure; questions about how South Africa will continue to move forward in democracy living into a future their beloved Nelson Mandela helped create and which they must now live into without him; uncertainty about how the structural reform of the Roman Catholic curia will transpire, as well as how Pope Francis's words about greater inclusion of women in leadership will materialize. Tensions continue all over

---

1 Massive Open Online Course.

the world: measured dance steps between North Korea and South Korea as reunions of separated family members ensue to ease strained relations and signify overtures for better relations.[2] At the same time there are ongoing delicate negotiations between Iran and the UN Security Council to create a framework for nuclear talks that can ease sanctions and reduce threats of military action.[3] The dances in all these areas and more are ongoing.

We walk a world which is the reign of God here and not yet.

The students I am privileged to walk with at Catholic Theological Union are involved in dances that require prophetic dialogue. One is working on a project to assist Rwandan youth whose parents are survivors, victims or perpetrators of the genocide of 1994 find a way to dialogue beyond violence, to incarnate 'never again' with another way to live together. Another is trying to create a process for education, 'conscientization' and socially just action of the people of Congo related to political matters. One person is working to get underneath the 'economics of impoverishment' in a part of Africa that brings early teenagers to clinics to become pregnant and then sells the infants in order to pay for education. A student is working to connect very diverse young people in an economically struggling neighbourhood of South Side Chicago. Another person is searching out the systemic causes and response to high unemployment among young adult black males who voice little hope for a better future or even a long adult life. Yet others are together looking at how parishioners might see their use of transportation as a communal effort at responsible use of resources and reducing their use of plastics as an act of faith in action. And there is more.

We walk a world which is the reign of God here and not yet.

Prophetic dialogue, developed marvellously and masterfully by Stephen Bevans and Roger Schroeder, has much to contribute towards the reign of God calling us in the midst of our world today. Prophetic dialogue is what Bevans and Schroeder describe in part as: 'an attitude of respect and friendship, which permeates or should permeate all those activities constituting the evangelizing mission of the church', an attitude that can be called 'the spirit of dialogue'.[4] The focus here is on

> a basic attitude, something that not only is practised in the specific *practice* of dialogue, but one that gives direction to each and all of the elements of mission, whether it be the way Christians give witness or proclaim the

---

2 Choe-Sang-Hun, 'Amid Hugs and Tears, Korean families Divided by War Reunite', *New York Times*, 20 February 2014, www.nytimes.com/2014/02/21/world/asia/north-and-south-koreans-meet-in-emotional-family-reunions.html?hp.

3 Steven Erlanger, 'Iran and 6 Powers Agree on Terms for Nuclear Talks', *New York Times*, 20 February 2014, www.nytimes.com/2014/02/21/world/middleeast/iran.html?hp.

4 Stephen B. Bevans and Roger P. Schroeder, *Prophetic Dialogue: Reflections on Christian Mission Today*, Maryknoll, NY: Orbis, 2011, 21.

gospel, celebrate liturgy or pray, do deeds of justice and peacemaking, engage in inculturation or in the process of reconciliation.[5]

They also remind us to respond as the prophets did, rooted in dialogue, 'someone who listens, who is attentive, who sees, who has a sensitivity to the world and to women and men', who 'speaks forth' in word or deed God's message of salvation, offering a 'vision of what God has in store for people in God's plan of salvation'.[6] Prophets speak out when people are not living out God's call.

We are called to prophetic dialogue in our world today, participating in God's mission; God's offer of life in abundance for all. Prophetic dialogue, both separately and together, is desperately needed in our world today, for we walk in a world which is the reign of God here and not yet.

So, what sustains us for prophetic dialogue? When we see that some of the challenges of today were here yesterday and many yesterdays before? When we realize that the changes called for are immense yet must begin at some moment? When we realize that we too must change if we expect change to happen? When we realize that prophetic dialogue is a process of transformation of all, ourselves and the other who is neighbour? What will sustain us, to be continually transformed and open ourselves to God transforming us and all of creation? What sustains us for prophetic dialogue in the long and the short haul?

Hope: The anthropology of prophetic dialogue is an anthropology of hope.

Hope is needed, hope is in fact, required, for prophetic dialogue. To live prophetic dialogue one must be a person of hope. When the mission we are about is God's mission of the Good News of love, mercy and reconciliation in relationships with one another and with God in all and when we are to live this mission in the world we see around us, hope (theological hope) sustains and animates us for prophetic dialogue. Hope naturally opens and moves us to prophetic dialogue and hope sustains us for prophetic dialogue.

Hope is intimately connected to prophetic dialogue and, in fact, grounds prophetic dialogue. Prophetic dialogue is manifestation of hope. Only a person of hope can live and sustain prophetic dialogue in our world. In what follows I would like to consider five dimensions of hope which a person of hope and even more, communities of hope, offer prophetic dialogue, particularly in the areas of justice and peacemaking. Attentive to the many avenues that prophetic dialogue engages, I focus on justice and peacemaking, because these are two areas in which I engage which consistently invoke prophetic dialogue yet where prophetic dialogue strains mightily to respond. Hope must hold all persons seeking prophetic dialogue or the strain wears down and breaks lasting efforts. I begin by defining hope within

---

5 Bevans and Schroeder, *Prophetic Dialogue*, 21–2.
6 Bevans and Schroeder, *Prophetic Dialogue*, 42.

the framework of a virtue and then open up five dimensions (rooted in reality; contemplative; paschal, imaginative, communal), which offer particular significant relevance and connection to prophetic dialogue.

Hope and Virtue

Hope is a virtue and as such it fits under the greatest virtue, which is love. A virtue is a disposition and habit, which flows out of who we are and who we want to become, and it offers a vision of how to get there. Virtues are teleological; that is, there is a goal or end towards which they strive. In Christianity, the ultimate end is union with God, and we live out this desire on a daily basis through our love of God, neighbour and self. Throughout our lives we strive towards this *telos* or end, and as long as we live our task is not complete. Virtues, like our human nature, are also dynamic; therefore, as we continue to learn, grow and mature, so our level of understanding and depth of living the virtues evolve.

Hope gives us a particular sustained moral and spiritual vision. In addition, it is the transcendent virtue that animates and informs the virtues which follow. Hope not only gives us the vision, it sanctions and sustains the vision. Christian hope tells us what type of vision we have.[7] Hope is also a prime Christian resource of the imagination. Hope offers a horizon for our expectations in both tangible and nontangible ways. Hope allows us to reshape our reality in a particular way. We begin this reshaping grounded in our first marker of hope.

Context of Hope: Grounded in Reality

Even as hope provides a horizon for our expectations, a person of hope is firmly grounded in reality, a reality in which movement forward is not easy to obtain yet within the realm of possible options. The reality towards which hope leans is that of the wounded heart of humanity and the wounded earth. Hope looks at reality through the lens of gospel faith and points to areas in need of prophetic dialogue. Not only does hope lean in towards *los pobres*, the poor, but towards what in parts of Latin America people call *los miserables*, the miserable. The Catholic social tradition urges us on, probably most famously exemplified in the opening lines of the Preface to the Pastoral Constitution on the Church in the Modern World (*Gaudium et Spes*): 'The joys and the hopes, the griefs and the anxieties of the men (people) of this age, especially those who are poor or in any way afflicted, these are the joys and hopes, the griefs and anxieties of the followers of

---

7 I distinguish Christian hope here from existential or humanistic hope. Some of this early pondering on hope came from my book *When God's People Have HIV/AIDS: An Approach to Ethics*, Maryknoll, NY: Orbis, 2005.

Christ.'[8] This is often the context of prophetic dialogue towards justice and peace-building. Reality invites us to have the other and the concerns of the other in as clear view as possible. What does hope offer a person here? Much.

Describing hope as rooted in reality, not easy to obtain yet possible, within the realm of possible options, flows from a reading of Thomas Aquinas's look at the virtue of hope.[9] Hope is not pie in the sky, inattentive to the realities present. Catholic social encyclicals begin with a wide-eyed look at reality around us. It is the standard format for bringing our faith to a situation. I cannot hope for peace in the city of Chicago if I do not realize that within a walk of where I live we have some of the highest gun violence rates in the country. And I need to know why this is so.

We hope only when the answer is not so easy, so visible. We turn to hope when we cannot see the road in front of us and our usual GPS is non-functional and actually ineffective. Hope is needed when the journey may be long or arduous and even when we are not sure what the outcome will be. Hope costs. It is not simple or easy. At times it is not even logical (to society).

At the same time, we hope only for what we think, imagine, long to be possible. If there is no chance at all, we do not hope. A 1 per cent chance is hope. We actually only lament because we hope, because we believe the future could be other than what the present is. That is the book of Lamentations. When we have no hope we simply despair. Nothing says this is going to be easy, or that we will not suffer. It is the long haul often enough, yet there are sparks that indicate something is possible. Prophetic dialogue happens under these very conditions and requires hope.

One of my burgeoning interests is peace-building and work towards reconciliation, both social and interpersonal. A story is told about Archbishop John Baptist Odama serving in northern Uganda, the region where the Lord's Resistance Army was primarily located. He regularly went into the camps of leader Joseph Kony and even spent the night there. When people ask why he does this – he could be killed! – he simply answers, 'He is a child of God. He is one of my sheep too.' Bishop Odama has hope, sees possibility.[10]

Yes, the hope offered, looking straight at reality, must be both outrageous (beyond what is initially deemed possible) and focused on needs and people outside ourselves. It was last year, in a course on contemporary vowed

---

8 Second Vatican Council, Pastoral Constitution on the Church in the Modern World (*Gaudium et Spes*), no. 1, www.vatican.va/archive/hist_councils/ii_vatican_council/documents/vat-ii_cons_19651207_gaudium-et-spes_en.html.

9 See Romanus Cessario, 'The Theological Virtue of Hope', in Stephen J. Pope (ed.), *The Ethics of Aquinas*, Washington, DC: Georgetown University Press, 2002, 232–43.

10 I am grateful to CTU colleague Robert J. Schreiter CPPS, who shared this narrative in his course, Reconciliation and Forgiveness, Fall 2013.

religious life, that Jerod, from Kenya, showed me again how outrageous hope can be. He wrote a reflection paper on the readings for that week, and on the back of the paper was a drawing. It was an image of the earth, and he put lines throughout it connecting human figures in the cities of Chicago, New York, Kampala, London, Paris, Johannesburg, Sydney, Rome and, at the centre, Nairobi. The title of the drawing was 'Hope Links Humanity'. This was all the more striking because he drew this the week after the terrorist killings in the mall in Nairobi on 21 September 2013. Jerod drew what peace and reconciliation expert John Paul Lederach writes: 'It is hope that links people half a world away',[11] and Jerod added, 'hope that somehow things will change because of the shared humanity'. Keenly aware of realities in his country, Jerod drew his hope.

Yet, even as one sees,[12] how does one go beyond seeing and acknowledging challenging realities and come to them with an open stance, willing to learn from all and see through the challenge to another reality? Contemplation.

Hope is Contemplative

Hope is contemplative, and a person who practises prophetic dialogue, too, can only exist within a contemplative spirit. Contemplative here is not to be equated (and thus dismissed if one is not part of it) with monastic or contemplative religious orders, but with an attitude of deep listening, reflectively and prayerfully seeking to hear what the Spirit might be inviting us to in dialogue.

Hope, real hope, is directed to God. Real hope is in God, is God. That must be the source of our hope. Anything else will crash in on us at some point. Hope requires that we keep our eyes on the horizon which is God. All else is held lightly or even let go of. In 2009 Carmelite Constance FitzGerald offered a plenary at the Catholic Theological Society of America in Halifax, Canada. The title of her address to theologians in all walks of life was 'From Impasse to Prophetic Hope: Crisis of Memory'.[13] In my estimation it is one of the most important articles for contemporary contemplative living today. What she writes is directly applicable and essential to prophetic dialogue.

FitzGerald, using John of the Cross's writings on 'purification of memory', writes that if we wish to get to the dawn of prophetic hope we will have to hold lightly, or even de-link, all our accolades as well as our painful experiences. Only when we can do this, so that we are not held back from

---

11 John Paul Lederach, *The Moral Imagination*, Oxford: Oxford University Press, 2005, 4.

12 I also want to note that these five elements may occur in various orders and in multiple layers.

13 Constance FitzGerald, 'From Impasse to Prophetic Hope: Crisis of Memory', *Catholic Theological Society of America Proceedings* 64 (2009), 21–42; www.ctsa-online.org/Convention%202009/0021-0042.pdf.

the future God is inviting by using the compass of the past, can we open ourselves to where God is leading. This is not easy, but the open stance of prophetic dialogue both requires contemplation and is a result or grace of contemplation. When God and what God is creating is the horizon we seek, then the future can emerge.

We must be aware, however, that, as Rahner says, there is no such thing as a real vacuum – something fills it. If we leave space for God, we have to hold that space and not use filler to fill it, as we are naturally apt to. (I think of the times I avoid something by checking email, surfing the web, getting up for something to drink or eat, going on the phone, etc.) However, if we do not fill the space, Rahner reminds us that there is God:

> There is no such thing either in the world or in the heart, as literal vacancy, as a vacuum. And whenever space is really left – by death, by renunciation, by parting, by apparent emptiness, provided the emptiness that cannot remain empty is not filled by the world, or activity, or chatter, or the deadly grief of the world – there is God.[14]

FitzGerald writes that 'You can see what a radical call this is. Those who answer it must be prepared to leave so much behind, to stop clinging to a security that has been taken away.'[15] The contemplative and the open stance required to navigate the shifts of our day is well described by Jan Richardson: 'You hollow us out, God, so that we may carry you, and you endlessly fill us only to be emptied again. Make smooth our inward spaces and sturdy, that we may hold you with less resistance and bear you with deeper grace.'[16]

If we can let go, which takes much effort because we often seek to hold on to what we can, so much more is possible. Again, FitzGerald writes:

> This dynamic of being able to yield unconditionally to God's future is what John of the Cross calls *hope*, a hope that exists without the signature of our life and works, a hope independent of us and our accomplishments (spiritual gifts or ordinary human achievements), a hope that can even embrace and work for a future without us. This theological hope is completely free from the past, fully liberated from our need to recognize ourselves in the future, to survive, to be someone ... The key insight here is that it is the limited self constituted by the past that needs to yield to the transforming power of God's call into the future.[17]

---

14 Daniel O'Leary, 'Space for Grace', *The Tablet*, 18 November 2006, quoted in FitzGerald, 'From Impasse to Prophetic Hope', 37.

15 FitzGerald, 'From Impasse to Prophetic Hope', 35.

16 Jan Richardson, *Night Visions: Searching the Shadows of Advent and Christmas*, Orlando, FL: Wanton Gospeller Press, 1998, 45.

17 FitzGerald, 'From Impasse to Prophetic Hope', 34.

It is important to note as well that the open stance is not one of being planted in shifting sands; rather it would be grounded in roots that are both deep and wide. This purification of memory may initially seem to be counter to prophetic dialogue. One may wonder whether de-linking could mean letting go of all you hold most dear. If that is the case, then what do you have to be prophetic about? This is not the case, however. The call and invitation is instead to let ourselves go into God and God's vision, which thus places our dialogue at the service of God's mission. When we open ourselves thus, the dialogue can truly be prophetic free, and possibilities emerge which were formerly not seen or imagined possible.

Hope is Paschal

We come now to the paschal nature of hope. As disciples, Jesus' life, suffering, death and resurrection are central to our paschal hope and our own lives. We are people who know Good Friday and also believe in Easter Sunday. The cross is part of our narratives and imagination. We know Good Friday and do not deny this. In fact, we are called to those very places of suffering, unmet need, anguish, to offer Jesus' love and to help the crucified people and the suffering earth community off the cross. We help as gently as we can, for we know nails bind in many ways. We do so because we are Easter people. Our humanity is grounded in the paschal mystery. We know Good Friday; we know the confusion of Holy Saturday. We also know and believe Easter Sunday and so we seek to live this vision of love and justice into the world. We are Easter people, and because we are so, we imagine differently even as we live in a world that still has suffering and injustice. Poet Denise Levertov beautifully reminds us that paschal people never tire of hope:

We have only begun
To imagine the fullness of life.
How could we tire of hope?
– so much is in bud.
How can desire fail?
– we have only begun
to imagine justice and mercy,
only begun to envision
how it might be
to live as siblings with beast and flower,
not as oppressors.[18]

---

18 Denise Levertov, 'Beginners', in *Candles in Babylon*, New York: New Directions Press, 1982.

Something of hope lives in us through the Holy Saturdays of our lives. While not denying the suffering and death of Good Friday and the empty spaces of Holy Saturday, we believe that Easter does live, exist. Resurrection stakes the claim that good is victorious over evil, that love is stronger than death, that joy overcomes sorrow.

The power of hope is very much in the resurrection. The resurrection offers a vision of freedom for prophetic dialogue that is difficult to dissipate. A faith tradition that claims the risen Christ offers a vision that allows risk and even 'apparent' failure to diminish nothing. Resurrection reminds us that more is possible than we see. The freedom here is great if we dare immerse ourselves in it.

Prophetic dialogue is possible for paschal persons precisely because they know both suffering and joy and live from joy. Discipleship, following the crucified and risen Christ, allows one to accompany others in both suffering and into a new life never imagined. Prophetic dialogue is possible through a paschal vision. Hope risks joy. Risking joy is utter freedom. Paschal persons of hope bring a particular freedom to their encounters. The centres and margins of society are equally places of dialogue, for the person is free to risk all, to risk joy, to risk failure, because Easter life is already given to us.

I deeply sense that Pope Francis's freedom is paschal freedom. He has known great suffering and made mistakes (see his interview in which he describes himself as 'a sinner whom the Lord has looked upon'),[19] and he also knows God's love, mercy and forgiveness. This is the type of person whose freedom invites others to the transformation God offers. He is able to offer this same love and forgiveness to others which he received, and he can risk much because the risk comes from knowing God's love. His words and actions embody prophetic dialogue as he both welcomes engagement and challenges a world with great wealth and great suffering. He also challenges the Church, the people of God: 'How I would like a Church that is poor and for the poor.'[20] Paschal hope opens up possibilities for prophetic dialogue.

Again, the freedom here is great if we dare immerse ourselves in it, for what is galvanized at this time is *disponibilité*, or radical availability. This is a freedom to serve, to offer, to dialogue from the 'centre of the tradition and the growing edges of the tradition'.[21] This availability is capable of transforming the person and the community. Such radical or root availability invites and fosters religious imagination and creativity, and it is to this that we now turn.

---

19 Antonio Spadaro SJ, 'A Big Heart Open to God', *America*, 30 September 2013, http://americamagazine.org/pope-interview.

20 Joshua McElwee, 'Pope Francis: "I would love a church that is poor"', *National Catholic Reporter*, 16 March 2013, http://ncronline.org/blogs/francis-chronicles/pope-francis-i-would-love-church-poor.

21 This phrase is attributed to John Courtney Murray SJ.

Hope Activates the Religious Imagination

Another important attribute of hope which is essential to the anthropology of prophetic dialogue is the religious imagination and creativity. Hope activates the imagination. Hope activates, galvanizes the imagination, and particularly the religious imagination. It is here that we move to what Walter Brueggemann has classically called the prophetic imagination.

Theologian Philip Keane describes imagination as 'the basic process by which we draw together the concrete and the universal elements of our human experience ... a playful suspension of judgment leading us toward a more appropriate grasp of reality'.[22] This 'playful suspension' is not of reality but of judgement on the reality. Imagination here is not fantasy, which makes up or creates an image to avoid or escape reality. Imagination instead takes various experiences and realities and places them into a context, an 'intelligible landscape'. Lynch reminds us:

> one of the permanent meanings of imagination has been that it is the gift that envisions what cannot yet be seen, the gift that constantly proposes to itself that the boundaries of the possible are wider than they seem. Imagination, if it is in prison and has tried every exit, does not panic or move into apathy but sits down to try to envision another way out. It is always slow to admit that all the facts are in, that all the doors have been tried, and that it is defeated. It is not so much that it has vision as that it is able to wait, to wait for a moment of vision which is not yet there, for a door that is not yet locked. It is not overcome by the absoluteness of the present moment.[23]

Imagination and rituals help us see what is with new eyes. The Jesus narratives, eucharistic celebrations and our reflections on Scripture all impact how we see and what is possible in our world, Church and more. Noted Scripture scholar John R. Donahue, SJ, writes how the parables, which contain frequent reversals (those working one hour receive same wage as those working all day; a Samaritan teaches love of neighbour; a prodigal son is received with the same love as a dutiful son, etc.) invite the imagination: 'These reversals challenge deeply held values and invite people to enter imaginatively into a different world, providing a paradigm for the manner in which a new vision of social justice can be presented to people today.'[24]

---

22 Philip S. Keane SS, *Christian Ethics and Imagination: A Theological Inquiry*, New York: Paulist Press, 1984, 81.

23 William F. Lynch, *Images of Hope: Imagination as Healer of the Hopeless*, Baltimore: Helicon Press, 1965, 35.

24 John R. Donahue SJ, 'The Bible and Catholic Social Teaching', in Kenneth R. Himes OFM (ed.), *Modern Catholic Social Teaching: Commentaries and Interpretations*, Washington: Georgetown University Press, 2005, 9–40 (25).

Imagination is part of our gospel narratives. In the narratives we see that Jesus healed, or at least offered healing. When healing happens, really happens, when forgiveness and reconciliation happen, hope changes even our narratives. The truth is not silenced or bent, but the narrative can be seen with new eyes. And I will again say that this is often arduous rather than easy and long term rather than short term.

When we find stories of hope, we usually want to find a way to share them. I offer two narratives of hope that invite ever more in prophetic dialogue.

'See how they love one another'

In April 2013, former president of Ireland Mary McAleese came to the Catholic Theological Union to receive the 'Blessed Are the Peacemakers' Award. In her remarks at a lunchtime community forum she shared that as she began her chosen task of bridge-building for peace, she said to her husband, 'Let's see if this great commandment to love one another really works.'[25] During her time in office she invited Queen Elizabeth to visit Ireland. While many saw this as a big risk, she saw it as necessary. In 2011, the Queen came to Ireland and in many symbolic ways opened up further spaces for a new relationship between England and Ireland. She wore green when she arrived. She went to the places of nationalistic significance to Irish nationalism, including the Garden of Remembrance and Croke Park, scene of the 1920 Bloody Sunday massacre. The impact of the visit was immense and part of the many ways the president worked to build bridges to peace. About whether the commandment to love one another really works, she said, '14 years later as we left, I said to him [her husband Martin], I think it worked.'[26] Mary McAleese incarnated prophetic dialogue, and hers is a story of hope which must be shared.

'You Are My Brother'

A friend of mine has worked at a camp for children in Uganda who have nowhere to go. Some children are there because they are orphans. Often it is because their families have been murdered by the Lord's Resistance Army (LRA) and they have nowhere to go. Some children are there for rehabilitation after being abducted in Uganda and used as child soldiers in the LRA. Some of these children cannot return to their families because their families no longer want them. The children, often under threat of death themselves if they refused, have mutilated, raped, killed and more. Much goes on in the

---

25 President Mary McAleese, Presentation videotaped at Catholic Theological Union is found on YouTube, www.youtube.com/watch?v=F4RiKYyvCvI.

26 Mary McAleese, see above.

rehabilitation programme and the road is often long and arduous, even as reintegration into society is a goal.

My friend was present when the following happened. Two boys at the camp were in the same small group and a friendship began forming. They called one another brother. One had been forced into the army and the other had his family killed by the LRA. As stories began to be shared, including particulars about their families and location, the boy forced into the LRA started distancing himself from the other boy. At one point he went to the boy and said, 'I do not deserve your friendship. I deserve your death. When you talked about your family, I realized I was the one in the village that day who killed them. I killed your mother and sister. I cannot be your friend.'

The boy, who now heard this truth from the one he called friend and brother, walked away, shaken. Sometime later he came back to him and said. 'You are my brother. I have lost my entire family. You are what I have left now. So you are my brother.'

One of the greatest gifts we are finding in hope right now is its capacity to help us imagine forgiveness, reconciliation. Forgiveness is one step. Reconciliation is a completely other step. Forgiveness acknowledges the wrong done and forgives the wrong doer. Reconciliation is at a whole new level, for it begins a new relationship.

Prophetic dialogue cannot exist without the hope that evokes the religious imagination. Steeping in these areas is essential. And we do not do this alone but together, bringing us to our final area.

Hope is Communal

So much in our world can be quite daunting if we think that we have to handle it on our own. The very examples used at the beginning of this chapter can create paralysis or flight. My dissertation was in the area of HIV/AIDS, and I knew very quickly that I would not get out of bed in the morning if I felt I had to take on alone the pandemic impacting over 40 million people. No one, from pope to president, can do alone what must be done. Together we imagine, hope, even see new life in the midst of suffering, so much better than alone. The anthropology of prophetic dialogue demands that we hope together.

Think for a few moments about the new Pope Francis on the day of his election. A few moments after Cardinal Jorge Mario Bergoglio is elected pope, the cardinal friend next to him hugs him and says, 'Do not forget the poor.' The new pope then decides his name shall be Francis. Hope is communal! Francis – his name is a daily reminder of the poor (and much more).

Hope is fostered in community and is communal. Using Trinitarian imagery, theologian Catherine Mowry LaCugna offers us an image of community and how we are to live: 'We were created for the purpose of glorifying God by living in right relationship as Jesus Christ did, by becoming holy through the power of the Spirit of God, by existing as persons in communion with God and every other creature.'[27]

Community is where we are supported in seeking hope and where hope also emerges. Community is necessary since what we hope for, the world we seek to help create, takes time to heal its broken places. In this way, we can hope together, both working and waiting and reminding ourselves of 'from whence comes our hope'.

The person of hope who can live out prophetic dialogue in areas of peace and justice will be marked by *convivir*, communion and solidarity. A few words about each. In Brazil the Myky people, a tribal people in the Amazon, do not have the word *vivir*, to live. They have only the word *convivir*, to live together.[28] Living can only be together. This is essential. Prophetic dialogue can only be done out of a deep belief that there must be a 'we'. What that looks like brings us to our second marker, communion.

We are called to be women and men who create communion,[29] and this is in all areas of life. The communal nature of hope is such that it not only imagines, but *imagines with*; it is inherently collaborative and promotes mutuality.[30] This communion will be both with one another across all lines and with God. This communion will include those who have gone before us as well as those living among us. Theologian Johann Baptist Metz writes of solidaristic hope, a hope that includes those who have gone before us.[31] We act out of a horizon of expectation that the sisters and others who have gone before us are not only part of our legacy but also part of our energy and drive in seeking to respond to God's call to love and serve. Even as the call to respond and live may differ in detail, hope remembers all and leaves none behind. We are part of this communion of saints.

Third, we are called to live solidarity. My salvation is caught up in your salvation and my cries are your cries. In defining solidarity, Roberto Goizueta writes: 'in order to truly serve the neighbour, [that] love must be born out of an identification or solidarity with the neighbour in his or her joys, suffering and struggles. The call to solidarity is a call to affirm in one's life the interdependence and unity of humankind before God; what happens

---

27 These words, taken from her book, *God For Us: Trinity and the Christian Life*, New York: HarperCollins, 1991, were on the remembrance cards given at her funeral.

28 This comes from a narrative shared by one of my sisters, Elizabeth (Beth) Amarante RSCJ from Brazil. For over 35 years her ministry has been among the Myky, an indigenous people in the Amazon. She shared this during a presentation to some members of my congregation, December 2013 in Brazil.

29 The phrase 'Women who create communion' is from the 1982 *Constitutions of The Society of the Sacred Heart of Jesus* (#6).

30 Lynch, *Images of Hope*, 23.

31 See Johann Metz, *Faith in History and Society: Toward a Practical Fundamental Theology*, trans. David Smith, New York: Seabury, 1980, 73.

to one happens to all.'[32] Solidarity identifies us with one another, honouring each 'other' as embodied agents, yet connected by bonds of our common humanity.

Church documents and liberation theologies closely connect solidarity to persons on the margins of society. Goizueta writes:

> If solidarity implies an affirmation of human community, then it implies a special affirmation of those persons who have historically been excluded or ostracized from the human community: the hungry, the naked, the sick, the 'least ones' (see Matt. 25.31–46). Chapter 25 of Matthew's Gospel speaks of Jesus Christ's identification with the powerless; hence the Christian's identification with Jesus Christ is verified by his or her own identification with the powerless.[33]

Because our community now includes the margins, an affirmation of persons requires that we go to the margins. We are to recreate communities without borders.

Solidarity on the 'margins' teaches us several things. Solidarity reminds us of our mutual need for one another as a constitutive dimension of our humanity. Our humanity is connected with our fully embodied relational agency. In his encyclical, *On Social Concern*, Pope John Paul II states:

> Solidarity helps us to see the 'other' – whether a *person, people, or nation* – not just as some kind of instrument, with a work capacity or physical strength to be exploited at low cost and then discarded when no longer useful, but as our 'neighbor', a 'helper', (cf. Gen. 2.18–20) to be made a sharer, on a par with ourselves, in the banquet of life to which we are all equally invited by God.[34]

Reflective of our theological anthropology, Sobrino writes that the Church has been 'an instrument for giving voice to the cry of the poor majority, who by their very existence are trumpeting the proclamation that today one cannot be a human being *and* disregard the sufferings of millions of other human beings'.[35] Our humanity is essentially connected to our interdependence, and so our hope is also connected to our solidarity. All can find meaning and hope in the mutual interaction. Prophetic dialogue is intimately interconnected here.

32 Roberto S. Goizueta, 'Solidarity', in Michael Downey (ed.), *New Dictionary of Catholic Spirituality*, Collegeville, MN: Michael Glazier, 1993, 906–7 (906).

33 Goizueta, 'Solidarity', 906.

34 John Paul II, *Sollicitudo rei socialis* (1987), no. 39. www.vatican.va/holy_father/john_paul_ii/encyclicals/documents/hf_jp-ii_enc_30121987_sollicitudo-rei-socialis_en.html.

35 Jon Sobrino, 'Bearing with One Another in Faith', in Jon Sobrino and Juan Hernandez Pico (eds), *Theology of Christian Solidarity*, trans. Philip Berryman, Maryknoll, NY: Orbis, 1985, 1–42 (11).

As prophetic dialogue by its very definition must invite the other, needs the other, each of these, *convivir*, communion and solidarity, deepen prophetic dialogue.

Conclusion

In concluding this look at the anthropological foundation of prophetic dialogue, I would like to (in the spirit of Bevans' and Schroeder's *Prophetic Dialogue!*) offer an image for hope that flows from what has been written. Hope is the *thin air*[36] that gives prophetic dialogue what it needs to cross divides and build bridges that are just and peaceful. Sometimes, like now, we take time to see some of what makes up the hope that a person who practises prophetic dialogue needs in order to function well: groundedness in reality, contemplative, paschal, imaginative, communal. Often we take such an anthropology for granted. However, it is exactly when situations become challenging, when justice, love and peacemaking are not quite so quick as we would wish to see enfleshed, that the thin air of hope reminds us that all is in motion even when we do not see clearly. Such is the nature of hope for a woman or man who commits themselves to prophetic dialogue.

---

36 I am grateful to Mary Sharon Riley RC for this most apt image.

12

Prophetic Dialogue and the Human Condition

JOE KAPOLYO

Introduction

Prophetic dialogue is a conversation between the prophetic, which is the word of God and human beings in their cultures. The word of God came into being when agents of God, the prophets, were carried along or moved by the Holy Spirit (cf. Isa. 59.21; Jer. 1.4–10; 20.7–10; 2 Tim. 3.16; 2 Peter 1.21) and so spoke or wrote that which was and still is the word of God.[1] For this reason the Scriptures, which are inspired by God, have God's authority even though they are expressed in human form. The cooperation between God and his agents, in the historical authorship of the Scripture does not in any way violate the agency of the prophets who wrote it down and vice versa; 'The paradox is that Scripture is the word of God as well as the words of mortals.'[2] In the present, a similar process takes place when modern day agents of God – preachers, authors, apostles or prophets,[3] – are carried along by the same Holy Spirit and so speak or write under the authority of God's word. The product is always in keeping and in line with and under the authority of the written word of God. In this interaction between the prophetic, the word of God and human beings, God's take on reality confronts human beings in a dialogue in order to help them see things and consequently be challenged to act in faith according to God's perspective.

If this prophetic dialogue is to be truly effective, transformative and life-changing, enabling the goal of mission to be realized, it needs to engage the human spirit both individual and corporate at its most profound level located in the deep structures of culture involving worldviews, beliefs and

---

[1] Only false prophets would presume to speak what their own minds prompted them to say as God's word (cf. Jer. 23.16; Ezek. 13.3) and the punishments for so doing were severe (Deut. 18.20–22).

[2] D. G. Bloesch, *Holy Scripture, Revelation, Inspiration and Interpretation*, Carlisle: Paternoster, 1994, 87.

[3] I am thinking here in terms of the prophetic function other than the ecclesiastical office in some denominations. The two meanings might coincide in any one person but this need not be the case. For a helpful discussion, see Wayne Grudem, *The Gift of Prophecy*, Eastbourne: Kingsway, 1988, 14ff.

values.[4] This fact is extremely significant for the fulfilment of the Great Commission (Matt. 28.18–20). The people of the nations to whom Jesus sent his followers, to convert them and teach them to obey everything he had taught, all have developed over time cultures which help them to view reality, organize their lives and integrate new experiences into their existing structures in order to meet the needs of their societies. Unless the word of God, the prophetic, engages that societal organizing entity at the core of people's human existence the results will tend towards the domination or domestication of the gospel by the culture.

Domestication of the gospel is a major problem created, in part, by missionary practice in the nineteenth and early twentieth centuries from which the African Church generally continues to struggle. At that time culture was understood in singular terms. There was one human culture and all human societies all over the world were to be located at some point on that continuum as they evolved from the most primitive to the most civilized. David Livingstone's missionary motto of the three 'C's; Commerce, Christianity and Civilization, reflects this mindset.[5]

Hiebert makes the same point when he says, 'Culture was seen as a single human creation in various stages of development in different parts of the world. Societies were thought to progress from simple to complex organizations, from irrational to rational thought, and from magic to religion and finally to science.'[6] Rapport and Overing add that culture in the singular was set in the framework of 'the social evolutionary thought linked to Western imperialism' where 'culture in the singular assumed a universal scale of progress and the idea that as civilizations developed through time, so too did human kind become more creative and more rational' thus increasing human beings' capacity for culture.[7]

The impact of this concept of culture and the practice of missionary work that it forged, compounded by European colonial aspirations and racial and cultural superiority complexes, meant that the Christianization of sub-Saharan Africa had a built-in fundamental weakness or barrier that made it very difficult for prophetic dialogue to take place between the word of God and the host cultures and their societies. What did take place instead was the transformation of the expressive elements of the host cultures, the human institutions that reveal a people's worldview. These changes reflected what was perceived to be European ideals and preferences, but did not have any real corresponding in-depth conversion or transformation of the deep structures of culture. Oger, a veteran Roman Catholic priest in Northern

---

4 See P. G. Hiebert, *Anthropological Insights for Missionaries*, Grand Rapids, MI: Baker, 1993, 21.

5 R. Mackenzie, *David Livingstone*, Fearn: Christian Focus Publications, 1993.

6 P. G. Hiebert, *Anthropological Insights*, 20.

7 N. Rapport and J. Overing, *Social and Cultural Anthropology: The Key Concepts*, London: Routledge, 2007, 110.

Zambia, states that '[t]he Christian spiritual import [from Europe], with its aim at *"bringing men to their ultimate goal in heaven"* may be a mere overcoat over traditional deep seated traditions and customs leaving them undisturbed'.[8]

For the most part, Christianity is therefore rather like a thin veneer covering the host cultural worldviews without interacting with them or disturbing or challenging them in any way. The concept of the African Church being likened to a river two miles wide but only two inches deep may very well be attributed to this historic oversight.

The concept of human progress and evolution that provided the sociological and intellectual underpinnings for that period of missionary work has been largely but not entirely abandoned. The two world wars dealt a heavy blow to the idea of inexorable human progress. In its place, the concept of cultural relativism first promulgated by Franz Boaz has become prominent. 'Very early on Franz Boaz (1886, 1911) firmly placed all cultures on an equal footing and scoffed at notions that wed technological might with social and cultural superiority. In his view, Chinese culture would be different from, but equal to, African Nuer or the Amazonian Yanomami.'[9]

A redefinition of culture after the rejection of theories of cultural evolution gave birth to cultural anthropology. 'Culture came to mean not merely the aggregates of human thought and behaviour, but both the system of beliefs that lie behind specific ideas and actions and the symbols by which those ideas and action are expressed. Cultures are seen as integrated wholes in which many parts work together to meet the basic needs of their members.'[10] Thus it is now generally recognized and accepted that there are different cultures and each culture has an integrated system of its own and must be judged within its own context.

In theory, this development has placed all cultures on an equal footing and provides a greater possibility for prophetic dialogue between the gospel and each of those cultures. It has the potential to avoid or minimize the hegemony of the assumed Western cultural and intellectual supremacy and oppression over other cultures and the forms of Christianity forged in those nations. That is where the potential for prophetic dialogue lies.

Western cultural hegemony is particularly acute in certain parts of Africa – both Anglophone and Francophone – where, during the period of colonialism, the colonized were not encouraged to develop confidence in using their local languages and cultures for formal education, which tended to have been developed by Westerners for Westerners but adapted and packaged for the colonies. This Eurocentric approach to education, history, culture and intellectual development excluded the possibility of serious engagement with indigenous thought patterns, categories, idiom and indeed general

---

8 L. Oger, *Where a Scattered Flock Gathered*, Ndola, Zambia: Mission Press, 1991, 231.

9 Rapport and Overing, *Social and Cultural Anthropology*, 110.

10 Hiebert, *Anthropological Insights*, 21.

concerns. This is especially true in countries in the areas ranging from East, Central and Southern Africa where white settler presence inculcated a near total abandonment of the local languages and their cultures for anything but personal and domestic use. The riches of African languages and cultures would not and did not form any serious part of educational curricula at either secondary or tertiary levels. 'Imperial western values and concepts ... were at one and the same time opening to African societies the intellectual and economic means of [modern] nationhood and also creating a universe where their traditional worldview found no place.'[11] To the detriment of the African Church, this state of affairs has been perpetrated even in the post-colonial era in life in general and especially so in the Church.

It is depressing to find many, perhaps even the majority, of educated sub-Saharan African Christian ministers preferring to preach or teach in their adopted colonial lingua franca instead of their mother tongues even when the context of such ministry, for example family funerals, is totally monocultural. Kalilombe, writing from the context of Malawi, emphasizes this point when he laments the dearth of grassroots theological reflection because 'the Christian masses tend to doubt whether they can do their own reflection on their faith'.[12]

Cone, writing from an African American context, makes a similar point when he says:

> I think that black professors are still too captivated by structures of white thought and therefore cannot think creatively. What we think and how we organize our ideas are too much determined by our training at Union, Harvard, Yale and other white schools that imitate them. The academic structure of white seminary and university curriculums require that black students reject their heritage or at least regard it as intellectually marginal.[13]

This inevitably leads to building one's theology, not on native cultural foundations but on the shifting sands of borrowed culture. Thus the prophetic dialogue does not easily happen because it is being mediated through a context that provides answers to questions that have not arisen out of a people's struggles of life. Theology thus understood is in danger of being irrelevant to life.

So, the academic teaching of theology is an area where Western hegemony is clearly established. This is true even when such teaching is done by Africans or other non-Westerners in their own cultural contexts. Most of

---

11 G. Molyneux, *African Christian Theology*, San Francisco: Mellen Research University Press, 1993, 27.

12 P. Kalilombe, *Doing Theology at the Grassroots*, Gweru, Zimbabwe: Mambo Press, 1999, 193. I would add African professional theologians and ministers to this assertion.

13 J. H. Cone, *My Soul Looks Back*, Maryknoll, NY: Orbis, 1993, 76.

my generation of theologians have been mentored directly or indirectly by Westerners in or from Western institutions.

Theological departments include in their curricula a course or modules on 'theology' (not 'theologies'). In some institutions, alongside 'theology' are offered modules or courses in so-called contextualized theologies. These latter theologies are generally viewed either as marginal, exotic or even deviant, closely wed to their contexts as if 'theology' is not itself contextualized. The cultural and intellectual framework of 'theology' was forged on the anvil of rationalism during the Enlightenment period based on ideas from Greek culture mediated through the philosophies of medieval European intellectual giants such as Anselm and Aquinas and the philosophers who followed them. It is an inescapable fact that all theologies emerge from a specific cultural and historic context. White or Western theology is contextualized in the European cultures of the latter centuries of the second millennium. Even the assumed value-free nature of 'theology' is in fact a matter that arises directly out of the dominance of science and scientism in the West.

Theological education in the Western academy over the past centuries has been grounded on a course(s) based on the study of ideas about God (*theos – logos*) in a systematic approach exploring the doctrines of God, man, Christ, the Holy Spirit, the word of God, salvation, the Church and eschatology.[14] This list of subjects is based on a general outline to be found in any of the ancient creeds such as the Athanasian (Antioch AD 341), Nicene (Nicea AD 325) or the Chalcedonian (Chalcedon AD 451). There have been variations of approach such as biblical and historical theologies, but the essence is the same.

Over the centuries and in the hands of an Enlightenment-driven intellectual and political agenda, Western theology has assumed a normative paradigmatic status; it has become theology with a capital T. This approach to the study of ideas about God, married as it is to Greek philosophy, fuelled by rationalism, committed to a monistic Eurocentric view of culture, has delivered a *theologia perennis,* a seemingly objective truth accessible to all who are equipped with the right hermeneutical tools. But this can only be a 'false theology' for it does not 'reflect our time, our culture and so our current concerns'.[15]

All this amounts to a huge problem for the African Church in particular; for the Church has not yet developed the skills to engage in grassroots reflection. The end result is that little or no prophetic dialogue takes place or can take place between the prophetic, God's word and the human subject, in this case Africans in their God-given cultures. Theology or the gospel is denied the possibility of transforming the hidden bases or foundations of

---

14 See, for example, Louis Berkhof, *Systematic Theology*, Edinburgh: Banner of Truth Trust, 1958.

15 S. Bevans, *Models of Contextual Theology*, Maryknoll, NY: Orbis, 1992, 5.

these cultures. It is at this point that anthropology offers the Church a tool or set of tools by which real prophetic dialogue can take place.

Anthropologists define culture as 'the integrated system of learned patterns of behaviour, ideas, and products characteristic of a society'.[16] An important distinction is made between the hidden or deeper levels of culture including beliefs, worldviews and values and the human structures they give rise to in expressive forms of behaviour and existence.

Deep and Surface Cultures

The common onion cut across at its widest part, exposing the concentric rings or the bases of its leaves swelled with food, provides us with the imagery to help us mentally visualize the complexity we call culture. The innermost or core circle represents the heart of any particular culture: the deep culture. This consists of the values, beliefs and worldviews. Here we can expect to find a people's religious convictions and the essential elements of the group's vision of life, the way a particular people views themselves, the world and their place in it, as well as values and norms that characterize their worldview. And what is true of the whole group is also true of each individual within that society, for individuals are microcosms of the whole. Moving outwards, the next set of circles encompass material and spiritual creations; the expressive culture, such as marriage, initiation rites, work, family, health and healing, the Church and the state with its laws, customs, behaviour, habits, etc. In most sub-Saharan African cultures – and this is true of my own culture, the Bemba culture of Northern Zambia – the content of the first circle, the heart of culture, is not visible but completely permeates and regulates the nature and content of all elements of the expressive culture. The 'inner, deeper cultural layers determine and direct the outward layers'.[17] Whereas the latter is easier to describe for it is clearly discernible, the inner core, the vision of life, is more difficult to identify and describe.

Turner developed a helpful metaphor: deep and surface levels of cultures.[18] The surface or expressive or visible cultures relate to personal and public forms within human social existence. Some of these forms will be highly localized while others will be more widespread both nationally and internationally. This is particularly so for a country like Zambia and no doubt many others which were created by decree of Western imperial colonists; Belgium, Britain, France, Germany and Portugal in Berlin in 1884–5. 'Some of the frontiers claim no rationale other than the convenience of lines of longitude and latitude. Ethnic linguistic entities in Africa were thereby often

---

16 P. G. Hiebert, *Cultural Anthropology*, Grand Rapids, MI: Baker, 1976, 25.

17 B. J. Van der Walt, 'Being Human: A Gift and a Duty', 20–1. A series of lectures given in Kinshasa in 1988 and published in a series of pamphlets by the Instituut Vir Die Bevordering Van Calvinisme, PU vir CHO Potchefstroom 2520 South Africa.

18 H. Turner, *Frames of Mind*, Auckland: Deepsight Trust, 2001, 74ff.

severed in two.'[19] The national boundaries drawn very often cut through whole ethnic groups consigning them to different countries. For example the Chokwe people occupy land where three borders converge: Angola, Congo and Zambia. Other similarly divided groups include the Ndebele of Zimbabwe and South Africa, the Ndau of Zimbabwe and Mozambique and the Tumbuka of Zambia and Malawi. 'The new state boundaries usually took little account of ethnic considerations, or the special "belongingness" of African societies.'[20]

Bemba Deep Culture

Deep Culture is Not Readily Visible

It is a complex for which we use many different descriptive terms – a complex of axiomatic, unconsciously assumed convictions, belief systems, values, mindsets, stances, reference points, frameworks, paradigms, etc. These form the ultimate creative and motivating forces and controlling factors operating at the expressive or surface levels, whether in parent or subcultures.[21]

This is the illusive, inner, deeper, foundational culture which forms the core in which resides a people's vision of life, the home of their worldviews. Most ethnographic descriptions of culture are dealing at the surface level although the studies of myth and ritual have led the way into a deeper understanding of what lies below the surface. A veteran missionary and indefatigable world traveller was giving advice to a colleague about to visit Korea for the first time. He advised him never to drink water in public while facing the audience or congregation. This is an illustration of the superficial nature of most attempts to teach intercultural studies to those about to cross cultural boundaries with the gospel. All too often the instructions tell them to avoid making mistakes at the surface level. It is indeed important not to drink water in public while facing the crowd or to blow your nose in public even if one has a handkerchief, or hand over items with one's left hand, or cross one's legs revealing the soles of one's shoes, etc. But these are surface issues. Much more needs to be done in order to deeply affect the people with the gospel of Christ. It may well be that the 'conversion' of deep culture is something which only the Christian natives can bring about with the help of the Spirit of God as he leads them in discovering God's will through his word.

---

19 Molyneux, *African Christian Theology*, 23–4.

20 A. F. Walls, 'Africa in Christian History – Retrospect and Prospect', a paper given at the gathering of the Africa Theological Fellowship, September 1997 at the Akrofi-Christaller Memorial Centre, Ghana.

21 Turner, *Frames of Mind*, 75.

Foundational Cultural Values of the Bemba[22]

Here are some of the values that belong to the core, the foundational culture that constitute a vision of life for an African people group; the Bemba of north-eastern Zambia.

Religion and Spirituality

The first is what we may call *religion*. This term is most probably misapplied to sub-Saharan Africans. The Bemba people do not have a word for religion in their vocabulary. There are words for praising God (*Ukulumbanya Lesa*), serving God (*Ukubombela Lesa*), thanking God (*Ukutotela Lesa*), but there is no word for religion.

Mbiti is perhaps the first African to attempt a thorough systematization of what in my view is erroneously called African religions. Mbiti himself admits this much in saying that this not an easy task. 'Africans are notoriously religious ... religion permeates into all the departments of life so fully that it is not easy or possible always to isolate it.'[23] But then he proceeds to treat 'religion' as if it were a separate category from other entities in life, a category that can be systematized. This was his first mistake. For there is no substantial body of orthodoxy preserved either orally or literally in the so-called African traditional religions. The thousand or so African ethnic groups (tribes) do not share a monolithic system of religion. Instead, they have different beliefs expressed variously depending on need. This is not to say that some beliefs and practices are not more widespread, or that they do not bear any resemblance to expressions of spirituality found elsewhere in the world. Migrations, similarity in kinship systems, wars, famines, witchcraft eradication movements, inter-tribal trade and warfare all combined to ensure cross-fertilization of ideas and practices. In this regard Taylor is right in suggesting that 'we may reasonably claim that we are dealing with the universal, basic elements of man's understanding of God and of the world'.[24] But this recognition does not amount to a promulgation of a religious system, which can be systematized around the theme, for example, of the African concept of time.

But Mbiti, along with many other Africanists, is wrong in calling the collection of 'traditional beliefs, attitudes and practices' of African peoples a religion. The isolation of beliefs in deities and the whole spiritual side of human existence is a Cartesian creation imposed on a description of

---

22 Much of the material below formed part of my book *The Human Condition* (Downers Grove, IL: InterVarsity Press, 2005) and is used here with permission from Langham Partnership. I have made some minimal revisions to suit this project.

23 J. Mbiti, *African Religions and Philosophy*, London: Heinemann, 1969, 1.

24 J. V. Taylor, *The Primal Vision: Christian Presence amid African Religion*, London: SCM Press, 1963, 26.

African experiences. The Enlightenment demands classification. But life for the African must be embraced in its totality. Rationalism demands that life be broken up and classified in order to be labelled and thereby presumably understood better. Classification in itself is not a bad thing. It depends on what one does with what is so classified. In modernity, classification almost invariably leads to the process of the privileging of human minds over everything else including the emotional and spiritual realm. Spiritual practices are therefore classified in the category of religion, which is then deemed a private pursuit, which belongs to the area of personal subjective opinion. It is divorced from ordinary life in the public domain. African practice until the onset of Christianity knew no such classification. In fact one of the major weaknesses of Christianity in sub–Saharan Africa, as we will seek to demonstrate, is precisely because it is a religion, 'a classroom religion' for that matter.[25] It therefore fits not into the inner person, the deep culture which is the locus of the vision of life, and where it naturally should belong, but rather, and disastrously, into the expressive elements of culture, in the area of a people's material and spiritual creations. It is not thus an integrating element in life. For these reasons it is more accurate to speak not of African religions but African spiritualities, living faiths. Spirituality, unlike popular types of religion, does have those qualities of control and of powerful influence over life in its totality. Spirituality is an integrating principle of life. If this understanding and practice of spirituality in Africa had been transferred to the practice of Christianity, the Church would be healthier, authentically African and exerting greater impact upon life in its totality, not just personal but public as well. As it is, African spirituality controls, certainly permeates life in its totality, even the practice of Christianity. 'Christianity thus seemed like an ideal which people wanted to aspire to, but practically they continued living according to the normative system of their ethnic groups.'[26] Van der Walt states that 'Westernisation has not touched their essential being.'[27]

Traditional Africans do not maintain a dichotomy between spiritual and secular values. 'No distinction can be made between sacred and secular, between natural and supernatural, for nature and the unseen are inseparably involved in one another in a total community.'[28] For many Africans the material world is firmly connected to the spiritual world and spirituality is the tie that binds human beings to the world of ancestral spirits and gods. The practices of many African peoples show that they strongly believe in God and in the spiritual world. An illness for instance is never considered, let alone treated, in isolation. Contrary to normal biomedical practice, an illness is treated as part of the person suffering within the context of the

---

25 Taylor, *The Primal Vision*, 22.
26 Women and Law in Southern Africa Research Trust (WLSA), *The Changing Family in Zambia*, Lusaka: WLSA, 1997, 53.
27 Van der Walt, 'Being Human', 21.
28 Taylor, *The Primal Vision*, 72.

community, which includes both the living people and the spirits of the ancestors.

That is why for example the Bemba say, *Ukwimba akati: kusanshyako na Lesa* (*Ukwimba* – to dig – *akati* – a small stick [or perhaps more accurately a small medicinal plant], *kusanshyako* – it is necessary to add – *Lesa* – God). This means that to be a successful herbalist, who finds the right roots for medicinal application, one needs more than just knowledge of the relevant bushes. One needs the efficacious presence of God and the good will of the spirits of the ancestors in the digging of the roots, or presentation of sacrifices, as well as in the application of the medicine.[29] What was true of treating bodily disorders was also true of endeavours like hunting, preparing gardens for planting, going on long journeys and deprivations like lack of food in times of drought.[30]

Spiritual Activities

The second core value, which derives from the first, is the growth of varieties of *spiritual* activities, such as rainmaking, healing, witch-hunting and sorcery (more widely referred to as witchcraft – a term Mbiti disparages and desires not to be used ever at all).[31] Africans are very spiritual. They have no need to be convinced of the existence of God. Many are even monotheistic. Phenomena like death are always both natural and spiritual.[32] Many if not most African peoples believe that lots of human beings have power to tap into the supernatural realm and use such power mysteriously for harm or good. Many Christians of good standing are intimidated and often unnerved by threats of witchcraft.

The typical African person is wide open to the spirit-world. It is precisely this openness to spiritual things that accounts for the phenomenal growth of the Church in sub-Saharan Africa. The important question is not, are Africans spiritual but with which spirit are they in fellowship?

Commitment to the Group

The third value is commitment to the *group*. One of the hallmarks of Western Christianity from the time of the Reformation and the Industrial Revolution is the concept of faith as a highly personalized and most individualized decision both in its inception and application. This is what John Taylor calls the 'isolated man with his intensely private world'.[33] On the contrary, for the African person such individual isolationism, even in matters of faith, is

---

29 Taylor, *The Primal Vision*, 103–4.
30 Taylor, *The Primal Vision*, 105.
31 Mbiti, *African Religions*, 166.
32 Mbiti, *African Religions*, 155.
33 Taylor, *The Primal Vision*, 93.

unimaginable. Taylor is so captivated by the all-embracing presence of the group that his chapter on an African anthropology, entitled 'What is Man', is simply a description of an African person's incorporation into and existence within the extended family. He says:

> The sense of the personal totality of all being, and of a humanity which embraces the living, the dead and the divinities, fills the background of the primal world-view. But the foreground in which this solidarity becomes sharply defined and directly experienced is the life of the extended family, the clan, and the tribe. This is the context in which an African learns to say I am because I participate. To him the individual is an abstraction; Man is a family.[34]

A typical African extended family comprises the nuclear families of a couple and their siblings. That number can often exceed 200 people. But when one includes all the collateral relations and their families – for they are also members of these extended families – the figures often reach up to several hundreds. This is what is called in Bemba *Ulupwa* – one's paternal and maternal relatives. Legally defined a family is 'a socially recognized union of two people and any offspring from that union'.[35] This is what the Bemba would call 'those of one house', that is to say, they have one mother and one father; the African equivalent of the European nuclear family. Culturally and practically among the Bemba this is the least significant of the definitions of family. It corresponds to what is called a household, although even a household would normally be greater in that it includes all the people who live together and share the same dwellings, food and other basic essentials. *Ulupwa*, among the Bemba, corresponds more to the kinship group and that really only to the matrikin (the Bemba are matrilineal). In practice, however, bilateralism is common. Two proverbs will illustrate this: *Abana ba mfubu: bangala amatenga yonse* (literally: *Abana* – Children – *ba* – of a – *mfubu* – hippo – *bangala* – play – *amatenga yonse* – in all the pools of water in the river or lake). The application is that children belong to both their paternal and maternal kin. Similarly, *Umutembo: ufinina konse* (literally: *Umutembo* – a heavy burden – *ufinina* – weighs heavily – *konse* – on both sides). This means the duty and cost of bringing up children must be shared equally between the two sides of the family. Both sides of the family should recognize their obligations to the child as a member of the two families.

The extended family combines all the benefits of a fully fledged social security system without any bewildering red tape. The system is flexible, efficient and user friendly.

The sense of solidarity in the extended family is a felt thing. Nowhere is this more real than at a family funeral when multitudes of relatives gather

---

34 Taylor, *The Primal Vision*, 93.
35 WLSA, *The Changing Family*, 30.

for several days to mourn and bury the departed. The physical presence of all relatives is imperative. It is the duty of relatives to attend all funerals. At the funeral house itself, the sheer number of relatives makes the burden of grief light. Physical duties like baby care, cooking, cleaning, laundry, are all done by the many willing helpers gathered. Babies become the focus of particular attention as they are introduced and passed around to the relatives they have never seen. The prosperous members of the family will make contributions to pay for the gathering and the funeral expenses related to the actual burial. The camaraderie is also very significant. Lots of family stories are told and family histories may be recited for the benefit of the young. This process of socialization accounts for why identity crisis is not really a problem on the African continent, although it may be so in the African 'diaspora', scattered among the impersonal cities of Europe, America and elsewhere.

There are difficulties with the extended family system. Some unscrupulous people can easily abuse it. Lazy people can opt out of their obligations and instead move from one relative's house to another in search of a more comfortable life. But abuses do not outweigh the true benefits of the system. There are however, some important issues in relation to the Church. These include the matter of fellowship, support for the church, hospitality, individuality (personal and in relation to any given marriage) and priority of relatives. Let me deal with just two of these, fellowship and priority of relatives.

Christian fellowship can also be a victim of the African extended family system. Fellowship is an essential part of what it means to be Christian. The Apostle John considers it to be the grounds for the incarnation (1 John 1.3–7). Jesus came into the world that he might create the basis for fellowship. The word fellowship translates the Greek word *koinonia*. It is used in the New Testament to describe the Church in terms of community, participation and of course, fellowship. At the basis of the use of this word group is the idea of a common and shared background. In the Christian sense this stems from our 'being united in Christ ... participation in the Spirit' (Phil. 2.1). The Christian heritage includes primarily a participation in the life of the Father, the Son and the Holy Spirit. These things cannot be changed because they are bestowed on us by God.

Similarly, Christian fellowship is not just what church members share in common, it must issue in community of goods (Acts 2.43–47) and the giving and receiving of hospitality (Acts 9.43). These attributes find much common ground with the African extended family. All who belong to any extended family share a common biological ancestry. Their blood, their names and to a large extent their culture can all be traced back to a common ancestor or set of ancestors. The extended family gives people identity and a strong sense of family or clan solidarity. The relationships between members result not only in words of affirmation but especially in deeds of solidarity that include many of the attributes of a fully functioning social security system in the West. But more than that there is a very strong personal social support structure to meet the needs of the members at all times.

One would have assumed that these similarities in attributes between the African extended family and the body of Christ, the Church, would make it easier for the African Church to more fully live out the concept of fellowship. But sadly the reality in many places is that the experience of 'fellowship' in the natural family is so real and exclusive that it hinders and discourages fellowship in the Church across the traditional dividing walls of hostility, for example, family, clan, tribe and nation. The sense of solidarity stemming from common ancestry is so strong that it acts as a big barrier to the idea of extending the same sense of community to total strangers. Tribal churches thrive on this weakness. No prophetic dialogue has taken place to redeem this wonderful cultural provision for the benefit of the kingdom of God.

There are at least two important principles to aid prophetic dialogue in this regard. These include first the example of Jesus, who in coming into our world embraced us in our fallen humanity even though our nature of sin was completely contrary to his nature and to the Father's holiness. We were by nature objects of his wrath (Eph. 2.3). But God reached out to us and at great cost to himself God in Christ bore the burden of sin so that we might go free (Rom. 5.8; 2 Cor. 5.21; Eph. 2.14–18; 1 Peter 2.24). Second, tribal churches have mistakenly made absolute their tribal identities and turned them into insurmountable barriers to fellowship with non-members of the tribe. Every cultural value is relative. The word of God alone, the prophetic utterance, is absolute. Every culture comes under the scrutiny of the gospel and is judged by it. We have no right to maintain or rebuild the barriers that Christ has torn down at great cost to himself.

Priority of relatives is the term I choose to use to describe the fact that in life – personal, social and public – relatives always assume a place of priority over all others. In public life nepotism blights the political and social land-scapes of the African continent. Priority of relatives distorts a proper sense of justice and fair play. But it is also and maybe especially so in marriage where this priority of relatives can have a devastating effect on personal relations. This is a clear example of the ability of unredeemed culture to negate the teaching of Scripture. The Bemba always say '*Umwanakashi: mwina fyalo*' (literally: *Umwanakashi* – A woman or wife – *mwina fyalo*' – is a foreigner). That means she must never be allowed to assume a place of importance in relation to her husband prior to his relatives. The woman on the other hand will never allow her sisters-in-law to assume a place of prominence prior to her in relation to her brothers. The unfortunate result in many cases is that marriages can be little more than convenient arrangements for increasing the number of people in the extended family and may thus lack the rich mix of love, care and sharing that the Bible envisages.

In an atmosphere like this biblical teaching on subjects like marriage often falls on very deaf ears indeed.

Ukulilapo

The fourth core value is what I call *Ukulilapo*. This is a Bemba word derived from the word *ukulya* – to eat. The word implies that in every situation it is one's duty to exploit the circumstances for one's personal (by extension one's extended family's) advantage. The attitude may well have arisen at a time when eating was the preoccupation of most people during the days of hunting and gathering and feasting was to be desired for it was so rare. However it came about, it is a fact that this attitude, and nepotism is an expression of it, makes public and social accountability very difficult indeed. Take the spread of orphanages as a case in point. Many of these institutions have sprung up in response to the great numbers of orphans owing to the scourge of the HIV/AIDs pandemic. The suffering of children attracts a lot of sympathy from donors all over the world. And yet it is not uncommon to see the children for whom such aid is sought and procured still languishing on scraps while the person running the orphanage grows wealthier as do his or her relatives. Such abuse of public trust would not be understood for what it really is, stealing, but as a duty that one has to himself and his or her relatives. Dare I suggest it that some of the resources of many local churches and denominations are misused in this way?

Life after Death

The fifth core value is belief in the afterlife. Qoheleth says that God has put eternity in the heart of people (Eccles. 3.11). Whatever else this verse means; it certainly suggests that it is part of the human condition not only to long for but to seek for life after death. In many parts of Africa there are two very clear lines of thought in considering what happens to a person after death. The first is the translation of the dead into the *living dead*. These are the spirits of the departed who are nevertheless very much alive and well and resident in the neighbourhood either in a physical reality like a tree or simply as a disembodied spirit. The living dead are still part of the family. Care must be taken not to ignore them or be negligent of duty to them. Libations and foods must be left for them. In times of crises they can be consulted and appealed to for protection. Although they are invisible, they are very much alive and part of the family. Eventually they will pass on when their memory is completely erased from human consciousness after the demise of the last remaining relative who remembers them in physical form. From then on they become part of the corporate identity of the spirits of the forefathers.

The second line of thought in dealing with the afterlife has to do with inheritance. After the death of a man or woman, the relatives gather to appoint the person who will inherit the deceased. It is important to establish that inheritance in this case has very little to do with receiving bequests and all to do with 'becoming' in a mysterious and spiritual way the person that has died. Through the inheritance ceremony the family symbolically invite back the departed and renew contact with him or her.[36] At the appointed time a younger relative will be nominated. In matrilineal ethnic groups the line of inheritance goes through a man's sisters and their children, his uterine nephews and nieces.[37] This is perhaps what makes the sisters of a man so special and important. They bear him the boys who will take his name after his death. Bemba inheritance does not focus on wealth but people inherit other people, effectively becoming the deceased.

Accordingly, from that moment on, all who had relationships with the departed transfer those to the candidate so that they relate to him or her in the same way they would have related to the departed. A man whose daughter has inherited his grandmother will always treat her with the same reverential love and respect as he would his departed forebear. This person will henceforth be the representative of the departed among the living. The living dead are immanent and actively involved among their people in this way.

A third way of conceiving of the afterlife involves the naming of children. Names of the newborn are sometimes discerned through dreams and visions or divination. Such names will invariably belong to some ancestor whose spirit is seen to want to continue their existence in the material world through a newborn child.

These then are the three ways of conceiving of the afterlife: the living dead, people who have inherited others and the giving of ancestral names to newborn children. Such afterlife is bound firmly to this present earth and existence in the afterlife is conceived in terms of an earthly human body. This might be called existence by proxy. This hope for immortality is very different from the Christian hope. The glory of the Christian message is seen not only in the resurrection body – incorruptible, imperishable and spiritual – but also in existence in the very presence of God eternally, without any fear of death (1 Cor. 15.51–57).

Theologians and preachers, whether local or cross-cultural missionaries need to take these values and look at them in the light of Scripture in order to facilitate the prophetic dialogue that must take place between the word of God and the Bemba culture. Only then can the Church be relevant to the African constituencies they serve.

We could add to this list still more significant core values such as concepts of seniority and authority, definitions of truth, the African concept of time,

---

36 Mbiti, *African Religions*, 152.

37 A. I. Richards. 'Some Types of Family Structure amongst the Central Bantu', in A. R. Radcliffe-Brown and D. Forde (eds), *African Systems of Kingship and Marriage*, London: KPI/ IAI, 1950, 207–51.

the good image syndrome, guilt and shame, etc. All these values are to be found in the spiritual core of one's life, the deep or foundational culture, and they form the integrating principle of life. They fundamentally affect how the Bemba view the world. They also affect how the Bemba perceive and practise Christianity for better or for worse.

Around such a core of values any culture builds its essential expressive or surface institutions such as marriage and family, work, play, relationships, methods of healing, even the Church; these are the human creations that appear as the culture of any given people. The question is how does the core affect the institutions any cultural group sets up? For the African situation, because the core of values, which are spiritual in orientation, are in effect an integrating principle of life and because there is no secular/sacred divide in public and private conception of life, the core values affect every one of the essential cultural institutions. So for instance, as seen above, treatment of any illness is both a physical and a spiritual exercise. Unlike medical science, African systems of healing treat illnesses in a social context in which the spiritual element plays an integral part. Similarly priority of relatives encourages nepotism in public office and at the same time makes it difficult for marriages to attain the ideal as spelled out in Genesis 2.24–25 where a man and woman must leave their respective parents – physically, mentally, emotionally and spiritually – in order to be united together in an indissoluble union. The desire for children often means a person's worth is judged by his or her ability to bear children. Childless men and women are the object of great community derision. Childless couples come under intolerable pressure to break up.

What is the effect of these core values on the establishment of the Church? Ideally, at conversion one would hope that it is the core values that are 'converted' and replaced by biblical values, derived from the Bible and enshrined in our hearts by the Holy Spirit. Because the core values are already both spiritual in orientation and an integrating principle in life, it is often stated that when an African gets converted, the core values are somehow transformed to reflect new allegiances and immediately, following established patterns, become the new integrating principle of life in its totality. The unavoidable inference is that the African Church should therefore reflect biblical values through and through.

This is obviously too simplistic a formula. Processes of conversion are truly complex and when they occur they do so for a variety of reasons quite apart from the straightforward desire to follow another religion. Aguilar says: 'African processes of conversion are fluid, and they also include processes of reconversion to religious practices socially present in the eras preceding the world religions.'[38] Fear, opportunities for commercial and political advancement, desire to create cohesion around a tribal identity, economic survival,

---

38 M. I. Aguilar, 'Reconversion among the Baroona', *Africa* 65:4 (1995), 525–44, 526.

all can play significant parts in the decision made especially by groups of people to convert from traditional beliefs to a world religion.

Since core values change very slowly at the presuppositional philosophical level, it takes a long time before 'true' religion of the heart corresponds with what takes place at the expressive or surface-level culture.[39] In the intervening period we can expect to see a kind of localization of the new religion as expressive cultural forms superficially change to correspond to the new-found faith. Certainly this is the case in much of Africa where Christianity appears as a veneer, which is itself thoroughly affected by the original African core values. 'The Christian spiritual import, with its aim at bringing men to their ultimate goal in heaven may be a mere overcoat over traditional deep seated beliefs and customs leaving them undisturbed.'[40]

Conclusion

This I believe is the reason why so often the Church in Africa has been compared to the proverbial river two miles wide but only two inches deep! This is an admission of the failure of African Christianity to root adopted surface cultural changes; singing Christian hymns (for a long time these could only be Christian if they were in the traditional Western linguistic forms and idiom), meeting on Sundays, reading the Bible, adopting 'Christian' names, forms of dress, taking communion, undergoing baptism, etc., into the foundational or deep cultural level of the host cultures on the African continent. Unless this happens, and I fear that it rarely happens at a systemic level, then no prophetic dialogue is possible.

The Church in sub-Saharan Africa is growing phenomenally. Theological processes happening in places such as Soweto, Kinshasa, Kibera, Kampala and Lagos will inevitably affect the quality of the nature and appearance of Christianity worldwide. The baton of leadership for the Church is firmly passing to the Southern continents including Africa. The quality of that leadership, upon which the very outlook of the Church will hang, depends on the quality of the prophetic dialogue between the word of God and the deep cultures of the African people groups.

---

39 D. R. Jacobs, 'Conversion and Culture: An Anthropological Perspective with reference to East Africa', in J. R. W. Stott and R. T. Coote (eds), *Gospel and Culture*, Pasadena, CA: William Carey Library, 1979, 175–94 (181).

40 Oger, *Where a Scattered Flock*, 231.

PART 6

Culture: Mission and Culture in Prophetic Dialogue

13

Prophetic Dialogue and Contemporary Culture

JONNY BAKER

Introduction: Pioneering in Western Contexts

It is a surprise to me that I find myself working for the Church Mission Society (CMS). My memory of CMS as a child was that on mission Sundays in the village church I attended, a visiting missionary would show slides of an exotic location in the world with tales of different foods and dress and customs with news of sharing stories of Jesus Christ with them and growing the Church there. I did not pay it a second thought – it seemed very far away from my own world and experience.

My interest in mission arose later when I was in my twenties, and I had begun a role in youth ministry seeking to share Christ in England with teenagers who had not grown up in church. It was easy enough to be with young people, build friendships and begin to share Christ naturally with them, but getting these young people to join church, which we all assumed was required, was a seemingly impossible task and it seemed to have something to do with the question of culture. They lived in one culture and Church in another – bridging that cultural gap rarely seemed to produce any lasting fruit. While it was a short geographical journey it was a huge cultural one. Youth ministers began to reflect that this was the same challenge faced by missionaries travelling overseas to share Christ with people of other cultures, only it was on our doorstep.[1] In the same way that missionaries had sought to grow indigenous expressions of Church in the various countries and cultures they travelled to, we needed to engage in the same mission challenge but in Britain, our own culture.[2] The incarnation quickly became a unifying theological theme. I have been on that quest ever since. Initially this was with young people but subsequently in relation to adults seeking to

---

1 For example, see Pete Ward, *Youth Culture and the Gospel*, London: Marshall Pickering, 1992.

2 Vincent Donovan, *Christianity Rediscovered*, London: SCM Press, 1982 became something of a must-read for all youth ministers engaged in this type of ministry seeking to emulate what he had done among the Masai with various youth subcultures.

follow Christ in the emerging postmodern culture(s) for whom the cultural challenges were just as real, albeit played out in different ways.[3]

There have now been 30 years or so of this current wave of exploration in mission in the UK out of which a whole plethora of youth churches, missional communities, alternative worship, new takes on monasticism, emerging churches, fresh expressions of church, pioneering ministries, have grown. This has been paralleled in other Western contexts to varying degrees proving Stephen Johnson's rather lovely idea of the 'adjacent possible'.[4] I joined CMS 11 years ago as part of a team to encourage mission in the emerging culture. The latest development has been a training programme for pioneers done through the lens of cross-cultural mission. Pioneer ministry is the term I will use for those seeking to engage in prophetic dialogue inculturating the gospel in Western contexts. This term is used in the UK for those planting fresh expressions of Church.[5] Reading cultures and contexts is as much part of their training as it is for those travelling overseas. It is a pleasant surprise that this would be taken seriously enough to be considered for a missiology text on culture.

New Vistas for Reading Cultures

Various writers have documented the developing complexity of what is meant by the term 'culture' and noted the shifts in anthropology and cultural studies as we have moved from modern to postmodern times.[6] Kathryn Tanner suggests that postmodern understandings of culture open up new vistas for theology, inculturation and even how Christianity understands its own identity in relation to culture as theologians have tended to work with modern assumptions and definitions. Cultures are no longer thought of as fixed entities, but sites in which there are multiple meanings and ways of viewing the world, which are most likely contested or at least not unified. They are fluid, dynamic and alive. These patterns of meaning are encased in networks of myths, symbols, narratives and rituals. And they carry deep assumptions, nearly always implicit rather than explicit, about what is the correct way to feel, behave, think and act in the world. Genesis 1.28 is sometimes referred to as the cultural mandate as humans are entrusted to be culture formers as part of what it means to image God in the world, and

---

3 Emerging culture and postmodern culture were the two most common terms at the time being used to describe the wider cultural changes.

4 Stephen Johnson, *Where Good Ideas Come From*, New York: Penguin, 2010, 25–42, suggests that when one idea is developed it opens up a series of adjacent possibilities. This is why sometimes you get simultaneous developments in different locations.

5 See http://pioneer.cms-uk.org.

6 See for example Kathryn Tanner, *Theories of Culture*, Cambridge: Cambridge University Press, 1997 and Gerald Arbuckle *Culture, Inculturation and Theologians: A Postmodern Critique*, Collegeville, MN: Liturgical Press, 2010.

postmodern notions of culture highlight that the directions in which culture is unfolded are manifold.

It can be helpful to think of contemporary culture as a shared environment, in which people develop practices and resources for everyday life in a given society.[7] One of the most significant features of the culture in which we live in Britain is that it is an environment based on the logic of consumption in which people live and move and have their being. Practices are constructed and resources flow, are mediated and used in everyday life to make sense of being and living in this world. Whereas in modernity, identity and social integration were found through production and the work place, in postmodernity we have made stuff the dominant prerequisite of organized society. Things 'R' Us consumption has become production or 'you are not what you make, you are what you buy'.[8] This way of conceiving of culture as a mix of environment, practices and resources in everyday life in a society is helpful as it creates space to make sense of various groups and communities within the wider culture who may be fragmented or hybrid or subcultures and resists reducing culture to something homogeneous which it clearly is not. It also allows for difference, diversity and contestation. That difference might be along ethnic, religious, political, sexuality or gender lines, which are familiar subjects of cultural studies. It might be on the basis of access to resources. Lots of pioneers are working in mission with communities who have little by way of resources and access but they still share the environment and develop their own practices within it. It might also be on the basis of taste. The sociologist Bourdieu described the significance of taste in the way people make distinctions.[9] Several theorists have shown how his insights, which were based on a high/low class distinction, are relevant to the way in which everybody is involved in making distinctions.[10] 'The exercise of taste and aesthetic discrimination is as important in popular as in high culture.'[11] One of the most significant ways in which this is taking place is through the consumption of mediated texts and artefacts in popular culture. It is in this way that people construct some notion of identity (both individually and in terms of what subcultural groups they identify with and/or belong to) and how they position themselves in relation to other people and their subcultures or 'taste communities'. The environment itself as well

---

7 Gordon Lynch, *Understanding Theology and Popular Culture*, Oxford: Blackwell, 2005 suggests this way of conceiving of popular culture as it encompasses both those approaches that attend to popular cultural texts such as films and music, alongside those that focus on the practice of everyday life beyond just the texts of popular culture.

8 James Twitchell, *Lead Us Into Temptation*, New York: Columbia University Press, 1999, 286, 196.

9 Pierre Bourdieu, *Outline of a Theory of Practice*, Cambridge: Cambridge University Press, 1977.

10 See for example Sarah Thornton, *Club Cultures*, Cambridge: Polity Press, 1995, 10–14. H Mackay (ed.), *Consumption and Everyday Life*, London: Sage, 1997, 4–5.

11 Simon Frith, *Performing Rites*, Oxford: Oxford University Press, 1996, 11.

as the resources and practices are not static. It too is alive and able to be adapted, changed and continually remade.

Dialogue: Do It from the Inside

How does mission as prophetic dialogue play out in relation to contemporary culture? Expanding on what they mean by dialogue, Bevans and Schroeder suggest that mission is imagined and practised as 'gentle among', recognizing that God is present before our arrival and that it is about being with people, listening and sharing with them. It is characterized by respect, openness, willingness to learn, attentiveness, vulnerability, hospitality, humility and frankness. And they offer images of treasure hunter, guest, stranger and someone entering into someone else's garden.[12] This is a posture, a spirituality, a way of being rather than a strategy. There are very few texts about consumer culture or popular culture written from a theological or mission perspective that embody this posture, that take seriously the notion that God might be present in this space, rather than over and against it.[13] Even texts and journal articles on mission and Western culture tend to hold up a theology of the incarnation at the local or neighbourhood level, while simultaneously problematizing the macro level of postmodernity or consumer culture or both. But this macro level is the amniotic fluid or environment within which neighbours at the local level have been formed and within which they construct meaning and identity.

The starting place for dialogue in contemporary culture is the same as it is for any culture – leaving your own culture and being present in the new culture, listening and discerning where God might be at work and joining in. That listening needs to pay attention to the wider environment, resources and practices of everyday life. When travelling to another culture that is geographically far away, another country, it is obvious that this requires a letting go of your own ways of doing things and learning a new language. It can take quite a long time to begin to feel at home in the new culture. The spirituality of the pioneer requires a constant practice of letting go, of shutting up, of resisting taking up power, of really seeing and really listening. It also can practically mean giving up many of the practices that have

---

12 Stephen Bevans and Roger Schroeder, *Prophetic Dialogue*, Maryknoll, NY: Orbis, 2011, 19–39.

13 There are exceptions. The first book I came across that took a different posture towards popular culture was Tom Beaudoin, *Virtual Faith*, New York: Jossey Bass, 1998, which took seriously the idea that people were experiencing the sacred mediated through their use and consumption of popular culture whether that was body piercing, music videos, or the Internet. A spirituality of irreverence and bricolage were held up as practices for 'Xers'. Lynch, *Understanding Theology and Popular Culture*; Pete Ward, *Participation and Mediation*, London: SCM Press, 2008; Robert Johnson, *Reel Spirituality*, Grand Rapids, MI: Baker, 2000; Craig Detweiler and Barry Taylor, *Matrix of Meanings*, Grand Rapids, MI: Baker, 2003 are proof that there are others and hopefully growing interest in the area.

hitherto fuelled their own faith, especially if they are embedded in resources from another culture (songs, texts, liturgies). And it can mean letting go of certainties regarding the content of the gospel itself. The gospel always comes culturally robed so, without this letting go, the gospel will not be free to find new indigenous robes and language. In contrast with this, the local insider is to speak up and to speak out boldly finding God in the cracks and corners, the signs and symbols of their own context, to feel proud about using the resources of their culture and location, of taking the risk of robing the gospel in new language and clothes.[14]

John Taylor in his book *The Primal Vision*, having travelled in tribal areas in Africa with a primal worldview, reflects on mission in that context and develops a rich and radical array of themes and nuances around mission which get pretty close to this notion of mission spirituality.[15] Like many mission books he reflects on issues of gospel and culture, suggesting that gospel and Western culture have mistakenly been thought of as the same gift and need separating out. The challenge in mission is to go on an adventure of the imagination that enables mission to be done from the inside of the primal worldview and cultures. This leads to an articulation of the gospel that is local and indigenous rather than foreign and imposed. He then underlines the necessity of hearing from and encouraging the voices of African poets, artists who are able to articulate in the vernacular of their culture as opposed to the vernacular of Western cultures. This is so important because it breaks down the dualism that locates God in only one aspect of life and culture. Finally in the book he suggests that sin is the last truth to be told. In other words in dialogue, judgement comes late in the process and is best brought by the Spirit speaking to insiders.

In contemporary culture the same kinds of issues are at play – there are certain tastes that sit with church cultures. In many cases this is what used to be termed high culture – classical music, a literary culture, classical paintings, stained glass, church architecture and in some cases a particular kind of contemporary culture loved by the Christian media industries. While there is nothing wrong with that kind of culture, its dominance has meant that you are unlikely to find much in the way of other popular taste cultures in the aesthetics of church life or they are frowned upon. So for the sake of dialogue this will all need to be let go, at least initially, however much it is loved, for the sake of the gospel with the same commitment that Taylor articulates to do it from the inside of a culture.[16] As a resource, some of those things may be offered back at a later stage if and when people are ready to be opened up to other traditions in intercultural dialogue but initially this

---

14 This is elucidated in chapter 7 of *Prophetic Dialogue*, which explores a spirituality of inculturation.

15 John Taylor, *The Primal Vision: Christian Presence amid African Religion*, London: SCM Press, 1963.

16 Taylor, *Primal Vision*, 24.

is to be resisted. Outsiders need to immerse themselves in the resources and practices that the insiders use to make meaning and seek to find God present there. This may mean a different newspaper, listening to dubstep, joining in karaoke, developing a dark sense of humour, sharing stories through asking about tattoos, going to the fish and chip shop on a Thursday night, playing bingo, doing yoga or whatever it is in the local culture. All the while prayerfully asking to see rumours of glory, hints of God at work, noticing when the sacred is being mediated in and through the everyday stuff of the local culture. This is a sacramental view of all of life and culture, closest to anthropological in Bevans' models of contextual theology.[17] Ignatian spirituality's catchphrase 'finding God in all things' needs to be tested to the limit. Clemens Sedmak suggests seeing our cultural environment as a kind of fifth gospel from which to draw insights.[18] It is essential to find out the songs, TV, films, books, websites, usage of mobile phones being listened to, used, watched and practised, but also to find the local artists and poets and filmmakers who articulate in the vernacular as opposed to the Church or middle class vernacular of another outsider culture. As the Christian sub-culture is left behind, it is surprising what treasure can be unearthed in the everyday of cultural texts and practices that are not the outsider's previously acquired taste or habit. When the previous cultural texts and practices are taken along, the pioneer is unlikely to ever find the treasure. This *kenosis* is likely to entail grief because what is lost is real and there is a liminal space to be gone through which can be a creative and formative space but is difficult nonetheless. In the listening and waiting it is important to notice, to pay attention to what comes near and discern where the Spirit may be at work. There are most likely particular insiders with whom there is an openness and a sense of peace who may become those who God is calling to speak out at some future point. I do not want to suggest or pretend that outsiders do not have a significant role to play – they definitely have agency, but it is in humility that gently brings the resources of the gospel to bear in genuine prophetic dialogue.

Many pioneers are on this journey in contemporary culture. Gav is a Methodist pioneer in North Wales. He was seeking to listen and be present and discern when he saw an outdoor piece of art by a local artist which was a mix of poetry and film. He managed to track him down and rang to tell him that he thought he was a local prophet. This was something of a surprise to him but since then they have developed a friendship and worked together to develop a community of local artists around a disused hotel in Colwyn Bay and put on several events and exhibitions together. This has included inviting local artists to interpret aspects of the Easter story in the Gospels. For his piece the aforementioned 'local prophet' carried a

---

17 Stephen Bevans, *Models of Contextual Theology*, Maryknoll, NY: Orbis, 1992.
18 Clemens Sedmak, *Doing Local Theology*, Maryknoll, NY: Orbis, 2002, 140.

cross several miles and filmed people's reactions to him. They have also had spoken word, music and comedy nights. The Occupy movement in London had barrier tape around its camp with the words 'another world is possible', which several of us, including Gav, received as a provocative sign of the Spirit of prophecy at work in the world; of treasure.[19] Gav hosted a discussion panel with an artist, poet and theologian to explore together what indeed this might mean or could look like. It is early days for this project and community but it seems to me to have embodied this spirituality of prophetic dialogue – pioneers letting go and insiders speaking out.

Theology that Risks Thinking, Dreaming and Praying another Language

A question that quickly arises in inculturation in popular culture surrounds theology. How do you theologize, have conversation about God? The same risks are at play here – of imposing outside categories and bringing too much to bear that silences the conversation with insiders before it has even begun. Doing local theology is most likely a process of asking questions and uncovering issues with and among local people in a posture of humility again. Language is key in crossing cultures. This is obvious when the language is different, and pioneers sense a breakthrough when they start to think or pray or dream in a different language. But the same is true in contemporary culture – local theologies need to pay attention to the particularities of local language and use local language as a sign of respect for the local culture to the point where the pioneer can think and pray and dream those particularities.[20] Stephen Bevans outlines the risk that was taken in theology in Antioch using a new local Greek term for Lord.[21] We need to be open to this kind of risk-taking in mission and in theological reflection in contemporary culture. Richard Passmore has named God as Flow with a group of skaters in England and developed a series of parables that explored this further.[22] In the West we have grown to love representations of Christ from other cultures, but it is still something of a surprise to see contemporary representations of Christ, icons of the present and the local. Western images tend to be drawn from art in centuries that are long gone. I live in London and can think of the reaction to Jesus as a life-size statue of a young adult on a plinth in Trafalgar Square,[23] or Jesus represented as a

---

19 Treasure hunter is one of the images of prophetic dialogue offered in Bevans and Schroeder, *Prophetic Dialogue*.

20 Sedmak, *Doing Local Theology*, 81.

21 Stephen Bevans and Roger Schroeder, *Constants in Context*, Maryknoll, NY: Orbis, 2004, 26.

22 Richard Passmore, *Here Be Dragons*, Porthouse: Frontier Youth Trust, 2013, 6–8; 37–8.

23 Mark Wallinger's *Ecce Home*, July 1999.

brand in among a sea of brands.[24] We are slowly aware of and energized by theological reflection from elsewhere in the world though admittedly that is long overdue. Notions such as God is rice or water buffalo theology are certainly de rigueur for people studying mission in Asia for example and perhaps even old hat.[25] But 'the kingdom of God is like the Tour de France ...', 'the church is like an open source platform for apps', is still unusual. In a module we teach on cross-cultural skills, pioneers visit a different culture or community and as part of that imaginatively rewrite a passage of Scripture in the vernacular, embodying some of the particularities of language of that culture. This has produced some really creative risky pieces, which are exactly the kinds of risks required in inculturation, in prophetic dialogue. By way of an example, I wrote one myself, which is a reworking of the famous passage on the body of Christ in 1 Corinthians 12.12–31. I used the metaphor of the network of Christ drawing particularly on small world theory. It was written in response to or in prophetic dialogue with Clay Shirky's book *Here Comes Everybody*.[26]

The Network of Christ

Just as a network, though one, has many small worlds, but all its parts interconnect, so it is with Christ. For we were all baptized by one Spirit and given a portal into the wider network of Christ – whether Orthodox, Emerging, Missional, New Monastic, Catholic, Anglican, Post-denominational, Pentecostal, Baptist, Anabaptist, etc. or any blend of the above, the Spirit flows through our networks. So the network of Christ is not made up of one small world but of many interconnected small worlds and hubs.

If the Australian missional communities should say 'because I am not focused on worship I don't connect into the wider network' it would not cease to be part of the global network of Christ. And if the French Catholic Church should say 'because I can't feasibly imagine homogeneous missional church planting I don't belong to the wider network' it wouldn't cease to be part of the global network of Christ either. If the whole network lived in the small world of alternative worship where would the growth of African churches be? If the whole network lived in the Anglican small world where would the prophetic passion for justice of the Anabaptists be? But in fact in the network of Christ God has catalysed and flows in lots of small worlds just as God wills. And the network is such that the Spirit creates an environment where she flows and small worlds emerge as the Spirit beckons the network into the future.

---

24 This was an exhibit as part of an exhibition Brand New in London at the Victoria and Albert Museum, in 2000.

25 Masao Takenaka, *God is Rice*, Eugene, OR: Wipf and Stock, 2009, Kosuke Koyama, *Water Buffalo Theology*, London: SPCK, 1971.

26 Clay Shirky, *Here Comes Everybody*, London: Allen Lane, 2008.

If there were just one small world with no external connectors where would the network be? The redemptive gifts that the Spirit has distributed throughout the wider network of Christ would not flow. They would remain static. So don't let the small world of which you are a part ever say 'I don't need you' to another small world and don't despise the gift of external connection. To be in Christ is to connect to Christ and to participate in the Network of Christ where the Spirit flows. And be careful that you don't just notice the hubs that seem important or powerful or branded and neglect the weaker or less connected small worlds. God flows in these parts, distributes gifts there and has a special love for them. And the small world in which you mostly participate is most likely to be energized by connection to other small worlds which are the most different to you so don't be tempted to just connect to others who seem like you.

You are the network of Christ and each one of you is connected and participates. And the Spirit flows in and through you and has distributed different kinds of gifts and roles – pioneers, catalysts, networkers, artists, mission leaders, loyal radicals, local practitioners, environmentalists, guardians of flow. Are all external connectors? Are all local practitioners? But eagerly desire the greater gifts to flow throughout the network of Christ.

Gordon Lynch's preferred method of theological reflection in relation to popular culture is a revised correlational method.[27] In this, the conversation between culture and tradition is a two-way street, and in particular it lays itself open to the possibility that contemporary culture can be a mediator of truth and goodness in its own right generating insights that challenge ideas which are part of the tradition. Robert Johnson in his book on theology and film insists that a film be first viewed and understood on its own terms before stepping back and getting analytical.[28] He has a schema of various postures of theology towards culture. The last of these is epiphany, which allows for the idea of revelation in and through the stuff of culture (in this case film) and not simply the other way round.

Prophecy as Imagination, Speech, Embodiment and Enactment of Another Possible World

I have observed the tension pioneers experience in seeking to inculturate the gospel surrounding the degree to which they let go and let go of the gospel as they have conceived of it elsewhere and the sharing of the story of Christ enabling that to be discovered in the new context. For example, one pioneer wrote a wonderful contemporary parable that was a reworking of Moses' encounter with the holy through the burning bush set into the context of an

---

27 Lynch, *Understanding Theology and Popular Culture*, 103.
28 Johnson, *Reel Spirituality*.

English housing estate. But in the assignment he explained why he had ended up feeling it was inappropriate at the current moment to share it with the young people on the estate he is working on. Because of the acute awareness of mistakes missionaries have made unwittingly (or wittingly!) imposing their own culture in crossing cultures, they are genuinely hesitant about saying too much, about speech and would rather that the story of Christ somehow just emerged! I think this hesitancy and vulnerability, patience and waiting is healthy and entirely in keeping with the spirituality of prophetic dialogue. But there is a story to be told, to be shared, and the pioneer comes with gifts from the tradition. Prophecy does require speech, and by speech that could be any number of ways of communicating or voicing. It is interesting in theological education how so much focus goes into preaching as a means of speech to the detriment of almost any other kind of speech. But voice might just as easily (or better) be conversation, photography, painting, storytelling, film, poetry, parables, icons, ritual, installations and so on. I always think that art and prophecy are close friends and tend to look for artistic kinds of speech.

The best way to understand Jesus is as a prophet, which is most likely how he saw himself and how he was understood by his contemporaries.[29] He announced that his mandate was to proclaim good news to the poor, the recovery of sight to the blind, freedom for captives and liberating the oppressed (Luke 4). The liberation of the kingdom of God was at hand in his life and ministry. He proceeded to enact and embody this vision as well as announcing that one day all things would be made new. Bosch suggests that the challenge in mission is to prolong the logic of the ministry of Jesus in imaginative and creative ways, which must include this prophetic dimension as the prophethood of all believers.[30]

Mission as prophecy is an exciting new way of conceiving of mission in contemporary culture though the way prophetic dialogue is conceived could lead to a false dichotomy if the prophetic and dialogue parts get separated too much. I hope that dialogue does not end up being thought of as the culture friendly part where we listen and be and discern in mission, and then prophetic is simply countercultural. This would be a mistake or at least it is not the way the prophetic always flows in culture. It is all too easy to imagine prophets as outside cultures or over and against them, which seems to me to be a false imagining. Jesus was very much loved by the people as a prophet, who was fully inside the culture. Sedmak points out that Jesus only raised his prophetic voice after being embedded in the local culture and that genuine prophecy has to use familiar concepts in order to have an impact.[31] 'Only a theology firmly rooted in a culture can be genuinely prophetic in

---

29 Bevans and Schroeder make this point in chapter 3 of *Prophetic Dialogue*.
30 David Bosch, *Transforming Mission*, Maryknoll, NY: Orbis, 1991, 34.
31 Sedmak, *Doing Local Theology*, 17.

that same culture ... Prophecy is effective when it reorganizes knowledge already part of the culture. To stand completely outside is to be ignored. Thus the more contextually rooted a theology the more acute can be its prophetic voice and action.'[32] It was from within the culture that he spoke up and spoke truth to power.

Reflecting on Jesus the prophet and the prophetic church in Acts, Johnson says that the marks of prophets are being inspired by the Holy Spirit, speaking God's word, embodying God's vision for humans, enacting that vision through signs and wonders and bearing witness to God in the world.[33] This seems to be a pretty good agenda for pioneers in mission in contemporary culture although there is no blueprint, no answer that can be looked up in a book of how this can be done. It is a process of imagination, discerning and participating with the Spirit of prophecy in a never-ending adventure. It will begin to be at its most creative as a local, missional community begins to emerge, gathers around the stories of Christ and does the imaginative work of what it means for them together to prolong the logic of the ministry of Jesus in their community. Together they will dream of how another world might not only be possible but enacted and embodied in their midst.

Finding Local Prophets of the Unpopular Popular

Popular culture is a site for a whole array of meanings, some of which are competing or contested. There is a strain of art within its flow that is prophetic in and of itself. It tends to be tucked away in more marginalized spaces rather than in the flow of the mainstream and is usually resistant to the more dominant consciousness or meanings. Brueggemann describes the role of prophecy as nurturing, nourishing and evoking a consciousness and perception alternative to the consciousness and perception of the dominant culture.[34] Music critic Simon Frith refers to it as the 'unpopular popular' and suggests it is about culture as transformation rather than reconciliation. He suggests, 'Culture as transformation must challenge experience, must be difficult, must be unpopular ... the unpopular popular, the "difficult" appeals through the traces it carries of another world in which it would be "easy".'[35] This use of culture empowers people to change rather than simply providing a means of escape through leisure from the drudgery of daily work. David Dark names it as apocalyptic, revealing what is hidden,

---

32 Robert Schreiter, 'Some Conditions for a Transcultural Theology', in P. Knitter (ed.), *Pluralism and Oppression: Theology in World Perspectives*, Lanham, MD: University Press of America, 1991, 22–8 quoted in Sedmak, *Doing Local Theology*, 17.

33 Luke Johnson, *Prophetic Jesus Prophetic Church*, Grand Rapids, MI: Eerdmans, 2011, 4.

34 Walter Brueggemann, *The Prophetic Imagination*, Minneapolis: Augsburg Fortress, 1978, 13.

35 Simon Frith, *Performing Rites: Evaluating Popular Music*, Oxford: Oxford University Press, 1996.

showing what we are not seeing, naming what the sustainers of the way things are do not want to be spoken, 'cracking the pavement of the status quo'.³⁶ It can shock and surprise and pull the rug from under our feet, blindsiding us. Marshall McLuhan suggests that the role of the artist (and he is clearly describing this strain) is to create an anti-environment as a means of perception and adjustment, because without an anti-environment all environments are invisible.³⁷ Art and prophecy are close friends, which is why totalitarian regimes often silence artists – they are dangerous because they see and speak in this way!

A tactic in prophetic dialogue is to listen and discern those activists, dreamers, vagabonds, poets and unpopular popular artists who are already prophets in their own culture and to join in with what they are doing in liberation, in service to the healing of creation. It is to dig out the treasure of popular cultural resources that are apocalyptic, the unpopular popular and to use them as dialogue partners, or as the building blocks of liturgy and spirituality in the new emerging missional community. By doing so, we are joining in with what God is already doing in the culture. Once you start to see, this is going on in all sorts of places, both in local contexts and in the wider mediated spaces of popular culture. It is all around us. Let me give an example.

'Everything is Going According to Plan' was a performance of film and music made by Adam Curtis with 'Massive Attack' at Manchester International Festival in 2013. It took place in a disused railway station, which gave it a very industrial feel, and the audience was surrounded by 11 huge screens from floor to ceiling – a totally immersive visual environment. 'Massive Attack' was playing a soundtrack behind one of the screens. The film, which played sometimes simultaneously and sometimes with different parts on different screens, roamed through cultural footage over the last 50 years weaving global narratives unmasking many of the paradigms or worldviews of that era. It was made from material produced in common culture, like news clips, music videos or sound bites. They were used to generate meaning that subverted and resisted the capitalist system in which it was produced. Capitalist society ironically has created the ideal conditions for this because there are lots of resources available for the symbolic work.³⁸ This is a sort of creative poaching constructing devious and tactical ways of 'making do' through ways of using the products that flow in the wider economic order to create different meanings. 'Readers are travellers; they move across lands belonging to someone else, like nomads poaching their way across fields they did not write.'³⁹

36 David Dark, *Everyday Apocalypse*, Grand Rapids, MI: Brazos, 2002.

37 Marshall McLuhan, *Probes*, Berkeley, CA: Gingko Press, 2002.

38 Paul Willis, *Common Culture*, Milton Keynes: Open University Press, 1990, 19.

39 Michel De Certeau, *The Practice of Everyday Life*, Berkeley, CA: University of California, 1984, 174.

One of the phrases projected said 'we have opted to manage the world rather than change the world' which is why we are stuck. What an extraordinary insight! This is true in many businesses, much of the social/charity sector and the Church. We elevate managers, we prefer and feel safer with them rather than visionaries and dreamers in top leadership positions. This may be because of fear of money, the future or simply we want to feel that we can control things as best we can. After the concert I was seeing it everywhere whereas the week before I had been used to business as usual. Adam Curtis and Robert del Naja (of 'Massive Attack') were interviewed on BBC Radio 6 Music by Mary Anne Hobbs and she asked the question, 'Are we really free?' In response, Curtis said that the issue he is trying to explore in the film is how power works, how it pervades our lives – not just through Westminster but through popular culture. One of the examples he gave is the feedback loops that are going on around us all the time through websites tracking our tastes – you like this, so you'll like that. We have probably got so used to it now that we do not think about it. We are continually being given what we liked yesterday. The idea of the film/experience he said was to pull back like a helicopter to enable people to stop and see this static managed world, the pervasive ideology of our time. And he then mused whether we are really free? 'We're free to have what they think you like. Is that freedom? It's a kind of static or limited freedom where you are stuck in your own yesterday.'[40] I thought this was such a good line – stuck in your own yesterday. With this approach to reality, ideas and possibilities that are new will never emerge – they will be perceived as risky, unprovable, unmeasurable and a threat. Yet when we are stuck precisely what we need is this genuine kind of newness. The last thing to be projected were these words:

the future is full of POSSIBILITY
It is not predictable
You can make anything happen
You can change the world
Please find your own way home.

The twofold task of the prophet is to evoke grief about the current situation to break numbness through the shedding of tears and to use the language of amazement to open up the possibility for hope and newness. For Brueggemann the reasons for criticizing and energizing are rooted in the tradition and story of God, but it seems to me that Curtis and 'Massive Attack' are engaged in a similar task of prophetic imagination.[41] Ironically the thought that was uppermost in my mind for the next few months, as I reflected on it, was how the Church as institution is all too often stuck in its own yesterday in precisely this way, opting to manage the world out of fear rather than

40 The interview by Mary Anne Hobbs was aired on BBC Radio 6 Music on 14 July 2013 on Stuart Maconie's *Freak Zone* show.
41 Brueggemann, *The Prophetic Imagination*.

change the world. Examples of this might be in relation to the cultural forms of worship, hesitancy around new technologies, but also in deeper questions such as women bishops in the Church of England, or the debates around sexuality. One of the tasks for pioneers is to find ways themselves, together with the communities they are part of, to live in a consumer culture, while at the same time developing some notion of resistance to consumerism living out of a different imaginary formed by the gospel. A lot of approaches fall down because they criticize the culture while pretending they are outside it, but then find it impossible to escape from it, often generating a false sub-culture that is equally working under the logic of capitalism. 'Everything is Going According to Plan' manages to resist and be prophetic without withdrawing from engagement in the culture. It uses the resources and practices of culture itself to question and suggest alternatives to the environment itself in order that it might be remade.

Prophetic Dialogue: The Last and Most Difficult Area

Prophetic dialogue in relation to culture is extremely challenging. Gerald Arbuckle, who in many ways is the leading voice in the area of inculturation, highlights one last area in which prophetic dialogue is necessary. This is in relation to the Church institutions and traditions themselves.[42] While the importance of inculturation is accepted in theory among missiologists (some) theologians and (some) Church authorities, in practice it can be extremely difficult to do something that is genuinely experimental in theology, mission and ecclesiology. It is variously seen as a threat, novelty, a waste of resources, or even heretical. There are refreshing exceptions to this, of course. I think it is made doubly difficult for pioneers in mission in Western cultures because they have not got the benefit of distance. At least when you travel to a culture a long way away you are out of sight! We are finding that pioneers need to be formed and located in a prophetic community truly to sustain and nurture the mission spirituality required for this difficult task.[43] But part of their challenge is to embody the spirituality and posture of prophetic dialogue in relation to the wider Church – to be gentle among, listening and discerning what the Spirit is doing but also to be reforming religious tradition in a prophetic spirit, beckoning the Church into the future.

---

42 Arbuckle, *Culture, Inculturation and Theologians*, xx.

43 Gerald Arbuckle, *Refounding the Church: Dissent for Leadership*, Maryknoll, NY: Orbis, 1993 and *From Chaos to Mission: Refounding Religious Life Formation*, London: Geoffrey Chapman, 1996 has been incredibly helpful in gaining insight into prophetic ministry and formation.

14

Prophetic Dialogue and Interculturality[1]

ROGER SCHROEDER

In *Constants in Context: A Theology of Mission for Today* (2004) Stephen Bevans and I proposed six theological constants which shape a mission theology and practice.[2] This article develops in more depth the dynamic intersection of one of those constants, namely 'culture', from the perspective of interculturality, with the idea of 'prophetic dialogue' which was introduced in *Constants in Context* and developed in more depth in a later publication.[3] I will describe, first of all, interculturality from the social science and missiological perspectives, and second, prophetic dialogue as 'prophecy' and 'dialogue' separately, and then as the two dimensions together. The chapter then brings the two concepts into conversation with each other and proposes how prophetic dialogue and interculturality can mutually shape, enrich and complement each other. In conclusion, I will briefly draw missionary implications.

Interculturality

The term 'multicultural' describes the factual situation where members of different cultures are living, working or worshipping together in the same space. 'Cross-cultural' dynamics imply that there is an attempt, to varying degrees, to take the next step of appreciating, understanding and interacting with another culture. This often, but not always, is understood and experienced as unidirectional. The newer idea of 'intercultural' relationships or 'interculturality' explicitly moves beyond mere peaceful coexistence or one-directional movement 'to emphasize and make more explicit the essential mutuality of the process of cultural interaction on both the personal and social level'.[4] In order to establish a more in-depth and foundational

---

[1] Earlier versions of this chapter were published in *Verbum SVD* 54:1 (2013), 8–21, and in *Perspektif*, 8:1 (2013), 67–79.

[2] Stephen B. Bevans and Roger P. Schroeder, *Constants in Context: A Theology of Mission for Today*, Maryknoll, NY: Orbis, 2004, 33–4.

[3] Bevans and Schroeder, *Constants in Context*, 348–52; Stephen B. Bevans and Roger P. Schroeder, *Prophetic Dialogue: Reflections on Christian Mission Today*, Maryknoll, NY: Orbis, 2011.

[4] Robert Kisala, 'Formation for Intercultural Life and Mission', *Verbum* 50:3 (2009), 331–45 (335).

understanding of the meaning of interculturality, I will draw from the disciplines of the social sciences and missiology.

Social Science Perspective

Social scientists have been studying the phenomenon of interculturality for some time. First of all, they describe and analyse the universal human tendency for *ethnocentrism*, whereby an individual, group or nation consider their culture as superior and normative in relation to others. Accordingly, they 'prejudge people's behaviour and explain differences as if they were the result of perceived physical and mental differences (racism) or spiritual and moral differences (elitism)'.[5] The counterpoint to ethnocentrism is cultural relativism, which presupposes that 'each culture can be understood and appreciated only in its own context'.[6] This perspective of course is a key component for mutual interculturality.

A second and more recent approach that is generating much attention is in the area of *de-coloniality*. While the external forms of political colonialization have for the most part been dismantled, this period of post-colonialism is still marked by 'colonial' actions and 'colonial' thinking in the areas of economics, social organization, and I would add, church life and mission. Ethnocentrism is of course underlying this phenomenon. Interculturality offers a new counter-colonial framework, which substitutes attitudes and actions of superiority and paternalism with those of self-determination and mutual interdependence. In other words, interculturality fosters a situation 'where differences are not cast in terms of values of plus and minus degrees of humanity'.[7]

A third major study in the social sciences focuses on the phenomenon of *globalization*. One of the major consequences of globalization is the creation of a universal metaculture, often at the expense of local culture and identity. At the same time, the world is experiencing many radical movements for local autonomy through culturally rooted violent conflicts, usually at the expense of others and the common good. The idea and practice of interculturality is intended to avoid the dangers of this polarization between globalization and fundamentalism. Franz Xaver Scheuerer describes interculturality as 'a third way between monoculturalism and radical pluralism, or between a centralist universalism and a relativistic ethnophilosophy'.[8]

---

5 Michael Rynkiewich, *Soul, Self, and Society: A Postmodern Anthropology for Mission in a Postmodern World*, Eugene, OR: Cascade Books, 2011, 24.

6 Rynkiewich, *Soul, Self, and Society*, 27.

7 Walter D. Mignolo, 'Delinking: The rhetoric of modernity, the logic of coloniality and the grammar of decoloniality', *Cultural Studies* 21:2–3 (2007), 499–514 (499). For an excellent article on the implications of decoloniality from a philosophical perspective, see Enrique Dussel, 'A new age in the history of philosophy: The world dialogue between philosophical traditions', *Philosophy and Social Criticism* 35:5 (2009), 499–516.

8 Franz Xaver Schererer, *Interculturality: A Challenge for the Mission of the Church*,

These sociological studies point to the potential destructiveness of ethno-centrism, post-colonialism and globalization in promoting systems and relationships based on superiority, uniformity and exclusive self-interest. And these systems and relationships are not only in the areas of personal interactions, politics, economics and social/cultural identity, but they also can shape the understandings and practices within missionary life and work. At the same time, it is very interesting that the social sciences highlight the potential of true interculturality for contributing to the creation of a world in which individuals, communities and nations interact in a more appropri-ate and mutually enhancing fashion.

Missiological/Theological Perspective

The cornerstone for a missiological/theological foundation for intercultur-ality was laid with the Second Vatican Council. The operative missionary theology before the Council reflected two primary motivations for mission. First of all, the Catholic Church was focused on the salvation of souls and it saw itself as bringing God in a one-directional movement to people in a lost world and bringing them safely on board the 'ark of salvation'. The second motivation for mission was the establishment of the visible presence of the Church, which considered its Western form as normative and non-Western cultures as inferior. However, in the opening paragraphs of the missionary decree *Ad Gentes*, the Vatican Council grounded mission and the Church itself in the *mission of God (missio Dei)*, who, in ways only God knows, had from the beginning been actively present in all of history and creation, drawing all people and every created thing to Godself, the source of life. The Church plays a key role in God's mission by being a faithful witness to and sacrament of God's salvation, love and justice (*Lumen Gentium* 1, 5), but God is bigger than the Church. As an instrument of God's mission, the Church is to acknowledge and engage God's Spirit somehow already present in other Christian churches and denominations, all religions and secular society, all cultures, the world and all of creation. The Church recog-nized a need for a shift 'from the old heroic, paternalistic model of mission – reaching down to "save" and "help" another person – to a model of humility and mutuality – developing a reciprocal relationship out of respect for how God is already present in the other'.[9]

Of particular importance for our treatment of interculturality was the Vatican II shift to a more *positive assessment of culture*, especially non-Western cultures. It was actually the first time the term 'culture' appeared in a conciliar document. The Council encouraged Christians and local churches to 'be familiar with their national and religious traditions and uncover with

Bangalore, India: Asian Trading Corporation, 2001, 35.

9 Roger P. Schroeder, *What is the Mission of the Church? A Guide for Catholics*, Mary-knoll, NY: Orbis, 2008, 4.

gladness and respect those seeds of the Word which lie hidden among them' (*Ad Gentes* 11). Post-conciliar developments over the past 50 years have further refined the process of what has become known as inculturation.[10] This is based on the theology that *every* culture/society contains *both* the seeds of the Word of God and those elements which are contrary to God's reign. Therefore, the intercultural interaction among individuals, cultures and local churches is crucial for mutual enrichment and for the recognition of the continual call to conversion for all.

The basic idea of mutual exchange is reflected in the post-conciliar understanding of mission. Before the Second Vatican Council, missionary activity was basically seen in geographical terms – from Europe, North America and Australia to the rest of the world. With Vatican II's understanding that the entire Church and every local church is 'missionary by its very nature' (*Ad Gentes* 2) and that God's mission is stirring on all six continents, every local church is to be both mission-sending and mission-receiving. In order to express this multidirectional mutual exchange in mission around the globe, a number of people now propose complementing the phrase '*ad gentes*' (to the nations) with '*inter gentes*' (among the nations).[11] Former Superior General of the Society of the Divine Word (SVD) Antonio Pernia described 'mission inter gentes' as 'mission as dialogue WITH people, mission as encounter BETWEEN peoples, mission as finding a home AMONG the people'.[12]

Much more can be written to develop more fully and appropriately the missiological/theological, as well as the sociological/anthropological (and one could add the biblical, historical and spiritual), foundations for interculturality.[13] Sufficient for this chapter is the brief overview of the understanding of interculturality from the perspectives of the social sciences and missiology/theology. They indicate converging and complementary conversations about the potentiality, challenges and need for transformation in order to foster and create real in-depth mutual relationships and exchanges among cultures, on both the individual and communal levels. We will now describe prophetic dialogue.

---

10 See Bevans and Schroeder, *Constants in Context*, 385–9; Gerald Arbuckle, *Culture, Inculturation, and Theologians: A Postmodern Critique*, Collegeville, MN: Liturgical Press, 2010.

11 For example, see Jonathan Tan, 'Missio Inter Gentes: Towards a New Paradigm in the Mission Theology of the Federation of Asian Bishops' Conferences (FABC)', *Mission Studies* 21:1 (2004), 65–95; William Burrows, 'Formation for Mission "Missio Ad et Inter Gentes"', *Sedos Bulletin* 39:5–6 (2007), 106–18.

12 Antonio Pernia, 'Missio Inter Gentes', *Arnoldus Nota*, November 2009, 1–2 (2).

13 Refer to other articles in *Verbum SVD* 54:1 (2013).

Prophetic Dialogue

Origin of the Term

While Indian missiologist Michael Amaladoss used the term 'prophetic dialogue' in passing in 1992,[14] it surfaced more clearly as an expression of the missionary response to varied contexts in the General Chapter of the Society of the Divine Word (SVD) in 2000. It was accepted by the entire assembly and served as a central idea of the final chapter document.

> It is in dialogue that we are able to recognize 'the signs of Christ's presence and the working of the Spirit' (*Redemptoris Missio*, 56) in all people, that we are called to acknowledge our own sinfulness and to engage in constant conversion, and that we witness to God's love by sharing our own convictions boldly and honestly, especially where that love has been obscured by prejudice, violence, and hate. It is clear that we do not dialogue from a neutral position, but out of our own faith. Together with our dialogue partners we hope to hear the voice of the Spirit of God calling us forward, and in this way our dialogue can be called prophetic.[15]

While the individual SVD source for the initial coining of the term is unclear and probably unimportant since it was created and adopted through a communal process, some have proposed that it represented the combination and complementarity of two different perspectives and contexts regarding the understanding and practice of mission. The large group of Asian SVD delegates at the chapter understood mission primarily as 'dialogue' – reflecting the post-Vatican II reflections of the Federation of Asian Bishops' Conferences (FABC) in terms of dialogue with the poor, cultures and religions. The large group of Latin American SVD chapter delegates primarily understand mission as 'prophecy' – reflecting the post-Vatican II reflections of the Latin American Episcopal Council (CELAM: Consejo Episcopal Latinoamericano) in terms of confronting injustices and embracing a 'preferential option for the poor'. Although the use of the idea of 'prophetic dialogue' did not generate an in-depth theological discussion at its inception by the SVD, further reflection and study has shown that this term brings together two essential dimensions of the practice and theology of mission in all contexts.

For example, Stephen Bevans and I have developed and proposed 'prophetic dialogue' as an insightful way to synthesize current mission theology and

---

14 Amaladoss used the phrase in this way: 'Religion is called to enter into a prophetic dialogue with the world.' See Michael Amaladoss, 'Mission as Prophecy', in James A. Scherer and Stephen B. Bevans (eds), *New Directions in Mission and Evangelization 2: Theological Foundations*, Maryknoll, NY: Orbis, 1994, 64–72 (the quotation is from 72). The original article appeared in French in *Spiritus* 128 (1992), 263–75.

15 Society of the Divine Word, In Dialogue with the Word, Documents of the 15th General Chapter SVD 2000, Rome: SVD Publications, No. 1, September 2000, par. 54.

practice not only for the SVD, but also for the broader Christian world.[16] I shall briefly describe dialogue and prophecy separately as two essential dimensions of the *missio Dei* and then look at them together.

Mission as Dialogue[17]

Reflecting the shift in the Church's attitude to the world during the Second Vatican Council, described above, Paul VI wrote: 'it seems to Us that the sort of relationship for the Church to establish with the world should be more in the nature of a dialogue'.[18] For example, *Nostra Aetate*, the Council's declaration on non-Christian religions, described the presence of 'rays of Truth which enlightens all human beings' (2) who are followers of world religions.[19] Almost 20 years after Vatican II, the Vatican's Secretariat for Non-Christians stated: 'Dialogue is thus the norm and necessary manner of every form of Christian mission, as well as every aspect of it, whether one speaks of simple presence and witness, service, or direct proclamation. Any sense of mission not permeated by such a dialogical spirit would go against the demands of true humanity and against the teachings of the gospel.'[20] Dialogue is based on the *missio Dei*. Just as God is dialogical in Godself and is engaged in the world, so the Church needs to give of itself in service to the world and to learn from the world, its cultures, its religions – and so learn more about God's unfathomable riches. Just as God's missionary presence is never about imposition but about persuasion and freedom, so must the Church never neglect the freedom and dignity of human beings. Finally, just as God 'humbled' Godself in the incarnation, so the Church needs to do mission not out of superiority, but in humility and vulnerability.

---

16 Bevans and Schroeder, *Constants in Context*, 281–395; Bevans and Schroeder, *Prophetic Dialogue*.

17 For a fuller development, see Bevans and Schroeder, *Prophetic Dialogue*, chapter 2, 'We Were Gentle among You: Christian Mission as Dialogue', 19–39.

18 Paul VI, Encyclical Letter Ecclesiam Suam, 78, www.vatican.va/holy_father/paul_vi/encyclicals/documents/hf_p-vi_enc_06081964_ecclesiam_en.html.

19 'Christian theology had always had a strong, if perhaps subaltern, tradition of the possibility of grace and salvation outside the boundaries of the church and explicit faith in Jesus Christ – from the second-century theologian Justin Martyr through Thomas Aquinas to Pius XII in the 1940s.' (Bevans and Schroeder, *Prophetic Dialogue*, 23). See Jacques Dupuis, 'A Theological Commentary: Dialogue and Proclamation', in William Burrows, *Redemption and Dialogue: Reading* Redemptoris Missio *and* Dialogue and Proclamation, Maryknoll, NY: Orbis, 1993, 123 and 133–5.

20 Secretariat for Non-Christians, 'The Attitude of the Church toward the Followers of Other Religions: Reflections and Orientations on Dialogue and Mission', *Bulletin Secretariatus pro non Christianis* 56:2 (1984), 29.

Mission as Prophecy[21]

While mission is dialogical, 'mission is and must be prophetic because God's inner nature is also prophetic, and because God is prophetic in dealing with creation'.[22] To begin, a prophet must be grounded in dialogue. A prophet strives to listen to God's Word, to discern God's presence in the 'signs of the times' (*Gaudium et Spes*, 4) and to dialogue with the worldview and context of the people. Second, a prophet 'speaks forth' a message about the future. However, rather than 'fortune telling', it is an *annunciation* of God's plan of salvation – as Ezekiel prophesied over the dry bones (Ezek. 37) and Jesus prophesied about the immanent reign of God (Matt. 5.1–11) – both of which were happening but people did not see it. Prophecy includes telling the world about Jesus. Third, a prophet is involved in 'speaking against' or pronouncing a *denunciation* of something that is contrary to the reign of God – as Amos denounced injustices towards the poor (Hos. 6.1–11) and Jesus denounced a very narrow understanding of religious stipulations (e.g. Matt. 12.1–14; Mark 2.13–17). This must be done with a spirit of love for God and the people, and the prophet must always be aware of his/her own sinfulness. Finally, it is important to note that both *annunciation* and *denunciation* can be done with and without words.[23]

Mission as Prophetic Dialogue

Dialogue and prophecy are understood here not as two totally separate actions, but rather they are *complementary* dimensions of the *missio Dei*, which should underlie *every* form of Christian mission/ministry. In other words, every theology and practice of mission needs to be both dialogical and prophetic as a part of the *missio Dei*. For example, proclamation is not only a prophetic non-forceful presentation of the good news of the gospel, but as stated by the late Archbishop Marcello Zago, proclamation 'presupposes and requires a dialogue method in order to respond to the requirements of those to be evangelized and to enable them to interiorize the message received'.[24] At the same time, interreligious dialogue is not only dialogical in its many forms, but is also prophetic in that Christians maintain and respectfully witness to their own Christian beliefs with those of other faiths, just as the other does with their religious beliefs. I have addressed this particular relationship of proclamation and interreligious dialogue in more

---

21 For a fuller development, see Bevans and Schroeder, *Prophetic Dialogue*, chapter 3, 'I Am Not Ashamed of the Gospel: Mission as Prophecy', 40–55.

22 Bevans and Schroeder, *Prophetic Dialogue*, 41.

23 See Bevans and Schroeder, *Prophetic Dialogue*, 43–8.

24 Marcello Zago, 'The New Millennium and the Emerging Religious Encounters', *Missiology: An International Review* 28:1 (2000), 5–18 (17).

detail elsewhere.[25] While dialogue and prophecy are always theologically fully present, in practice it is better to think of these two dimensions in terms of a continuum, whereby the dialogical dimension may be more prominent in some contexts, while the prophetic dimension is prominent in others. However, Christian participation in the *missio Dei* always includes both the dialogical and prophetic dimensions to some degree.

Balancing dialogue and prophecy at the same time as 'prophetic dialogue' is parallel to the insightful and challenging call for '*bold humility*' by the late renowned South African missiologist David Bosch over 20 years ago. 'It is ... a bold humility – or a humble boldness. We know only in part, but we do know.'[26] J. N. J. (Klippies) Kritzinger, former colleague of Bosch, maintains that Bosch's ecumenical missionary paradigm, including 'bold humility', needs to be understood in terms of 'creative tension'.[27] At first, Bevans and I considered the two dimensions of 'prophetic dialogue' more as a synthesis.[28] However, after conversations with those who understand and experience this more as creative tension, we are beginning to image 'prophetic dialogue' as a '*synthesis in creative tension*'.[29] No matter how it is phrased, this theological foundation shapes and is shaped by mission practice. Furthermore, in paraphrasing Robert Schreiter,[30] 'prophetic dialogue functions more as a *spirituality* than a strategy'.[31] And it requires ongoing conversion to be both dialogical and prophetic.

Interculturality and Prophetic Dialogue

I shall now bring these two concepts of interculturality and prophetic dialogue into conversation with each other and propose how a mutual interrelationship between them can be complementary and fruitful.

---

25 Roger Schroeder, 'Proclamation and Interreligious Dialogue as Prophetic Dialogue', *Missiology: An International Review* 41:1 (2013), 50–61.

26 David Bosch, *Transforming Mission: Paradigms in Theology and Mission*, Maryknoll, NY: Orbis, 1991, 489. See also Willem Saayman and Klippies Kritzinger (eds), *Mission in Bold Humility: David Bosch's Work Considered*, Maryknoll, NY: Orbis, 1996.

27 J. N. J. (Klippies) Kritzinger, '"Mission as ..." Must we choose? A dialogue with Bosch, Bevans, Schroeder and Schreiter in the South African context', unpublished paper delivered at a conference on 'Mission as Prophetic Dialogue?' at the University of South Africa (Unisa), Pretoria, on 16 April 2010. See Bosch, *Transforming Mission*, 367, 381–9, 507–10.

28 Bevans and Schroeder, *Prophetic Dialogue*, 2.

29 Schroeder, 'Proclamation and Interreligious Dialogue', 54. Theologically, Catholics tend to strive for a synthesis, while some Christians of other traditions seem to prefer holding them in creative tension. David Tracy describes and contrasts these two approaches in terms of an 'analogical imagination' and a 'dialectical imagination', respectively. See *The Analogical Imagination: Christian Theology and the Culture of Pluralism*, New York: Crossroad, 1981.

30 Robert J. Schreiter, *The Ministry of Reconciliation: Spirituality and Strategies*, Maryknoll, NY: Orbis, 1998.

31 Bevans and Schroeder, *Prophetic Dialogue*, 2.

Prophetic Dialogue Shaping Interculturality

The vision of prophetic dialogue has the potential to enhance and complement the pursuit of interculturality, through its mission theology, practice and spirituality. *Missio Dei* theology provided interculturality with a solid foundation for a positive attitude towards culture and for a mutual exchange among cultures on an equal basis. Prophetic dialogue with this same Trinitarian *theology* clarifies the necessary interplay of the two dimensions in any intercultural exchange/relationship: (a) dialogical acknowledgement of the presence of the seeds of God's Word in all cultures, and (b) prophetic acknowledgement of those elements contrary to God's reign (denunciation) and of blindness to God's movement (annunciation) in all cultures. This theological background provides a framework for the *practice* of interculturality that aims for a middle path between universal monoculturality and exclusive particularity. In the face of ethnocentrism, post-colonialism and globalization, the theological/sociological/missiological challenge is to (a) promote mutual enrichment and critique among all individuals, groups and nations and (b) to avoid claims of cultural superiority and dominance, by either a global power of influence or a particular individual/group. In other words, it promotes unity-in-diversity, and it avoids uniformity and fundamentalism in intercultural dynamics and relationships. The idea of prophetic dialogue finally, and perhaps most importantly, provides a profound and inspiring *spirituality* for those striving for true interculturality. Being a person of dialogue and prophetic vision within an intercultural context demands deep attention and response to God's stirring among others and within oneself. Holding prophetic dialogue in those same settings like a synthesis in creative tension requires a real spirit of discernment spirit. Striving for mutual interculturality requires openness and self-confidence, vulnerability and courage and in the words of David Bosch, 'humility' and 'boldness'.

Interculturality Shaping Prophetic Dialogue

Now by reversing the perspective, let us see what the idea of interculturality has to offer to the understanding and practice of prophetic dialogue through its content, methodology and training. The current *content* of the general study of culture – as something dynamic and changing and not a harmonious integrated whole – and the more particular studies of interculturality – such as on ethnocentricism, post-colonialism and globalization – provide excellent information for understanding the many different contexts of mission today.[32]

---

32 For anthropological resources for mission, see Louis Luzbetak, *The Church and Cultures: New Perspectives in Missiological Anthropology*, Maryknoll, NY: Orbis, 1988; Rynkiewich, *Soul, Self, and Society.*

Bevans and I have proposed prophetic dialogue as the underlying framework for the understanding and practice of every form of Christian mission today – witness and proclamation; liturgy, prayer and contemplation; justice, peace and the integrity of creation; interreligious and secular dialogue; inculturation; reconciliation.[33] Not only the basic knowledge of the theory but also the *methodology* of studying culture, context and interculturality can serve as essential tools for an in-depth contextualization of every element of mission – mission as prophetic dialogue.

In returning to the case of the Society of the Divine Word (SVD), one of the distinguishing characteristics of its work and charism was the importance placed on the social sciences for mission already in the late nineteenth and early twentieth century. This vision originated with the SVD founder Arnold Janssen, was carried out in the academy and field work through the organization of SVD ethnologist Wilhelm Schmidt, and it was enfleshed in practice by SVD missionary Joseph Freinademetz in China. Antonio Pernia called this the SVD 'Anthropos Tradition' and described it in this way:

> Our Anthropos tradition is really a way of doing mission which considers an appreciation of people's culture as a necessary precondition for genuine evangelization. A way of doing mission whereby the gospel message is not simply parachuted from outside, but enters into dialogue with the culture of the people. And so, a way of doing mission whereby the missionary is ready not just to change people but to be changed himself, or as *Evangelii Nuntiandi*[34] (e.g. no. 15) puts it, a way of evangelizing whereby the evangelizer not only evangelizes but allows himself or herself to be evangelized.[35]

In this powerful statement, Pernia proposes the study of culture as 'a necessary precondition' for mission and for an intercultural encounter, which enables enrichment and change – that is prophetic dialogue – within both parties.

In the first part of the twentieth century, the study of culture by missionaries was primarily focused on rural communities of people of traditional religions. Today, missionaries are living in different contexts on all six continents, where an understanding of migration, ethnic identity, family life, youth culture, globalization, urbanization and post-colonialism, is relevant. The theme of interculturality provides an excellent opportunity not only for missionaries but for all ministers in differing contexts to use the content and

---

33 See Bevans and Schroeder, *Prophetic Dialogue*, chapter 5, 'Unraveling a "Complex Reality": Six Elements of Mission', 64–71.

34 Paul VI, Apostolic Exhortation Evangelii Nuntiandi, www.vatican.va/holy_father/paul_vi/apost_exhortations/documents/hf_p-vi_exh_19751208_evangelii-nuntiandi_en.html.

35 Antonio M. Pernia SVD, 'Expectations of the Generalate of the Anthropos Institute', *Verbum SVD* 45:1 (2004), 19–37 (34).

methodology of the social and religious sciences for both their mission *ad extra* and their community, parish, or congregational life *ad intra*.

The third area of interculturality that can benefit all aspects of mission is *training*. Training is understood here not so much in terms of learning content and methodology, but rather being trained or formed with the appropriate perspectives and attitudes. In other words, how do we understand the world of the other from the perspective of the other? For example, Milton J. Bennett has developed an excellent training programme for developing intercultural sensitivity, whereby participants move along a continuum, from wherever they begin the process, between six stages from ethnocentrism to ethnorelativism.[36] Such a process would dovetail with the spirituality of prophetic dialogue described earlier.

Missionary Implications

Missionary anthropology, or anthropology for the sake of mission, was often understood in the past on the level of using the tools of the social sciences to accomplish the goals of mission. However, bringing together interculturality and prophetic dialogue moves beyond a mere instrumentalist understanding of the relationship of the social sciences with mission. Rather than considering the social sciences as only a secular pursuit, interculturality and prophetic dialogue, as presented in this article, are both grounded in a post-Vatican II *missio Dei* theology and both are based on the principle of mutual enrichment and exchange. Furthermore, each is concerned with the essential interplay between theory/theology and practice, and I propose that they can enrich, complement and challenge each other. Philip Gibbs described the intersection in this way: 'In order to take *anthropos* [humanity] seriously we need both a theological and a cultural anthropology that informs our missiology, and we need an intercultural hermeneutics to help us navigate through multiple cultural identities.'[37] A recent publication *Cross-Cultural Mission*, edited by Raymundus Sudhiarsa, includes in-depth studies of the experience of present-day Indonesian, Filipino and Indian missionaries in a variety of cross-cultural settings and insightful implications regarding appropriate formation for intercultural life and mission.[38]

Finally, both prophetic dialogue and interculturality see the need for a process of transformation and conversion of perspectives and attitudes. This

---

36 Milton J. Bennett, 'Toward Ehnorelativism: A Developmental Model of Intercultural Sensitivity', in R. Michael Paige (ed.), *Education for the Intercultural Experience*, Yarmouth, ME: Intercultural Press, Inc., 1993, 21–71. Consult the link for Bennett's Intercultural Development Inventory: www.idiinventory.com/.

37 Philip Gibbs, 'The Context of God's Mission in Papua New Guinea: Intercultural Relations and an SVD Tradition', *Verbum SVD* 53:1 (2012), 69–85 (84).

38 Raymundus Sudhiarsa SVD (ed.), *Cross-Cultural Mission: Problems and Prospects*, Malang, Indonesia: Bayumedia Publishing, 2012.

is the fundamental point of convergence that occurs not only in the head, but primarily in the heart. Jon Kirby calls this 'cross-cultural conversion', while John Prior 'intercultural conversion'[39] – out of the contexts of Ghana and Indonesia, respectively. Missiologist and anthropologist Darrell Whiteman describes Peter's encounter with Cornelius in Acts 10 as an ideal example of such a conversion that is essential for a missionary, when Peter realized that God does not have favourites (Acts 10.34).[40] VanThanh Nguyen has treated the entire Peter–Cornelius incident as a story of conversion and mission in an insightful way.[41] And this was also a moment of prophetic dialogue for Peter, in that he recognized God's stirring in the life of the Gentile Cornelius (dialogue) and he witnessed to and proclaimed the gospel of Christ (prophetic). Hopefully, this chapter has pointed to the significant potentiality of how prophetic dialogue and interculturality can mutually shape, enrich and complement each other.

---

39 John Mansfield Prior, 'Learning to Leave: The Pivotal Role of Cross-Cultural "Conversion"', *Verbum SVD* 53:2 (2012), 225, 232.

40 Darrell Whiteman, 'The Conversion of a Missionary: A Bible Study from Acts 10', unpublished manuscript.

41 vanThanh Nguyen, *Peter and Cornelius: A Story of Conversion and Mission*, Eugene, OR: Pickwick Publications, 2012.

15

Contextual Theology and Prophetic Dialogue

STEPHEN B. BEVANS

Introduction: Contextual Theology as Prophetic Dialogue / Prophetic Dialogue as Contextual Theology

Doing contextual theology is an exercise of prophetic dialogue. Prophetic dialogue is practised in a dialectic of openness to the new, surprising and sometimes disturbing, and fidelity to the traditional, kerygmatic, and sometimes confrontative. Contextual theology is done with the same dialogical openness, prophetic fidelity and creativity. At Nicea, for example, there had to be an openness to a term beyond biblical language that would answer a question that only the Hellenistic context of Alexandria had given rise – *homoousios*; but at the same time this new term had to be faithful to what the Bible proclaimed and the Christian people firmly yet rather instinctively believed – that Jesus was Lord, that he had revealed the true face of God, that God had touched human life and so redeemed it fully.[1] In our own day, to give another example, we search for ways to affirm the insights of contemporary physics and evolutionary theory without abandoning our faith in biblical and traditional faith that 'in the beginning ... God created heaven and earth' (Gen. 1.1).[2]

At the same time, prophetic dialogue is an exercise of contextual theology. When do we keep silent and learn from the situation around us? When and how do we explain 'the reason for [our] hope' (1 Pet. 3.15) or decide to organize a demonstration against a nation's military action? When do we organize a liturgy of lament after a tragedy like a bush fire or a typhoon, and when do we celebrate a liturgy of hope in a country torn apart by violence? When do we agree to accept an offer to celebrate a day of thanksgiving in an interfaith service, and when do we invite non-Christians to join us in

---

1 See Bernard Lonergan, *The Way to Nicea: The Dialectical Development of Trinitarian Theology*, trans. Conn O'Donovan, Philadelphia: The Westminster Press, 1976, 105–37, esp. 134–7. See also the translator's introduction, xxvii–xxviii.

2 See, for example, Ilia Delio, *The Emergent Christ: Exploring the Meaning of Catholic in an Evolutionary Universe*, Maryknoll, NY: Orbis, 2011 and John F. Haught, *God after Darwin: A Theology of Evolution*, Boulder, CO: Westview Press, 2000.

celebrating Christmas or Easter? Each one of these decisions depends on the context in which we live. The wonderfully moving film *Of Gods and Men* depicts how the monks of Tibhirine in Algeria made the prophetic decision to remain in their monastery despite almost certain capture and death by Algerian rebel forces. Such a decision was hardly a casual one. It was taken with a deep understanding of the meaning of their dialogical missionary presence among the local people, one that gave them the authority to confront a corrupt government as well as the rebels who menaced them.[3]

This chapter will reflect on this close connection between the practice of prophetic dialogue and the doing of theology that is rooted in a particular context. Good theologizing is a reflection on faith that learns from experience, that illuminates it and that sometimes challenges it. An attitude and spirituality of prophetic dialogue is rooted in the practice of theological reflection that honours, reflects on and critically appropriates present human experience – or context. The chapter will have three parts. Part I will reflect briefly on the practices of contextual theology and of prophetic dialogue themselves. Part II will then reflect on contextual theologizing as a practice of prophetic dialogue. Finally, Part III will reflect on the practice of prophetic dialogue as a practice of contextual theologizing.

Contextual Theology and Prophetic Dialogue

Contextual theology – or, perhaps better, contextual *theologizing*, since theology is more an activity than a content – is, as I have described it in my book *Models of Contextual Theology*, a way of doing theology that takes into account both past and present. It is a result of vigorous, mutually critically dialogue between the experience of the Christian past, preserved in Scripture and tradition and Christian experience in the present, in other words, in a particular context. Such a context might consist of personal or social experience (a death in my family, Typhoon Yolanda in the Philippines), social location (male, female, rich, poor, disabled, gay), the web of meanings and power relations involved in culture and social change (technology, changing attitudes towards sexuality) in a culture. Depending on how Scripture, tradition and context interact in this dialogue, I have suggested, there will emerge various models or combinations of models that guide and shape the theological process.[4] While doing theology in a reflexively conscious way is something that is rooted in the modern and perhaps especially postmodern 'turn to the subject', it is not really new. I would argue that *any* authentic theology – in the past (e.g. Origen, Augustine,

3 See also John Kiser, *The Monks of Tibhirine: Faith, Love, and Terror in Algeria*, New York: St Martin's Griffin, 2003.

4 See Stephen B. Bevans, *Models of Contextual Theology*, revised and expanded edn, Maryknoll, NY: Orbis, 2002.

Aquinas, Luther) or in the present (e.g. contemporary efforts of African, Asian or feminist theologies) – has always been done contextually.[5]

Cathy Ross and I have already offered an understanding of prophetic dialogue in the Introduction to this volume, and other contributors have no doubt added to that understanding. Nevertheless, for the purposes of this chapter, it might be good to offer a brief explanation of what has become such an important concept in missiological practice and thinking. First of all, prophetic dialogue is more of an attitude, a *habitus* or spiritual discipline, than anything else. It requires developing, on the one hand, in the words of the African American poet and novelist Alice Walker, 'a heart so open that the wind blows through it'.[6] Such a heart has to cultivate the skills and attitudes of deep listening, of 'docility' or the ability to learn from those among whom we work, of respect and word of vulnerability. On the other hand – and only within the context of such dialogue as the condition for the possibility – the *habitus* of prophetic dialogue demands the cultivation of clarity of speech and thought, the courage to confront evil and injustice and the dogged conviction of hope in what might seem like hopeless situations. Prophecy is twofold: it is about 'speaking forth' in both word and deed and 'speaking out' in word and deed as well. Every authentic act of missionary activity contains both prophecy and dialogue, and discernment is always needed to determine when and to what extent prophecy or dialogue is the more appropriate practice. In some cases, as is the case of the monks of Tibhirine, being open to dialogue is already a prophetic act.[7]

Contextual Theology as Prophetic Dialogue

The entire reason for doing theology contextually is so that the gospel, transmitted in Scripture and tradition, can be understood as clearly as possible, both by those hearing the gospel for the first time and those believers who constantly need to grow in their faith and be more and more evangelized by it. The goal of contextual theology, in other words, is prophecy. That doing theology contextually is an exercise of prophetic dialogue is evidenced in the mutually critically dialogue that the contextual theologizing process entails. Dialogue is the way that the prophetic message of the gospel is developed and communicated.

In an important article – first given as a keynote address at the annual meeting of the American Society of Missiology in 1996 – anthropologist

---

5 I argue this briefly in *Models of Contextual Theology*, 7–9, and more at length in my *Introduction to Theology in Global Perspective*, Maryknoll, NY: Orbis, 2009, 205–323.

6 Alice Walker, 'A Wind through the Heart: A Conversation with Alice Walker and Sharon Salzberg on Loving Kindness in a Painful World', *Shambhala Sun* (1997), 1–5.

7 In addition to Cathy Ross's and my introduction, see chapters 2 and 3 of Roger Schroeder's and my book *Prophetic Dialogue: Reflections on Christian Mission Today*, Maryknoll, NY: Orbis, 2011, 19–55.

Darrell Whiteman offers three ways that the prophetic message of the gospel is served by the dialogue demanded by contextual theologizing.[8] Whiteman recognizes that the dialogue between the gospel message and context is something that goes back to the beginning of Christianity, when the early community made the decision, recorded in Acts 15, that one could be a Christian without first taking on the culture of Judaism. Contemporary concern with contextual theologizing, he says, is 'getting us back in touch with this principle, for at nearly every era of the Church's history, Christians have had to return to this principle'.[9]

The first way, says Whiteman, that doing contextual theology makes the gospel a prophetic message is that it makes it possible for women and men to follow Christ faithfully while remaining full members of their own culture. Like the Word made flesh, the gospel does not take women and men out of their culture, but moves them towards its centre and calls them to be full participants in it. Vatican II's document on mission encourages Christians who have received the gospel to 'share in cultural and social life by the various exchanges and enterprises of human living', to 'be familiar with their national and religious traditions, gladly laying bare the seeds of the Word which lie hidden in them'.[10] Whiteman gives an example here of a student of his, a Thai woman, who exclaimed in one of his courses: 'Now that I have been studying contextualization and have discovered how the Gospel relates to culture, I am realizing that I can be both Christian and Thai.'[11] Her experience showed the error in thinking that Thai culture was completely synonymous with Buddhism, and so anyone who became a Christian had to turn their backs on Buddhist relatives and denounce their culture.

Several of the 'models of contextual theology' that I have proposed – for example, the translation model, the anthropological model, the synthetic model and in some ways the praxis model – function to make the gospel message prophetic in its particular context.[12] Each of these models, in its own way, enters into a dialogue with a particular context and attends to the Christian message as the prophetic message that it is, the 'two edged sword' that is 'able to discern reflections and thoughts of the heart' (Heb. 4.12).

Second, the dialogue with context in contextual theologizing becomes prophetic as a challenge to that context. Whiteman writes that in this way contextualization *offends ' – but only for the right reasons, not the wrong*

---

8 Darrell Whiteman, 'Contextualization: The Theory, the Gap, the Challenge', *International Bulletin of Missionary Research* 21:1 (1997), 2–7.

9 Whiteman, 'Contextualization', 3

10 Second Vatican Council, Decree on the Missionary Activity of the Church (*Ad Gentes*), 11, www.vatican.va/archive/hist_councils/ii_vatican_council/documents/vat-ii_decree_19651207_ad-gentes_en.html.

11 Whiteman, 'Contextualization', 2.

12 See Bevans, *Models of Contextual Theology*, 37–53, 54–69, 70–87, 88–102.

ones'.[13] A preaching of the gospel that does not come out of a 'sincere and patient dialogue'[14] with the culture or context may indeed offend, but it is not really prophetic. It comes across as anti-cultural, which the gospel never is, rather than countercultural, like the gospel sometimes should be. So often people reject the gospel for the wrong reasons, often because of preaching that offends their cultural and human sensitivities. The gospel contains plenty of material that offends. Gustavo Gutiérrez remarked rather famously that the gospel is at once the *annunciation* of good news and the *denunciation* of anything that is not human or liberating.[15] When the gospel is preached rightly the Holy Spirit can 'convict the world in regard to sin' (see John 16.8). When it is not, it comes across as insensitive, foolish, irrelevant. 'When people are offended for the wrong reason, the garment of Christianity gets stamped with the label of "Made in America [or Britain] and Proud of It", and so it is easily dismissed as a "foreign religion".'[16]

The 'countercultural model' of contextual theology and in some ways the 'praxis model' as well offer the possibility of a critical yet honest dialogue with a context that makes the gospel 'challengingly relevant' to it, contributing to a context's 'subversive fulfilment'.[17]

Whiteman speaks of a third way that contextual theologizing helps articulate the prophetic nature of the gospel: it allows the universal Church to come to a deeper and broader understanding of the very message it proclaims. As people of various cultures, of various locations and of particular historical contexts receive the gospel and by that 'sincere and patient dialogue'[18] that Vatican II encourages, discover new and astonishing facets of the gospel (e.g. its fundamental 'option for the poor' through twentieth-century Latin American theology, its call to radical equality through contemporary feminist theologies), not only particular contexts will benefit. These new facets of the gospel will enhance the entire, global Church. As Andrew Walls expresses it with his customary eloquence, each culture, gender, generation and social location becomes 'a building block belonging to a new temple still in process of construction. Like them, each is an organ necessary to the proper functioning of a body under Christ's direction. Only together will

---

13 Whiteman, 'Contextualization', 3. Italics in original.

14 *Ad Gentes* 11.

15 Gustavo Gutiérrez, *A Theology of Liberation*, Maryknoll, NY: Orbis, 1973, 265–72.

16 Whiteman, 'Contextualization', 3–4.

17 See Bevans, *Models of Contextual Theology*, 88–102 and 117–37. The phrases in quotation marks are from Alfred G. Hogg, *The Christian Message to the Hindu: Being the Duff Missionary Lectures for Nineteen Forty-Five on the Challenge of the Gospel in India*, London: SCM, 1945, 9–26; and Hendrik Kraemer, *The Authority of Faith: The Madras Series*, vol. 1, New York, London: International Missionary Council, 1939, 4. These are quoted from Michael Goheen, *'As The Father Has Sent Me, I Am Sending You': J. E. Lesslie Newbigin's Missionary Ecclesiology*, Zoetermeer, Netherlands: Boekencentrum Publishing House, 2001, 357.

18 *Ad Gentes* 11.

they reach the fullness of Christ which is the completion and perfection of humanity.'[19] Vatican II speaks of how those who preach the gospel, as they listen carefully to the world's cultures, discover 'what treasures a bountiful God has distributed among the nations'.[20]

Today one talks not only of *contextual* theologizing, but of the *inter-contextual* or *intercultural* dialogue of theology in global perspective. Not only is the dialogue of Christian tradition with particular contexts necessary to discover the prophetic articulation of the gospel, a dialogue *among* the contextual theologies is also necessary.[21]

Contextual theology is a theology born of dialogue, but, most ironic-ally, that dialogue is itself a prophetic activity. The dialogical character of contextual theologizing bears witness to the fact that Christianity is not a religious way that calls women and men out of the world, out of their con-texts. Rather, its concern with all that is truly human, its passion to discover the 'seeds of the Word'[22] in human experience and history, its determin-ation to discover the Spirit's 'hidden presence'[23] in movements and persons, its labour to heal, ennoble and perfect 'the hearts and minds ... the rites and cultures peculiar to various peoples'[24] is a clear and powerful prophetic expression of the God who loved the world so much as to send the Beloved Son (see John 3.16). Contextual theologizing is indeed a practice of proph-etic dialogue.

Prophetic Dialogue as Contextual Theology

If mission is imaged as Christians' participation in God's joyful, life-giving and healing dance through the world (planet earth and the entire creation), then prophetic dialogue might be imaged as well as the rhythm of that dance, a rhythm that has constantly to be discerned as holy mystery moves through the world through the Spirit and embodied in the incarnate Word.[25] God is the first one to dance in prophetic dialogue. God's dance through creation is guided by creation's various rhythms and by women and men in all their variety growing, changing, developing, regressing – to which God is con-stantly responding. Pope Paul VI expressed this long ago when he described God's saving, prophetic work in the world in terms of dialogue: 'the whole

---

19 Andrew F. Walls, 'Afterword: Christian Mission in a Five-Hundred-Year Context', in Andrew F. Walls and Cathy Ross (eds), *Mission in the Twenty-First Century: Exploring the Five Marks of Global Mission*, London: Darton, Longman and Todd, 2008, 195.

20 *Ad Gentes* 11.

21 See Roger P. Schroeder, 'Interculturality and Prophetic Dialogue', *Verbum SVD* 54:1 (2013), 8–21; Stephen Bevans, 'A Theology for the Ephesian Moment', *Anvil* 27:2 (2011), http://anviljournal.org/174.

22 *Ad Gentes* 11.

23 *Ad Gentes* 9.

24 *Ad Gentes* 9.

25 See Bevans and Schroeder, *Prophetic Dialogue*, 9–18, 156.

history of humanity's salvation is one long, varied dialogue, which marvellously begins with God and which God prolongs with women and men in so many different ways'.[26] Pope Paul wrote these words in 1964; in 1991 they were echoed by the important document *Dialogue and Proclamation*. The foundation of the Church's commitment to dialogue is not simply anthropological. It is theological: 'God, in an age-long dialogue, has offered and continues to offer salvation to humankind. In faithfulness to the divine initiative, the Church too must enter into a dialogue of salvation with all men and women.'[27]

As Christians enter this dialogue of 'Trinitarian practice',[28] therefore, discernment of God's rhythm is a theological task and even more precisely a *contextual* theological task. Such contextual theological reflection is a continual requirement of women and men in mission, because the work of mission is never a one-size-fits-all activity. Mission involves, as Roger Schroeder and I have argued, a number of *Constants*, but these constants have always and must always be realized *in Context*.[29] This has been evident, as we have shown, throughout the Church's history, and it remains a task for today as well. Theological reflection on how the constants of mission need to be expressed and lived out is the discernment of how the Church should engage in prophetic dialogue in particular times and places – in particular contexts.

Mission always involves a witness to and a proclamation of Jesus the Christ, but how and when Christ is to be witnessed to and proclaimed is a matter of theological wisdom and discernment. Some contexts, for example, in places where there is a Muslim majority or a high level of secularism, might allow for nothing but a simple but clear Christian witness.[30] But how might that be carried out? Engaging with sincere people in working for social justice? Running schools or hospitals? Being a welcoming Christian

---

26 Paul VI, Encyclical Letter *Ecclesiam Suam*, 70, www.vatican.va/holy_father/paul_vi/encyclicals/documents/hf_p-vi_enc_06081964_ecclesiam_en.html.

27 Pontifical Council for Interreligious Dialogue and Congregation for the Evangelization of Peoples, *Dialogue and Proclamation*, 38, www.vatican.va/roman_curia/pontifical_councils/interelg/documents/rc_pc_interelg_doc_19051991_dialogue-and-proclamatio_en.html.

28 See Stephen Bevans, 'Missiology as Practical Theology: Understanding and Embodying Mission as Trinitarian Practice', in Clare Wolfteich (ed.), *Invitation to Practical Theology: Catholic Voices and Visions*, New York/Mahwah, NJ: Paulist Press, forthcoming.

29 See Stephen B. Bevans and Roger P. Schroeder, *Constants in Context: A Theology of Mission for Today*, Maryknoll, NY: Orbis, 2002, 32–72.

30 John Paul II, Encyclical Lettter *Redemptoris Missio*, 42, www.vatican.va/holy_father/john_paul_ii/encyclicals/documents/hf_jp-ii_enc_07121990_redemptoris-missio_en.html. I believe that a particular witness of the Church in the secular world should be that of deep listening and silence. I believe some of that is wonderfully exemplified in the actions, attitudes and some of the writing of Pope Francis. On this witness of respectful listening and silence, see Stephen B. Bevans, 'Revisiting Mission at Vatican II: Theology and Practice for Today's Missionary Church', *Theological Studies* 74:2 (2013), 280.

community with liturgies that are beautiful and that address the issues of daily life? And if and when Christ is preached, how is he to be presented? Some situations of oppression might require a Christology of liberation. Asian Christologies might focus on Jesus as Teacher or Guru. Preaching Christ in Western contexts might focus on his revelation of God's humanity that emphasizes God's commitment to persuasion and vulnerability. African Christology might develop the image of Jesus as ancestor, or master of initiation, or chief. Christian witness and proclamation of Christ may draw on the social location of a group of participants in a particular context, or on local culture, or engage in particular debates or discussions taking place in a situation. Or Christian witness and preaching might challenge certain attitudes or practices in a context, like equality for women or white privilege. An attitude of prophetic dialogue can shape Christology for a particular context.

Mission is also a profoundly ecclesiological reality. But what kind of Church should be manifested in each particular circumstance? What image of the Church might best suit a particular situation? What should be the role of the Church in countries where it has been shamed by scandals of clergy sexual abuse? What is the mission of the Church in countries overwhelmed by HIV/AIDS? Should it cultivate its identity as a 'little flock' in a larger, non-Christian context? Do Western yearnings for meaningful community shape its pastoral planning? In places like the Philippines, Mexico and Fiji it might be a voice of justice. In Nicaragua, South Africa and Argentina it might be a voice of reconciliation. In India it might be a voice of dialogue and openness to Hinduism. The African Church has tried to define itself – not without some controversy – with the image of the extended family.[31] The Federation of Asian Bishops' Conferences (FABC) has written repeatedly of a Church in a triple dialogue with the poor, cultures and other religions.[32] How does the Church embody itself as a community where life is cultivated and thrives? Welsh pastor Peter Cruchley-Jones writes challengingly about the shape of the Church's mission in a situation like Britain where God and the Church are not associated at all with life, which it professes to bring.[33]

---

31 See John Paul II, Apostolic Exhortation *Ecclesia in Africa*, esp. 63, www.vatican. va/holy_father/john_paul_ii/apost_exhortations/documents/hf_jp-ii_exh_14091995_ecclesia-in-africa_en.html. See also Teresa Okure, 'Church-Family of God: The Place of God's Reconciliation, Justice, and Peace', in Agbonkhianmeghe E. Orobator (ed.), *Reconciliation, Justice and Peace: The Second African Synod*, Maryknoll, NY: Orbis, 2011, 13–24.

32 A good summary of the FABC's writings on this is found in Thomas C. Fox, *Pentecost in Asia: A New Way of Being Church*, Maryknoll, NY: Orbis, 2002.

33 Peter Cruchley-Jones, '"You Have Not Sought the Lost": A Reflection from Europe on the WCC Theme', *International Review of Mission* 102:1 (396) (2013), 69–81. Jones is responding to the recent Mission Statement of the World Council of Churches, entitled 'Together towards Life: Mission and Evangelism in Changing Landscapes', 2012, www. oikoumene.org/en/resources/documents/wcc-commissions/mission-and-evangelism/together-towards-life-mission-and-evangelism-in-changing-landscapes?set_language=en, 20.

Once again, an attitude of prophetic dialogue, questioning and dialoguing with the context, can point to the way the Christian community needs to be and act.

Eschatology shapes thinking about missionary practice as well. In *Constants in Context* Roger Schroeder and I distinguish two basic types of eschatological perspectives. A first focuses on the basic meaning and goal of history symbolized by the kingdom or reign of God. A second perspective focuses on the inevitable future of individual human beings: death, judgement, purgatory, heaven and hell.[34] Depending on the particular context in which the Church participates in God's mission, one or the other aspect of these two perspectives will be emphasized in preaching, liturgical celebration and pastoral practice. A missionary practice of liberation will certainly emphasize the already-but-not-yet presence of God's reign as Christians struggle for freedom from political or economic oppression. In situations of extreme poverty or oppression the missionary task might be to focus on a more future-oriented and apocalyptic understanding of history, which might help people cope with daily drudgery and offer them a spark of hope and meaning. This can never be a mere spiritualization or 'pie-in-the-sky' eschatology, however, but always connected to justice and human wholeness.[35] In any case, a more apocalyptic eschatology can be one that allows people to lament, vent pent-up anger and express hope in creative ways. While a holistic eschatology may be appealing to more affluent situations, what might serve God's saving and healing work in this context might be a sober reminder of human finiteness and individual responsibility for personal, political and economic decisions. African, Asian and some cultures in Oceania may profit from a personal eschatology that explores the veneration of ancestors. Indian preaching and catechetics might reflect on connections between purification after death and Hindu beliefs in reincarnation.[36] Eschatological perspectives will shape how funeral liturgies are planned and celebrated. Some eschatological beliefs and practices will draw from the context. Others will offer it a stringent critique. Still others might draw on eschatological imagery as a relevant way to present God's saving work in Jesus. All these decisions are the result of a rich theologizing in context for the practice of prophetic dialogue.

Closely related to eschatology is the understanding of salvation. Should Christians in mission emphasize personal salvation, or a salvation that is more communal?[37] This will depend on the context – more individualistic

---

34 Bevans and Schroeder, *Constants in Context*, 42.

35 Christopher Rowland, *Liberating Exegesis: The Challenge of Liberation Theology*, Louisville, KY: Westminster/John Knox, 1990, 131–55.

36 Eminent Catholic theologian Karl Rahner hints at this connection in his *Foundations of Christian Faith: An Introduction to the Idea of Christianity*, New York: Seabury Press, 1978, 441–2.

37 Bevans and Schroeder, *Constants in Context*, 44, 68–9.

Western societies will be more interested in what happens to the individual; other socio-centric societies will be attracted to a salvation that includes family, clan and ancestors. A well-known story narrates how members of a certain African tribe told a missionary that, while they believed in Jesus, they would not be baptized because they wanted to be with their families and ancestors who had not had the opportunity to know about him. On the other hand, will a particular context call the Church to critique an excessive individualism? Or an excessive socio-centrism? Will the context demand that the gospel be preached in a way that acknowledges the possibility of salvation outside the boundaries of explicit Christian faith and Christian baptism. Will salvation emphasize more the Spirit's work of leading all peoples toward a participation in the paschal mystery?[38] Will salvation be more holistically understood as achievement of full humanity, healing from disease and sickness or reconciliation with enemies? In these days, as the new (2012) Mission Statement from the World Council of Churches points out forcefully, 'We do not believe that the earth is to be discarded and only souls saved; both the earth and our bodies have to be transformed through the Spirit's grace.'[39]

Christian mission has ever and will ever need to wrestle with questions of anthropology and the closely related constant of culture. Christian mission in the past was fuelled both by a negative concept of human persons as evil and sinful and in need of Jesus' satisfactory and substitionary death (another aspect of the constant of Christology). Correlatively, mission was motivated by the need to exorcise diabolical cultures and to bring what to their minds was civilization. Today, while these theologies are still somewhat prevalent among some churches, many other churches work with a very different anthropology and understanding of culture. While women and men are inherently flawed and cannot save themselves, many Christian churches acknowledge that they are basically good, enjoy certain 'inalienable rights' and possess a basic human dignity. It is in promotion of this basic humanity that motivates many Christians in mission to work for justice, peace and reconciliation throughout the world, and it is because of their work in contexts that do not fully recognize such rights and dignity that many have given their lives. Theological discernment of missionary action in such places has resulted in churches and communities adopting a vigorously prophetic lifestyle, as exemplified by women and men like Janani Luwum, Oscar Romero, Jean Donovan and Dorothy Kazell.[40]

---

38 Vatican Council II, Pastoral Constitution on the Church in the Modern World, *Gaudium et Spes*, 22, www.vatican.va/archive/hist_councils/ii_vatican_council/documents/vat-ii_cons_19651207_gaudium-et-spes_en.html.

39 World Council of Churches, 'Together Towards Life', 20.

40 See Robert Ellsberg, 'Janani Luwum, Anglican Archbishop of Uganda, Martyr (1924–1977)', 'Oscar Arnulfo Romero, Archbishop and Martyr of San Salvador (1917–1980)', 'Maura Clarke and Companions, Martyrs of El Salvador (d. 1980)', in *All Saints: Daily Reflec-*

Today, as well, culture is regarded by many churches as something that, while not perfect and subject to prophetic criticism and healing, is basically good and holy. 'Respect for people and their cultural and symbolic life-worlds', the WCC Mission Document asserts, 'are necessary if the gospel is to take root in those different realities.'[41] Vatican II calls for the development of contextual theologies rooted in local culture: 'From the customs and traditions of their people, from their wisdom and their learning, from their arts and sciences, these churches borrow all those things that can contribute to the glory of their creator, the revelation of the Savior's grace, or the proper arrangement of Christian life.'[42] As the Church in mission works at a clear and prophetic inculturation of the gospel, it does it by theologizing in a way that is through-and-through dialogical. The practice of prophetic dialogue leads to what Paul Hiebert has famously called 'critical contextualization'.[43]

Mission done with the spiritual discipline of prophetic dialogue is not simply *doing*. Mission in all its elements – witnessing and proclaiming; celebrating liturgy, engaging in prayer and contemplation; working for justice, peace and the integrity of creation; participating in interfaith, secular, and ecumenical dialogue; developing a theology and pastoral practice that is inculturated; ministering for reconciliation[44] – must be guided by a praxis of action guided by reflection and reflection motivated by action. The work of mission is always grounded in a theology. Unfortunately in the past that theology was often the theology of the West, of Geneva or of Rome. What a commitment to contextual theologizing offers to that work is a constant reflection and critique that anchors that theology in the concrete realities of the people and times in which missionaries or ministers work. The practice of mission as prophetic dialogue demands constant and thorough contextual theologizing.

Conclusion

Contextual theology is an exercise of prophetic dialogue. Prophetic dialogue is an exercise of contextual theology. Both contextual theology and prophetic dialogue are done in a dialectic of openness and critique, fidelity to Christian tradition and human experience. Both reflect the mission of God, whose Spirit pervades the universe and calls us to truth and whose Word is found in all human contexts and who is the greatest of the prophets.

---

tions on Saints, Prophets, and Witnesses for Our Time, New York: Crossroad, 1997, 79–80, 131–3, 526–7.

41 'Together Towards Life', 97.

42 *Ad Gentes* 22.

43 Paul Hiebert, 'Critical Contextualization', *International Bulletin of Missionary Research* 11:3 (1987), 104–12.

44 See Bevans and Schroeder, *Constants in Context*, 348–95; *Prophetic Dialogue*, 64–71.

Bibliography

Abukhater, A., *Water as a Catalyst for Peace: Transboundary Water Management and Conflict Resolution*, Earthscan Studies in Water Resource Management, New York: Routledge, 2013.

Adedibu, B., *Coat of Many Colours: The Origin, Growth, Distinctiveness and Contributions of Black Majority Churches to British Christianity*, Gloucester: Wisdom Summit, 2012.

Adeney, F., *Christian Women in Indonesia: A Narrative Study of Gender and Religion*, Syracuse, NY: Syracuse University Press, 2003.

Adeney, F., *Graceful Evangelism: Christian Witness in a Complex World*, Grand Rapids, MI: Baker Academic, 2010.

Adeney, M., *Daughters of Islam: Building Bridges with Muslim Women*, Downers Grove, IL: InterVarsity Press, 2002.

Adeney, M., *Kingdom Without Borders: The Untold Story of Global Christianity*, Downers Grove, IL: InterVarsity Press, 2009.

Adeney, M., 'Telling Stories: Contextualization and American Missiology', in W. Taylor (ed.), *Global Missiology for the 21st Century*, Grand Rapids, MI: Baker Academic, 2001, 377–88.

Adogame, A., *The African Christian Diaspora: New Currents and Emerging Trends in World Christianity*, London: Bloomsbury Academic, 2013.

Adogame, A., 'Up, Up, Jesus! Down, Satan! African Religiosity in the Former Soviet Bloc: The Embassy of the Blessed Kingdom of God for All Nations', *Exchange* 37:3 (2008), 310–36.

Aguilar, M. I., 'Reconversion among the Baroona', *Africa* 65:4 (1995), 525–44.

Aizpurua, F., 'Following Francis: A Catechism of Franciscan Spirituality', *Greyfriars Review* 17, supplement (2003), 3–102.

Alexander, L., 'What is a Gospel', in S. C. Barton (ed.), *The Cambridge Companion to the Gospels*, Cambridge: Cambridge University Press, 2006, 13–30.

Allenby, B., 'The Industrial Ecology of Emerging Technologies: Complexity and Reconstruction of the World', *Journal of Industrial Ecology* 13:2 (2009), 168–83.

Allison, S., 'Fixing China's Image in Africa one Student at a Time', theguardian.com, 5 July 2013, www.theguardian.com/world/2013/jul/31/china-africa-students-scholarship-programme.

Alonso, P., *The Woman Who Changed Jesus: Crossing Boundaries in Mark 7.24–30*, Biblical Tools and Studies 11, Leuven: Peeters, 2011.

Amaladoss, M., 'Mission as Prophecy', in J. Scherer and S. Bevans (eds), *New Directions in Mission and Evangelization 2: Theological Foundations*, Maryknoll, NY: Orbis, 1994, 64–72.

Anderson, A., *An Introduction to Pentecostalism*, Cambridge: Cambridge University Press, 2004.

Arbuckle, G., *Refounding the Church: Dissent for Leadership*, Maryknoll, NY: Orbis, 1993.

Arbuckle, G., *From Chaos to Mission: Refounding Religious Life Formation*, London: Geoffrey Chapman, 1996.

Arbuckle, G., *Culture, Inculturation and Theologians: A Postmodern Critique*, Collegeville, MN: Liturgical Press, 2010.

Armstrong, R. J., 'Francis of Assisi and the Prisms of Theologizing', *Greyfriars Review* 10:2 (1996), 179–206.

Armstrong, R. J. and Brady, I. (eds), *Francis and Clare*, Mahwah, NJ: Paulist Press, 1982.

Armstrong, R. J., Hellmann, J. A. W. and Short, W. J. (trans. and eds), *Francis of Assisi: Early Documents*, vol. 1, *The Saint*, New York: New City Press, 1999.

Armstrong, R. J., Hellmann, J. A. W. and Short, W. J. (eds), *Francis of Assisi: Early Documents*, vol. 2, *The Founder*, New York: New City Press, 2000.

Armstrong, R. J., Hellmann, J. A. W. and Short, W. J. (eds), *Francis of Assisi: Early Documents*, vol. 3, *The Prophet*, New York: New City Press, 2001.

Atkins, J. D., 'The Trial of the People and the Prophet: John 5:30–47 and the True and False Prophet Traditions', *Catholic Biblical Quarterly* 75:2 (2013), 279–96.

Barbour, C. M., 'Seeking Justice and Shalom in the City', *International Review of Mission* 73 (1984), 303–9.

Barth, K., *The Word of God and the Word of Man*, New York: Harper Torchbooks, 1957.

Beaudoin, T., *Virtual Faith*, New York: Jossey Bass, 1998.

Bennett, M. J., 'Toward Ethnorelativism: A Developmental Model of Intercultural Sensitivity', in R. M. Paige (ed.), *Education for the Intercultural Experience*, Yarmouth, ME: Intercultural Press, 1993, 21–71.

Bennington, G. and Derrida, J., 'Politics and Friendship, A Discussion with Jacques Derrida', Centre for Modern French Thought, University of Sussex, 1 December 1997, http://hydra.humanities.uci.edu/derrida/pol+fr.html.

Bergant, D. and Nothwehr, D. M., 'The Earth Is the Lord's and All It Holds (Psalm 24:1)', *The Bible Today* 47:1 (2009), 185–91.

Berkhof, L., *Systematic Theology*, Edinburgh: Banner of Truth Trust, 1958.

Bevans, S. B., *An Introduction to Theology in Global Perspective*, Maryknoll, NY: Orbis, 2009.

Bevans, S. B., *Models of Contextual Theology*, Maryknoll, NY: Orbis, 1992.

Bevans, S. B., *Models of Contextual Theology*, revised and expanded edn, Maryknoll, NY: Orbis, 2002.

Bevans, S. B., 'Missiology as Practical Theology: Understanding and Embodying Mission as Trinitarian Practice', in C. Wolfteich (ed.), *Invitation to Practical Theology: Catholic Voices and Visions*, Mahwah, NJ: Paulist Press, forthcoming.

Bevans, S. B., 'A Theology for the Ephesian Moment', *Anvil* 27:2 (2011), http://anviljournal.org/174.

Bevans, S. B., 'Revisiting Mission at Vatican II: Theology and Practice for Today's Missionary Church', *Theological Studies* 74:2 (2013), 261–83.

Bevans, S. B. and Schroeder, R. P., *Constants in Context: A Theology of Mission for Today*, Maryknoll, NY: Orbis, 2004, 2009.

Bevans, S. B. and Schroeder, R. P., *Prophetic Dialogue: Reflections on Christian Mission Today*, Maryknoll, NY: Orbis, 2011.

Bloesch, D. G., *Holy Scripture, Revelation, Inspiration and Interpretation*, Carlisle: Paternoster, 1994.

Boff, L., *Cry of the Earth, Cry of the Poor*, Maryknoll, NY: Orbis, 1997.

Bonaventure of Bagnoregio, *Opera Omnia: Doctoris Seraphici S. Bonaventurae opera omnia*, 10 vols, Quaracchi: Collegium S.Bonaventurae, 1882–1902.

Bonaventure of Bagnoregio, *Sancti Bonaventurae Sermones Dominicales, Bibliothca Franciscana Scholastica Medii Aevi*, 27, ed. J. G. Bougerol, Rome: Grottaferrata, 1977.

Boff, L., *Trinity and Society*, trans. Paul Burns, Maryknoll, NY: Orbis, 1988.

Borg, M., *Meeting Jesus Again for the First Time*, San Francisco: HarperSanFrancisco, 1994.

Bosch, D., *Transforming Mission: Paradigms in Theology and Mission*, Maryknoll, NY: Orbis, 1991.

Bourdieu, P., *Outline of a Theory of Practice*, Cambridge: Cambridge University Press, 1997.

Bowman, L. J. 'The Cosmic Exemplarism of Bonaventure', *The Journal of Religion* 55 (1985), 181–98.

Bretherton, L., *Hospitality as Holiness: Christian Witness amid Moral Diversity*, Farnham: Ashgate, 2006.

Brink, L., 'In Search of the Biblical Foundations of Prophetic Dialogue: Engaging a Hermeneutics of Otherness', *Missiology: An International Review* 41:1 (2013), 9–21.

Browning, D. S. and Cooper, T. D., *Religious Thought and the Modern Psychologies*, 2nd edn, Minneapolis: Fortress Press, 2004.

Brueggemann, W., *The Prophetic Imagination*, Philadelphia: Augsburg Fortress Press, 1978.

Brueggemann, W., *Theology of the Old Testament*, Philadelphia: Fortress, 1997.

Brunette, P., *Francis of Assisi and His Conversions*, trans. Paul La Chance and Kathryn Krug, Quincy, IL: Franciscan Press, 1997.

Bühlmann, W., *The Chosen People*, Slough: St. Paul Publications, 1982.

Burridge, R. A., *What Are the Gospels?: A Comparison with Graeco-Roman Biography*, 2nd edition, Grand Rapids, MI: Eerdmans, 2004.

Burrows, W., 'Formation for Mission "Missio Ad et Inter Gentes"', *Sedos Bulletin* 39:5–6 (2007), 106–18.

Capra, F., *The Web of Life: A New Scientific Understanding of Living Systems*, New York: Doubleday, 1996.

Carney, J. 'Roads to Reconciliation: An Emerging Paradigm of African Theology', *Modern Theology* 26 (2010), 549–59.

Centre for the Study of Global Christianity, *Christianity in its Global context, 1970–2020, Society, Religion, and Mission*, South Hamilton, MA: CSGC, 2013, wwwgordonconwell.com/netcommunity/CSGCResources/ChristianityinitsGlobal Context.pdf.

Certeau, M. de, *The Practice of Everyday Life*, Berkeley, CA: University of California Press, 1984.

Cessario, R., 'The Theological Virtue of Hope', in S. J. Pope (ed.), *The Ethics of Aquinas*, Washington, DC: Georgetown University Press, 2002, 232–43.

Charette, B., '"And Now for Something Completely Different": A "Pythonic" Reading of Pentecost?', *Pneuma* 33 (2011), 59–62.

Charlesworth, J. H., *The Historical Jesus: An Essential Guide*, Nashville, TN: Abingdon, 2008.

Choe-Sang-Hun, 'Amid Hugs and Tears, Korean families Divided by War Reunite', *New York Times*, 20 February 2014, www.nytimes.com/2014/02/21/world/asia/north-and-south-koreans-meet-in-emotional-family-reunions.html?hp.

Cimperman, M., *When God's People Have HIV/AIDS: An Approach to Ethics*, Maryknoll, NY: Orbis, 2005.

Commission of the Bishops' Conferences of the European Community (COMECE), 'A Christian View on Climate Change: The Implications of Climate Change for Lifestyles and EU Policies', Brussels: COMECE, 2008.

Cone, H. J., *My Soul Looks Back*, Maryknoll, NY: Orbis, 1993.

Congar, Y., *I Believe in the Holy Spirit*, trans. David Smith, New York: Crossroad, 1983.

Cousins, E. H. 'Francis of Assisi and Bonaventure: Mysticism and Theological Interpretation', in Peter Berger (ed.), *The Other Side of God: A Polarity in World Religion*, Garden City, NY: Anchor Press, 1981, 74–103.

Croatto, J. S., 'Jesus, Prophet like Elijah, and Prophet–Teacher like Moses in Luke–Acts', *Journal of Biblical Literature* 124:3 (2005), 451–65.

Crockett, W. V. and Sigountos, J. G. (eds), *Through no Fault of Their Own? The Fate of Those Who Have Never Heard*, Grand Rapids, MI: Baker Book House, 1991.

Crossan, J. D. and Reed, J. L., *Excavating Jesus: Beneath the Stones, Behind the Texts*, revised and updated, New York: HarperOne, 2001.

Cruchley-Jones, P., '"You Have Not Sought the Lost": A Reflection from Europe on the WCC Theme', *International Review of Mission* 102:1 (396) (2013), 69–81.

Cruz, G. T., *An Intercultural Theology of Migration: Pilgrims in the Wilderness*, Leiden: Brill, 2010.

Culpepper, R. A., 'The Gospel of Luke', in *The New Interpreter's Bible Commentary*, vol. IX, Nashville, TN: Abingdon Press, 1995, 3–490.

Dark, D., *Everyday Apocalypse*, Grand Rapids, MI: Brazos Press, 2002.

Darragh, N., *At Home in the Earth*, Auckland, New Zealand: Accent Publications, 2000.

De Gruchy, J. W., *Reconciliation: Restoring Justice*, Minneapolis: Fortress Press, 2002.

Delio, I., *Simply Bonaventure: An Introduction to His Life, Thought, and Writings*, Hyde Park, NY: New City Press, 2001.

Delio, I., *The Emergent Christ: Exploring the Meaning of Catholic in an Evolutionary Universe*, Maryknoll, NY: Orbis, 2011.

Derrida, J., *Of Hospitality: Anne Dufourmantelle invites Jacques Derrida to respond*, Stanford, CA: Stanford University Press, 2000.

Detweiler, C. and Taylor, B., *Matrix of Meaning*, Grand Rapids, MI: Baker, 2003.

Donahue, J. R., 'The Bible and Catholic Social Teaching', in K. R. Himes (ed.), *Modern Catholic Social Teaching: Commentaries and Interpretations*, Washington: Georgetown University Press, 2005, 9–40.

Donovan, V., *Christianity Rediscovered*, London: SCM Press, 1982.

Dowsett, R., 'Dry Bones in the West', in W. Taylor (ed.), *Global Missiology for the 21st Century*, Grand Rapids, MI: Baker Academic, 2001, 447–62.

Doyle, E., 'Duns Scotus and Ecumenism', in C. Bérubé (ed.), *De Doctrina I. Duns Scoti*, vol. III, Acta Congressus Scotistici Internationalis Oxonii et Edimburgi, 11–17 September 1966 celebrati, Roma: Cura Commissionis Scotisticae, 1968, 633–52.

Dries, A., *The Missionary Movement in Catholic History*, Maryknoll, NY: Orbis, 2003.

Dunn, J., *Jesus and the Spirit: A Study of the Religious and Charismatic Experience of Jesus and the First Christians as Reflected in the New Testament*, London: SCM Press, 1997.

Dupuis, J., 'A Theological Commentary: Dialogue and Proclamation', in William Burrows (ed.), *Redemption and Dialogue: Reading* Redemptoris Missio *and Dialogue and Proclamation*, Maryknoll, NY: Orbis, 1993, 119–58.

Dussel, E., 'A New Age in the History of Philosophy: The World Dialogue Between Philosophical Traditions', *Philosophy and Social Criticism* 35:5 (2009), 499–516.

Edwards, D., *Breath of Life: A Theology of the Creator Spirit*, Maryknoll, NY: Orbis, 2005.

Edwards, D., 'Final Fulfillment – The Deification of Creation', *SEDOS Bulletin* 41:7–8 (2009), www.sedosmission.org/web/en/sedos-bulletin/cat_view/93-bulletin/253-sedos-bulletin-2009/283-july-august-2009-seminar.

Effa, A., 'The Greening of Mission', *International Bulletin of Missionary Research* 32 (2008), 171–6.

Elliott, J. H., *1 Peter, A New Translation with Introduction and Commentary*, New Haven, CT: Yale University Press, 2000.

Ellsberg, R., *All Saints: Daily Reflections on Saints, Prophets, and Witnesses for our Time*, New York: Crossroad, 1997.

Erlanger, S., 'Iran and 6 Powers Agree on Terms for Nuclear Talks', *New York Times*, 20 February 2014, www.nytimes.com/2014/02/21/world/middleeast/iran.html?hp.

Fackre, G., Nash, R. H. and Sanders, J., *What about Those Who Have Never Heard? Three Views on the Destiny of the Unevangelized*, Downers Grove, IL: InterVarsity Press, 1995.

Fiddes, P., *Participating in God: A Pastoral Doctrine of the Trinity*, London: Darton, Longman & Todd, 2000.

Finch, R., 'Missionaries Today', *Origins* 30:21 (2000), 327–32.

Finn, D. K., 'Theology and Sustainable Economics', in R. W. Miller (ed.), *God, Creation, and Climate Change: A Catholic Response to the Environmental Crisis*, Maryknoll, NY: Orbis, 2010, 95–6.

FitzGerald, C., 'From Impasse to Prophetic Hope: Crisis of Memory', *Catholic Theological Society of America Proceedings* 64 (2009), 21–42, www.ctsaonline.org/Convention%202009/0021-0042.pdf.

Fitzmyer, J. A., *The Gospel according to Luke I–IX*, Garden City, NY: Doubleday, 1981.

Forrester, D., *Christian Justice and Public Policy*, Cambridge: Cambridge University Press, 1997.

Fox, T. C., *Pentecost in Asia: A New Way of Being Church*, Maryknoll, NY: Orbis, 2002.

Francis, Apostolic Exhortation, *Evangelii Gaudium* of the Holy Father Francis to the Bishops, Clergy, Consecrated Persons and the Lay Faithful on the Proclamation of the Gospel in Today's World, www.vatican.va/holy_father/francesco/apost_exhortations/documents/papa-francesco_esortazione-ap_20131124_evangelii-gaudium_en.html.

Francis, World Day of Peace Message, 1 January 2014, www.vatican.va/holy_father/francesco/messages/peace/documents/papa-francesco_20131208_messaggio-xlvii-giornata-mondiale-pace-2014_en.html.

Frith, S., *Performing Rites: Evaluating Popular Music*, Oxford: Oxford University Press, 1996.

Garces-Foley, K., *Crossing the Ethnic Divide: the Multi-ethnic Church on a Mission*, New York: Oxford University Press, 2007.

Gärtner, B. E., *The Areopagus Speech and Natural Revelation*, Acta Seminarii Neotestamentici Upsaliensis 21, Uppsala and Lund: C. W. K. Gleerup, and Copenhagen: Ejnar Munksgaard, 1955.

Gaventa, B. R., 'Initiatives Divine and Human in the Lukan Story World', in G. N. Stanton, B. W. Longenecker and S. C. Barton (eds), *The Holy Spirit and Christian Origins: Essays in Honor of James Dunn*, Grand Rapids, MI: Eerdmans, 2004, 79–89.

Geivett, R. D. and Phillips, W. G., 'A Particularist View: An Evidentialist Approach', in D. L. Okholm and T. R. Phillips (eds), *More than One Way? Four Views on Salvation in a Pluralistic World*, Grand Rapids, MI: Zondervan, 1995, 211–45.

George, S., *Called as Partners in Christ's Service: The Practice of God's Mission*, Louisville, KY: Geneva Press, 2004.

George, S., 'From Missionary to Missiologist at the Margins: Three Decades of Transforming Mission', in P. Lloyd-Sidle and B. S. Lewis (eds), *Teaching Mission in a Global Context*, Louisville, KY: Geneva Press, 2001, 40–53.

Gibbs, P., 'The Context of God's Mission in Papua New Guinea: Intercultural Relations and an SVD Tradition', *Verbum SVD* 53:1 (2012), 69–85.

Goheen, M., *'As the Father Has Sent Me, I Am Sending You': J. E. Lesslie Newbigin's Missionary Ecclesiology*, Zoetermeer, Netherlands: Boekencentrum Publishing House, 2001.

Goizueta, R. S., 'Solidarity', in M. Downey (ed.), *New Dictionary of Catholic Spirituality*, Collegeville, MN: Michael Glazier, 1993, 906–7.

Golley, F. B., *A Primer for Environmental Literacy*, New Haven, CT: Yale University Press, 1998.

Gonzales, J. L., *Acts: Gospel of the Spirit*, Maryknoll, NY: Orbis, 2001.

Gregersen, N. H. 'The Cross of Christ in an Evolutionary World', *Dialog: A Journal of Theology* 40:3 (2001), 197–207.

Groody, D. G., *Globalization, Spirituality and Justice*, Maryknoll, NY: Orbis, 2007.

Groody, D. G., *Crossing the Divide: Foundations of a Theology of Migration and Refugees*, Oxford: Crowther Centre Monographs, 2010.

Groody, D. G. and Campese, G. (eds), *A Promised Land, A Perilous Journey: Theological Perspectives on Migration*, Notre Dame IN; University of Notre Dame Press, 2008.

Grudem, W., *The Gift of Prophecy*, Eastbourne: Kingsway, 1988.

Guattari, F., *As Três Ecologias*, Campinas, Brazil: Papirus, 1988.

Guelke, J. K. 'Looking for Jesus in Christian Environmental Ethics', *Environmental Ethics* 26:2 (2004), 115–34.

Gunkel, H., *The Influence of the Holy Spirit: The Popular View of the Apostolic Age and the Teaching of the Apostle Paul*, Minneapolis: Fortress Press, 2008 [1888].

Gutierrez, G., *A Theology of Liberation*, Maryknoll, NY: Orbis, 1973, revised edn, 1988.

Haar, Gerrie ter, *Halfway to Paradise: African Christians in Europe*, Cardiff, Cardiff Academic Press, 1998.

Hanciles, J. J., *Beyond Christendom: Globalization, African Migration and the Transformation of the West*, Maryknoll, NY: Orbis, 2008.

Haney, M. S., 'Toward the Development of a New Christian Missiological Identity', in P. Lloyd-Sidle and B. S. Lewis (eds), *Teaching Mission in a Global Context*, Louisville, KY: Geneva Press, 2001, 79–92.

Haney, M. S., 'Afrocentricity: A Missiological pathway toward Christian Transformation', in M. S. Haney and R. E. Peters (eds), *Afrocentric Approaches to Christian Ministry: Strengthening Urban Congregations in African America Communities*, Lanham, MD: University Press of America, 2006, 151–65.

Haney, M. S. and Peters, R. E. (eds), *Afrocentric Approaches to Christian Ministry: Strengthening Urban Congregations in African American Communities*, Lanham, MD: University of America Press, 2006.

Hardy, T., *The Complete Poems*, ed. J. Gibson, London: Macmillan, 1976.

Harris, P., 'Nestorian Community, Spirituality, and Mission', in W. Taylor (ed.). *Global Missiology for the 21st Century*, Grand Rapids, MI: Baker Academic, 2001, 495–502.

Hathaway, M. and Boff, L., *The Tao of Liberation: Exploring the Ecology of Transformation*, Maryknoll, NY: Orbis, 2009.

Hauerwas, S., *After Christendom*, Nashville, TN: Abingdon, 1991.

Haught, J. F., *God after Darwin: A Theology of Evolution*, Boulder, CO: Westview Press, 2008.

Hayes, Z., *The Hidden Center: Spirituality and Speculative Christology in St. Bonaventure*, Franciscan Pathways, St. Bonaventure, NY: The Franciscan Institute, 1992.

Hays, R. 'Justification', in *Anchor Bible Dictionary Volume 3*, New York: Doubleday, 1992, 1129–33.

Healy, N. M., *Church, World and the Christian Life, Practical–Prophetic Ecclesiology*, Cambridge: Cambridge University Press, 2000.

Heim, S. M., *The Depth of the Riches: A Trinitarian Theology of Religious Ends*, Sacra Doctrina, Grand Rapids, MI: Eerdmans, 2001.

Heim, S. M., *Saved from Sacrifice: A Theology of the Cross*, Grand Rapids, MI: Eerdmans, 2006.

Heron, A. I. C., *The Holy Spirit: The Holy Spirit in the Bible, in the History of Christian Thought, and in Recent Theology*, London: Marshall Morgan & Scott, 1983.

Hershberger, M., *A Christian View of Hospitality, Expecting Surprises*, Scottdale, PA: Herald Press, 1999.

Herzog II, William R., *Jesus, Justice, and the Reign of God: A Ministry of Liberation*, Louisville, KY: Westminster/John Knox, 2000.

Hiebert, P. G., *Cultural Anthropology*, Grand Rapids, MI: Baker, 1976.

Hiebert, P. G., 'Critical Contextualization', *International Bulletin of Missionary Research* 11:3 (1987), 104–12.

Hiebert, P. G., *Anthropological Insights for Missionaries*, Grand Rapids, MI: Baker Book House, 1993.

Hobson, C., Cox, J. and Sagovsky, N., *Fit for Purpose Yet? The Independent Asylum Commission's Interim Findings*, www.citizensforsanctuary.org.uk/pages/reports/InterimFindings.pdf.

Hogg, A. G., *The Christian Message to the Hindu: Being the Duff Missionary Lectures for Nineteen Forty-Five on the Challenge of the Gospel in India*, London: SCM Press, 1945.

Holden, A., *Religious Cohesion in Times of Conflict: Christian–Muslim Relations in Segregated Towns*, London: Continuum, 2009.

Horsley, R., *Jesus and the Spiral of Violence*, San Francisco: HarperSanFrancisco, 1987.

Iammerrone, G. 'Franciscan Theology Today: Its Possibility, Necessity, and Values', *Greyfriars Review* 8:1 (1994), 103–26.

Ingham, M. E., 'Integrated Vision', in K. B. Osborne (ed.), *The History of Franciscan Theology*, St. Bonaventure, NY: The Franciscan Institute, 1994, 185–230.

Intergovernmental Panel on Climate Change (IPCC), *Climate Change 2007: Synthesis Report Summary for Policymakers*, www.ipcc.ch/ publications and_data/ar4/syr/en/spm.html.

Jackson, G. S., *'Have Mercy on Me': The Story of the Canaanite Woman in Matthew 15.21–28*, Journal for the Study of the New Testament Supplement series 228, London: Sheffield Academic Press, 2002.

Jacobs, D. R., 'Conversion and Culture: An Anthropological Perspective with reference to East Africa', in J. R. W. Stott and R. T. Coote (eds), *Gospel and Culture*, Pasadena: William Carey Library, 1979, 175–94.

Jagessar, M., *URC Mission Council Report*, London: United Reformed Church, 2011.

John Duns Scotus, *God and Creatures: The Quodlibetal Questions*, trans. Felix Alluntis and Allan B. Wolter, Washington, DC: Catholic University of America Press, Paperback Edition, 1981.

John Paul I, General Audience, 20 September 1978, www.vatican.va/holy_ father/john_paul_i/audiences /documents/hf_jp-i_aud_20091978_en.html.

John Paul II, Apostolic Exhortation *Ecclesia in Africa*, www.vatican.va/holy_father/john_paul_ii/apost_exhortations/documents/hf_jp-ii_exh_14091995_ecclesia-in-africa_en.html.

John Paul II, Apostolic Letter *Inter Sanctos: Franciscus Assisiensis Caelestis Patronus Oecologiae Cultorum Eligitur*, www.vatican.va/holy_father/john_paul_ii/apost_letters/1979/documents/ hf_jp-ii_apl_19791129_inter-sanctos_lt.html.

John Paul II, Encyclical Letter *Redemptoris Missio*, www.vatican.va/holy_father/john_paul_ii/encyclicals/documents/hf_jp-ii_enc_07121990_redemptoris-missio_en.html.

John Paul II, *Sollicitudo rei socialis*, www.vatican.va/holy_father/john_paul_ii/encyclicals/documents/hf_jp-ii_enc_30121987_sollicitudo-rei-socialis_en.html.

Johnson, E. A., *She Who Is: The Mystery of God in Feminist Discourse*, New York: Crossroad, 1992.

Johnson, E. A., *Friends of God and Prophets: A Feminist Reading of the Communion of Saints*, London: SCM Press, 1998.

Johnson, E. A., 'An Earthy Christology: "For God So Loved the Cosmos"', *America* 200: 12 (13 April 2009), 27–30.

Johnson, K. E., *Rethinking the Trinity and Religious Pluralism: An Augustinian Assessment*, Downers Grove, IL: IVP Academic, 2011.

Johnson, L. T., *The Gospel of Luke*, Sacra Pagina Series 3, Collegeville, MN: Liturgical Press, 1991.

Johnson, L. T., 'The Christology of Luke–Acts', in M. A. Powell and D. R. Bauer (eds), *Who Do You Say That I Am? Essays on Christology*, Louisville, KY: Westminster John Knox Press, 1999, 49–63.

Johnson, L. T., *Prophetic Jesus, Prophetic Church: The Challenge of Luke–Acts to Contemporary Christians*, Grand Rapids, MI: William B. Eerdmans, 2011.

Johnson, R., *Reel Spirituality*, Grand Rapids, MI: Baker, 2000.

Johnson, S., *Where Good Ideas Come From*, London: Penguin, 2010.

Jonge, H. J. de, 'The Historical Jesus' View of Himself and of His Mission', in Martinus C. de Boer (ed.), *From Jesus to John: Essays on Jesus and New Testament Christology in Honour of Marinus de Jonge*, Sheffield: Sheffield Academic Press, 1993, 21–37.

Kalilombe, P. A., *Doing Theology at the Grassroots*, Gweru, Zimbabwe: Mambo Press, 1993.

Kapolyo, J. M., *The Human Condition*, Downers Grove, IL: InterVarsity Press, 2005.

Karris, R. J., *Luke: Artist and Theologian*, New York: Paulist Press, 1985.

Katangole, E., 'Mission and the Ephesian Moment of World Christianity: Pilgrimages of Pain and Hope and the Economics of Eating Together', *Mission Studies* 29:2 (2012), 183–200.

Kato, J-K., *How Immigrant Christians Living in Mixed Cultures Interpret their Religion*, Lewiston, NY: Edwin Mellen Press, 2012.

Kay, J., 'Concepts of Nature in the Hebrew Bible', in D. M. Nothwehr (ed.), *Franciscan Theology of the Environment: An Introductory Reader*, Quincy, IL: Franciscan Press, 2002, 23–45.

Kaylor, R. D., *Jesus the Prophet: His Vision of the Kingdom of God*, Louisville, KY: Westminster/John Knox Press, 1994.

Keane, F., *Letter to Daniel*, London: Penguin, 1996.

Keane, P. S., *Christian Ethics and Imagination: A Theological Inquiry*, New York: Paulist Press, 1984.

Kim, K., *The Holy Spirit in the World: A Global Conversation*, Maryknoll, NY: Orbis, 2007.

Kim, K., *Joining in with the Spirit: Connecting World Church and Local Mission*, London: SCM Press, 2010.

Kisala, R., 'Formation for Intercultural Life and Mission', *Verbum SVD* 50:3 (2009), 331–45.

Kiser, J., *The Monks of Tibhirine: Faith, Love, and Terror in Algeria*, New York: St. Martin's Griffin, 2003.

Knitter, P. F., *One Earth Many Religions: Multifaith Dialogue and Global Responsibility*, Maryknoll, NY: Orbis, 1995.

Knitter, P. F., *Jesus and the Other Names: Christian Mission and Global Responsibility*, Maryknoll, NY: Orbis, 1996.

Knitter, P. F., *Introducing Theologies of Religion*, Maryknoll, NY: Orbis, 2002.

Koenig, J., *New Testament Hospitality: Partnership with Strangers as Promise of Mission*, Eugene, OR: Wipf and Stock, 2001.

Koyama, K., *Water Buffalo Theology*, London: SPCK, 1971.

Koyama, K., '"Extend Hospitality to Strangers": A Missiology of Theologia Crucis', *International Review of Mission* 83:327 (1993), 283–95.

Kraemer, H., *The Authority of Faith: The Madras Series*, vol. 1, London: International Missionary Council, 1939.

Kritzinger, J. N. J., '"Mission as . . ." Must we choose? A dialogue with Bosch, Bevans & Schroeder and Schreiter in the South African context', *Missionalia: South African Journal of Missiology* 39:1–2 (2011), 32–59.

Kritzinger, J. N. J., 'Black Theology: Challenge to Mission', unpublished DTh dissertation, University of South Africa, Pretoria.

Kurz, W. S., *Reading Luke–Acts: Dynamics of Biblical Narrative*, Louisville, KY: Westminster/John Knox Press, 1993.

LaCugna, C. M., *God for Us: The Trinity and Christian Life*, New York: HarperCollins Publications, 1991.

LaCugna, C. M., *Freeing Theology: The Essentials of Theology in Feminist Perspective*, San Francisco: Harper Collins, 1993.

Lederach, J. P., *The Moral Imagination: The Art and Soul of Building Peace*, New York: Oxford University Press, 2005.

Letham, R., *The Work of Christ*, Downers Grove, IL: InterVarsity Press, 1993.

Levertov, D., *Candles in Babylon*, New York: New Directions Press, 1982.

Levison, J. R., *Filled with the Spirit*, Grand Rapids, MI: Eerdmans, 2009.

Levison, J. R., '*Filled with the Spirit*: A Conversation with Pentecostal and Charismatic Scholars', *Journal of Pentecostal Theology* 20 (2011), 213–31.

Levison, J. R., 'A Stubborn Missionary, a Slave Girl, and Scholar: The Ambiguity of Inspiration in the Book of Acts', in A. Yong, K. Kim and V-M. Karkkainen (eds), *Interdisciplinary and Religio-cultural Discourses on a Spirit-filled World: Loosing the Spirits*, New York: Palgrave Macmillan, 2013, 15–27.

Lewis, B. S., *Creating Christian Indians: Native Clergy in the Presbyterian Church*, Norman, OK: University of Oklahoma Press, 2003.

Lloyd-Sidle, P. and Lewis, B. S. (eds), *Teaching Mission in a Global Context*, Louisville, KY: Geneva Press, 2001.

Lohfink, Gerhard, *Jesus and Community*, Philadelphia: Fortress Press, 1984.

Lonergan, B., *The Way to Nicea: The Dialectical Development of Trinitarian Theology*, trans. C. O'Donovan, Philadelphia: The Westminster Press, 1976.

Longenecker, B. W., 'Rome's Victory and God's Honour: The Jerusalem Temple and the Spirit of God in Lukan Theodicy', in G. N. Stanton, B. W. Longenecker and S. C. Barton (eds), *The Holy Spirit and Christian Origins: Essays in Honor of James Dunn*, Grand Rapids, MI: Eerdmans, 2004, 90–102.

Luzbetak, L., *The Church and Cultures: New Perspectives in Missiological Anthropology*, Maryknoll, NY: Orbis, 1988.

Lynch, G., *Understanding Theology and Popular Culture*, Oxford: Blackwell, 2005.

Lynch, W. F., *Images of Hope: Imagination as Healer of the Hopeless*, Baltimore: Helicon Press, 1965.

McDonagh, S., 'Trees and "God Talks"', *SEDOS Bulletin* 43:7–8 (2011), 208–21.

McElrath, D. (ed.), *Franciscan Christology: Selected Texts: Translations and Essays*, Franciscan Sources No. 1, St. Bonaventure, NY: The Franciscan Institute, 1980.

McElwee, J., 'Pope Francis: "I would love a church that is poor"', *National Catholic Reporter*, 16 March 2013, http://ncronline.org/blogs/francis-chronicles/pope-francis-i-would-love-church-poor.

McGavran, D., *How Churches Grow*, London: World Dominion Press, 1959.

McGavran, D., *Understanding Church Growth*, Grand Rapids, MI: Eerdmans, 1970, 1980, 1990, etc.

McGinn, B., *Meister Eckhart and the Beguine Mystics*, New York: Continuum, 1983.

McGinn, B., *The Flowering of Mysticism: Men and Women in the New Mysticism, 1200–1350*, New York: Crossroad, 1998.

MacIntyre, A., *Whose Justice? Which Rationality?* Notre Dame, IN: University of Notre Dame Press, 1988.

Mackay, H. (ed.), *Consumption and Everyday Life*, London: Sage, 1997.

Mackenzie, R., *David Livingstone*, Fearn: Christian Focus Publications, 1993.

McLuhan, M., *Probes*, Berkeley, CA: Gingko Press, 2002.

Manahan, R., 'Christ as Second Adam', in C. DeWitt (ed.), *The Environment and the Christian: What Does the New Testament Say about the Environment?*, Grand Rapids, MI: Baker House, 1991, 45–56.

Mbiti, J., *African Religions and Philosophy*, London: Heinemann, 1969.

Meier, J. P., *A Marginal Jew: Rethinking the Historical Jesus*, 4 vols, New York: Doubleday, 1991, 1994, 2001, 2009.

Menzies, R. P., *Empowered for Witness: The Spirit in Luke–Acts*, London: T & T Clark, 2004.

Merrick, J. R. A., 'The Spirit of Truth as Agent in False Religions? A Critique of Amos Yong's Pneumatological Theology of Religions with Reference to Current Trends', *Trinity Journal* 29:1 (2008), 107–25.

Metz, J., *Faith in History and Society: Toward a Practical Fundamental Theology*, trans. David Smith, New York: Seabury, 1980.

Migliore, D., *Faith Seeking Understanding*, 2nd edition, Grand Rapids, MI: Eerdmans, 2004.

Mignolo, W. D., 'Delinking: The Rhetoric of Modernity, the Logic of Coloniality and the Grammar of Decoloniality', *Cultural Studies* 21:2–3 (2007), 449–514.

Miles, S., *Take This Bread: A Radical Conversion*, New York: Ballantine, 2007.

Miles, T., *A God of Many Understandings? The Gospel and Theology of Religions*, Nashville, TN: B & H Academic, 2010.

Moltmann, J., *The Spirit of Life: A Universal Affirmation*, trans. Margaret Kohl, London: SCM Press, 1992.

Molyneux, G., *African Christian Theology*, San Francisco: Mellen Research University Press, 1993.

Montague, G. T., 'Review of J. R. Levison, *Filled with the Spirit*', *Catholic Biblical Quarterly* 72 (2010), 831–2.

Moynagh, M., *Church for Every Context: An Introduction to Theology and Practice*, London: SCM Press, 2012.

Muck, T. and Adeney, F. S., *Christianity Encountering World Religions*, Grand Rapids, MI: Baker Academic, 2009.

Naish, T, 'Mission, Migration and the Stranger in our Midst', in S. Spencer (ed.), *Mission and Migration*, Calver: Cliff College, 2008, 7–30.

Newbigin, L., *The Gospel in a Pluralist Society*, Grand Rapids, MI: Eerdmans, 1989.

Newlands, G. and Smith, A., *Hospitable God: The Transformative Dream*, Farnham: Ashgate, 2010.

A New Zealand Prayer Book, He Karakia Mihinare o Aotearoa, Auckland: William Collins, 1989.

Nguyen, vanThanh, *Peter and Cornelius: A Story of Conversion and Mission*, Eugene, OR: Pickwick Publications, 2012.

Nguyen, vanThanh, 'Luke's Passion as Story of Good News', *The Bible Today* 48:2 (2010), 61–7.

Nguyen, vanThanh, 'Biblical Foundations for Religious Life: A Prophetic Vision', *Verbum SVD* 53:2 (2012), 263–73.

Nguyen, vanThanh, 'Speaking in Parables', *Give Us This Day* (July 2012), 240–1.

Nile, D. P., 'Justice, Peace and the Integrity of Creation', November 2003, *World Council of Churches, Ecumenical Dictionary*, www.wcc-coe.org/wcc/who/dictionary-article11.html.

Nothwehr, D. M., *Mutuality: A Formal Norm for Christian Social Ethics*, San Francisco: Catholic Scholars Press, 1998.

Nothwehr, D. M., *Ecological Footprints: An Essential Franciscan Guide for Sustainable Living*, Collegeville, MN: Liturgical Press, 2012.

Nothwehr, D. M. (ed.), *Franciscan Theology of the Environment: An Introductory Reader*, Quincy, IL: Franciscan Press, 2002.

Nothwehr, D. M. 'Mutuality and Mission: A "No Other" Way', *Mission Studies* 21:2 (2004), 249–70.

Nouwen, H., *Reaching Out: The Three Movements of the Spiritual Life*, Glasgow: William Collins, 1976.

Nussbaum, M. C., 'Women and Cultural Universals', in *Sex and Social Justice*, New York: Oxford University Press, 1999, 29–54.

O'Toole, R. F., *Luke's Presentation of Jesus: A Christology*, Rome: Editrice Pontificio Istituto Biblico, 2004.

Oger, L., *Where a Scattered Flock Gathered*, Ndola, Zambia: Mission Press, 1991.

Okure, T., 'Church—Family of God: The Place of God's Reconciliation, Justice, and Peace', in Agbonkhianmeghe E. Orobator (ed.), *Reconciliation, Justice and Peace: The Second African Synod*, Maryknoll, NY: Orbis, 2011, 13–24.

Osborne, K. B., *Christian Sacraments in a Postmodern World: A Theology for the Third Millennium*, New York: Paulist Press, 1999.

Padilla, E. and Phan, P. C. (eds), *Contemporary Issues of Migration and Theology*, New York: Palgrave Macmillan, 2013.

Palmer, P., *The Company of Strangers: Christians and the Renewal of America's Public Life*, New York: Crossroad, 1986.

Panikkar, R., *The Intra-Religious Dialogue*, revised edn, New York: Paulist Press, 1998.

Passmore, R., *Here Be Dragons*, Porthouse: Frontier Youth Trust, 2013.

Pasura, D., 'Modes of Incorporation and Transnational Zimbabwean migration to Britain', *Ethnic and Racial Studies* 36:1 (2011), 199–218.

Paul VI, Apostolic Exhortation *Evangelii Nuntiandi*, www.vatican.va/holy_father/paul_vi/apost_exhortations/documents/hf_p-vi_exh_19751208_evangelii-nuntiandi_en.html.

Paul VI, Encyclical Letter *Ecclesiam Suam*, www.vatican.va/holy_father/paul_vi/encyclicals/documents/hf_p-vi_enc_06081964_ecclesiam_en.html.

Paul VI, 'A Hospitable Earth for Future Generations', Address at the Stockholm Conference on Human Environment, 1 June 1972, Conservation Catholic, http://conservation.catholic.org/pope_paul_vi.htm.

Pernia, A., 'Expectations of the Generalate of the Anthropos Institute', *Verbum SVD* 45:1 (2004), 19–37.

Pernia, A., 'Missio Inter Gentes', *Arnoldus Nota* (2009), 1–2.

Phan, P. C., 'The Experience of Migration as a Source of Intercultural Theology', in E. Padilla and P. C. Phan (eds), *Contemporary Issues of Migration and Theology*, New York: Palgrave Macmillan, 2013, 179–210.

Pieris, A., *An Asian Theology of Liberation*, Faith Meets Faith Series, Maryknoll, NY: Orbis, 1988.

Pohl, C., *Making Room: Recovering Hospitality as a Christian Tradition*, Grand Rapids, MI: Eerdmans, 1999.

Pontifical Academy of Sciences, 'Fate of Mountain Glaciers in the Anthropocene', 11 May 2011, www.vatican.va/roman_ curia/ pontifical_academies/acdscien/2011/PAS_ Glacier_110511_ final.pdf.

Pontifical Council for Inter-Religious Dialogue and the Congregation for the Evangelization of Peoples, *Dialogue and Proclamation: Reflection and Orientations on Interreligious Dialogue and the Proclamation of the Gospel of Jesus Christ*, Rome: Holy See, 1991.

Pontifical Council for Justice and Peace, *Compendium of the Social Doctrine of the Church*, www. vatican.va/roman_curia/pontifical _councils /justpeace/documents/rc_pc_justpeace_doc_20060526_compendio-dott-soc_en.html.

Pontifical Council for Justice and Peace, 'Water: An Essential Element for Life', www.vatican.va/roman_curia/pontifical_councils/justpeace/documents/rc_pc_justpeace_doc_20030322_kyoto-water_en.html.

Pontifical Council for Religious Dialogue and Congregation for the Evangelization of Peoples, *Dialogue and Proclamation: Reflection and Orientations on Inter-religious Dialogue and the Proclamation of the Gospel of Jesus Christ*, 1991, www.vatican.va/roman_curia/pontifical_councils/interelg/documents/rc_pc_interelg_doc_19051991_dialogue-and-proclamatio_en.html.

Prior, J. M., 'Learning to Leave: The Pivotal Role of Cross-Cultural "Conversion"', *Verbum SVD* 53:2 (2012), 219–35.

Prior, M., *Jesus the Liberator: Nazareth Liberation Theology (Luke 4.16–30)*, Sheffield: Sheffield Academic Press, 1991.

Quell, G. and Schrenk, G., *Righteousness*, London: A & C Black, 1951.

Raguin, Y., *I am Sending you: Spirituality and the Missioner*, Manila: East Asian Pastoral Institute, 1973.

Rahner, K., *Foundations of Christian Faith: An Introduction to the Idea of Christianity*, New York: Seabury, 1978.

Rapport , N. and Overing, J., *Social and Cultural Anthropology: The Key Concepts*, 2nd edn, London: Routledge, 2007.

Reid, D., 'Enfleshing the Human', in D. Edwards (ed.), *Earth Revealing – Earth Healing: Ecology and Christian Theology*, Collegeville, MN: Liturgical Press, 2000, 69–83.

Richards, A., 'Some Types of Family Structure amongst the Central Bantu', in A. R. Radcliffe-Brown and D. Forde (eds), *African Systems of Kingship and Marriage*, London: KPI/IAI, 1950, 207–51.

Richardson, J., *Night Visions: Searching the Shadows of Advent and Christmas*, Orlando, FL: Wanton Gospeller Press, 1998.

Richie, T., *Speaking by the Spirit: A Pentecostal Model for Interreligious Dialogue*, Wilmore, KY: Emeth Press, 2011.

Richie, T., *Toward a Pentecostal Theology of Religions: Encountering Cornelius Today*, Cleveland, TN: CPT Press, 2013.

Richie, T., 'The Spirit of Truth as Guide into All Truth: A Response to R. A. James Merrick, "The Spirit of Truth as Agent in False Religions? A Critique of Amos Yong's Pneumatological Theology of Religions with Reference to Current Trends"', *Cyberjournal for Pentecostal-Charismatic Research* 19 (2010), http://pctii.org/cyberj/cyber19.html.

Ritschl, D., 'Historical Development and Implications of the Filioque Controversy', in L. Vischer (ed.), *Spirit of God, Spirit of Christ: Ecumenical Reflections on the Filioque Controversy*, Geneva: World Council of Churches, 1981, 46–65.

Robert, D. L., *American Women in Mission: A Social History of Their Thought and Practice*, Macon, GA: Mercer University Press, 1997.

Robert, D. L., *Christian Mission: How Christianity Became a World Religion*, Chichester: Wiley-Blackwell, 2009.

Robert, D. L. 'Historical Trends in Missions and Earth Care', *International Bulletin of Missionary Research* 35:3 (2011), 123–8.

Roberts, J. D., *Liberation and Reconciliation: A Black Theology*, Philadelphia: Westminster Press, 1971.

Ross, C., Prado, O., Wood, J., Fountain, J., Giron, R., Stamoolis, J., Anyomi, S. and Castillo, M., 'The Iguassu Affirmation: A Commentary by Eight Reflective Practitioners', in W. Taylor (ed.), *Global Missiology for the 21ˢᵗ Century*, Grand Rapids, MI: Baker Academic, 2001, 521–48.

Rowland, C., *Liberating Exegesis: The Challenge of Liberation Theology*, Louisville, KY: Westminster John Knox Press, 1990.

Rynkiewich, M., *Soul, Self, and Society: A Postmodern Anthropology for Mission in a Postmodern World*, Eugene, OR: Cascade Books, 2011.

Saayman, W. and Kritzinger, K. (eds), *Mission in Bold Humility: David Bosch's Work Considered*, Maryknoll, NY: Orbis, 1996.

Sagovsky, N., *Christian Tradition and the Practice of Justice*, London: SPCK, 2008.

Sanders, E. P., *The Historical Figure of Jesus*, London: Penguin, 1993.

Satyavrata, I., *God Has Not Left Himself without Witness*, Oxford: Regnum International, 2011.

Schererer, F. X., *Interculturality: A Challenge for the Mission of the Church*, Bangalore, India: Asian Trading Corporation, 2001.

Schreiter, R., *The Ministry of Reconciliation: Spirituality and Strategies*, Maryknoll, NY: Orbis, 1998.

Schreiter, R., 'Some Conditions for a Transcultural Theology', in P. Knitter (ed.), *Pluralism and Oppression, Theology in World Perspective*, Lanham, MD: University Press of America. 1991, 22–8.

Schreiter, R., 'Migrants and the Ministry of Reconciliation', in D. G. Groody and G. Campese (eds), *A Promised Land, A Perilous Journey: Theological Perspectives on Migration*, Notre Dame, IN: University of Notre Dame Press, 2008, 107–23.

Schroeder, R. P., *What is the Mission of the Church? A Guide for Catholics*, Maryknoll, NY: Orbis, 2008.

Schroeder, R. P., 'Interculturality and Prophetic Dialogue', *Verbum SVD* 54:1 (2013), 8–21.

Schroeder, R. P., 'Proclamation and Interreligious Dialogue as Prophetic Dialogue', *Missiology: An International Review* 41:1 (2013), 50–61.

Schüssler Fiorenza, E., *In Memory of Her: A Feminist Theological Reconstruction of Christian Origins*, New York: Crossroad, 1984.

Schüssler Fiorenza, E., *Jesus: Miriam's Child, Sophia's Prophet: Critical Issues in Feminist Christology*, New York: Continuum, 1994.

Schweiker, W., *Responsibility and Christian Ethics*, New Studies in Christian Ethics, Cambridge: Cambridge University Press, 1995.

Schweitzer, A., *The Quest of the Historical Jesus: A Critical Study of Its Progress from Reimarus to Wrede*, revised edn; New York: Macmillan, 1968.

Schweizer, E., 'On Distinguishing Between Spirits', *Ecumenical Review* 41:3 (1989), 406–15.

Second Vatican Council, Decree on the Missionary Activity of the Church (*Ad Gentes*), www.vatican.va/archive/hist_councils/ii_vatican_council/documents/vat-ii_decree_19651207_ad-gentes_en.html.

Second Vatican Council, Pastoral Constitution on the Church in the Modern World (*GaudiumetSpes*),1965,www.vatican.va/archive/hist_councils/ii_vatican_council/documents/vat-ii_cons_19651207_gaudium-et-spes_en.html.

Secretariat for Non-Christians, 'The Attitude of the Church toward the Followers of Other Religions: Reflections and Orientations on Dialogue and Mission', *Bulletin Secretariatus pro non Christianis* 56:2 (1984).

Sedmak, C., *Doing Local Theology: A Guide for Artisans of a New Humanity*, Maryknoll, NY: Orbis, 2002.

Seifrid, M., *Christ, Our Righteousness*, Leicester: Apollos, 2000.

Selak, A., 'The Church Young Catholics Want', www.washingtonpost.com/blogs/guest-voices/post/the-church-young-catholics-want/2013/02/14/de08eae2-760a-11e2-95e4-6148e45d7adb_blog.html.

Shelton, J. B., 'Delphi and Jerusalem: Two Spirits or Holy Spirit? A Review of John R. Levison's *Filled with the Spirit*', *Pneuma* 33 (2011), 47–58.

Sherman, R., *King, Priest, and Prophet: A Trinitarian Theology of Atonement*, New York: T & T Clark, 2004.

Shirky, C., *Here Comes Everybody*, London: Allen Lane, 2008.

Snyder, S., *Asylum-Seeking, Migration and Church*, Farnham: Ashgate, 2012.

Sobrino, J., 'Bearing with One Another in Faith', in J. Sobrino and P. J. Hernandez (eds), *Theology of Christian Solidarity*, trans. Philip Berryman, Maryknoll, NY: Orbis, 1985, 1–42.

Society of the Divine Word, *In Dialogue with the Word*, Documents of the 15th General Chapter SVD 2000, Rome: SVD Publications, No. 1, September 2000.

Society of the Divine Word, Statement of the 15th General Chapter 2000, 'Listening to the Spirit: Our Missionary Response Today', Rome: Society of the Divine Word, 2000.

Spadaro, A., 'A Big Heart Open to God', *America Magazine*, 30 September 2013, http://americamagazine.org/pope-interview.

Stanley, B., *The World Missionary Conference, Edinburgh 1910*, Grand Rapids, MI: Eerdmans, 2009.

Stanley, D. and Young, K., 'Conceptualizing Complexities of Curriculum Developing a Lexicon for Ecojustice and the Transdisciplinarity of Bodies', *Journal of Curriculum Theorizing* 27:1 (2011), 35–47, http://journal.jctonline.org/index.php/jct/ article/ view/306.

Stanton, G. N., Longenecker, B. W. and Barton, S. C. (eds), *The Holy Spirit and Christian Origins: Essays in Honor of James Dunn*, Grand Rapids, MI: Eerdmans, 2004.

Sudhiarsa, R. (ed.), *Cross-Cultural Mission: Problems and Prospects*, Malang, Indonesia: Bayumedia Publishing, 2012.

Summers, S., *Friendship: Exploring its Implications for the Church in Postmodernity*, London: T&T Clark, 2009.

Takenaka, M., *God is Rice*, Eugene, OR: Wipf and Stock, 2009.

Tan, J., 'Missio Inter Gentes: Towards a New Paradigm in the Mission Theology of the Federation of Asian Bishops' Conferences (FABC)', *Mission Studies* 21:1 (2004), 65–95.

Tanaka, H., 'North Korea: Understanding Migration to and from a Closed Country', 7 January 2008, www.migrationpolicy.org/article/north-korea-understanding-migration-and-closed-country.

Tannehill, R. C., *The Narrative Unity of Luke–Acts: A Literary Interpretation*, vol. 1, Philadelphia: Fortress Press, 1986.

Tannehill, R. C., *Luke*, Abingdon New Testament Commentaries, Nashville, TN: Abingdon Press, 1996.

Tanner, K., *Theories of Culture*, Cambridge: Cambridge University Press, 1997.

Taylor, J. V., *The Primal Vision: Christian Presence amid African Religion*, London: SCM Press, 1963.

Taylor, J. V., *The Go-Between God, The Holy Spirit and the Christian Mission*, London: SCM Press, 1972.

Taylor, W. D. (ed.), *Global Missiology for the 21ˢᵗ Century: The Iguassu Dialogue*, Grand Rapids, MI: Baker Academic, 2001.

Thomas, J. C., *The Spirit of the New Testament*, Leiden: Deo Publishing, 2005.

Thorne, B., *Infinitely Beloved*, London: Darton, Longman & Todd, 2003.

Thornton, S., *Club Cultures*, Cambridge: Polity Press, 1995.

Tiede, D. L., *Luke*, Augsburg Commentary on the New Testament, Minneapolis: Augsburg Publishing House, 1988.

Toolan, D., *At Home in the Cosmos*, Maryknoll, NY: Orbis, 2001.

Tracy, D., *The Analogical Imagination: Christian Theology and the Culture of Pluralism*, New York: Crossroad, 1981.

Turner, H., *Frames of Mind*, Auckland, New Zealand: Deepsight Trust, 2001.

Turner, M., *Power from on High: The Spirit in Israel's Restoration and Witness in Luke–Acts*, Sheffield: Sheffield Academic Press, 1996.

Turner, M., 'The Spirit and Salvation in Luke–Acts', in G. N. Stanton, B. W. Longenecker and S. C. Barton (eds), *The Holy Spirit and Christian Origins: Essays in Honor of James Dunn*, Grand Rapids, MI: Eerdmans, 2004, 103–16.

Turner, M., 'Jesus and the Spirit in Lucan Perspective', *Tyndale Bulletin* 32 (1981), 3–42.

Turner, M., 'Levison's *Filled with the Spirit*: A Brief Appreciation and Response', *Journal of Pentecostal Theology* 20 (2011); 193–200.

Turner, R. E. 'Doubt and the Values of an Ignorance-Based World View for Restoration: Coastal Louisiana Wetlands', *Estuaries and Coasts* 32 (2009), 1054–68.

Tutu, D., *No Future without Forgiveness*, New York: Doubleday, 1999.

Twitchell, J., *Lead Us Into Temptation*, New York: Columbia University Press, 1999.

US Conference of Catholic Bishops (USCCB), 'Global Climate Change: A Plea for Dialogue Prudence and the Common Good', 15 June 2001, www.usccb.org/issues-and-action/human-life-and-dignity/environment/global-climate-change-a-plea-for-dialogue-prudence-and-the-common-good.cfm.

USCCB, 'Renewing the Earth: An Invitation to Reflection and Action on Environment in Light of Catholic Social Teaching', 14 November 1991, www.usccb.org/issues-and-action/human-life-and-dignity/environment/renewing-the-earth.cfm.

USCCB, *To the Ends of the Earth*, New York: Society for the Propagation of the Faith, 1986.

Van der Meer, A. L., 'The Scriptures, the Church, and Humanity: Who Should Do Mission and Why?', in W. D. Taylor (ed.), *Global Missiology for the 21st Century: The Iguassu Dialogue*, Grand Rapids, MI: Baker Academic, 2000, 149–62.

Van der Walt, B. J., 'Being Human: A Gift and a Duty' (a series of lectures delivered in Kinshasa in 1988) and subsequently published in a series of pamphlets by the Instituut Vir Die Bevordering Van Calvinisme, PU vir CHO Potchefstroom 2520 South Africa, 1988.

Vanier, J., *Community and Growth*, New York: Paulist Press, 1989.

Vanier, J., *Signs of the Times: Seven Paths of Hope for a Troubled World*, London: Darton, Longman & Todd, 2013.

Vermes, G., *The Religion of Jesus the Jew*, Minneapolis: Augsburg Fortress, 1993.

Volf, M., *After Our Likeness: The Church as the Image of the Trinity*, Sacra Doctrina, Grand Rapids, MI: Eerdmans, 1998.

Wahrish-Oblau, C., *The Missionary Self-Perception of Pentecostal/Charismatic Church Leaders from the Global South in Europe: Bringing Back the Gospel*, Leiden: Brill, 2009.

Walker, Alice, 'A Wind through the Heart: A Conversation with Alice Walker and Sharon Salzberg on Loving Kindness in a Painful World', *Shambhala Sun* (January 1997), 1–5.

Walls, A. F., *The Cross-Cultural Process in Church History*, Maryknoll, NY: Orbis, 2002.

Walls, A. F., 'Africa in Christian History – Retrospect and Prospect', a paper given at the gathering of the Africa Theological Fellowship, September 1997 at the Akrofi-Christaller Memorial Centre, Ghana.

Walls, A. F., 'Afterword: Christian Mission in a Five-Hundred-Year-Context', in A. F. Walls and C. Ross (eds), *Mission in the Twenty-First Century: Exploring the Five Marks of Global Mission*, London: Darton, Longman & Todd, 2008, 193–204.

Ward, P., *Youth Culture and the Gospel*, London: Marshall Pickering, 1992.

Ward, P., *Participation and Mediation*, London: SCM Press, 2008.

Warner, K. D. 'Franciscan Environmental Ethics: Imagining Creation as a Community of Care', *Journal of the Society of Christian Ethics* 31:1 (2011), 143–60.

Warren, K. A., *Daring to Cross the Threshold: Francis of Assisi Encounters Sultan Malek al-Kamil*, Rochester, MN: Sisters of St. Francis, 2003.

Whiteman, D., 'Contextualization: The Theory, the Gap, the Challenge', *International Bulletin of Missionary Research* 21:1 (1997), 2–7.

Wild-Wood, E., 'The Experience of Migrants in a Native British Church: Towards Mission Together', in H. Chandler and A. Yong (eds), *Global Diasporas and Mission*, Oxford: Regnum Books International, 2014, 175–90.

Willis, P., *Common Culture*, Milton Keynes: Open University Press, 1990.

Witherington III, Ben, *The Jesus Quest: The Third Search for the Jew of Nazareth*, new expanded edn, Downers Grove, IL: InterVarsity Press, 1997.

Witherington III, Ben, *The Many Faces of the Christ: The Christologies of the New Testament and Beyond*, New York: Crossroad, 1998.

Wolter, A. B. 'John Duns Scotus on the Primacy and Personality of Christ', in Damian McElrath (ed.), *Franciscan Christology: Selected Texts: Translations and Essays*, Franciscan Sources 1, St. Bonaventure, NY: The Franciscan Institute, 1980, 138–82.

Women and Law in Southern Africa Research Trust (WLSA), *The Changing Family in Zambia*, Lusaka: WLSA, 1997.

World Commission on the Ethics of Scientific Knowledge and Technology (COMEST) and UNESCO, *The Precautionary Principle*, http://unesdoc.unesco.org/images/ 0013/001395/139578e.pdf.

World Council of Churches, 'Statement on Water for Life', adopted at Porto Alegre, 2006, www. oikoumene.org/en/resources/documents/assembly/2006-porto-alegre/1-statements-documents-adopted/international-affairs/report-from-the-public-issues-committee/water-for-life?set_language=en.

World Council of Churches, 'Together Towards Life: Mission and Evangelism in Changing Landscapes', 2012, www.oikoumene.org/en/resources/documents/wcc-commissions/mission-and-evangelism/together-towards-life-mission-and-evangelism-in-changing-landscapes?set_language=en.

Wright, N. T., *The New Testament and the People of God: Christian Origins and the Question of God, Vol. 1*, London: SPCK, 1992.

Wright, N. T., *Jesus and the Victory of God: Christian Origins and the Question of God, Vol. 2*, London: SPCK, 1996.

Wright, N. T., *Paul and the Faithfulness of God: Christian Origins and the Question of God, Vol. 4*, London: SPCK, 2013.

Yong, A., *Beyond the Impasse: Toward a Pneumatological Theology of Religions*, Grand Rapids, MI: Baker Academic, 2003.

Yong A., *The Spirit Poured Out on All Flesh: Pentecostalism and the Possibility of Global Theology*, Grand Rapids, MI: Baker Academic, 2005.

Yong, A., *Theology and Down Syndrome: Reimagining Disability in Late Modernity*, Waco, TX: Baylor University Press, 2007.

Yong, A., *Hospitality and the Other: Pentecost, Christian Practices, and the Neighbor*, Faith Meets Faith series, Maryknoll, NY: Orbis, 2008.

Yong, A., *In the Days of Caesar: Pentecostalism and Political Theology*, Sacra Doctrina, Grand Rapids, MI: Eerdmans, 2010.

Yong, A., *The Bible, Disability, and the Church: A New Vision of the People of God*, Grand Rapids, MI: Eerdmans, 2011.

Yong, A., *Who is the Holy Spirit? A Walk with the Apostles*, Brewster, MA: Paraclete Press, 2011.

Yong, A., *Spirit of Love: A Trinitarian Theology of Grace*, Waco, TX: Baylor University Press, 2012.

Yong, A., *Pneumatology and the Christian-Buddhist Dialogue: Does the Spirit Blow through the Middle Way?* Studies in Systematic Theology, Leiden: Brill, 2012.

Yong, A., 'Guests, Hosts, and the Holy Ghost: Pneumatological Theology and Christian Practices in a World of Many Faiths', in D. H. Jensen (ed.), *Lord and Giver of Life: Perspectives on Constructive Pneumatology*, Louisville, KY: Westminster John Knox Press, 2008, 71–86.

Yong, A., 'The Inviting Spirit: Pentecostal Beliefs and Practices regarding the Religions Today', in S. Studebaker (ed.), *Defining Issues in Pentecostalism: Classical and Emergent*, Eugene, OR: Wipf & Stock, 2008, 29–44.

Yong, A., 'Jesus, Pentecostalism, and the Encounter with (Religious) Others: Pentecostal Christology and (the Wider) Ecumenism in North America', in D. Coulter and K. Archer (eds), *North American Pentecostalism*, Global Pentecostal & Charismatic Studies series, Leiden and Boston: Brill, forthcoming.

Yong, A., *Discerning the Spirit(s): A Pentecostal-Charismatic Contribution to Christian Theology of Religions*, Journal of Pentecostal Theology Supplement Series 20, Sheffield: Sheffield Academic Press, 2000.

Yong, A., 'A P(new)matological Paradigm for Christian Mission in a Religiously Plural World', *Missiology: An International Review* 33:2 (2005), 175–91.

Yong, A., 'The Spirit, Christian Practices, and the Religions: Theology of Religions in Pentecostal and Pneumatological Perspective', *Asbury Journal* 62:2 (2007), 5–31.

Yong A., 'The Spirit of Hospitality: Pentecostal Perspectives toward a Performative Theology of the Interreligious Encounter', *Missiology: An International Review* 35:1 (2007), 55–73.

Yong, A., 'Primed for the Spirit: Creation, Redemption, and the *Missio Spiritus*', *International Review of Mission* 100:2 (2011), 355–66.

Zago, M., 'The New Millennium and the Emerging Religious Encounters', *Missiology: An International Review* 28:1 (2000), 5–18.

Index of Names and Subjects